I WAS WRONG: THE MEANINGS OF APOLOGIES

Apologies pervade our news headlines and our private affairs, but how should we evaluate these often vague and deceptive rituals? Discussing numerous examples from ancient and recent history, *I Was Wrong: The Meanings of Apologies* argues that we suffer from considerable confusion about the moral meanings and social functions of these complex interactions. Rather than asking whether a speech act "is or is not" an apology, Smith offers a nuanced theory of apologetic meaning. Smith leads us with a clear voice through a series of rich philosophical and interdisciplinary questions, arguing that apologies have evolved from a confluence of diverse cultural and religious practices that do not translate easily into pluralistic secular discourse. After describing several varieties of apologies between individuals, Smith turns to collectives. Although apologies from corporations, governments, and other groups can be profoundly significant, Smith guides readers to appreciate the kinds of meaning that collective apologies often do not convey and warns of the dangers of collective acts of contrition that allow individual wrongdoers to obscure their personal blame.

Dr. Smith is an assistant professor of philosophy at the University of New Hampshire. A graduate of Vassar College, he earned a law degree from SUNY at Buffalo and a Ph.D. in philosophy from Vanderbilt University. Before coming to UNH, he worked as a litigator for LeBoeuf, Lamb, Greene, and MacRae and as a judicial clerk for the Honorable R. L. Nygaard of the U.S. Court of Appeals for the Third Circuit. He specializes in the philosophy of law, politics, and society, and he writes on and teaches aesthetics. He is working with Cambridge University Press on the sequel to *I Was Wrong*, applying his framework for apologetic meanings to examples in criminal and civil law. His writings have appeared in journals such as the *Continental Philosophy Review*, *Social Theory and Practice*, *The Journal of Social Philosophy*, *Culture, Theory & Critique*, the *Rutgers Law Journal*, and the *Buffalo Law Review*.

I Was Wrong: The Meanings of Apologies

Nick Smith, J.D., Ph.D.
University of New Hampshire

DISCARD

CAMBRIDGE
UNIVERSITY PRESS

CAMBRIDGE UNIVERSITY PRESS
Cambridge, New York, Melbourne, Madrid, Cape Town, Singapore, São Paulo, Delhi

Cambridge University Press
32 Avenue of the Americas, New York, NY 10013-2473, USA

www.cambridge.org
Information on this title: www.cambridge.org/9780521865524

First published 2008

Printed in the United States of America

A catalog record for this publication is available from the British Library.

Library of Congress Cataloging in Publication Data

Smith, Nick, 1972 Jan. 14–
I was wrong : the meanings of apologies / Nick Smith.
  p. cm.
Includes bibliographical references and index.
ISBN 978-0-521-86552-4 (hardback)
ISBN 978-0-521-68423-1 (paperback)
  1. Apologizing. 2. Ethics I. Title.
BF575.A75S65 2008
155.9′2–dc22   2007031595

ISBN 978-0-521-86552-4 (hardback)
ISBN 978-0-521-68423-1 (paperback)

Cambridge University Press has no responsibility for
the persistence or accuracy of URLs for external or
third-party Internet Web sites referred to in this publication
and does not guarantee that any content on such
Web sites is, or will remain, accurate or appropriate.

For Nicole and Ulysses

"over and beyond ourselves
in which our love will outlive us"

Please forgive me, sir,
for getting involved

in the music—
it's my innate weakness

for the cello: so human.
Please forgive me
for the attention

I've given your wife
tonight, sir.

I was taken by her
strand of pearls,
enchanted by piano
riff in the cortex,
by a secret

anticipation. I don't know
what came over me, sir.

After three Jack Daniel's
you must overlook

my candor, my lack of
sequitur.

I could talk
about Odysseus

& Athena, sexual
flowers, autogamy
or Nothingness.

I got carried away
by the swing of her hips.

But take no offense
if I return to the matter
as if hormonal.
I must confess
my love for black silk, sir.
I apologize for
the eyes in my head.

Yusef Komunyakaa, "When in Rome – Apologia," from
Neon Vernacular[1]

Contents

Acknowledgments

It can be easy to forget what an extreme luxury it is to work as a professor of philosophy, especially when we become habituated to its daily routines. As we stare at our screens, often tired and alone, we can also lose sight of what a great privilege it is to have one's work published, read, and discussed. The opportunity to follow my mind and conscience, rather than the orders of an employer, has been a life-defining gift from many people in my life.

Above all others, I must thank my wife, Nicole. Before I came to the University of New Hampshire in 2002, I worked as an attorney at a large firm in Manhattan. My career change meant not only a precipitous decline in our family's income, but also a move away from Nicole's beloved home city, family, and friends. She embraced this transition with her usual enthusiasm, and in her extraordinary work as a teacher at a local public elementary school we share our commitments to social justice through education. I hope that our students see us as an example of two people enjoying deeply meaningful lives together doing inherently valuable work. In many respects, my relationship with Nicole led me to the topic of apologies. We learn the most about apologies in intimate and vulnerable moments, and much of this book explains how these interpersonal meanings often translate poorly into axioms of social and political philosophy. Our relationship has been a laboratory for apologies, not only in my clumsy attempts to get them right but also through interacting with an exemplar of sincerity like Nicole. Nicole was also the closest reader of this book, saving readers from many ham-fisted, overwrought, and repetitive passages. Our first child was born during the final stages of preparing the text, and my memories of Nicole cheerfully editing the chapters on collective apologies with Ulysses asleep on her lap evoke pangs of profound gratitude in me. She has made my life almost unbearably good.

I would also like to thank my parents, my grandparents, my brother, and his family. They always told me that white lie that I could be whatever I wanted when I grew up, but I doubt that they had philosophy professor in mind as one of the outcomes. They believe in me more than I believe in myself, and I am just now learning how to pass this on to my own family and students.

My students have continually inspired and grounded my work. They infuse me with energy while continually reminding me of just how fragile we all are even in our most triumphant moments. The gifts they have given me eclipse the devotion I show them. Several of them provided substantive commentary of this manuscript, and there are few things more rewarding than watching your students become your peers. In particular, I want to thank Ryan Abbott, Jennifer Bulcock, Mark Joseph, Jacob Skinner, Julian Torres, Dave Turner, Hannah Varn, and Michaela Wood for their various contributions to this project.

My friends also had quite a bit to say about this topic and their delightful eccentricities helped me to appreciate the different ways that apologies convey meaning. It helps to have such an interdisciplinary group of friends when writing a book on apologies. Even if they do not realize it, the exhaustive commentary or offhanded quips of the following people shaped portions of this text: Scott Bakker, Albert Chang, Kyung Cho, Chris Colocousis, Amanda Howerton, Rebecca Johnson, Woo Shik Kim, Mana Kia, Cesar Rebellon, Misha and Liza Risin, Alexis Roberson, Andy Russell, Stefan Sobolowski, Corbin Stevens, Colin Stewart, Emilie Stewart, Karen Van Gundy, George Williams, and Seth Young. As usual, Cesar's engagement with the project helped me to think systematically about the darkest underlying questions.

Just as I argue that one can apologize to a pet in certain respects, I should also thank our dog, Grady. He has been a constant source of joy in our lives, and he appears in many examples.

After the dog, I should thank the philosophers. My colleagues at UNH have lovingly scrutinized this project from its inception, and sharing my work with this diverse group of philosophers has led me to think twice about every claim in the book. I learn something every day from them. I especially want to thank Bill deVries, whose thorough review of the manuscript at a crucial moment helped me to improve the project considerably. Comments from Paul McNamara added needed precision, and Alan Ray's thoughtful comments encouraged me to expand the portions on repentance and religious traditions. Without David Hiley's reminder that "a finished book isn't a bad thing," I might still be revising. I note specific contributions from others within the text.

I began working on this project with Jay Bernstein and Gregg Horowitz, who encouraged me to explore what may have initially looked to them like an odd direction. I assure them that if you scratch any of these arguments, they bleed Adorno. Other than my wife, Guyora Binder did the most to make this book possible. Guyora shepherded me through law school and became my strongest advocate. I continue to struggle with the fundamental questions he asked of this project at its inception. I would also like to thank Roger Gottlieb for recommending that I study the notion of *teshuva*, Stephen Trzaskoma for his help with my *Iliad* references, and Markus Dubber for his support of the project. For introducing me to the Law and Society Association and for her persistent championing of interdisciplinary research in justice studies, I also thank Ellen Cohn.

In addition, I want to express my appreciation to Amanda Moran at Stanford University Press, Deborah Gershenowitz at New York University Press, and John Berger at Cambridge University Press. The confidence that you all expressed in this work fortified me. John proved to be a wise editor, providing time, space, and moral support without transferring onto me any of the pressures that come with the business of selling ideas. His decision to divide this project into two books, with this one outlining the meanings of apologies and the second applying this theory within legal contexts, allowed me to think of this research program in much more ambitious terms. Peter Katsirubas masterfully guided the book to completion.

Finally, this work benefited from the generous support of the University of New Hampshire Roland H. O'Neal Professorship, the University of New Hampshire Graduate School Summer Faculty Fellowship, the University of New Hampshire Junior Faculty Research Fellowship, and the University of New Hampshire Liberal Arts Summer Faculty Research Fellowship. I also want to express my deepest appreciation to those who work in and support the institutions providing my education, including the primary and secondary public school systems of New York, Vassar College, the Baldy Center for Law and Social Policy at the State University of New York at Buffalo School of Law, and the Vanderbilt University Department of Philosophy. Earlier versions of some of the arguments in the text appeared in the *Journal of Social Philosophy*.

Introduction: Apologies as a Source of Moral Meaning in Modernity

Maimonides' *Hilchot Teshuvah*, compiled between 1170 and 1180, arguably provides the most recent philosophical monograph devoted to apologies.[1] Considering the relevance of apologies to moral philosophy and current general interest in acts of contrition, this surprised me. Philosophers have long delighted in scrutinizing suspect social practices, and apologies now seem more than ripe. We share a vague intuition that something has gone afoul with this ubiquitous gesture, a sense that apologies are rotting on the vine.

The arguments in this book track that intuition at various levels. We might think of our standards for apologies as buried deep within our evolutionary hardwiring, as primatologists have documented reconciliation protocols between chimpanzees. These "natural conflict resolutions" can look uncannily similar to handshakes, and from this perspective we might measure the quality of an apology by the amount of oxytocin released by the hominid on its receiving end.[2] Bad apologies, like spoiled fruit, do not satisfy our primal needs.

Alternatively, we might consider the steady stream of odd apologies in the daily news to be like hiccups of etiquette, passing symptoms of normative dyspepsia as we become accustomed to a multicultural buffet of beliefs and manners. Taking the long view of history, we live in a transitional age for apologies and we will eventually settle into more stable habits. Technological shifts accelerate these growing pains, as a connected world creates more opportunities to offend each other, capture these transgressions digitally, and reproduce them on command for anyone across the globe who might take umbrage.[3] Gestures of contrition are also more likely to be captured in the public record, providing armchair moralists with more opportunities to scrutinize what they perceive as faulty apologies. Thus we have two opportunities to disparage wrongdoers: one for the offense and another for providing what we almost always find to be a flawed apology. If either George W. Bush or Hillary Clinton apologizes for a transgression, we can be fairly sure that their critics will seize the occasion to further question their character regardless of the quality of the apology offered. Such is the nature of contemporary politics.

From an even more disconcerting perspective, perhaps our dissatisfaction results from the decay of vestigial customs once essential for religious rituals of repentance but now increasingly obsolete. According to this view, contemporary apologies signify the death twitches of expiring moral systems and those who complain about "disingenuous," "inauthentic," or "commodified" apologies suffer from nostalgia for a more principled age that probably never existed. We can diagnose the general health of our shared values by examining apologies, and something diseased courses through our cultural veins. I do not mean to suggest that the current state of apologies is symptomatic of the decline of Western civilization or something so dramatic, but surely its pulse beats in rhythm with the often-conflicting conditions of modern life. Regardless of my conclusions here, I hope that others will soon join me in thinking through the philosophical substance of these complex and occasionally spectacular moral phenomena.

Law, Commodification, and Apology

I began thinking systematically about apologies while working on another project considering the trend toward increasing commodification in law. When legal actors and institutions convert so many harms – from racial discrimination to the wrongful death of a child – into economic cost-benefit analyses, they can jeopardize certain forms of meaning incommensurable with money. Although money may offer a convenient means of measuring value in a complex and pluralistic world, many of us experience a vague moral discomfort when legal systems convert the worth of human life into dollars and cents. Something seems to be lost in the translation between moral and economic value. Given my sympathies for the Frankfurt School, one can imagine the contours of such an analysis.

In this context I thought that apologies might present opportunities for legal systems to honor meanings and values that seem incompatible with trends toward increasing commodification. In a legal system overrun with commercial logic, a simple apology might convey substantial meaning. A failure to apologize might compound an injury. Examples seemed to corroborate my pedestrian intuition. A close relative, for instance, was fired from her job the day after her employers learned she was pregnant. Although outraged by this transgression and suffering from considerable economic hardship as a result of losing her job, she did not want to pursue a legal claim because she imagined that the process would simply convert the moral offense into some form of economic compensation. As a woman of strong moral and religious values, for her the situation was "not about the money." Instead, she wanted something like an apology. She wanted the employers to admit they had treated her unfairly and to promise they would never cause another woman to suffer such an injustice. This was a matter of principle.

Her sentiments resonated with my experiences in civil and criminal law: despite the common conception that greed motivates litigants, many seek primarily moral rather than economic redress. If you can imagine the horror of having a loved one killed by a faulty product or a grossly negligent surgeon, receiving a monetary award for your loss might be significant for many reasons. This would be so even if the offender refused to admit wrongdoing, as we would expect within an adversarial legal system. Although money can be useful in many ways, however, no amount of cash could provide the sorts of meaning that you might receive if the offender apologized, accepted blame, took moral as well as fiscal responsibility for the loss, and then honored a commitment never to cause such harm again. Money may provide a common denominator for some losses, but often the most significant meanings cannot be reduced to a cash value. This seems like more than facile moralism.

We find the idea that apologies convey meaning beyond financial compensation in the oldest texts of the West. In *The Iliad*, for example, Achilles refuses to fight at Troy despite King Agamemnon's offer to mend their disagreement over Briseis by providing Achilles with gifts fit for a god. Agamemnon offers vast material wealth, the return of Briseis, and the choice among Agamemnon's own daughters in marriage. Achilles rebuffs the offer: "Not if he offered me ten times or twenty times as much as he possesses or could raise elsewhere ... not if his gifts were as many as the grains of sand or particles of dust, would Agamemnon win me over." Instead, Achilles demands, "he must pay me in kind for the bitter humiliation I endured."[4] Rather than material wealth, Achilles believes only something like a sufficiently painful apology could restore his relationship with the king. Thousands of years later, the words of a recent Canadian victim of child abuse echoes Achilles' sentiments: "I got an apology, and you can't put a price on that."[5]

At one level, it might seem that apologies would be incompatible with law, especially the sorts of law predominantly practiced in the contemporary United States. Adversarial law typically creates legal combatants engaged in a struggle to maximize self-interest, but apologies seem better suited to a context of moral reconciliation. My initial research into the role of apologies in law, however, indicated that certain kinds of apologies were increasingly common within legal institutions. Legal actors do in fact put a price on apologies. Expressions of contrition within legal institutions have increasingly become another commodity. Studies suggest that a few words of contrition, regardless of their sincerity by any measure, can dramatically decrease the likelihood of costly litigation. Thus if one were to say something like "I am sorry that the lawn mower we manufacture injured your child," evidence suggests that this provides a highly cost-effective means of avoiding litigation.[6] Considering that a refusal to accept blame for an injury often provides the fundamental grounds for a dispute arriving in the courts in the first place, these findings encourage attorneys and litigants to offer apologetic words without admitting guilt. It can be lucrative to apologize, in other words, so long as you avoid accepting blame.

Legislators recognize the tension between the disincentive to apologize or even offer gestures of compassion in legal proceedings (because of their often-ambiguous relation to admissions of guilt) and the ability of apologies to decrease litigation rates. To resolve this, legislation in numerous jurisdictions codified the notion that apologies can be mere expressions of sympathy – such as "I am sorry that your child was killed" – and need not accept blame for the injury. Settlement agreements may now explicitly negotiate the monetary value of an apology, for example offering compensation of $10 million without any form of apology or $7 million with an apology. The Federal Sentencing Guidelines allow judges to reduce punishment if a criminal defendant expresses remorse, giving convicts incentive to utter words of contrition penned by their attorneys but leaving the judiciary with little means of differentiating between profound expressions of regret and perfunctory attempts to please the court.[7]

Like me, you may be confused at this point. Can we really describe a statement that does not accept blame or admit wrongdoing as an "apology"? What counts as a "proper" apology in these situations? Who are the final arbiters? What standards do they apply? Do the powerful exploit our uncertainties about apologies to their benefit?

Apologies in Culture

These trends in law appear to parallel a broader social phenomenon. Nearly every day someone appears in headline news apologizing for something. Whether a politician, religious leader, corporate executive, celebrity, athlete, or anyone else who finds herself or someone she represents in disfavor, displays of contrition have become routine. As specious apologies become ubiquitous in contemporary culture, their value seems to decline like a form of inflated moral currency. Now when we bear witness to yet another famous person apologizing, our reflexes have become cynical. We question intentions. Does she apologize only to garner votes in the next election? To placate teammates or fans? To brace falling stock values after a corporate controversy? To take the blame for someone more powerful? To avoid or minimize incarceration?

The words and deeds of the apologizers often corroborate our suspicions. Something seems not quite right about many of the apologies we hear. What does it mean for the Pope to apologize for two thousand years of church-sponsored violence? Can he do that? Why does he offer this now? How can Bill Clinton apologize for the Rwandan genocide without accepting personal blame for his own calculated decisions not to intervene? Can a leader claim that she takes personal responsibility for a policy failure yet refuse to admit that she has done anything wrong? How can an executive appear on national television apologizing for the misdeeds of her corporation while simultaneously denying in legal proceedings that any members of the institution committed the alleged wrongdoing? What should we make of the apology from a celebrity who seems to reoffend and apologize every few months? Self-help and corporate leadership manuals like *The Power of Apology: Healing Steps to Transform All of Your Relationships* and *The One Minute Apology* seem to profit from our confusions.[8]

Media outlets reproduce apologies in clips too brief to capture their subtleties, rewarding public figures who provide sound bite apologies and tuning out those who take time to develop the substance of their gesture. The same media also tear offenses from their contexts, leaving the falsely accused in delicate situations. If someone tries to defend herself, headlines will announce that she "refuses to apologize." Within such a culture, the best strategy for damage control may be matching one distorting sound bite with another, saying that you are "sorry" but then explaining that you deserve no blame. Such exchanges typify the impoverished state of moral discourse in modern culture.

Sometimes these apologies seem laughably insincere, disingenuous, deceptive, manipulative, confused, or simply wrong. Since 2001, comedian Harry Shearer – responsible for *This is Spinal Tap* and many voices on *The Simpsons* – has riffed on the seemingly ridiculous nature of public acts of contrition in the "Apologies of the Week" portion of his radio show. Apologies, it seems, have become something of a joke.

We should not fail to appreciate the gravity underlying what may at times seem like a farcical comedy of apologies. The importance of these questions and the extent of our disagreements about apologies were dramatically evident in September of 2006. In an address at the University of Regensburg, Pope Benedict XVI included the following quotation, attributed to Byzantine emperor Manuel II Paleologus circa 1391: "Show me just what Muhammad brought that was new and there you will find things only evil and inhuman, such as his command to spread by the sword the faith he preached." Although we could discuss at length the disclaimers, nuances, and judgments surrounding the Pope's inclusion of this quotation, many took offense to the address. The Vatican quickly released the following statement:

As for the opinion of the Byzantine emperor Manuel II Paleologus that he quoted during his Regensburg talk, the Holy Father did not mean, nor does he mean, to make that opinion his own in any way. He simply used it as a means to undertake – in an academic context, and as is evident from a complete and attentive reading of the text – certain reflections on the theme of the relationship between religion and violence in general, and to conclude with a *clear and radical rejection of the religious motivation for violence, from whatever side it may come.* [The Pope] sincerely regrets that certain passages of his address could have sounded offensive to the sensitivities of the Muslim faithful and should have been interpreted in a manner that in no way corresponds to his intentions.[9]

Here the Vatican effectively claims that if those offended had read more closely, then they would not be offended. Regardless of whether we agree with the substance of the Church's response, we can notice that the Vatican offers something akin to what we might expect from an annoying boyfriend: "I'm sorry you feel that way, you are mistaken to feel that way, and I did not do anything wrong."

Some found the Vatican's statement unsatisfactory. Mohammed Habib, deputy leader of the Society of Muslim Brotherhood, questioned the Vatican: "Has he presented a personal apology for statements by which he clearly is convinced? No. We want a personal apology. We feel that he has committed a grave error."[10]

In an attempt to stem the growing tension created by his address, the day after the Vatican released its statement the Pope included the following comments in his weekly Angelus prayer:

At this time, I wish also to add that I am deeply sorry for the reactions in some countries to a few passages of my address at the University of Regensburg, which were considered offensive to the sensibility of Muslims. These in fact were a quotation from a medieval text, which do not in any way express my personal thought. I hope that this serves to appease hearts and to clarify the true meaning of my address, which in its totality was and is an invitation to frank and sincere dialogue, with great mutual respect.[11]

Although major Western media outlets such as *Reuters* and *The New York Times* described this as an "apology" from the Pope without much reflection on the meaning of the term, others refused to recognize it as such.[12] Yusuf al-Qaradawi, an influential Egyptian Sunni scholar and host of a popular Al-Jazeera program, claimed that the Pope's statements "were no apology" but rather amounted to "an accusation against Muslims that they didn't understand his words."[13] Mehmet Aydin, the Turkish religious affairs minister with a doctoral degree in philosophy from the University of Edinburgh, expressed similar reservations: "You either have to say this 'I'm sorry' in a proper way or not say it at all. Are you sorry for saying such a thing or because of its consequences?"[14] Aydin thus wonders if we should read the Pope's statements as we would if someone explained that she was "sorry you feel that way" and thus regrets not her wrongdoing but your unfortunate response to her justified actions. Grand Sheikh of Al-Azhar Mosque Mohammed Sayed Tantawi, whom the BBC described as "the highest spiritual authority for nearly a billion Sunni Muslims,"[15] insisted that the Pope still must "apologize frankly and justify what he said."[16] Iraq parliamentary speaker Mahmoud al-Mashhadani described the Pope's statements as "inadequate and not commensurate with the moral damage caused to Muslims' feelings."[17] Sheikh Mohammad Hussein, Grand Mufti of the Palestinian Territories, called for the Pope to issue "a personal and clear apology to 1.5 billion Muslims in this world for the insult."[18]

Others appeared openly uncertain. A leader of the Muslim Brotherhood first described the Pope's statements as a "sufficient apology," but later in that same day reversed course: "It does not rise to the level of a clear apology and, based on this, we're calling on the Pope of the Vatican to issue a clear apology that will decisively end any confusion."[19] Still others, including Iranian President Mahmoud Ahmadinejad and Malaysian Prime Minister Ahmad Badavi, took more favorable views of the Pope's clarifying gestures. A representative from the Muslim Council of Britain called the Pope's statements a "good first step." Ajmal Masroor of the Islamic Society of Britain described the Pope's statement as "greatly noble."[20] According to the president of Rome's Islamic cultural center, Italian Muslims had accepted the Pope's apology and this was "a closed chapter."[21]

As religious leaders and heads of state debated the incendiary remarks and subsequent statements, students in Islamabad burned effigies of the Pope.[22] Christian establishments were bombed in Nablus and Gaza City.[23] The Lashkar-e-Toiba allegedly issued a Fatwa calling for the Pope's death. According to one source, the Islamic Salafist Boy Scout Battalions promised to kill all Christians in Iraq if the Pope did not apologize properly.[24] Iraqi Al-Qaeda threatened to punish all "worshippers of the cross" for the Pope's remarks.[25] Two days after the Angelus prayer, two Somalis murdered a nun and her bodyguard in Mogadishu, allegedly in response to the Regensburg address.[26] According to Al-Jazeera, those who kidnapped and beheaded Christian priest Paulos Iskander had demanded a denunciation by his church of the Pope's statements in addition to a ransom of $350,000.[27] To some degree, all of this resulted from perceived deficiencies in the Pope's remarks.

Might we appeal to some measure of apologies to adjudicate between these competing interpretations? This book explores the issues underlying these questions: What is an apology? What are its constitutive elements? Must it convey moral substance? How does it bear social meaning in various traditions and contexts? Has its meaning been subverted or abused within modern public and private life? Are its moral meanings – which surely evolved from notions of repentance shared by ancient religious traditions – becoming obsolete in a secular and multicultural era? Is our dissatisfaction with many contemporary apologies a form of nostalgia for the moral certainties of the past? Must we agree on the answers to these questions if we are to be morally compatible?

Apologies: A Philosophical Genealogy

Unfortunately, the history of philosophy offers little guidance in answering these questions and in fact only seems to confuse us further. The *Confessions* of both St. Augustine and Rousseau offer moments of contrition but do not give much explicit thought to the nature of apologies as such. Montaigne expressed his skepticism for the related practice of repentance.[28] Austin and

Searle offered some analysis of apologies as speech acts, but most research influenced by their discussions migrated into the field of linguistics. Levinas' notion of "apologetic discourse" in response to the violence of reducing the Other has become quite influential within Continental philosophy and various forms of Cultural Studies, but this notion of apology has become a rather technical concept typically invoked in radical contrast to the traditions of freedom and moral responsibility that inform more common usage of the term. Perhaps the most critical attention to the subject in the history of philosophy has been devoted to Heidegger's failure to apologize for his service to the Nazi Party.

Given the dearth of analyses of apologies in Western philosophical traditions, it is especially ironic that so many introductory philosophy courses begin with Plato's *Apology*. Socrates is anything but apologetic as the term has come to be understood. Instead, he provides an apologia (απολογια) as was customary in the classical Greek legal system in rebuttal to the prosecution's accusations. Apologia still finds use in this sense of offering a defense of one's position, and the field of apologetics has come to be associated with the long tradition of defending and reinforcing religious doctrine – particularly Christian beliefs – through argumentation. Montaigne intends this justificatory use in his *Apology for Raymond Sebond*.[29] In modern parlance we consider an "apologist" to be a sort of spokesperson who promotes and defends causes by using various rhetorical strategies to spin facts and influence an audience, sometimes performing this service for pay. A White House press secretary or a corporate defense attorney comes to mind as a modern apologist compensated for her ability to forward partisan arguments.

The modern use of apology as an admission of wrongdoing rather than a defense seems to have gained momentum around the sixteenth century, when Shakespeare used it in *Richard III* to imply a kind of regret.[30] Johnson's 1755 dictionary noted the historical tension and steered the definition toward the modern sense: "Apology generally signifies rather excuse than vindication, and tends rather to extenuate the fault, than prove innocence."[31] Hence the common usage of apology may have drifted from a general notion of a defense to a particular kind of defense in the form of an excuse. Johnson noted that this trend was "sometimes unregarded by writers," citing Milton's *Paradise Lost* for this insensitivity. Although I am no authority in historical linguistics, perhaps the secularization of morality occasioned the advent of modern notions of apologies to supplant ancient religious practices of repentance. Broadly influential philosophers like Maimonides facilitated this transition by speaking of apologies to god and fellow humans within the same text.

Thus even the etymology of apology pulls in two directions. On the one hand, we associate apologizing with repentance, confession, remorse, blame, and moral *defenselessness*. On the other hand, a considerable period of history understood the practice precisely as a *defense*. A third convention came into usage around 1754 and defined "apology" and "sorry" as a poor substitute, as in a "sorry excuse for a friendship" or "crackers served as but an apology for dinner."[32] *The Oxford English Dictionary* recognizes each of these forms as acceptable definitions of "apology."[33] Given this, consider the complex role of an attorney acting as a paid apologist in the old sense instructing her client to offer something like an apology in the modern sense because this may be her best rhetorical strategy for the optimal legal outcome. Now imagine the attorney carefully calibrating the apology to avoid admitting wrongdoing. It would not be surprising if the offended party in such a claim suffered from uncertainty about the meaning of such an "apologetic" exchange. Add to this the arguments in the two pioneering books on apologies – one by sociologist Nicholas Tavuchis and the other by psychiatrist Aaron Lazare – that both understand apologies primarily as social tools.[34] Lazare and Tavuchis provide extremely thoughtful analyses and I do not wish to underestimate the importance of the many pragmatic functions of apologies. Use, however, is only one source of apologetic meaning. In addition, not all of the uses of apologies and their imitators – even those leading to apparently beneficial consequences – are entirely good. How can we make sense of apologies as they transform from the ancient notion of a legal defense to the modern notion of contrition for wrongdoing, but then occasionally return to their roots as a kind of concealed legal, political, and personal rhetorical stratagem?

Why Study Apologies?

Readers might legitimately ask whether we should expend effort to understand apologies better. A thought experiment may provide the best way to answer that question: take a moment to identify the apology that would be most meaningful for you to receive.

Perhaps you think of an apology from a parent, a spouse, a sibling, a colleague, or an estranged friend. Perhaps the person who defrauded, disfigured, or humiliated you comes to mind. Perhaps you think of the leader of the platoon that bombed your town. Maybe an apology from the president of your own country would matter most to you. You might want an apology from a group, like the Nazi Party, the United Nations, the Janjaweed, or Enron Corporation.

I do not have any unusually traumatic events in my past, but when I consider the apologies that would be most meaningful to me I imagine that they would directly address my deepest pains, fears, values, and hopes. My life and my relationships would be fundamentally different after these apologies. Things would be better and more just. This book attempts to explain how an apology, which at first glance may seem like an artifact of old-fashioned etiquette, can have such power.

The following chapters describe the various ways that apologies can have meaning for us, but we can preview a few here. An apology can recognize that we have been harmed, helping us to understand what happened and why. The person apologizing accepts blame for our injury and she explains why her actions were wrong. This validates the victim's beliefs, and she can begin or resume a relationship based on these shared values. The offender also treats us differently at the most fundamental level when she apologizes to us: instead of viewing us as an obstacle to her self-interests, we become a person with dignity. If the apologizer regrets her actions and promises not to repeat them, we can take some security in the hope that she will not harm us again. This provides a reason to trust the offender and may be terribly important if she is someone for whom the victim cares deeply. An apology can also provide the victim with relief for her injury, ranging from nominal gestures of communion to considerable economic compensation. An apology may also punish injustice.

When we think of apologies in these respects, we can appreciate why personal and political relationships may hinge on them and why a penitent act has the power to mend a broken family or avert a war. If we think of all of the festering injuries that cause so much pain in our intimate lives as well as our global conflicts, apologies often seem like the best means of cleaning and stitching those wounds. Whether a petty insult that has poisoned family dynamics for generations or an era of brutal oppression against a racial minority that haunts a nation, what I describe as a categorical apology can often serve as the most effective means of mitigating social conflicts.

Although apologies serve numerous purposes and we can think of their value in terms of these utilitarian benefits, they often strike at the heart of our deontological commitments and call on us to honor our basic duties. Apologies can also speak directly to our character and integrity. At a time when value and meaning seem to erode into a morass of selfish and nihilistic commercial culture, we often demand an apology when we refuse to allow an offender to disregard a moral principle. Apologies flag when someone crosses a line, patrolling the limits of our commitments to shared principles. In this respect, apologies have inherent as well as instrumental value.

Although apologies can be profoundly meaningful, many of us know all too well that this is usually not the case. At least three factors cloud our ability to judge apologies: 1) we are uncertain about what a full apology is and lack a framework for analyzing acts of penitence; 2) we often consider any gesture with a family resemblance to an apology – such as the bare utterance of the word "sorry" – to be equal to a full apology; and 3) given this confusion, we may accept whatever satisfies our lowest standards for apologies so that we can consider ourselves "apologized to." I describe how apologies often convey muddled or deceptive sentiments and I prescribe a means of decoding such gestures. With this, we can understand the subtleties of apologies, be clear about what we want from apologies, and determine how particular apologies measure up to our expectations. If we desire a categorical apology for a serious injury, we need not settle for less because of our confusion. Although it might seem harmless if someone provided an insubstantial apology for stepping on my toe, it could be a grave injustice for an offender to dupe a victim of abuse into settling for a purposefully deceptive apology. Whether an innocent mistake or an intentional manipulation of our confusion about apologies, this occurs regularly in quarrels among friends, expressions of remorse from convicts, and declarations between nations. When a victim knows what kinds of meanings she wants from an apology, she can hold the offender to these standards rather than artificially inflate the meaning of a few sympathetic words offered to mollify her. If she expects a categorical apology in a romantic or criminal context, vacuous or manipulative language will not deceive her. In addition, apologizing begrudgingly, equivocally, or evasively can embrace or compound the initial wrongdoing rather than repudiate and correct it. Fluency in the language of apologies should provide a defense against politicians, corporate executives, attorneys, criminals, or lovers who seek to use the illusion of their moral transformation to win our favor.

Under my theory we should view the words "I am sorry" with the same scrutiny we would apply to the words "I love you" spoken on a first date – the declaration may be meaningful in some senses but we would need to know much more before we could make a well-informed judgment. This renders the slogan from Erich Segal's *Love Story* claiming that "love means never having to say you're sorry" doubly problematic. Although I have some difficulty interpreting this statement, I suspect he intends it to convey the idea that those who love each other will always necessarily reconcile (or perhaps never need reconciling). Because love presupposes reconciliation and apologies provide but a tool to achieve reconciliation, apologies are of no use to those who love each other. Yet notice how such a statement elides the complexities of love and the complexities of apologies, compounding two banalities into a third regarding the relationship between love and apologies. With such adages lodged in our cultural memory we should not find it surprising that apologies within intimate relationships can be such a source of befuddlement and contention.

I should also emphasize the prescriptive component of my theory here. My point is not only to help us measure the apology we get against the apology we want. We might be entirely confused about apologetic meaning, and our desire alone does not determine what makes for a suitable apology. As we reflect on apologetic meaning, I expect that we will want more from apologies in our lives. Instead of seeking only an expression of sympathy, we might realize that we deserve much more and demand it. I hope that thinking about apologies in the ways I suggest will empower victims to some degree. Those who understand the contours of apologetic meaning should probably receive better apologies.

We can appreciate the meanings of apologies for the apologizer as well as for the victim. As the lucid work of Trudy Govier and Wilhelm Verwoerd emphasizes, apologies are not only for victims.[35] Becoming literate in the dialects of apologetic meaning seems essential for our moral development. Apologies can anchor our moral lives, promising that our actions never drift too far from our values. As children, we learn about morality in large part when our parents and teachers admonish us to apologize so that we will reflect on the nature of our behavior and become integrated into a normative community. As we mature, apologizing can mark an occasion when we pause and self-consciously honor our abstract moral beliefs – we have wronged or have been wronged and we must denounce the trespass or risk losing the value jeopardized by it. Because of their importance to our moral growth, apologies have become integral to twelve-step programs such as Alcoholics Anonymous that attempt to reorient the moral lives of their members.

Understanding when and how to apologize can provide invaluable insights into our relationships with others. Since working on these issues, I have found myself increasingly aware of the moral dimensions of my daily interactions. Instead of tossing out half-hearted "sorrys" when I fail to take out the trash as my spouse requested, for instance, I can now identify the deeper underlying harm (such as not listening to or respecting her), appreciate why I have indeed committed an offense that should not be taken lightly, and explain to her why I am really remorseful. Instead of arguing about the garbage, we realize that this spat really concerns how we treat each other. An increased apologetic acuity can provide insights into the moral core of our relationships and make us more socially wise. This does not entail that every apology in our lives must be categorical. We may take comfort in a mere expression of sympathy and we may appreciate the sentiment of a confused but well-intentioned attempt to apologize. In all of these cases, however, deciphering the apology should help us to understand our interactions better.

The Meanings and Complexities of Apologies

Apologies are far more complex than they seem and this study, like all of my favorite books, raises more questions than it answers. As I will discuss at length in the subsequent chapters, we face considerable temptation to apply some binary standard and declare whether something "is or is not" an apology. Instead of worrying whether an example "is or is not" an apology, I wonder how well it serves certain purposes and to what extent it conveys certain kinds of subtle social meanings. I will refer to these as a "loose constellation of interrelated meanings," but others may prefer Wittgenstein's notion of "family resemblance."[36] In some cases, a victim may desire each of the forms of meaning I mention. In others, she may only seek one sort of meaning such as a sincere expression of sympathy or a remorseless payment to cover the cost of repair.

In the initial portions of this book I attempt to defend why I prefer speaking of the various "forms" of apologetic meaning rather than "is or is not" binary conceptions. I then consider the forms of meaning that I find most illuminating, with much of my work devoted to the inexact science of parsing the distinct spheres of meaning from each other. I begin by considering how an apology can explain the history of an injury. Contested facts often lie at the heart of moral conflicts, and this meeting of the minds between the offender and offended can in certain circumstances be the most significant and hardest-earned aspect of an apology. I then brave the knotty question of the relation between apologies and responsibilities. I subdivide this into concerns regarding 1) the distinction between accepting blame and expressing sympathy, as we often find in the form of "I am sorry that X happened to you"; 2) the general relationship between causation and moral responsibility and how debates within this complex field relate to apologetic meaning; 3) the status of accidents and surprisingly common denials of intent in the form of "I didn't mean to X"; and 4) the problem of standing, where one person apologizes for another.

I then note the significance of identifying each moral wrong in the act to be apologized for. This entails both explicitly naming the offense as a blameworthy violation of a moral value and naming each violation rather than covering over a host of wrongs with an undifferentiated and generic statement of contrition. Categorical regret also plays a role. The categorically regretful offender believes her actions were wrong and she would not undertake them again if confronted with similar circumstances and temptations, which differs from a belief that the harm she caused was justified but unfortunate. I then consider the various ways in which the performance of the apology can alter meaning. The problems of reform and reparation present numerous points of discussion, as do questions regarding the emotions and intentions of the apologizer. Each of these spheres of meaning invokes lively debates within contemporary philosophy that I cannot hope to resolve here. Instead, I note their relevance by explaining how various presuppositions would color one's view of apologetic meaning.

After outlining these spheres of apologetic meaning, I consider the relationship between apologies and gender and the often-cited presumption that women apologize more than men do. The different meanings of apologies also track various religious and cultural traditions, and I briefly suggest how contemporary notions of apologies map onto diverse practices of repentance. From here I entertain the possible meaning of unusual cases of apologizing to animals, infants, machines, the deceased, and oneself. I conclude the initial sections by examining the relationship between apologies and forgiveness. In an attempt to reconstruct some helpful shorthand for thinking about different kinds of apologies, I then classify a few different types of apologies. Rather than a set of predigested answers or a checklist, I attempt to offer a guide to how we can think about individual apologies within particular contexts.

With this framework in place, I devote considerable space to identifying the sorts of meaning possible for collective apologies, such as those offered by heads of states and corporate leaders. Such apologies, I argue, are often quite confused and face very serious objections if they claim to offer the sorts of meaning desired from individual apologies. The conclusion previews my next book, which will be devoted entirely to apologies in law.

I intend this introduction to prepare readers for an intricate account of apologies. For those seeking a succinct guide to apologizing, you might first read the section titled Varieties of Apologies and then consult other sections for clarification. If you have a strong stomach for moral nuances and would like to see how the sausage is made, I hope reading on repays your efforts.

PART ONE

Apologies from Individuals

In speaking of lies, we come inevitably to the subject of truth. There is nothing simple or easy about the idea. There is no "the truth," "a truth" – truth is not one thing, or even a system. It is an increasing complexity. . . .

This is why the effort to speak honestly is so important. Lies are usually attempts to make everything simpler – for the liar – than it really is, or ought to be. . . .

It is important to do this because it breaks down human self-delusion and isolation.

It is important to do this because in so doing we do justice to our own complexity.

It is important to do this because we can count on so few people to go that hard way with us.

Adrienne Rich, from "Women and Honor: Some Notes on Lying"[1]

CHAPTER ONE

The Meanings of Apologies

Much of our private and public moral discourse occurs in the giving, receiving, or demanding of apologies, yet we rarely make explicit precisely what we expect from a gesture of contrition. As a result, apologizing has become a vague, clumsy, and sometimes spiteful ritual. We intuitively understand that certain kinds of apologies can be life transforming for both victims and offenders. Some apologies, however, can be worse than none at all. Empty gestures may masquerade as soul-searching apologies, sometimes because this seems like the least burdensome means of restoring a relationship to its status quo. On other occasions, an offender may intentionally wish to deceive or manipulate a victim with an apology. Such duplicity occurs not only between adversaries but also among friends, relatives, and lovers. Whether an unrepentant executive orders her attorney to feign contrition so that an injured party will settle a claim or an abusive husband with no intention to reform says to his wife that he is "sorry that" she is upset, we can see how victims stand to suffer further injuries if they attribute more meaning to an apology than warranted.

This brings me to the passage from Adrienne Rich quoted at the outset of this chapter: "Lies are usually attempts to make everything simpler – for the liar – than it really is, or ought to be." Apologies are complex interactions, and many attempts to simplify them use 'sorry' to obscure injustices rather than to accept blame for wrongdoings. Many apologies lie.

Although I certainly have not discovered the "one true essence" of the gesture, I consider in some detail various elements central to historical practices of apologizing. By isolating these different aspects of apologies, we can gain a more honest understanding of how they form the nexus of meaning to which we refer in English as "apologizing."

I will use the neologism "categorical apology" to describe an apology that achieves meaning across each of the elements I discuss. We can understand a categorical apology as a kind of *prescriptive stipulation*, or, if you prefer, a regulative ideal. According to my account, a categorical apology amounts to a rare and burdensome act. Under certain circumstances, some forms of apologetic meaning may not be possible regardless of how badly we desire them. This is not to say that we should dismiss anything short of a categorical apology as worthless, and I will provide classifications for typical noncategorical apologies as well. I hope that these distinctions will guide us toward the sorts of meaning we can strive for in any particular apology and help us to compare the apologies we receive with our expectations.

Rather than focusing on the semantics or definition of the term "apology," I am primarily concerned with the various kinds of *social meanings* of apologies. Instead of emphasizing the social significance of apologies as I do, one might approach their meaning from a different direction. A linguistic analyst might expect me to answer the question "What is the meaning of the word 'apology'?" Here "meaning" refers to something like the *definition* of the term "apology." From this perspective, the important philosophical work consists of determining the necessary conditions for belonging to the group of things called "apologies" and then measuring particular examples against this standard. The title of Louis Kort's essay "What Is an Apology?" captures the spirit of this methodology. Kort frames his evaluations according to the following calculus: "Let X and Y be people, and U be an utterance. Then, in saying U to Y, X apologizes to Y for something, A, if and only if the following conditions obtain. . . ."[1] One type of question guides such an analyst: "Is U an apology?" The answer to this question is either yes or no. Because it effectively presents us with two choices, I describe such approaches to apologies as binary.

Consider a few definitions from diverse methodological perspectives. Lazare, a professor of psychiatry, offers the following "basic definition" of an apology: "an acknowledgment of an offense and an expression of remorse."[2] While finding its primary inspiration in philosophers like J. L. Austin and John Searle, the "speech-act" tradition pervades treatments of apologies in linguistics and other social sciences.[3] Austin classifies apologies as performative utterances because, under certain conditions, the act of uttering, "I apologize" is constitutive of the act of apologizing. Speaking the words "I apologize," to some extent, makes it so. This differs from uttering a statement like "I am flying" because speaking those words does not constitute the act of taking flight. For Searle, an apology is an example of an expressive illocutionary act and the "point of this class is to express the psychological state specified in the sincerity condition about a state of affairs specified in the propositional content."[4] Searle believes that feeling is regret in cases of apologies.[5]

Some, like Marion Owen and other contributors to the academic literature on politeness, combine speech-act theory with the "face-saving" or "remedial interchange" theories of sociologist Erving Goffman.[6] Goffman believes an apology in its "fullest form" has "several elements":

expression of embarrassment and chagrin; clarification that one knows what conduct had been expected and sympathizes with the application of negative sanction; verbal rejection, repudiation, and disavowal of the wrong way of behaving along with vilification of the self that so behaved; espousal of the right way and an avowal henceforth to pursue that course; performance of penance and the volunteering of restitution.[7]

Like the preponderance of speech-act theorists, Goffman argues that apologies in all facets of existence are "drawn from a single logically coherent framework of possible practices."[8]

Despite the fact that Searle and Goffman devoted but a few pages between them to the subject of apologies, they inform many of the subsequent definitions. Following Goffman, linguist Janet Holmes defines an apology as "a speech act addressed to B's face needs and intended to remedy an offense for which A takes responsibility, and thus to restore equilibrium between A and B (where A is the apologizer, and B is the person offended)."[9] Philosopher Kathleen Gill, also citing Goffman, provides the following "necessary conditions for apologizing":

1. At least one of the parties believes that the incident actually occurred.
2. At least one of the parties involved believes that the act was inappropriate. If the person offering the apology does not believe the act inappropriate, she must be willing to accept the legitimacy of the addressee having taken offense.
3. Someone is responsible for the offensive act. And either the party offering the apology takes responsibility for the act, or there is some relationship between the responsible actor and the apologizer such that her taking responsibility for offering the apology is justifiable.
4. The apologizer must have an attitude of regret with respect to the offensive behavior and a feeling of remorse in response to the suffering of the victim.
5. The person to whom the apology is offered is justified in believing that the offender will try to refrain from similar offenses in the future.[10]

Originating as a means of measuring the competence of those learning a second language, the Cross-Cultural Speech Acts Realization Project developed a system for analyzing apologetic speech acts across cultures and divides apologies into five components described as the "apology speech act set."[11] The system includes an "illocutionary force indicating device" (such as the words "I'm sorry"), an account of what caused the violation, the speaker's acceptance of responsibility for the harm, an offer to redress the injury, and a promise to forbear from reoffending.[12] Within such works we find tables indicating the "Operationalization of Apology Components and Definitions for Strength Ratings" and quantitative data measuring the outcomes.[13]

My own attempts to provide a definition of apologies collapsed under a barrage of questions. What if I express remorse for events that I did not cause in any obvious sense, for example the African slave trade or Rwandan genocide? Should this "count" as an apology? Have I apologized if I admit to causing the harm and provide some compensation, but I fear that I lack the self-restraint to act differently in the future? If I reoffend after uttering heartfelt apologetic words and providing generous redress, do I annul my apology in some sense? Must I experience certain emotions to have apologized properly? If so, which emotions and to what degree of intensity? Or consider philosopher Glen Pettigrove's sensible view that "if we have no intention of making reparation, doing penance, and acting justly in the future, then the offer of an apology is infelicitous." Thus, he argues, "while an apology absent reparation may be an apology in form, it is not one in substance."[14] But what if I apologize on my deathbed, understanding that I will regrettably never be able to complete penance, reform my behavior, or compensate the victim for the harms I caused her? If I am too poor to provide commensurate restitution, is an apology beyond my means? What if the person to whom I apologize is already dead? Can this "restore equilibrium" between us? What if my family practices a tradition requiring a repentant offender to bake an apple pie for the wronged relative, and no words are needed given the symbolic meaning of the pastry as a gesture of reconciliation? Would it be a mistake to describe an offering of this sort as an apology? More confounding questions surface when we ask about whether collectives can apologize. Does it make sense, for instance, to think of a nation as apologizing for events in its distant past? Questions of this sort riddled my attempts to offer a satisfying definition and left me with a sense that determining whether something is or is not an apology was not the question that most interested me.

I also came to realize that I wanted to think about more than speech and language. Language may relate to nearly all aspects of human social life, especially as understood by philosophers like Wittgenstein and Brandom. Searle, however, is the philosopher exerting the strongest influence on most interdisciplinary studies of apologies. He explicitly claims that to "study speech acts of promising or apologizing we need only study *sentences* whose literal and correct utterance would constitute making a promise or issuing an apology."[15] Regardless of the importance of speech acts in the study of apologies, there are other aspects to rituals of contrition. In many apologies, the words exchanged provide but a glimpse into their meanings and their predominant social value unfolds in the gestures, actions, habits, and emotions of the participants. It also seems possible that one could convey considerable apologetic meaning without the presence of anything like a conventional speech act, as the earlier apologetic baking example suggests.

Some theorists limit their studies not only to the language of apologies, but also to specific words. Marion Owen's book devoted entirely to apologetic language studies "only those utterances that include phrases 'I'm sorry' or 'I apologise' and variants of these."[16] For Owen, the "use of one of these key words guarantees that the move is remedial almost as unequivocally as the use of 'thank' constitutes thanking."[17] Bruce Fraser agrees: "When the speaker utters, 'I apologize for...' there is no question that an apology has been made, or perhaps offered."[18] This may be true according to some technical sense, but I suspect that few of us would find a speaker appropriately contrite if she states "I apologize for your stupidity" after an intense argument. Similarly, linguistic analyses have focused on the locutionary structure of apologies to such an extent that some consider disingenuous acts of contrition to be legitimate examples of apologies, just as a broken promise remains a promise and a false assertion remains an assertion.[19] Although this makes sense within a project that seeks only to determine what "counts" as an apology, it leaves unconsidered the fine-grained differences between apologies that make them significant to us.[20]

Occasions also arise when an offender explains that she was morally wrong for causing harm to you, deeply regrets the pain you have suffered, provides generous compensation for the injuries, undergoes a radical transformation, and never commits the offense again. All of this could take place without the words "sorry" or "apologize" being uttered and the interaction could thus fall outside the scope of some studies of apologies. I expect such examples are quite common. Instead of offering the words "apology" or "sorry," we sometimes employ different methods to convey similar meaning. We might cognitively restructure the event, perhaps thanking a person we have wrongly delayed ("Thank you for your patience") rather than apologizing for our tardiness ("I apologize for making you wait").[21] Alternatively, we might skip to requesting to be excused or granted forgiveness, as in "Please excuse me for wasting your valuable time." As numerous articles on obstacles faced by non-native speakers suggest, apologizing in other languages and between languages further complicates matters.[22] Indeed, some cultures have no equivalent terms for "I'm sorry" and instead the offender self-denigrates or expresses appreciation for the victim's ability to bear the imposed burden.[23]

I do not fault studies of the language of apologies for focusing on the proper domains of their areas of expertise to the exclusion of other perspectives. Indeed, I find their contributions invaluable. Because the philosophical study of apologies has focused on apologies as speech acts, however, I want to advise readers that I approach the subject from a different perspective. Instead of defining apologies and then judging what actions fall within the scope of this definition, I seek a theory of apologies capable of illuminating how this potentially profound interpersonal gesture can transform our understanding of our social world and ourselves. This shifts the focus from the *definition* of the term to its *value* within our lives. I want to know not only whether something is an apology, but also whether it performs certain functions and conveys desired meanings.

The Meanings of "Meanings"

In his 2003 book *Meaning*, David Cooper takes a broad view of meaning that I find compelling and applicable to the study of apologies.[24] In addition to the canonical texts in the philosophy of language, Cooper takes his cues from Continental philosophers like Merleau-Ponty who understand humans as "traffickers in meaning" and words as things "into which the history of a whole language is compressed."[25] For Cooper, in order "to gauge the reach of meaning, we should attend to the use of the English word 'significance' and its cognates as well as to that of 'meaning.'"[26] In this sense, we can speak of the meaning of works of art and everyday objects like the bowler hat that repeatedly returns to a Kundera character, "each time with a different meaning."[27] As Cooper argues, *"anything at all* may, in the appropriate context, be spoken of as having meaning."[28] Cooper continues: "Just as a terrain may contain, but extend beyond, the fields that have been cultivated upon it, so the terrain of meaning extends beyond the fields of made-to-measure items." "Is there a name for that terrain?" he asks. "We might call it 'the world,' in the sense made familiar by phenomenologists...the world of things and events as...taken up into and related to our lives."[29] Here the study of meaning considers not only locution or syntax but also existence in its many layered and diverse forms. To underscore the point that all things can have different meanings depending on the contexts in which we find them and the frameworks through which they are viewed, we need think only of the diverse senses of meaning invoked by Grice's analysis of utterances, Heidegger's excursus on a broken hammer, Van Gogh's depiction of a wheat field, or Clov's jest in *Endgame*: "Mean something! You and I mean something! Ah, that's a good one!"[30] Even silence or nonsense will have different meaning depending on where we find it.

My primary question is not "What is the meaning of 'apology'?" but rather "What are the social meanings of apologies?" We share a sense that an apology can be monumental or insignificant, just as we might consider the day of our marriage ceremony more meaningful than a typical day at the office. This sense of "meaning" as a descriptor of the value or worth of an apology interests me most. Unless they restrict their study to a biological classification of "life," philosophers do not use "meaning" to refer to a definition when they speak of the "meaning of life." Instead, meaning invokes a "sense" of how the world and our experiences in it come to have importance for us. Meaning here includes not only what is signified, but also what is significant, valued, worthy, and interesting. Such existential meaning considers, as phenomenologists refer to it, *lived human experience* as well as the linguistic conventions that contribute to such experiences. From this perspective, we can see how a question like "What is marriage?" differs from asking, "What does it mean to be married?" Understanding the meaning of marriage requires conversations about the subjective beliefs, ambitions, and emotions of specific individuals as they occur within vast networks of social values, religious and political histories, gender roles, and economic forces. The same is true regarding the meaning of a first kiss, a dollar bill, or an apology. I therefore explore not only the question "What is an apology?" but also the broader issue "What does it mean to give and receive an apology in a given context?" Here the significance of an apology relates to a broader cradle of meaning in which it nests, including ultimate frameworks such as those provided by religious worldviews. A benefit of this approach arises from its attention to how underlying social conditions inform nuanced interactions like apologies. The meaning of an apology does not exist exclusively within the minds of victims and offenders, but also within and because of the elaborate social space between them. This should also help us to remember that apologies hold meaning for offenders and communities as well as for victims.[31]

I argue that apologetic meaning can span several different "forms," "kinds," or "spheres" of value (to reference Michael Walzer's *Spheres of Justice*).[32] Apologies can be valuable in diverse and distinct ways. I devote the bulk of the initial portions of this book to explaining the various kinds of meanings apologies can have, but they include things like the offender admitting that she did something wrong, accepting responsibility for the harm she caused, and experiencing appropriate emotions. Others have noted several of the elements of apologies that I will consider, but I enjoy the luxury of examining each element and the relations between the elements in more detail than previous treatments.

Some apologies offer considerable significance across all of the central forms of meaning, and I describe these as categorical apologies. Other apologies provide limited meaning for a few of the forms, and some expressions offer little or no apologetic meaning in any of the forms. Some meanings are primarily instrumental and serve other purposes; some apologetic meanings are inherently valuable. An apology can be highly meaningful in one way while being almost meaningless in another, for instance by accepting blame for an injury but failing to provide any redress for the harm. As in Walzer's *Sphere of Justice*, the meanings between the forms of apologetic meaning are largely incommensurable. If a tycoon injures me and writes me a generous check but refuses to admit wrongdoing, the meaning associated with accepting blame will be absent regardless of how much she pays me. Inversely, an admission of wrongdoing without redress would lack a certain kind of meaning regardless of how emphatically the offender denounces her actions.

We can use the following terms, some of which may resonate a bit differently across disciplines, to describe aspects of my methodology: multivariable, multidimensional, contextualist, and both descriptive and prescriptive without committing to a single moral theory. We might think that we can locate every apology on a single one-dimensional scale from the meaningless to the meaningful, but I claim that apologies achieve varying degrees of diverse forms of meanings in contextually specific fields of significance. The forms of meaning interrelate, but they can be sufficiently parsed for study. It also seems unhelpful to describe separate instances of even categorical apologies as "equally" meaningful. Perfunctory apologies for grievous injuries may be more meaningful in some respects than apologies for minor harms that cover all of the forms. It is also possible that some apologies will be meaningful for reasons other than their quality as apologies, as I can imagine that an apology from my favorite celebrity for stepping on my toe could be significant for me even though I care little about its "apologetic" meaning.

The meaning of any apology derives from its particular actors and context, and I doubt it would be useful to argue for the existence of a necessary and universal essence of a social practice like apologizing in light of its range of meanings and cultural nuances. I do believe, however, that apologies can provide a core of coherent and profound meanings when we maintain the thick conception of them offered here. If we are "traffickers in meaning," to play on Merleau-Ponty's phrase, I offer something like an overhead view of the patterns of traffic in the sprawling cultural landscape of apologies. I try not only to describe those patterns but also to improve the signage and suggest better routes.

For the most part, we do not need to commit to any single underlying ethical theory when analyzing apologies. In some instances, our conceptions of apologies rest on foundational accounts of morality or endure as residue from times of greater normative certainty. Our commitments to shared principles can have many sources. Some understand their moral beliefs to be universally grounded while others live with a relativistic conception of their values. In order for us to share a value, however, we need not share a foundational account of that value. One's commitment to racial equality, for instance, may spring from any number of competing worldviews. Although I attempt to flag instances where a divergence in ethical frameworks might be salient, in most cases my claims should be equally compelling or disagreeable to Kantians, utilitarians, virtue ethicists, rational choice economists, and others. I try to note where consequentialists would take a distinct approach to an issue, and my account may occasionally appear Kantian when referencing dignity, respect, objectification, or instrumentalization. I invoke these notions not as a presupposed metaphysics of morals but because many readers will consider them essential reference points when evaluating social practices. To this end, I will also consider the relationships between apologies and various religious and cultural practices.

Despite these qualifications, I hope to demonstrate that for each injury there exist possibilities for more and less meaningful apologies. Approximations of categorical apologies – gestures that do not provide certain of the available kinds of apologetic meaning – can prove meaningful in their own right. We should take care, however, to understand how they fall short of categorical apologies because many mimic the meaning of full apologies without doing the required work.[33] I believe the elements outlined here are implicit in our commonsense expectations of apologies but that various social forces have caused slippages in meaning. We should correct this if we hope to achieve a better understanding of the practice and preserve its more meaningful expressions. Rather than asking what an apology *is*, I hope to provide some insight into what an apology *should be* in various contexts.

Responding to Preliminary Objections

I should attempt to forestall a few potential confusions here. The notion of a categorical apology appears to belie my claim that I want to focus on social meanings rather than definitions: Ultimately, something is a categorical apology because it satisfies certain necessary conditions or it is not. Although I believe we – and I will say more later about who belongs in this "we" – have such a categorical apology in mind when we seek a "full" apology, I use the notion of a categorical apology as a matter of rhetorical convenience rather than as a metaphysical assertion. In other words, I offer a prescriptive stipulation to create a kind of shorthand for an apology that rises to a certain level of comprehensiveness and intensity. I could have raised or lowered the standard somewhat without losing its prescriptive force. My determination of what counts as categorical, I admit, is entirely contestable and the definitional questions raised against other theories can challenge my notion of the categorical apology as well. I leave readers to ask these questions of my account as they arise in particular contexts. I imagine that the substance of my analysis will be of value primarily in sensitizing us to the gritty details of apologetic meaning, and I would be delighted if this leads to more interesting questions about these enigmatic gestures. If someone desires a "full" apology, this text may help her think through what sorts of meaning that might require. Characterizing an offender's actions as a categorical apology amounts to perhaps the least significant aspect of the analysis, and I hope that my neologism does not prove too distracting.

One might object that my lack of a final definition of apology renders me incapable of authoritatively describing actions that obviously do not amount to apologies as such. Some statements, we might think, are just clearly not apologies. Suppose my wife tells me that she will not share a meal with me until I apologize for a recent infraction. I respond by asking her to "please pass the salt." By most accounts, my request for the salt surely does not deserve to be considered an apology. Notice the work we must do to explain why this seems so obvious. We will probably recite a list of meanings that my request does not satisfy, claiming that such meanings are essential components of an apology. Not only does my request not satisfy these criteria, but it also seems to fall short in every sense.

But what if the argument that gave rise to her ultimatum concerned my poor table manners, as my boorish habits have grown intolerable to her and she refuses to eat with me until I become more polite? In this light, my request that she "*please* pass the salt" takes on more significance as an indication that I have at least momentarily made an effort to reform. Perhaps from this moment forward I am a model of etiquette. What seemed like a clear example of something that was not an apology now drifts into a recognizable realm of apologetic meaning. Alternatively, imagine that I said, "Sorry, please pass the salt." Does the presence of the word "sorry" make the gesture more apologetic? Would it now be "enough" of an apology to qualify? We need to know more. How did I intone the word? What were my intentions and emotions at the time? Did I reform my behavior? Or did I use "sorry" here as I might ask a stranger at the next table in a restaurant, "Excuse me, please pass the salt." Whether either gesture satisfies my wife will depend on the meaning she seeks. We can also imagine even less apologetic cases, for instance, if I responded to my wife's complaints about my manners by telling her that I find her sensibilities bourgeois and if she does not like eating with me she can file for a divorce. It would be difficult to find any apologetic meaning here, but I suspect we have little need for a framework like mine in such cases because neither of us contests "whether I have apologized or not."

As with all interesting philosophical discussions, each of these questions leads to more fundamental and difficult issues. Do my intentions determine the worth of my actions, or should my wife's perceptions and the consequences of my statement provide the best measure? What are emotions, are we in control of them, and must requisite emotional states accompany moral acts? Does our exchange around the dinner table represent an intricate moral drama between autonomous agents or an absurd struggle for power between petty and vindictive automatons? Fundamental questions of this sort haunt all social interactions, and I hope to explain how a robust treatment of apologies cannot ignore them.

According to my account, there are no precise boundaries regarding the significance of apologies. Just as they have throughout history, the meanings of apologies will surely change once again. As Nietzsche put it, we tend to act "as if every word were not a pocket, into which now this, now that, now several things at once have been put!"[34] Ultimately, "apology" provides but an artifact of human intellectual organization bobbing in the confluence of streams of meaning. Like a continually transforming river, no absolute boundaries mark its banks. We can, however, map the contours of the terrain and study the conventions and practices that run through its many tributaries.

Although a degree of indeterminacy seems prudential in any philosophical treatment of this kind, I hope to convince readers that it can be especially misleading to understand apologies as providing closure, finality, or even balance to the scale of justice. As Martha Minow has warned regarding political forgiveness, "[t]here are no tidy endings following a mass atrocity."[35] Whether there exists a ledger in the heavens against which we can compare the meaning of an apology and the meaning of injury may be an open question for some, but I know of no such standard on Earth. Instead, apologies provide another ritual within the infinitely complex nexus of life's meaning. I do not mean to imply that there are never clear examples of apologies or that apologies leave us drowning in a sea of indeterminateness. Instead, we can appreciate that the dialectical nature of apologies immerses us in the richness of human experience.

A few further terminological notes may prove useful before we begin considering the various apologetic elements. As I discuss further in the sections on intentions and emotions, note that an apology can be "sincere" without being categorical. One can apologize, for instance with sincerity and in good faith to the wrong person or for something for which they have no standing to apologize. In other words, an apology can lack certain kinds of meaning even if the apologizer "really means it." I similarly avoid using "genuine" because of its definition as either authentic in origin or motivated by sincere intentions. Finally, I could place nearly every reference to the term "apology" in scare quotes given the contested status of many of the examples. That would be quite annoying, and I will instead trust readers to sustain their critical sensitivity to the complexities of the many usages of the term.

CHAPTER TWO

Elements of the Categorical Apology

A. Corroborated Factual Record

Contested facts often lie at the heart of moral injuries. From the outset, apologies stand a better chance of bearing significant meaning if the offender and the offended share an understanding of the facts relevant to the transgression at issue. Although our interpretations of events may evolve over our lifetimes, much of our understanding of our selves and our world results from piecing together ambiguous fragments of information into a moral narrative. Not only do we want to understand what happened after a confusing or traumatic event, but we also want the offender to share our understanding. With this, my version of events becomes more than my biased perspective. In truth and reconciliation tribunals, for instance, establishing an official account corroborating victims' claims provides a primary function of the proceedings. Family members want to know how their loved ones suffered or died, who pulled the trigger, who issued the orders, and other information relevant to their understanding of the injury. Such information not only allows victims to reconstruct and judge the transgressions, but it can serve to memorialize the event and elevate its status above rumor and hearsay. Confronting this record can also bring offenders to appreciate the full gravity of the injury, awakening them to the reality and scale of suffering at issue. Denial and minimization become increasingly difficult.

On some occasions, this may simply be a matter of the offender admitting what the offended already knows or believes: I clearly saw you destroy my property, and I want you to admit doing so either to me or to a third party. At other times, we may enjoy less certainty about the events. Suppose my wife and I return from a vacation to find the cherished rocking chair from my great-great grandmother destroyed. If my neighbor informs me that my eighteen-year-old son had an unauthorized party in our house while the rest of us were away, I will want to hear more from my son. Although I may not need to know all of the details regarding what transpired at the party, I will want to know the morally salient ones. Did he plan the party? Did the party consist of him and his two best friends, or was the house full of people he barely knew? How was the chair broken, and who broke it? We can imagine the various sorts of information we might find pertinent in such a situation.

It can be difficult to distinguish the process of gathering information from the act of assigning blame. At this stage, we try to establish a record upon which we can judge wrongdoing; once we know what happened, we have a factual record to evaluate. Exculpatory facts may emerge in the process of learning about the events. My son might explain that he was studying with his two friends when several uninvited classmates stormed the house. If credible, such information would likely shift our moral judgments and thereby alter the meaning of – and perhaps the need for – an apology from my son. Again, we need a factual record to consider before an apology can go much further.

I should emphasize that the offender's mental states at the time of the offense will often amount to significant facts. What, for instance, were the offenders' intentions and emotions? Did my son throw the party to spite me in response to being punished? Knowing the symbolic meaning of the heirloom chair, did he intentionally destroy it as an act of contempt for our family? Did he mistakenly believe that he had permission to have a party while we were away, and the destruction of the chair resulted from an unforeseeable accident? I consider the role of these distinctions at length later, but I mention them here in order to point to their status as elements of a thorough factual account of an offense. Given the number of apologies that claim the offender "did not mean to" cause the harm at issue, it seems especially important to include this information in the record to the best of our ability.

This fact-gathering dimension of apologies may seem so obvious that we often miss it completely. If I confront my son about the party and broken chair and he responds by saying "I'm sorry" or even "I'm really sorry and it will never happen again," I have limited means of judging just what he did. For what does he apologize? What will he never do again? If I do not know what he apologizes for, then the meaning of the apology remains inscrutable to some degree. Consider a similar gap in the apology provided by scuba instructor Karl Jesienowski, who failed to notice that he returned to shore after an outing with two fewer customers than he departed with, leaving them to die on the Great Barrier Reef. "Somehow they fell through the system," he stated, "I apologize, I sincerely apologize."[1] Based on this statement, we do not know the circumstances surrounding the deaths. For just what, specifically, is he apologizing? Was he drinking on the job? Was the boat overcrowded and understaffed? Did the divers engage in risky behavior that might shift culpability to them and away from Jesienowski? Alternatively, perhaps an unforeseeable equipment failure played a prominent role in the accident. As I consider later, such details can be quite significant when assigning blame and evaluating the worth of an apology.

A crucial absence of information can occur even when the offender expresses considerable contrition, for example when Chinese Premier Zhu

Rongji responded to allegations that an explosion in a rural school killing thirty-eight children resulted from the underfunded school's efforts to raise money by manufacturing fireworks. He stated: "I believe that, no matter what the facts are, the State Council and I both bear unshirkable responsibility."[2] Although Lazare finds this a "successful apology" according to his criteria, it would convey more meaning if it explained precisely what occurred and stated Zhu's own as well and his government's role in the tragedy.[3] Otherwise we do not know what Zhu accepts responsibility for, as he could be apologizing for initially denying the story, for not funding the schools adequately, for forcing the children to work, or for failing to promulgate safety standards that would have prevented such a catastrophe. Without the factual record established in this manner we also cannot judge if Zhu and the council have standing to apologize, as discussed later.

If the accused denies facts material to the offense, the discrepancy must be resolved before some forms of meaning will be possible. An apology will occasionally admit to general wrongdoing while strategically concealing or misrepresenting facts, and we should be wary of subreption in these cases. During his gubernatorial campaign, six women accused Arnold Schwarzenegger of sexually harassing them earlier in his career. He responded with the following statement:

I want to say to you, yes, that I have behaved badly sometimes. Yes, it is true that I was on rowdy movie sets and I have done things that were not right which I thought then was playful but now I recognize that I have offended people. And to those people that I have offended, I want to say to them that I am deeply sorry about that and I apologize because this is not what I'm trying to do.[4]

Notice the generality of his admission, as he confesses to "behaving badly" and doing "things that were not quite right." What exactly did he do? Did he sexually harass the six women or not, and how do we define that offense? Is he apologizing for such serious offenses, or merely expressing regret that his "playfulness" has been misconstrued? Is he admitting that he committed wrongful acts, but denying wrongful intent? Surely this matters not only for the meaning of Schwarzenegger's apology, but also for his political career and the underlying legal claims against him. Does he craft his words to limit his legal liability while still appearing like a reformed and sensitive man? Also note how Schwarzenegger spins the facts, apologizing for his behavior on "rowdy movie sets." Perhaps he offers this fact because we might believe that lewd behavior is more acceptable in the hypersexualized and objectifying backrooms of Hollywood, thus mitigating the offensiveness of his actions. Perhaps, in his estimation, his suggestion that he was involved in such sexual escapades would further enhance his status as an icon of machismo rather than a bumbling molester of the women who rejected his unwelcome advances. According to the harassment allegations, however, several of the acts in question occurred in a gym, a café, a hotel room, and on a public street rather than on the mythological movie set.[5]

Another common strategy to frustrate a victim's attempt to establish a factual record involves a conditional apology, stating something to the effect of "if I did X, as you claim I did but I deny, then I am sorry for X." Senator Robert Packwood's public statements after being accused of sexually harassing at least a dozen women provide an infamous example of this. "I'm apologizing," Packwood said, "for the conduct that it was alleged that I did."[6] Packwood insinuates that if the allegations were true then he would apologize, but he denies their truth. This allows him to recognize the norm at issue – that sexual harassment is indeed wrong – while denying that he has breached it. Although commentators often cite Packwood's statement as an example of a "bad apology," similar tactics are more common than we might think. Alleged offenders often say something like "If anyone was hurt by my actions, then I apologize." Whereas such a statement may confirm that the offender did *something* that some *may* consider offensive (I consider later the failure to affirm that others would be justified in taking offense), the offender refuses to recognize or name the injury at issue. This leaves open the possibility that there is no injury to speak of, and failing to confirm the existence of an injury may infuriate someone who claims to have been injured by the apologizer. We commonly find speakers of sexist or racist remarks prefacing their apologies in this way, speculating that "if anyone was offended by my comments, then I apologize." Setting aside the question of whether the remark indeed offended someone, an apology may be appropriate from a deontological perspective regardless of the consequences of a morally insensitive statement because not every wrong involves injury or offense to someone. One might need to apologize because she has breached a moral duty, and this could be the case even if no one claims to be injured. For these reasons we should be wary of apologies making use of an "if" in these ways. I will say more about this later.

There may be cases in which the accused genuinely does not know what transpired, for instance if she were to awaken from a violent accident having no memory of committing a transgression attributed to her. An apology under such circumstances may not be able to provide the victim with meaningful information, and the offender might resort to apologizing on a record of events reconstructed by others. We can also be wary of those who claim not to have knowledge of the facts as a passive means of implying that no transgressions occurred. This returns us to Packwood, who later claimed that he "didn't know" three of the seven women accusing him of harassment and did not "recognize" their stories.[7] Thus he offered another apology: "If I did things I can't remember, didn't know, or to people I didn't know, I'm embarrassed and I apologize."[8] Packwood appears to apologize for *not remembering* rather than for the acts he allegedly fails to remember, but even if he stated that he apologized if he harassed anyone, this would still surely lack most apologetic meaning. Suppose I state: "I apologize if I murdered Abraham Lincoln." We all know that I did not commit this transgression, and therefore I do not apologize. I merely recognize that if I were the murderer, then it would be appropriate to apologize. Again, I affirm the value at issue without implicating myself in transgressing it.

Like offenders, victims and accusers may also face temptations to misrepresent facts relevant to an apology. Victims might embellish their injuries for various reasons, and beyond cases of an offender's memory loss we can imagine situations in which a victim or her advocates hold power over the accused and coerce her into offering an apology for acts she knows she did not commit. A parent may command a child to apologize for something she did not do, and a sentencing judge might require a convict to apologize for an offense even if she maintains her innocence. An offender might also offer an apology based on facts later proven wrong or that both parties know to be inaccurate. In the former, parties may revise meaning across the spheres of apologetic value depending on the significance of the new information. In the latter, the apology may maintain various forms of meaning primarily oriented to the community without providing much of the meaning usually specific to the apologizer and recipient of the apology. In order to deflect blame within a political administration, for example, a cabinet member might stage a public apology to the president for committing an offense that both know is actually the president's fault.

Legal proceedings undertake factual discovery of varying degrees of breadth and depth in order to establish an official account sanctioned by the state. For some, this corroboration of their story and memorialization of their injury may constitute the primary benefit of the legal action. According to one study, most victims of crime consider learning what transpired and why as more important than restitution for the injury.[9] In this light, Minow discusses Judge Marilyn Patel's 1984 *coram nobis* opinion reconsidering the U.S. Supreme Court's original decision in *U.S. v. Korematsu* upholding the constitutionality of the U.S. government's forced relocation of approximately 120,000 Japanese and Japanese-Americans to internment camps during World War II. For Patel, these proceedings allowed her to correct history not only by vacating Fred Korematsu's conviction but also by revising the factual record regarding Japanese internment within the law books of the United States.[10] Such meaning is distinct from and incommensurable with that provided by the Civil Liberties Act of 1988, which provided an apology for the internment as well as $20,000 for each surviving internee. Sir Hartley Shawcross, the lead British prosecutor at the Nuremberg War Crimes Tribunal, appreciated that his objectives consisted not only in convicting the accused Nazi offenders but also in recording facts for the ages: "This tribunal will provide a contemporary touchstone and an authoritative and impartial record to which future historians may turn for truth and future politicians for warning."[11] Of course, problems of objectivity, indeterminacy, revisability, and inexplicability riddle all attempts to write history. As new facts and interpretations come into light or favor after an offender has issued an apology, meanings will shift accordingly.

We should notice that an offender might confess and recount her deeds without offering anything recognizable as an apology. Many conflicts never move past this stage, as the alleged offender may admit the deeds but dig in her heels and defend them. To use a humorous example, such a scenario unfolds over the course of a *Seinfeld* episode as George badgers an acquaintance progressing through the steps of the Alcoholics Anonymous program to apologize to him. George alleges that his friend refused to lend him his sweater because he said that George would "stretch out the neck hole." When George confronts him, the friend admits his deed, defends it, and offers sarcastic sympathy: "I'm so sorry that I didn't want your rather bulbous head struggling to find its way through the normal-size neck hole of my finely knit sweater."[12] Admissions and explanations may help us understand what happened and perhaps even why it occurred such that we can take measures to avoid similar harm in the future, but we can achieve this without anything like regret or remorse. In this light, consider G. H. W. Bush's defiant statement during the 1988 presidential campaign after a U.S. cruiser shot down an Iranian plane and killed 290 civilians: "I will never apologize for the United States of America, I don't care what the facts are."[13]

Lastly, *how* these facts become known will also influence their meaning. If the offender freely comes forward and provides an account that proves to be honest, accurate, and potentially ruinous in terms of economic, social, or legal consequences, this differs from learning about the events against the offender's will. If someone came to my door, explained to me that she had stolen my car many years ago, and wanted to apologize, this would be quite different from hearing an apology from her after she was convicted and awaiting sentencing for the offense. An admission of the former sort – if accompanied by other considerations discussed later – could be so morally significant that I might forgo legal action altogether.

B. Acceptance of Blame

1. Distinguished from Expression of Sympathy

I should first distinguish several senses of "moral responsibility" that apologetic discourse tends to conflate. First, I may have a *duty* – or what we can describe as a moral responsibility – to help others even if I did not cause their injuries. If I find a badly injured person lying in the street, by most accounts I should help her even if I did not cause her injury. Providing such aid is my moral responsibility regardless of whether I deserve blame for her condition. Notice how we can use this sense of moral responsibility as duty to describe my obligations to provide charity or disaster aid relief even if I did not cause the unfortunate circumstances in any obvious sense.

Second, I might also have a nonmoral responsibility to remedy situations caused by others, for instance if my job requires me to fix problems that others create. This might apply to a janitor who cleans up after others or a president left to fix the problems created by her predecessor.

Third, moral responsibility can also mean that I caused a state of affairs and therefore any praise or blame for this should be directed at me. We can call this *causal moral responsibility*. I might explain that I am morally responsible for the injuries of the person lying in street because I forcefully restrained her when she attacked a child. Here I am responsible for the injury in the same sense that a police officer is morally responsible for a heroic rescue: I caused the state of affairs and I may deserve praise for doing so. Note that I can accept causal moral responsibility even if some disagree that my actions are praiseworthy or blameworthy, as a president may assert causal moral responsibility for an initiative regardless of its popularity.

Blameworthiness, which is most applicable to categorical apologies, admits both causation and wrongdoing. Here I might admit that I caused the injury as I attempted to rob the person and therefore I deserve all of the blame.

With those distinctions in mind, we can notice the ambiguity of a spouse or a political leader's claim that she "takes responsible for X." Does she mean that she will fulfill her moral duty to remedy an injury that she did not cause, that she is bound by her position to solve the problems created by others, or that she caused the harm and accepts blame for it?

Some gestures do not assert responsibility in any of those senses. Notice the differences in meaning between the following statements: 1) "Your grandmother died"; 2) "I killed your grandmother"; 3) "I am sorry that your grandmother died"; and 4) "I am sorry that I killed your grandmother." An historian might state the first claim when tracing your family genealogy, for instance explaining that "your grandmother died in 1950." She would not accept responsibility in any of the stated senses. A state executioner might speak the second, coldly recounting the fact of death and its cause in stating that "I killed your grandmother in accordance with governing standards of capital punishment." The executioner accepts causal moral responsibility and believes that the act is justified. Although these two statements could be uttered without offering anything that we might ordinarily understand as an apology, the third and fourth statements cause more confusion. We can distinguish between expressions of sympathy, which often take the form of "I am sorry that X occurred" found in the third example, from apologies that accept blame for an injury. Unless I am confessing to wrongly killing your grandmother and accepting blame for her death, we would not think of a phrase like "I am sorry that your grandmother passed away" as an apology. It offers sympathy rather than contrition.

The difference between such statements would be stark, for instance, if a friend indicated that she "accepts my apology" after I expressed condolences for her grandmother's death.[14] Her response would indicate that she misunderstood my gesture, and it might provoke me to clarify that I did not intend to intimate that I harmed her grandmother. I might elaborate on how much I love the deceased, the depth of my sorrow, and perhaps my intentions to assist her family in this time of need. Conversely, if she responded to my gestures of condolences by exonerating me and explaining that I "hadn't done anything wrong," this would similarly reflect that we were miscommunicating. As referenced previously, these subtleties may cause particular difficulties for non-native speakers of English. Without minimizing the importance of sympathy, we can notice the clear difference between using the passive voice to state "I am sorry that your grandmother was killed" and the active voice to state "I am sorry that I killed your grandmother." The active voice claims responsibility. The passive does not. Thus when Cardinal Bernard Law states that "[j]udgments were made regarding the assignment of [child sex offender] John Geoghan which, in retrospect, were tragically incorrect," the passive voice allows Law to avoid explaining precisely who made those incorrect decisions.[15] In this sense we can notice how factual questions (who made the decisions?) can be difficult to separate from assignments of responsibility.

The shared word "sorry" in statements three and four leads to a lack of clarity regarding the role of causation in apologies, which in turn creates a variety of confusions and possibilities for manipulation. It would seem comical to imagine criminal investigators misconstruing my condolences for my friend's grandmother's death as an admission of guilt, yet jurisprudential scholarship has paid considerable attention to questions regarding whether statements of sympathy should be excluded from evidence in legal proceedings.[16] In testament to just how misguided popular conceptions of apology can seem, several states have revised evidentiary law to exclude sympathetic language – distinguished from admissions of any kind – from evidence in some legal proceedings.[17] The need to legislate for such "safe apologies" suggests an astounding history of legal parties construing statements such as "I am sorry for your suffering" as an admission of guilt. Codifying measures to allow for expressions of compassion in legal contexts may reduce this confusion, but naming them "sympathy apologies" seems to perpetuate the conflation of sympathy and apology.

We can note here several examples in which officials attempt to deflect causal responsibility while still offering something like an apology. The effort to generate an on-line list where Australians can "apologize" (May 26 is "Sorry Day" in Australia) for their government's forcible removal of aboriginal people presents a clear case of eliminating causal responsibility from an apology. In order to encourage participation, the organizers state: "If you don't want to add your name to the list" you should not worry that your signature would amount to an admission of responsibility because "[a]n apology says 'This should not have happened; this should never happen again.' It doesn't say 'I was there and let it happen; I am guilty.'"[18] Nearly twenty-five thousand people have signed the petition. It seems difficult to discern how such an apology differs from the condolences offered for a deceased relative considered earlier. I might say "this should not have happened; this should never happen again" about any unfortunate historical event, including one such as the Holocaust that occurred before my birth. Yet until I accept blame for the event, such a statement looks more like a declaration than an apology. Few would construe an Auschwitz survivor's statement that the Holocaust was wrong and should never happen again as an apology for the Holocaust, unless she accepted some blame – perhaps for collaborating with or failing to resist the Nazis. This is not to say that contemporary Australians cannot take responsibility for their part in contributing to the continuing suffering of aboriginal people, perhaps by enjoying unjust benefits at the expense of previously exploited people or by allowing, failing to remedy, or committing further acts of discrimination. We can mark a clear distinction, however, between declaring that others committed wrongs in the distant past and accepting personal blame for the transgression. Both may provide important meaning, but the meanings provided are distinct in form.

Because it has crystallized as a linguistic symbol of everything that we associate with apologizing, the word "sorry" can serve as an effective stratagem given the common conflation of its various meanings. Some exploit the confusion between statements accepting and avoiding responsibility, hoping that including "sorry" will cause the victim to believe that she has received a more meaningful apology than what the offender offered. Understanding the meanings of "sorry" is in part the work of this entire book, but we can note *prima facie* how "sorry" can refer to pity, sorrow, or misfortune ("I feel sorry for you") on the one hand, or regret for causing a harm ("I am sorry for insulting you") on the other. The notion of "sorry" as inferior or without merit – as in "a sorry state of affairs" or a "sorry excuse for a newspaper" – further complicates the use of the term. A strategically inserted "sorry" therefore often works as a red herring when an accused party wishes to appear contrite without admitting wrongdoing.

The offender's acceptance of causal responsibility also releases the victim from doubts regarding her responsibility for her suffering. In domestic abuse cases, for example, the victim often mistakenly believes that her injuries are at least in part her fault. With moral responsibility delineated, we can properly transfer blame from a victim to the offender. Note, however, that a third party such as a judge can also accomplish this.

Consider President G. W. Bush's statements concerning the torture of prisoners at Abu Ghraib prison. In initial interviews with al-Hurra network and the al-Arabiya satellite channel, he stated: "People in Iraq must understand that I view those practices as abhorrent" and "that what took place in that prison does not represent the America that I know."[19] Many commentators found Bush's defensive statements inadequate and called for an apology. The following day White House spokesperson Scott McClellan told reporters that the president was "sorry for what occurred" in the prison.[20] National Security Advisor Condoleezza Rice similarly expressed "the United States' deep sorrow over the U.S. troops' abuses against the Iraqi prisoners."[21] Amidst a rising demand for Bush to personally utter an apology, later that week he included the word "sorry" in recounting his conversations with Jordan's King Abdullah II, stating that he was "sorry for the humiliations suffered by the Iraqi prisoners and the humiliations suffered by their families." He added: "I told him I was equally sorry that the people that have been seeing those pictures did not understand the true nature and the heart of America, and I assured him that Americans like me didn't appreciate what we saw and it made us sick to our stomachs."[22]

Setting aside questions regarding whether the president was in any sense causally responsible for the torture because of the policies encouraged or permitted by his administration, we can see that none of his statements provide more than an expression of sympathy and a refutation of charges that Americans enjoy Iraqi suffering. Instead of accepting blame for the harm, the president's statements deflect accusations that the causal chain leads back to high-ranking U.S. officials and attempt to diffuse the impression of a sadistic U.S. military left by the gruesome images. Thus Bush's use of "sorry" offers condolences and a defense rather than an acceptance of his own causal responsibility or blame for the atrocity. Defense Secretary Donald Rumsfeld maintained this strategy: "To those Iraqis who were mistreated by members of the U.S. armed forces, I offer my deepest apology. It was inconsistent with the values of our nation, it was inconsistent with the teachings of the military to the men and women of the armed forces, and it was certainly fundamentally un-American."[23] Rumsfeld offered what he calls an "apology" while implying that he cannot take responsibility for the offenses because they are contrary to the military training he oversees. Such a claim supports the administration's position that a few rogue soldiers performed the acts.

The work of accepting personal blame was left for low-ranking reservists like Sabrina Harman, who by her own account operated under the presumption that Army intelligence "made the rules [for detention and interrogation] as they went" and believed that the job of "the MP was to keep them awake, make it hell so they would talk."[24] "As a soldier and military police officer," Harman stated, "I failed my duties and failed my mission to protect and defend." She continued: "I not only let down the people in Iraq, but I let down every single soldier that serves today [because my] actions potentially caused an increased hatred and insurgency toward the United States, putting soldiers and civilians at greater risk." By emphasizing the harm to fellow U.S. soldiers rather than to the detainees, she invokes a common problem that I discuss later regarding naming the lesser wrong. It is also similar to the administration's tactic of responding to the torture primarily in relation to its impact on the United States' campaign rather than on those who were brutalized. After her conviction and during her sentencing hearing, Harman did not blur the issue of moral causation: "I take full responsibility for my actions.... The decisions I made were mine and mine alone."[25] We can notice here, as I consider later, the relevance of her audience. If she addresses fellow U.S. soldiers, they will be especially interested in an apology from her that appreciates the harm done to the U.S. effort.

Occasionally offenders will go so far as to utter words accepting personal responsibility only to retract their meaning. Bridgestone-Firestone CEO Masatoshi Ono offered the following statement in response to his role in the deaths and injuries of numerous drivers of vehicles equipped with his company's tires: "I come before you to apologize to you, the American people, and especially to the families who have lost loved ones in these terrible rollover accidents. I also come to accept full and personal responsibility on behalf of Bridgestone-Firestone for the events that led to this hearing."[26] Given that Ono claimed to accept full responsibility for the "events that led to this hearing," he appeared to accept blame rather than merely express sympathy or recognize a duty to assist the injured parties. As investigations unfolded, however, Ono explained that he intended this statement to offer merely "sympathy expressed for those individuals who operated vehicles using our products and got into accidents." Even though he was on the record explicitly accepting "full and personal responsibility," he explained that he meant only to offer condolences: "If we are deemed responsible for the accidents, that is another matter. However, there are maybe outside causes that caused the accidents. Then, I wouldn't say we're responsible for the accidents."[27] Thus even when the offender describes her statements as an apology and accepts responsibility, such statements may not be what they seem considering the ease with which we move between distinct notions of reponsibility. We can also view President Bush's statement after Hurricane Katrina in this respect. "Katrina exposed serious problems in our response capability at all levels of government," he confessed. "To the extent the federal government didn't fully do its job right," he declared, "I take responsibility."[28] Yet he leaves us to wonder about the nature of such responsibility if he admits no personal wrongdoing of any kind, not even for his appointment of an unqualified crony to head the Federal Emergency Management Agency.[29]

2. Causation and Moral Responsibility

In order to accept blame, the offender must parse precisely for what she is causally responsible. Although this may seem simple enough in many cases, assigning blame for injuries opens a range of notoriously knotty issues regarding the metaphysics of causation and its relation to moral responsibility. I cannot provide even a cursory overview of this broad and deep field, but I will mention a few concerns briefly here in order to flag areas where issues of causation can create contested meaning in apologies.

An example may help illuminate the sorts of difficulties I have in mind. Suppose I have an appointment to meet a friend for dinner, but at the last moment I decide to attend a film with other friends. In the rush to make the movie on time, I do not even call my friend to cancel our dinner meeting. As in many cases, issues of causation and blame are straightforward: I wronged my friend, she should trace any harm she suffers as a direct result of this wrong to me, and I should apologize to her. But what do we mean by "direct result" of my choice? Suppose that an attacker robs my friend while she stands waiting for me on the sidewalk outside of the restaurant a few minutes after our prearranged meeting time. Is this also my fault? Should I accept blame and apologize for the criminal offense as well as the missed meal? What if she begins to feel increasingly insecure in all of her relationships as she waits for me, triggering a severe bout of debilitating depression requiring years of therapy and medication? Am I to blame for this as well?

Although the questions raised by such examples may seem somewhat unusual, consider tobacco executive Nicholas Brookes' statement during a class action suit against his industry: "I have sincere regrets that many of the [remedial activities] we are now embarked on doing could have been done sooner." He continued: "To the extent that any of those things either changed your decision not to quit or would have allowed you to quit smoking sooner, or not to have taken up smoking in the first place, then I sincerely apologize to you."[30] In such a case, issues of causation and moral responsibility raise questions that can profoundly transform the meaning of his statement. Is he accepting blame for a slight increase in the probability that a few consumers may have smoked more cigarettes because of his corporation's actions, or does he accept responsibility for the long-term health consequences of his products on specific individuals? Should he apologize to the families of lung cancer victims and accept the economic responsibility for these losses, or should smokers bear this responsibility for failing to exercise their will to quit? What if one of these individuals died not from lung cancer, but rather from gross medical negligence when being treated for a minor smoking-related ailment? Such questions raise complex and contentious issues regarding the metaphysics, morality, politics, and law of causation, and the meaning of an apology of this sort hangs on these underlying conundrums. Given the political charge now conducted by the very idea of "personal responsibility," we should be wary of this polemical landmine.

Returning to the missed dinner example, in one sense I caused my friend to be robbed. If it were not for my violation – or "but for" my offense – that particular injury would not have occurred considering that we would have been safe inside the restaurant if I had kept my promise. According to what some refer to as "direct causation" or "causation-in-fact," personal responsibility attaches through physical causation in this way.[31] We might think of a hailstorm as being "responsible for" breaking a window in the same sense that a vandal might be "responsible for" the same damage. Different notions of responsibility are typically at work here. In the first case, we do not cast moral judgment on the natural cause when we think of the hail breaking the window. We do blame the vandal, however. Determinations of physical causation do not require us to mind our moral values as carefully as we do when assigning guilt. It is rather unhelpful, therefore, to analyze the dinner example from this perspective because under such a theory events are so interconnected that we cannot attribute responsibility to anyone in particular. According to some theories of direct causation, my friend's mother would also be responsible for her daughter's injury because "but for" her giving birth to her daughter she never would have suffered the injury.

One might argue that all events are caused by the sum of all of their antecedents, making the most distant causes of my friend's assault coterminous with the origins of the universe. If it were not for the cooling of the planet, European colonization, her parents' choice to attend the same college, the economic conditions that left the assailant jobless and poorly educated, and my decision to go to the movies, the robbery would not have occurred. Yet when we speak of moral causation and blame, we require more than tenuous physical connections. Assertions of moral responsibility require us to determine what we *should* hold someone responsible for because her agency best accounts for the outcome. Despite all of the background conditions required for people to be able to fail or succeed, our determinations of praise and blame rely on a belief that we find an individual's agency the most relevant factor in explaining the moral dimensions of life. Our conceptions of blameworthiness allow us to make causal delineations based on moral criteria, and therefore we can distinguish between wrongs rather than conflating all misfortunes into a stream of inevitable and inseparable ills. Even though I have done something wrong when I abandon my friend, it would seem intuitively mistaken to consider me responsible for any wrong that might subsequently befall her throughout her life. Yet how do we distinguish between the harms for which I *should* be considered responsible and those too remote to attribute to my actions?

Unlike the "but for" standard often referred to as the test for "causation in fact" or "direct causation," proximate causation is a legal construct fashioned according to moral and political considerations that serve to prevent moral causation from stretching back into an infinite regress.[32] H. L. A. Hart and A. M. Honore's landmark *Causation in the Law* describes proximate causation as a means of drawing sensible boundaries on webs of causation: "Whenever we are concerned with [causal] connection, whether for the purpose of explaining a puzzling occurrence, assessing responsibility, or giving an intelligible historical narrative, we employ a set of concepts restricting in various ways what counts as a consequence." Such limitations "colour all our thinking in causal terms; when we find them in the law we are not find-ing something invented by or peculiar to the law...."[33] As Justice Andrews stated in his classic dissent in *Palsgraf v. Long Island R.R.*, "[w]hat we mean by the word 'proximate' is that, because of...public policy...the law arbitrarily declines to trace a series of events beyond a certain point."[34] Prosser and Keaton restate *Palsgraf*'s conclusion: "The doctrine of proximate cause reflects social policy decisions based on shared principles of justice."[35] According to proximate causation, we attribute causal responsibility accord-ing to our moral beliefs regarding who should and should not be morally and legally responsible for harms. Inquiries into moral responsibility can-not merely trace an empirical chain of events to a source, but rather must judge where culpability should fall – it is a primarily prescriptive rather than descriptive task. Assignments of proximate causation, in other words, are determined according to stipulated norms more than discovered facts. Thus the nuanced norms regarding moral causation prevalent in our cultures guide our thinking about apologies.

The causal chain traced by a proximate-cause analysis can be broken by a supervening cause, which Prosser and Keaton describe as "an act of a third person or other force which by its intervention prevents the actor from being liable for harm to another which his antecedent negligence is a substantial factor in bringing about."[36] This legal doctrine maps onto com-monsense notions of blame. Just as a criminal court would not charge me with the assault of my friend after I missed our dinner, I am not proximately responsible for the assault because the attacker's decision to cause the harm is such a morally salient event in this story. Although my actions may be inconsiderate, within most moral lexicons we can distinguish my blamewor-thy actions from those of the robber because the latter result from a distinct blameworthy choice by another person that breaks the chain between my actions and the robbery. Even though I have done something wrong when I abandon my friend, it would overreach to charge me with the robbery committed by another. My apology can accept responsibility for breaking our appointment, but it might be a stretch to blame me for the robbery. My apology probably could not accept blame for the assault without tracing responsibility so far up the chain of causation as to risk rendering our notions of freedom, agency, and responsibility meaningless. Nevertheless, I could express my sympathy over the robbery. If, however, it was reasonably fore-seeable – noting the additional discussions required to determine a standard of reasonable foreseeability – that placing her in this situation would be dangerous, then I would deserve some blame for the injury. My apology should accept blame precisely for two separate wrongs: missing our meet-ing and placing her in danger. In such a case I should apologize for both wrongs even if an attack did not occur, which illustrates how we can accept moral responsibility for intangible harms such as exposing others to risk, committing various sins of omission, or indulging in "victimless" crimes.

One might object to the notion of responsibility informing this account of proximate causation by asserting that it is too thin and wedded to a liberal notion of agency that insulates individuals and groups from the remote consequences of their actions. One might assert, for example, that this narrow conception of responsibility allows wealthy nations to claim they are not to blame for global poverty, given the difficulty of tracing the actions of individual agents at one end of a complex economic system to the systemic indigence perpetuated at opposite ends. In such cases those sympathetic to the structural causes of destitution seek to extend the causal chain from the economic choices of rich Western corporations and individuals to the suffering of others. I take this worry seriously.

Suppose for the sake of argument that we can establish that a catastrophic flood like that experienced after Hurricane Katrina causes poverty in a region. The area enjoyed great wealth before the disaster, the disaster destroys the economic infrastructure, and the area suffers a bout of poverty while it is being rebuilt. Also presume that the flood did not result from global warming and therefore from the economic activity of developed nations. Then presume that the damage did not result from the failure of international agencies to meet their moral duty to provide better levy systems or flood preparedness programs. In addition, presume that the ensuing poverty does not result from exploitative development of the devastated area. Also set aside questions considered in the following chapters regarding whether we can attribute blame to collective agents like nations and corporations. These are many presumptions, which is my point. If we could make a bright-line determination that the president of the United States did not proximately cause the damage, then an apology from him would be limited with respect to his ability to accept blame for the disaster. Questions regarding moral causation are rarely so clean, especially in matters of poverty within interconnected global markets.

Consider how Marxists and Libertarians would debate questions regarding the nature of economic exploitation or the duties of international agencies to prevent such disasters. The ideologies would hold very different views on who bears responsibility and thus who should apologize for even such a "natural" event. As we have seen with Hurricane Katrina, the water and wind were only part of the problem. We now understand Katrina as a catastrophe of human failures instead of a mere natural disaster. This does not, I believe, make the underlying principle less persuasive: if we can determine that someone did not proximately cause something – however contested matters of causation may be in any given case – then an apology from her will lack meaning related to accepting blame for the harm. Yet if one could successfully argue that commercial practices in which I participate proximately caused the poverty at issue, we could attribute responsibility to me and an apology accepting such blame would be warranted.[37] Rather than jettison notions of responsibility and proximate causation, a successful argument of this sort would continue to operate within the framework of proximate causation by extending the operative moral categories to include remote victims. This also does not speak to whether the United States would have a moral duty to provide relief in such a situation, even if victims agreed that it was not causally responsible for the harm. It does clarify, however, the distinction between a duty to aid and a responsibility to apologize. Because not all of my moral responsibilities are triggered by my fault (I may have a duty to care for an ill parent even if I did not cause the sickness), I need not apologize for causing all injuries even if one were to make the claim that I have a duty to everyone who suffers. We can surely distinguish between accepting a moral duty for those we have not harmed and offering an apology that accepts blame for those we have harmed.

Notice here how questions regarding blame may fluctuate according to any number of formal or informal agreements that assign responsibility. If the United States had agreed to an international treaty that required its military to provide adequate levy systems to the area in question but then failed to do so, we can see where blame would fall according to such provisions. We often organize our private responsibilities according to similar arrangements, but with varying degrees of explicitness. Suppose I usually water the houseplants, but I forget to do so before we leave for a long vacation. We return to dead plants. My wife also forgot to water the plants, but the blame falls primarily on me because of our habits. If I refuse to accept exclusive blame for this loss (supposing that our plants had considerable value to us), we would need to navigate this set of previously implicit responsibilities.

Attributions of culpability remain central to apologies even when we operate with culturally diverse conceptions of responsibility or skepticism regarding the conceptions of freedom undergirding notions of personal choice. Given their dependence on the tradition of the autonomous individual taking causal responsibility for her breach of moral principles, the sorts of meanings I attribute to apologies seem like they might be a by-product of the European enlightenment. Our everyday notions of blame – for example those at work in romances, criminal justice systems, schools, and businesses – remain firmly bound to the voluntaristic notion of the discrete individual moral agent failing or succeeding even though the philosophical roots from which these notions grew have increasingly less cultural grip. Our conceptions of dignity remain wedded to notions of personal responsibility, even if some may be uncomfortable citing Kantian or religious traditions to justify such assertions. I suspect that even the hardened determinist wants an apology that apportions blame when someone wrongs her and the most reductive brain scientist holds her friends personally accountable for their wrongdoings.[38]

We typically act as if we possess moral freedom even if we think that this is an intellectually dubious presumption, perhaps because we are unwilling to part with the existential meaning provided by our conceptions of autonomy.

P. F. Strawson offered a powerful related argument, claiming that the practice of holding people responsible does not depend on a commitment to a metaphysical belief that people are free, but rather arises according to the degree to which we value the actions of others.[39] Thus our notions of responsibility spring from our experiences of concrete interpersonal relationships as well as from a quest for intellectual consistency. If we cannot reconcile our commonsense view with theoretical debates about determinism, lived practices of ascribing culpability typically win out. Marion Smiley pursues this emphasis on how a context structures conceptions of blameworthiness, considering in *Moral Responsibility and the Boundaries of Community* how our judgments of culpability track our social, political, and economic conditions and values.[40]

Competing notions of the intricacies of proximate causation may vary within the cultural traditions discussed later, but the practice of attributing blame in some sense appears to be an enduring aspect of human experience. Without this broadly held commitment to human agency, apologies would be devoid of a central aspect of their meaning. The details of how causation and moral responsibility unfold in any particular apology, however, can be a complex matter in that the process of assigning blame implicates many of our deepest and often unreflective beliefs. Some of us may think seriously about moral responsibility for the first time when we consider the nature of an injury we have suffered or caused, and this may not be the most effective occasion to reflect on the matter if we are eager to blame others or excuse ourselves. Thankfully, precision is not always essential in these matters. Parties can negotiate the sorts of meanings desired in each case, and a degree of uncertainty may be appropriate in private apologies in a manner foreign to criminal law.

The binary choice between conviction and exculpation in criminal courts leads to a range of causal conundrums, such as how to assign liability when two individuals separately deliver a lethal blow to the same individual. Or consider Leo Katz's example:

Henri plans a trek through the desert. Alphonse, planning to kill Henri, puts poison into his canteen. Gaston also intends to kill Henri but has no idea what Alphonse has been up to. He punctures Henri's canteen and Henri dies of thirst. Who has caused Henri's death? Was it Alphonse? How could it be, since Henri never swallowed the poison? Was it Gaston? How could it be, since he only deprived Henri of some poisoned water that would have killed more swiftly even than thirst? But if neither had done anything, Henri would still be alive. So who killed Henri?[41]

Although such examples may riddle criminal jurisprudence, apologies offer the flexibility for all of the malefactors to accept blame for their actions and intentions. Alphonse, Gaston, and any wrongdoers in such examples could apologize specifically for their role in the harm. If your bullet strikes a victim a millisecond after your accomplice has delivered the fatal blow, apologies from both of you could accept blame for your wrongdoing. Blame, in other words, is not exhausted once one person has claimed it. Accordingly, I can offer a meaningful apology to my friend for missing our meal and leaving her on the street where the assailant robbed her even if neither of us is certain about the precise degree to which I contributed to the likelihood of the robbery. She may simply wish for me to recognize that, in addition to skipping our dinner, I placed her in danger. Or perhaps we are both committed to Guido Calabresi's probabilistic theory of responsibility, in which case we could tailor the apology accordingly.[42] Or maybe she demands that I take full blame for the robbery, perhaps more than I am willing to accept.

In a climate where victims often take expressions of sympathy for apologies, a person expressing sympathy may be seen as accepting blame for wrongdoing that is not her fault. If more than one person should share blame for causing an injury but only one comes forward to either offer sympathy or accept responsibility, others may view her as absorbing all of the blame.[43] This relates to an interesting observation by Janet Holmes, who claims that women respond to apologies with counter-apologies more often than men do.[44] I consider the role of gender in apologies later, but the use of counter-apologies seems quite important. In my own experiences, I find that when someone offers me a robust apology I am more likely to offer an apology of my own than to merely "accept" her apology. If a friend apologizes for arriving an hour late to a meeting, I might minimize the offense against me by noting that I was able to catch up on my reading while I waited. I might also deflect some of the blame away from her and toward me, for example by claiming that I should have called to confirm the time or that I should not have insisted that we meet on a day when she was so busy. Why would I do this? Numerous reasons come to mind, including my desire to avoid confrontation, move beyond an uncomfortable situation, and restore the relationship as quickly as possible. I may also be acting out of politeness or generosity. I suspect, however, that counter-apologies also serve as recognitions of the difficulties of assigning moral responsibility and isolating fault. In response to the gray areas in questions of moral causation, at times we split the difference of blame. Sharing the burden in this way, even if one party clearly deserves the bulk of blame, makes us collaborators in the apology rather than adversaries. We can then understand the apology as mutually accomplished, and Deborah Tannen describes this gesture of accepting some responsibility (even if you must invent a fault to admit) as a "courteous way of not leaving the apologizer in a one-down position."[45] We should understand apologies as a collaborative and dialectical process, and at least one social scientist has noted how this complicates quantitative analyses of apologies that study only one speaker in an apologetic exchange.[46] If we combine this complication with each of the variables discussed in my account, we can sense some of the difficulties of conducting empirical research in this area.

My task here is merely to note how such questions of causation, responsibility, and blame impart meanings to apologies. An awareness of such subtleties should help us understand the sorts of meaning at stake when attributing blame within apologies. I also hope this helps to demonstrate the various shades of apologetic meaning.[47] Without being disingenuous or otherwise mistaken, I can consistently accept blame and apologize for committing a wrong even if I believe that the victim shares some responsibility with me or that I bear no culpability for some portion of the harm.[48]

3. Accidents and Denials of Intent

Apologies for non-negligent accidents typically deny intentionality and therefore do not accept blame.[49] This would be evident, for example, if I missed the aforementioned dinner meeting with my friend because a meteor struck me on the head while I was on my way to the restaurant. When I decide to skip the dinner in favor of viewing a film, this choice renders me responsible and blameworthy for the subsequent harm. I do not choose, however, for the meteor to strike me. As a result, we are disinclined to think that I caused the harm to my friend waiting for me because I have not done anything wrong. An act of nature, rather than my will, absorbs causal responsibility. If I attempted to apologize and accept blame after a meteor strikes me, I hope that my friend would understand that any harm she suffered was not my fault and therefore an apology accepting blame would be inappropriate. In this respect, Walt Whitman seems to consider himself a force of nature like a meteor when he declares in *Leaves of Grass*:

> I know I am august,
> I do not trouble my spirit to vindicate itself or be understood,
> I see that the elementary laws never apologize. . . .[50]

To return to the conflict between Agamemnon and Achilles in the *Iliad* mentioned earlier, this distinction appears to have a long tradition. After Nestor calls on Agamemnon to offer a "humble apology" to Achilles, Agamemnon admits to his counselors that Achilles' refusal to fight at Troy resulted from the king's wrongful taking of Briseis: "the account of my blind folly that you have given us is wholly true."[51] "Blinded I was – I do not deny it myself," he announces, and "since I did give in to a lamentable impulse and commit this act of folly, I am willing to go back on it and propitiate him with a handsome indemnity."[52] Despite offering great riches, Agamemnon's pride later prevents him from admitting his moral failure to Achilles: "I am older and more royal than himself. Therefore, let him now obey me." Achilles refuses to be bought, as his honor stands beyond price, but he returns to battle to avenge the death of Patroclus at the hands of Hector. At this point, Agamemnon asserts that he was "not to blame" for Achilles' grief: "It was Zeus and Fate and the Fury who walks in the dark that blinded my judgment." Given the power of the gods "that takes complete command," he asks, "What could I do?"[53] In comparing himself with a god, he recounts how Hera even deluded Zeus.[54] Here Agamemnon recasts the events not as a failure of his will but rather like being struck by a meteor. Like a natural event or a bout of insanity, on this account Agamemnon is not morally responsible for the interventions of the gods. Also notice that Agamemnon does not explain why the gods would conspire against him in this way other than their desire for Greek death, thus blocking an inference that Agamemnon somehow deserves this fate as punishment and is therefore indirectly responsible for the consequences.[55] According to Mark Edwards, "Agamemnon is not suggesting that any wrongdoing on his part" caused the gods to manipulate him and this accounts for his "ungracious and jealous, not humble or apologetic" and even "taunting" and "mean-spirited" tone.[56] Nevertheless, while Agamemnon deflects moral responsibility into the heavens, he willingly pays a "ransom" to return Achilles to the battlefield: "since I *was* blinded and Zeus robbed me of my wits, I am willing to make amends and pay you ample compensation."[57] He compensates Achilles for his loss while not exactly accepting blame for it.

In the exchange between Achilles and Agamemnon, Homer provides an insight taken up by Montaigne in the sixteenth century. Montaigne's argument seems worth reproducing here at length:

For myself, I may wish, on the whole, to be otherwise; I may condemn and dislike my general character, and implore God to reform me throughout, and to excuse my natural weakness. But I should not, I think, give the name of repentance to this, any more than I should to my dissatisfaction at not being an angel or a Cato. My actions are controlled and shaped to what I am, and to my condition in life. I can do no better. And repentance does not properly apply to things that are not in our power, though regret certainly does. I can imagine numberless loftier and better disciplined natures than mine: but this does not make me amend my character, any more than my arm or my mind grow stronger by my conceiving some other man's to be so. If to imagine and desire a nobler way of conduct than ours were to make us repent of our own, we should have to repent of our most innocent actions, in as much as we may rightly suppose that a more excellent nature would have performed them more perfectly and with more nobility; and we should wish to do likewise. When I look back on the conduct of my youth, I find that I generally behaved in an orderly manner, according to my lights; that is as much as my powers of control can manage. I do not flatter myself; in similar circumstances I should always be the same. It is not a single spot, but rather a general stain that dyes me. I know no superficial, middling, or formal repentance. It must touch me in every part before I can call it so. It must pierce my bowels and pain them as deeply and as completely as God sees into me.[58]

Here Montaigne affirms Homer's suggestion that repentance and apology apply most directly to events "in our power." If not within our power, it makes little sense to take responsibility for them. Yet what if, Montaigne suggests, we consider the totality of our natures as beyond our power? I can only be as good as I am, and "I can do no better." If I am "stained" throughout, Montaigne suggests repenting for a single spot – an isolated transgression – will always be superficial. Thus if I repent, I must repent for the entirety of my nature. Moreover, what if we consider the determination of my basic character as beyond my power, which might prove a sensible presumption for many worldviews? In this respect, Agamemnon might have blamed more than his momentary lapse of judgment on the gods. Again we see how conceptions of apologies and repentance buckle if not buttressed by modern notions of agency and responsibility.

These examples also mark the difference between being excused, justified, and forgiven. In Anglo-American criminal law since the early nineteenth century, "excuses admit that the deed may be wrong, but excuse the actor because conditions suggest that he is not responsible for his deed."[59] Thus even though an act is wrong, blame shifts away from this actor. A valid justification (like self-defense) establishes that there was no wrongdoing. Forgiveness, as I discuss in some detail later, takes many forms but typically pardons me in some sense after finding me guilty.

Common usage does not always conform to the legal definitions of the terms. If an injury was accidental, then an apology does not give the victim a reason to believe that it will not happen again because the threat is out of the apologizer's control. Here we can notice the subtle differences between someone saying "excuse me" and offering an apology. When requesting that you "excuse me," I typically assert that the harm or inconvenience I caused you is somehow justified and I seek your recognition of the legitimacy of this claim. According to legal concepts, I should probably say "I am justified" rather than "excuse me," but the former sounds abrasively self-righteous. If I serve tables in a crowded restaurant and need to carry a tray through a line of customers, asking patrons to excuse me as I bump into them would seem appropriate because they would understand that I am not committing a trespass against them. My actions are justified and I seek recognition and tacit permission rather than forgiveness.

This is not to say that moral wrongs must be intentional or that morally culpable intentional actions cannot contribute to accidents. Suppose I miss the meeting with my friend because I had too many drinks the night before, forgot to set my alarm clock, and overslept. I did not intend to break our date but I failed to honor the social engagement. It is tempting to consider missing the appointment an accident, but failing to set the alarm differs from being struck by the meteor because the results can be directly traced to my failure to meet my responsibilities. I also should foresee that overindulging the night before could lead to these consequences. When unintentional negligence contributes to harm, we can apologize and accept blame specifically for that. If I am carefully driving down the road and a nail punctures my tire, causing my car to swerve and collide with another vehicle, I will probably only express sympathy to those bearing the costs of this accident because it did not result from intentional or negligent moral error on my part. I did not do anything wrong. If, however, I was driving while intoxicated or over the speed limit and this caused me to run over the nail, I should apologize and accept blame for that specifically. An offender can be caught between offering an excuse and making an apology when she is uncertain if she has committed a moral trespass or been involved in an accident. The phrase "I'm sorry, but..." may fill this interim. If a legitimate excuse follows the "but," then an apology accepting blame may not be warranted.

This may illuminate another sort of exchange. Suppose I preface an apology to a friend by first explaining that just before I wronged her I missed the train, my migraine headaches struck, and I learned that she had insulted me the day prior. I continue to claim, however, that all of this is irrelevant; I was wrong for insulting her and I accept blame for doing so. If such information is irrelevant, why do we include it so often? I suspect this results from our ambiguity about the nature of apologies, which leaves us in a sort of penitential purgatory. On the one hand, we do not want to accept blame and hope the injured party will excuse us or find our actions justified. Hence we offer some evidence in support of this strategy. On the other hand, we realize that such information might appear as an attempt to diminish our responsibility and that this cuts against our ability to fully apologize. We offer the information to the offender for her to consider the possibility of our reduced agency or moral justification, but we then denounce it as irrelevant and affirm our agency so that we can try that strategy as well. In other words, we play both sides by asserting that we might not need to apologize, but if that argument is not convincing we will apologize anyway.

The factual components of apologetic statements often leave victims with insufficient information to evaluate whether harm was intentional, negligent, or accidental. U.S. National Park Director Bob Stanton, for example, offered this statement after a fire intentionally set by his agency to manage a forest grew out of control and destroyed more than two hundred homes: "I want to express on behalf of the National Park Service our deepest apology to the men and women of Los Alamos and all of New Mexico."[60] We are unclear if the destruction was truly accidental (perhaps because lightning or an unforeseeable wind contributed to the blaze) or if the agency was somehow negligent and thus morally culpable for the blaze. Until we know more, the moral status of the apology remains opaque. We can also notice here that I need not intend the precise harm in order to accept blame for it, for example if I aim to shoot person A but misfire and shoot person B. Shooting B would be accidental, but I have still committed a moral trespass because presumably I should not be shooting at anyone. I should, therefore, distribute my culpability to unintended consequences. In such a case, I would owe apologies to both A and B, and the apologies would differ in light of the mental states attached to the distinct wrongs of intentionally trying to shoot A and shooting B while aiming for A. Matters would be different still if I am a police officer with moral justification for shooting A but B unforeseeably jumps into my line of fire. If I have not done anything wrong, I cannot convincingly accept blame for B's injury.

This brings us to perhaps the most common rhetorical strategy for deflecting moral responsibility within apologetic statements: the caveat asserting "it was not my intention to. . . ." Although I will consider the importance of the motivations for apologizing later, here I am concerned with the offender's characterization of the mental states motivating the actions allegedly causing the harm under scrutiny. Many offenders attempt to deny intentionality in order to mitigate blame, for example by claiming that they "didn't mean to" cause the harm. If I did not intend the harm, then it seems like an accident for which I am not morally responsible. I found the frequency of this strategy rather astounding, and a few of the most egregious examples should bring to mind many more.[61] Assistant U.S. Attorney Kenneth Taylor, after referring to potential jurors from eastern Kentucky as "illiterate cave dwellers," asserted that the "comment was not meant to be a regional slur." "To the extent that it was misinterpreted to be one," he explained, "I apologize."[62] After MSNBC commentator Michael Savage stated to a caller, "Oh, you're one of the sodomites . . . [y]ou should get AIDS and die, you pig," he offered the following: "If my comments brought pain to anyone I certainly did not intend for this to happen and apologize for any such reaction. I especially appeal to my many listeners in the gay community to accept my apologies for any inadvertent insults which may have occurred."[63] In both instances the offenders attempt to convert a clear and grievous moral trespass into an accident for which we should not blame them. Such instances leave us to wonder what the offenders' true intentions could possibly have been if not to cause offense. If not to berate the potential jurors and the caller, why would Taylor or Savage utter these slurs? Rarely do offenders offer a window onto their allegedly misunderstood mental state and provide a convincing alternative intention. This also reminds us that the mental state of the offender before and at the time of the offense holds significance not only because it bears on her moral responsibility, but also because it fills in important details about the factual record. The offender's mental states can provide some of the most important historical facts that a victim seeks to understand, and in this respect the analysis of the offender's mind can be an important component of corroborating the historical record as discussed earlier.

A related ploy involves claiming that the injuries resulted from an accidental word choice for which we should excuse the transgressor. Consider former House Republican leader Dick Armey's statement after referring to openly homosexual Representative Barney Frank as "Barney Fag": "The media and others are reporting this as if it were intentional, and it was not. I repeat, this was nothing more than the unintentional mispronunciation of another person's name that sounded like something that it was not."[64] Frank's reply expresses an appropriate skepticism: "There are various ways to mispronounce my name, but that one, I think, is least common."[65] After Senator Trent Lott's apparent endorsement of Strom Thurmond's 1948 segregationist platform at the celebration of Thurmond's 100th birthday in 2002, on several occasions Lott attributed the controversy to "a poor choice of words,"[66] explaining that "his words were wrong"[67] and "conveyed things [he] did not intend."[68] Tom DeLay has blamed his offenses on speaking "in an inartful way,"[69] and Senator Orrin Hatch described one of his offenses as a "mix-up in words."[70] Representative John Cooksey cited an errant "choice of words" as the culprit in his stating that civil liberties should be suspended for anyone wearing a "diaper on his head." "If I offended Arab Americans, I regret my choice of words," Cooksey stated, as if he questioned whether his slur offended anyone.[71] Representative Robert Doran claimed that he was "not even aware that those words had come together in a sentence" after calling a Soviet news commentator "a disloyal, betraying little Jew."[72] In a further attempt to separate the core of their moral self from the wrongdoing, Lott and others often describe the accident as a "mistake of the head – and not the heart."[73]

Attempts to convert moral offenses into unintentional accidents seem especially common when the accused wishes to explain that, despite appearances, she is "not a racist." When J. Peter Grace, appointed by President Ronald Reagan to head a cost-cutting committee, argued that "900,000 [Puerto Ricans] live in New York, and they're all on food stamps, so this food stamp program is basically a Puerto Rican Program," Grace claimed that he was "deeply hurt by the misconceptions . . . that [he] is a racist." "I am not a racist," he asserted, "nothing could be further from the truth."[74] A Florida baseball umpire claimed that there "was no anti-Semitism whatsoever on [his] part" after calling an officiating administrator a "stupid Jew bitch."[75] Professional golfer Fuzzy Zoeller insisted that his comments "were not intended to be racially derogatory" after referring to Tiger Woods as "that little boy" and requesting that Woods – as the winner of the Masters tournament with the honor of setting the menu for the Champions dinner – "not . . . serve fried chicken . . . or collard greens or whatever the hell they serve."[76] Atlanta Braves pitcher John Rocker, who uttered some of the most racist statements by a public figure in recent memory, stated: "I am not a racist. I should not have said what I did because it is not what I believe in my heart."[77] A Florida sheriff explained that his letter advising hunters to prey on African Americans given the "shortage of big game animals" should not be construed as hateful because he "never thought of it not being taken as a joke because [he is] not a racist."[78] Even Jesse Jackson has played this gambit, making the following statement in response to his description of New York as "Hymietown": "However innocent and unintended, it was insensitive and wrong . . . I denied and do not recall ever making such a statement in any context that would be remotely construed as being either remotely anti-Semitic or anti-Israel."[79] In each of these examples, the offenders attempt to dissociate racist behavior from their "true" innocent selves by claiming that the offense was unintentional, accidental, or otherwise not a reflection of their "hearts." Offenders often fail to accept blame for their actions when resorting to this tactic, instead attempting to convert moral errors into morally neutral accidents within the very language of their apologies. I should also mention here how many offenses of this sort result from attempts at humor where the offender takes imprudent risks and then attempts to limit the damage caused by her poor judgment by claiming that she "was only joking."

Finally, we should note how these issues bear considerable importance for a Kantian given the centrality of intentions when assessing the moral worth of an act. Although a utilitarian may find the offender's mental state of secondary relevance compared with the consequences of her actions, the deontologist should believe that intentions are essential to assigning blame and evaluating the moral status of an apology.

4. Standing

These considerations regarding moral causation speak to what legal doctrine describes as "standing," a procedural requirement ensuring that only legitimate disputants adjudicate claims and that random parties cannot bring actions simply because they may hold an intellectual interest in the outcome. In the realm of apologies, I can only convey certain types of meaning if I am morally responsible for the harm.[80] As much as I might like to, I cannot accept blame and categorically apologize for civilian casualties during World War II because I was born after the conflict. I lack standing to convey such meaning. Likewise, if I harm my brother, my wife cannot categorically apologize for me no matter how sincere and sympathetic she may be. Only I, as the person causally responsible for the injury, have authority to accept blame for the harm and apologize accordingly. This parallels the similar notion that a victim has exclusive authority to issue certain types of forgiveness for harms against her, as I would have no standing to forgive Nazi executioners of a murder even if the victim was a relative of mine. I could forgive them for the harm they have done to me in leaving me without a grandparent, but presumably I cannot forgive for the entirety of the murder itself. I consider the relationship between apologies and various forms of forgiveness in more detail later.

Although they may not be able to accept causal responsibility, third parties can corroborate the victim's account of the event, apportion blame, vindicate her moral principles, legitimate her suffering, and provide reparations. Even these, however, will convey different meanings when performed by someone other than the offender. Only an offender accepting blame can provide much of an apology's possible meaning. Only the offender can undertake her own moral transformation. Only the offender can denounce her own commitment to the wrong. Only the offender can end the harm that she continues to perpetrate when she refuses to recognize the victim as a moral agent worthy of redress. Only the offender can promise that she will never commit the transgression again because it is wrong. Only the offender can build trust between her and the victim. We should also not forget that an offender might take as much meaning from providing an apology as a victim would.

In the desire to mend relationships, however, we often disregard concerns regarding standing. Families appear to suffer the most confusion in their attempts to bypass standing considerations, for instance when parents apologize for the acts of their children. If parents leave a young child alone when they should be supervising her and during this time the child damages a neighbor's property, the parents can apologize and accept blame precisely for their failure to supervise. Presumably the parents proximately caused the child to be alone, but if we can attribute some degree of moral agency to the child then we will likely consider her to have proximately caused the damage. Only she would have standing to provide certain forms of apologetic meaning. The reduced agency of children and parental desire to accept blame for their children's actions complicate cases of parents apologizing for young children, but these mitigating factors wane as children develop. According to conventional accounts of moral causation, a parent cannot categorically apologize for the acts of an adult child unless we can attribute independent moral responsibility to the parent for the transgression. If we claim that a parent who abused her child is partially blameworthy for any crimes that her child commits, the parent could categorically apologize for mistreating the child. Allowing the parent to accept full blame for the actions of the adult child, however, would eviscerate notions of blameworthiness in the same sense that imprisoning parents for the crimes of their adult children would offend our basic sense of justice.

The case of Susan Smith – the woman who drowned her two children by strapping them into her car and sinking it in a South Carolina lake – provides an example of an unmistakable standing failure. Smith initially claimed that a black kidnapper abducted her children, causing police to interrogate local African-American men during the investigation. In response to the racial tension caused by Smith's false accusation, her brother subsequently stated: "It's real disturbing to think that anyone would think this was even a racial issue. We apologize to all the black citizens here in Union and everywhere." An African-American resident understood that Smith's brother lacked standing to apologize, stating that "he didn't have to do it. She did."[81] Some forms of apologetic meaning attach to offenders – personally and inextricably – by their causal responsibility for the harm. Unlike money and other fungible commodities, we value apologies in their particularity of origin. As a nontransferable good, we cannot delegate the full work of apologizing to an attorney, a proxy, a successor, or an heir. Like forgiveness, this entails that the offender's death forecloses the possibility of a categorical apology. Many other sorts of apologetic meaning are available, but some are lost forever.

We can also notice in the Smith example how the apology from her brother functions not as an acceptance of blame for the racial injustice but rather as a declaration that he finds such acts unacceptable. When someone apologizes for the actions of someone closely identified with her, the apology may seek not to accept blame for the harm but to deny it. By publicly denouncing the actions of someone close to us, we distance ourselves from the person and behavior that would otherwise be associated with us. Thus if our parents make sexist comments to a houseguest in our presence, we might offer the guest an expression of sympathy in response to this behavior in order to block the assumption that we endorse our parents' offensive views because they raised us.[82] We could convey such sentiments simply by denouncing the wrong rather than couching it in apologetic language, but we often combine the condemnation with an expression of sympathy ("I am sorry you suffered through those disgusting comments.") and thus we tend to think of these exchanges as apologies even though the speaker lacks standing to accept blame for the harm.

Lazare appears to find a causal relationship between the apologizer and the inflicted harm to be less important, arguing that "just as people take pride in things for which they had no responsibility (such as famous ancestors, national championships of their sports teams, and great accomplishments of their nation), so, too, must these people accept the shame . . . of their family, their athletic teams, and their nations."[83] Although I appreciate his effort to cast both pride and shame widely, I question the substance of these notions when disconnected from moral causation. It seems like an odd form of emotional nepotism for one to take personal pride in the accomplishments of her ancestors, just as it seems mistaken to feel proud of one's inherited wealth or the accomplishments of her favorite professional sports team.[84] One could take personal pride if she did something to bring about this state of affairs – perhaps by contributing in some way to the team's success – but then her pride should be limited to that contribution. A mistake appears to be at work here between experiencing personal pride and being *proud of* others. I can feel proud of my ancestors for their role in the Underground Railroad, but I could be equally proud of your ancestors for such accomplishments. Pride attaches to a person via notions of proximate causation. I have nothing to be personally proud of with respect to the accomplishments of my ancestors unless I claim that a causal connection does exist, for example by asserting that I share my great grandmother's courage. Although religious notions of "original sin" would resist this, according to all secular accounts of moral responsibility that I am aware of I do not deserve praise for the feats of my ancestors just as I do not bear the same blame for their mistakes. I consider this in more detail in the context of collective responsibility in later chapters. If I have wrongly benefited from offenses of my predecessors, however, for instance if I knowingly spent an inheritance of wealth gained from slavery, I would be responsible specifically for that wrong and could categorically apologize accordingly.

One might object that this view underestimates the extent to which people identify themselves through narratives. Insofar as my self-understanding includes acts of heroism of my ancestors, I might take pride in a distinguished family history that I feel called upon to extend. My family history imposes a burden or calls upon me to uphold a tradition. Such normative views downplay the importance of causation. I address this concern in more detail in the context of collective apologies, but I can note two points here. First, certain morally robust versions praiseworthiness and blameworthiness must track causation. If my grandparent was a racist and a murderer, this does not entail that I am either. This insight drives our sense of injustice regarding punishing children for the sins of their parents. Second, we can distinguish between responsibilities to redress injuries we cause and for which we should accept blame and duties to care for those harmed by others. Thus even if we often do feel pride or shame for the deeds of our ancestors, we can question whether we should experience these emotions.

The identity of the person receiving the apology can also trigger concerns about standing. I may be the best person to accept blame and offer an apology, but apologize to the wrong person. If I harm you but then apologize to my therapist or in prayer to my god, this may provide little meaning for you. I might also apologize primarily for the benefit of or at the insistence of someone besides the victim, for instance because I realize that I will only be accepted by others if I apologize to you even though I would otherwise disregard your claims for an apology. This brings to mind a child commanded by a teacher to apologize to a classmate if she wishes to avoid further punishment, causing the child to utter an apology to meet the demands of the teacher rather than the needs of the injured peer. In some instances the person to whom I wish to apologize may be deceased, rendering certain forms of meaning between us forever lost. Even if President Bush wished to apologize for the civilian casualties in the Iraq War, his gestures would have limited meaning for the dead except perhaps in the deontological sense that I discuss later with an example from Kant. I consider these questions a bit further in relation to the process of performing an apology.

This requirement creates serious difficulties for collective and institutional apologies, as we can see how Pope John Paul II's apology for the Catholic Church's role in the Crusades and British Prime Minister Tony Blair's apology for the Irish potato famine present numerous questions regarding their standing to apologize for injuries that they clearly did not cause. I address these issues at length in the subsequent chapters. I also evaluate in that context the various means by which an individual member of a collective might delegate standing to apologize.

C. Identification of Each Harm

The next three sections consider the interrelated aspects of the apologizer identifying each harm, recognizing the values underlying each harm, and affirming the breached underlying value. First, I consider the surprisingly complex process of identifying precisely the harms at issue. We can subdivide this first concern into two issues: naming an offense other than the primary concern of the victim (what I call the "wrong wrong" problem) and conflating multiple wrongs into one general apology without recognizing each offense.

The initial problem arises when the offender addresses conduct other than the offense for which the victim seeks an apology, thus leading her to apologize for the incorrect offense or the "wrong wrong." In her report to the Law Commission of Canada, Susan Alter recounts Bishop Hubert O'Connor's response to sexual assault charges against him. Instead of apologizing for the sexual assaults, he apparently expressed regret for "breaking his vow of chastity."[85] O'Connor may have needed to apologize to his church and his god for violating their rules of conduct, but I doubt that the victims were primarily concerned by the fact *that* he had sex. An apology only for breaking the vow fails to identify the moral difference between consensual sex between adults and the alleged assaults. Also consider former Montana Senator Conrad Burns' response when he found himself under scrutiny after a constituent asked how Burns could live in Washington D.C. "with all those niggers" and Burns replied that doing so was "a hell of a challenge." Burns stated: "I deeply regret having related a story from the campaign trail which could have been interpreted that I share racist views."[86] Of course the primary harm at issue is not *that he told the story* but rather the racism motivating his response to such a hateful question. We likely want an apology specifically for the racism rather than for his poor political judgment that allowed the remark to slip into the public sphere. The same logic appears to be at work in former Houston city council member Jim Westmoreland's response to his complaint that the Houston airport be renamed "Nigger International." Westmoreland stated: "I'm truly sorry for the problems my actions have caused."[87] Like Burns, Westmoreland does not name the racism and the harm at issue but instead regrets the "problems" he may have caused. He leaves us to wonder what problems he refers to, as he may only regret the damage done to his political career. Perhaps if he lived in a district that rewarded racial hatred, he would have nothing to regret. Once again, this flags potential differences between consequentialist and deontological views of apologetic meanings by contrasting apologies that refer to the consequences of an act with those that denounce that inherent wrongness of an offense. Here we can also scrutinize apologies that refer only to the "tone" or form of a controversial statement in this respect.

My second concern relates to conflating multiple harms into one apology that fails to identify each offense. If I destroy my spouse's cherished tomato plant and then try to blame our dog, I have both lied and disrespected her efforts to cultivate a garden. If she learns of my actions and I offer a bare "I am sorry" instead of identifying each offense and explaining what

I am apologizing for, then she will be left to wonder which offense I intend the apology to address. Perhaps I am apologetic for lying, but I have no regrets about destroying the plant because I prefer to use the space for a horseshoes court. Unless I identify both wrongs in my apology, my wife will be limited in her ability to judge its meaning. In cases of historically significant harms or international disputes, it can be tempting to apologize for only the most grievous offenses while ignoring all of the lesser offenses contributing to and enabling them. Imagine, for instance, the difference between one statement from a U.S. president generally "apologizing for the Vietnam War" and volumes of apologies cataloguing every moral harm committed by Americans during the conflict. Whereas the former would surely carry meaning in some respects, the latter could achieve fine-grained significance for those victims who might otherwise go unacknowledged by a broad expression of contrition. These issues often arise in matters of collective apologies, which I consider later.

Bill Clinton's August 1998 public address regarding the Lewinsky scandal offers a further example of the subtleties of this element. He stated: "Indeed, I did have a relationship with Miss Lewinsky that was not appropriate. In fact, it was wrong. It constituted a critical lapse in judgment and a personal failure on my part for which I am solely and completely responsible."[88] Here Clinton isolated the personal rather than the political failure of the extramarital sexual relation and accepted blame for this private offense only. Clinton subsequently reinforced the personal nature of his offense and avoided apologizing for his perjury: "Now, this matter is between me, the two people I love most – my wife and our daughter – and our God. I must put it right, and I am prepared to do whatever it takes to do so." Under pressure to address the political nature of his actions, he later identified that specific wrong: "I know that my public comments and my silence about this matter gave a false impression. I misled people, including even my wife. I deeply regret that."[89] Now he names not only the affair, but also his subsequent deception regarding the affair. Perjury and infidelity are distinct harms, and we could add others in this case. Engaging in sexual relations with an intern, for example, might be considered an abuse of power similar to a professor sleeping with her students. Such behavior would be reproachable regardless of whether Clinton was married or lied about the affair under oath, yet this wrong goes unnamed.

D. Identification of the Moral Principles Underlying Each Harm

Suppose I say the following to my wife: "I was wrong for destroying your tomato plant and then blaming it on the dog. I am sorry." Now imagine that my wife asks me why I am sorry for destroying her plant, and I respond by saying that "I really wanted a salad for lunch and now I'm sorry I won't be able to have a tomato in it." This, I suspect, would be the wrong answer. My wife probably does not seek an expression of disappointment regarding the state of my lunch, but rather recognition that I disrespected her. Here we move from naming the harm to identifying the moral principle breached in committing the harm. For her, the tomato may be inconsequential but my trampling on the fruit of her labor may signify a general pattern of my denigration of her activities. Pairing the particular harm with the abstract principle raises the stakes of my apology by isolating the discrete nature of the wrongdoing so that we can denounce it as such. This discussion runs parallel to concerns that the offender determines precisely what she is responsible for so the parties can disentangle the causal chain and match each transgression with the moral principle violated.

Veronica Berlusconi, wife of former Italian Prime Minister Silvio Berlusconi, demonstrated considerable acumen with respect to this aspect of apologetic meaning after her husband quipped on a television program that he would marry a woman on the program if he were not already married. Veronica Berlusconi found the remarks "damaging to her dignity," and after her husband refused to apologize to her privately she publicly demanded an apology from him on the front page of a national newspaper.[90] Her husband crossed a line, she explained, and "this line of conduct has a sole limit, my dignity as a woman." She continued: "Today for my female children, already adults, the example of a woman capable of defending her own dignity in her relationships with men takes on a particularly significant importance." She found this an essential lesson for her son as well, teaching him "to never forget to keep among his fundamental values respect for women." By constructing her demands in this manner, Berlusconi made clear that she sought not only reconciliation with her husband but for the former prime minister to publicly recognize and honor her dignity as a woman. An apology that offered any less would not suffice.[91]

In this respect we can return to Sabrina Harman's statements regarding her role in Abu Ghraib. Recall her words: "I failed my duties and failed my mission to protect and defend. I not only let down the people in Iraq, but I let down every single soldier that serves today. My actions potentially caused an increased hatred and insurgency toward the United States."[92] Harman emphasizes "putting soldiers and civilians at greater risk" and thereby undermining the United States' efforts in Iraq, and indeed many wanted her to recognize and denounce this aspect of her actions. For others, however, Harman surely names the "wrong wrong." Even if her acts had advanced the United States' efforts, many still would have desired an apology for the inherent wrong of torturing detainees. Although she indicates that she "let down the people in Iraq," we are unsure if she refers only to her role in impeding U.S. progress. Her apology does not describe her actions as brutal, humiliating, and objectifying, and she does not identify the prohibition against torture as the moral principle at the forefront of judgments against her.

Contrast the response of Joseph Ellis, the Mount Holyoke history professor who lied to his students about his service as a platoon leader in Vietnam when in fact he avoided active duty and spent the time in question in graduate school:

I am solely responsible and wish to express my personal regret to all students, faculty, and administrators who have been affected. . . . By misrepresenting my military service to students in the course on the Vietnam War, I did something both stupid and wrong. I apologize to the students, as well as to the faculty of this institution, for violating the implicit covenant of trust that must exist in the classroom. Finally, I apologize to those Vietnam veterans who have expressed their understandable anger about my lie. I am truly sorry for the hurt I have caused.[93]

Notice how Ellis admits his wrongdoing with some specificity (though he does not say much about the content of his fabrications), and explicitly names his actions as lying rather than blunting the force of such a charge by describing it with a morally neutral euphemism. And rather than offering a justification for his lies, for example by claiming the deception served an arguably legitimate pedagogical purpose, he cites a breach in the "implicit covenant of trust that must exist in the classroom" as an explanation of why lying in this case is wrong. This brings us to the heart of the relationship between apologies and moral discourse.

Identifying the underlying value will often require a conversation about the level of abstraction or "scope" of the principle at issue. We might describe the principle very narrowly: never harm a tomato plant in this spot of our yard again. My wife might not care about the cucumbers or she may be especially protective of this portion of the yard because the sun shines directly here for most of the day. We could build this explanation into our understanding. Alternatively, we could describe the principle much more broadly: never disrespect me or my efforts again. This latter construction may require some unpacking. How do we define respect? Have I been disrespecting her in other ways, making the tomato incident but the latest in a series of transgressions that we should classify as breaches of the same principle? This can take some thought, but it may prove essential to the ultimate meaning of the apology. If we define the value too narrowly, the apologizer may violate the spirit of the apology but not the terms. A leader might apologize for allowing genocide against one ethnic group but then allow similar atrocities against another, claiming the ability to distinguish between the cases. Thus if the United States apologizes for its inaction in Rwanda, we should pay attention to the scope of the value endorsed. A categorical apology might commit it to intervene in all sufficiently similar cases.

E. Endorsing Moral Principles Underlying Each Harm

This element draws attention to the distinction between *identifying* the value in dispute and *endorsing* that value. I might understand that I lied, for instance, without believing that I have done anything wrong. With the historical record agreed upon, blame attributed, and the violated principles made explicit, a categorically apologetic offender will endorse the values at issue.[94] The offender will understand the victim's claim as legitimate, denounce her own behavior as flawed, and perhaps offer what can amount to the most significant words in an apology: "I was wrong." In the context of apologizing, these words express not only a cognitive error but also a moral lapse. If a six-year-old child just learning multiplication says, "I was wrong that seven multiplied by twelve equals ninety," in most cases we would not interpret this as her recognizing a moral failure. If spoken by a merchant who had intentionally taken advantage of a confused customer, however, the "wrong" would shift from an admission of mathematical error to a confession of a moral breach. Those who take their moral direction from religious sources may affirm their commitment to the violated principle by describing their trespass as a certain kind of sin.[95]

Whereas any like-minded person can confirm the victim's belief that she has suffered a wrong and deserves an apology, the offender's recognition of her transgression as such proves especially significant for the relationship between them. This signifies the point at which the offender accepts that the victim deserves an apology from her. An offender may stumble through the other aspects of an apology, but simply recognizing that the victim deserves an apology can convey profound meaning because it recognizes the victim not as a mere obstacle to the offender's self-interests but as a moral interlocutor who shares values with her. The victim can also take comfort in knowing that the offender's efforts to reform will be intrinsically motivated and thus more likely to succeed. It may require a considerable period of reflection for an offender to realize that she should apologize, and in some cases the victim may die waiting. Although an offender's apology to a deceased victim may convey important meaning to her as well as the community, in such circumstances this aspect of the moral debt will remain outstanding in perpetuity.

Apologies failing to endorse the underlying moral principle occasionally take the form of "I am sorry that X bothers you" or, perhaps even more galling, "I am sorry you feel that way." Like an asteism or a back-handed compliment ("You are much less annoying today than usual"), we might describe these as back-handed apologies. Such statements merely express regret that the victim does not conform to the offender's beliefs and reinforce the offender's commitment to her transgression. Similarly, conditional prefaces to apologies such as "If anyone was hurt by my actions" or "If you were offended" often question whether the perception of harm is warranted and therefore transfer some of the blame to the victim's fragility or flawed values.[96] A conditional apology may serve less deceptive ends if I am genuinely uncertain if I injured you. I might say "I apologize if I injured you" as an interrogative statement to determine if I harmed you and the extent of the injury. Rather than questioning the legitimacy of your injury, offering such a conditional apology can allow me to inquire into the extent of the harm for which I must accept responsibility.

We can also reinforce the difference here between expressing sympathy and admitting wrongdoing. I can sympathize with others even if I accept causal responsibility for their suffering but believe that they deserve to suffer or that I am justified in causing their suffering. The bombardier on the *Enola Gay*, for example, could sympathize with Japanese civilians while continuing to endorse dropping the bomb on them. A parent can sympathize with her child while punishing her, for example by commiserating with the child while she agonizes over being grounded. "Feeling bad" for the harm I visited upon the residents of Hiroshima or the punished child, however, is quite different from asserting that I acted immorally.

Accused parties may take a more direct route and explicitly reject the value at issue or forthrightly "refuse to apologize." If a host demands that I apologize for ruining her dinner by using the wrong fork, an apology from me would not endorse the value at issue because I find her sensitivity to matters of etiquette classist and puerile. If the host is bigoted and takes offense at my bringing a nonwhite guest to her table, apologizing in this sense would convey that I endorse her racism. I would instead identify the underlying value of racial bigotry and denounce it. In such a circumstance I would make a point of not apologizing and would likely counterclaim offense because I believe I am not morally wrong but she is. Disagreements do not require apologies, and disagreements regarding the value of the norm transgressed preclude categorical apologies.

I suspect that our reluctance to discuss where our pluralistic values diverge causes us to offer hasty apologies, and such gestures can replace normative discourse with social reflexes meant to relieve immediate tension rather than build mutual understanding. Consider if the host takes offense to my refusal to recite a prayer before dinner accepting her god as my savior. I am not prepared to convert, and therefore I would not apologize by renouncing my agnostic views. What are the consequences for our dinner? I would hope that we both share a commitment to religious tolerance, which could diffuse the conflict without the need for more than a conciliatory apology as described later. If she is willing to break bread with those who do not worship her god, then I could share a pleasant meal with her because doing so is consistent with my agnostic views. Excluding someone from even one meal because of her race is not consistent with my beliefs, and therefore if the host denied service to my nonwhite friend that would be the end of the meal for me as well.

However, what if these tensions have been building for years and I decide that this Thanksgiving I will bring the situation to a boil by bringing my nonwhite friend to dinner and emphatically denouncing Christ as the family says grace before the meal? The occasion results in predictable animosity, and I later consider my actions juvenile. I took the actions in order to make the family uncomfortable, ruin their holiday, and openly disrespect their values. All of this now seems to reflect poor judgment that warrants an apology on my part. I would remain unrepentant for rejecting their religion and racism, but I could identify and denounce the specific wrongs within my ill-advised stunt. National Public Radio commentator Andre Codrescu attempted this strategy after he insulted Christians who believe in the rapture by stating that the "evaporation of four million who believe in this crap would leave the world an instantly better place." After an NPR spokesperson announced that Codrescu had apologized, he clarified: "I certainly didn't apologize for what I said. Maybe the way I worded it was a bit strong."[97] Codrescu implies that he still harbors disparaging sentiments for these believers, but he is willing to consider that the tenor of his remarks may have breached some undisclosed principle. Former Reagan White House spokesperson Larry Speaks leaves us with similar uncertainty regarding his apology for controversial passages in his book regarding Reagan's occasional ineptitude during crucial moments of his presidency and Speaks' false attribution of statements to Reagan when he worked for him in order to make the president appear more astute. "I apologize not for the truth in my book nor the telling of it," he explained, because "the truth never requires apology."[98] While his claim that "truth never requires apology" provides an enigma in its own right, he then further confuses matters: "I do regret that I may have overstepped the bounds of propriety in some instances. It is for that I apologize." Among other things, this leaves us to wonder: 1) what are the bounds of propriety – or underlying moral principles – to which he refers; 2) which of his actions may have overstepped these bounds; 3) does he refer to his actions in publishing this book or in lying for Reagan; and 4) did the actions overstep those bounds or not, which would determine if he has done anything wrong by the standards of which he speaks?

Others have navigated similar complexities with a bit more finesse. When various values are at stake and one wishes to affirm some of the values but reject others, thoughtful apologies require some precision. We can consistently refuse to apologize for one of our beliefs while categorically apologizing for actions that the victim might believe are entwined with that belief so long as we can disentangle the web of values, actions, and causation. Consider James McGreevey's statements upon his resignation as governor of New Jersey in light of his extramarital homosexual affair:

I have to begin today with humility by simply saying I am sorry – so, so sorry that mistakes in my judgment made this day necessary for all of us. I am sorry that my actions have hurt those that I love in my personal and political lives. I am sorry to those who vested their careers with me and that this abrupt transition has caused them upheaval. And I am sorry that I have disappointed the citizens of the state of New Jersey who gave me this enormous trust. To be clear, I am not apologizing for being a gay American, but rather, for having let personal feelings impact my decision making and for not having had the courage to be open about whom I was.[99]

The final sentence isolates specifically what McGreevey believes he has done wrong and what he has not done wrong. By explicitly rejecting the notion that he should apologize for being gay, he redirects all blame to his fail-ures of courage and decision making. McGreevey can therefore simultane-ously express self-reproach for failures unrelated to his sexual orientation while challenging the homophobia of some of his critics. Some may reject McGreevey's attempt to separate his homosexuality from character flaws by making the stereotypical claim that promiscuity and deficiencies of courage are somehow causally related to homosexuality, but by attempting to block this assertion McGreevey can unrepentantly assert his position within the culture wars while expressing contrition regarding largely unrelated matters. In other words, adopting a tone of humility does not require the offender to concede to all of the moral beliefs of the harmed parties.

A further question arises here regarding the meanings of an apology for an offense I commit that breaches my ethical principles and that I believe the victim should find offensive, but at which she does not in fact take offense. Imagine that I, in a moment of gross stupidity, make a sexist comment to a woman who is a misogynist and applauds my remark. In a situation where I believe that the woman should have taken offense at an action that breaches my principles but not hers, it appears that I can offer an apology conveying meaning across each of the elements, but we will not share the appropriate value. I might attempt to persuade her that she should change her belief, which would in effect advise her to experience the injury I believe she has suffered from my actions as such. Barring a conversion, my apology may have meaning for me but perhaps very little for her. This would be akin to the stickler for etiquette insisting on apologizing profusely to me for a missing fork at her table when I had not noticed its absence and contentedly ate my salad with a dessert fork. If, however, this exchange occurred between people for whom cutlery signified social status and the missing fork amounted to a great disrespect, then we could imagine such an apology bearing considerable meaning for both. This would also be true between individuals holding truly insidious values, for example if one racist apologized to another racist for failing to be racist enough.

We can contrast my account with the terse but influential interpretation of apologies provided by sociologist Erving Goffman. Goffman claims that "apologies represent a splitting of the self into a blameworthy part and a part that . . . dissociates itself from the delict and affirms a belief in the offended rule."[100] Although Goffman agrees that the apologizer endorses the under-lying principle, this image of dividing her identity into a conforming self and a rebellious self risks stripping her of the intentionality required to accept blame as discussed earlier. When apologies include statements like "that wasn't me" or "I don't know what got into me," they imply that the apolo-gizer, speaking from her "good self," did not actually commit the act. She is a new person, and the old person caused the harm. Fracturing moral agency in this way drifts toward offering an excuse for the act or understanding it as a sort of intrapersonal accident. This type of self-deception occurs, for example, when someone makes racist comments but then claims not to be a racist. We can also see such dissociation at work in the self-description of a sailor who beat a homosexual shipmate to death: "It was horrible, but I am not a horrible person."[101] Moral agency, and by extension our practices of apologizing, makes less sense without unified moral agents possessing a suite of values and accepting blame for their violation of these values.

These two previous concerns point toward a rather serious problem for apologies that I take up later. If the affirmation of shared values constitutes such a central component of apologetic meaning, will pluralistic communities where members disagree about final vocabularies (to use Richard Rorty's term) be less likely to produce apologies that endorse underlying shared moral beliefs? Apologizers within insular communities with homogeneous value systems can easily identify breaches of shared values and reintegrate into the belief system by reaffirming those values. Few of us live in such environments where moral values remain stable, obvious, and compelling. Offenders may feel alienated from the prevailing moral norms – imagine a lapsed Catholic admonished for missing mass – even before they offend, and indeed this disaffection may be a central cause of their transgressions. Others may live with a fractured and contradictory set of values that only further unravels when one is called on to apologize and think through her moral commitments. This speaks not only to a conflict between pluralistic values in which an offender refuses to honor a competing norm because she finds her beliefs superior, but to a fragility or even absence of underlying values. Moral relativism does not extinguish apologetic meaning, as we saw in the mutual racist example earlier illustrating that fellow adherents to just about any belief system can endorse their shared underlying values. Given the state of contemporary culture, however, relativism may lead to a decrease in apologies recognizing what we might consider the "high moral values" and an increase in apologies affirming consumer values. In this respect we might envision apologies for failing to honor the "cultural imperative" of not presenting an expensive enough diamond engagement ring. Indeed, not all apologetic meaning requires reference to even a semblance of moral value but instead may be grounded in strictly instrumental objectives. We can view the loss of apologetic meaning in this respect as a by-product of the general decay of meaning and non-instrumental value in modernity, and I will refrain from further indulging in that conversation here. Beyond these worries with relativism, however, we should wonder about the meanings of apologies for the nihilists or sociopaths among us who function with a skepticism toward all moral commitments. From their perspective, apologies will be but a gambit in a meaningless game. Thus a scene of one nihilist apologizing to another nihilist for breaching values that neither holds sounds like joke from a Beckett dialogue.

F. Recognition of Victim as Moral Interlocutor

I can be brief here, but I wish to note the importance of one of the most meaningful aspects of apologies that we might overlook if we focus on the details of apologetic discourse to the exclusion of a broader perspective. When the offender engages the victim in this process of corroborating the factual record, accepting blame, identifying each harm and the principles underlying each harm, and expressing a shared commitment to those principles, she may undergo a radical transformation in her relation to the victim. Instead of viewing the victim as a mere means subordinated to the offender's ends, undertaking this process of apologetic dialogue may cause the offender to view and interact with the victim in an entirely new light. The offender may, perhaps for the first time, recognize and treat the victim as a moral interlocutor.[102] Otherwise she might believe that the value she breached deserves recognition, but the victim does not.

This helps to explain how failing to apologize for injuring someone can actually be more harmful than the injury itself. If someone steps on my toe and causes me some sharp but fleeting pain, I would consider this a small offense. If the offender refuses to offer even an expression of sympathy, however, then I might perceive this as disregarding me. Such a lack of respect or contempt for me would, in my mind, constitute a much more serious infringement on my well-being than the pain in my foot. Quarrels often escalate into serious conflicts for precisely this reason: the victim feels not only injured by the offender but also disrespected.

To some this may seem like an inconsequential definitional shift: of course when I discuss a moral question with someone she becomes, by definition, my moral interlocutor. Note the potential significance of this. The victim, whom the offender may have perceived as but a tool for her use, can become the primary conversant in the offender's task of reexamining and maintaining her core values. The offender comes to treat the victim as a being with *dignity* and equal moral worth to whom she must justify her actions. In what I take as the most profound existential sense of the Kantian term, the victim and offender recognize each other as people struggling to make sense of the very meaning of their lives and values. Rather than interacting with aloof certitude, the offender finds the victim worthy of engaging in such an intimate and identity-defining conversation. We acknowledge the person we mistreated as essential to our own well-being. I mean to emphasize something slightly different from the more common notion of recognizing the victim as a moral agent: she becomes my moral peer. This invokes the Hegelian notion of mutual recognition as well: I recognize when apologizing that my own dignity depends upon others and my treatment of them. Apologies foreground how my dialectical relationship with the other constitutes my own sense of meaning, value, and self. I can get straight with myself only by getting straight with the other.[103] If these Kantian and Hegelian notes do not resonate, we can register this thought in utilitarian terms. As I apologize, I appreciate that the victim is a being who suffers and I can no longer discount her pain against my own.

When I apologize, I acknowledge my own flaws, uncertainty, and vulnerability. Vulnerability refers here not only to my fear of sanction, but also to my moral confusion and my existential fragility. In this sense, victim and offender become equals at the most basic level as they try to explain what has meaning and value and recognize when one has strayed from those beliefs. Together they now engage in the process of revealing and shaping their ultimate values. This, in part, accounts for the demeanor of humility associated with contrition. It is not only that I have done something wrong, but also that I have become a person who does such wrongful things. This disrupts the very relationship between my values and my identity: I am not who I want to be. An apology can be so humbling in part because in this precarious moment of self-scrutiny I turn not to my closest confidant but to the person I may be most alienated from on account of my own actions. The Hegelian insight seems especially keen in this regard. However we describe this experience – as recognition of mutual interdependence, dignity, humanity, respect, rationality, equality, or even transcendence of the other (to use the favored Levinasian term) – it may provide the bedrock for all other apologetic meanings.

These points deserve special emphasis for those who may think of themselves as authorities in matters of morality, including ethical philosophers, clergy, members of the judiciary, and others. As a philosopher who regularly teaches classes in ethical theory, I occasionally find it especially humbling to cede authority on these matters in my personal life. The sense that I "should know better" than those who do not study moral problems professionally can present an additional obstacle to admitting my own failures and uncertainties and recognizing the person I have wronged as a worthy moral interlocutor. Just as knowledge of religious traditions does not necessarily make one pious, expertise in moral philosophy does not establish moral superiority. Although this may be utterly obvious to most, those who make their livelihood in such fields can be temporarily blinded to this fact. Such characters may also possess rhetorical tools that allow them to steer conversations regarding their own transgressions into more abstract and less personally challenging territory. Those offended by individuals with an alleged expertise in moral principles should be wary if the offender's apology begins to look more like a lecture than a discussion.

I consider this later with respect to the act of performing an apology by offering it to the appropriate recipient, but notice cases in which the offender directs her apology to someone other than the person she harms. Suppose, for instance, that a convict apologizes to the judge during sentencing for a crime committed against Person X. Here the convict could clearly admit wrongdoing, affirm the underlying value, and serve her sentence while continuing to ignore Person X and refusing to acknowledge her as more than a means to her ends. Also note various other situations in which transgressors offer their apologies to those who hold the greatest power over them rather than to their victims, like corporate executives apologizing to shareholders or consumers, professional athletes apologizing to league commissions, or sinners apologizing to priests instead of to those who most directly suffered the indignities. Continuing to fail to acknowledge the victim as a moral interlocutor – whether from an outright refusal to recognize her as worthy of engaging in such an exchange or from an ignorance of the meaning of such an interaction – can cause the victim to experience still further harm against her. The victim may perceive the initial harm as well as the secondary offense of failing to recognize her as a moral interlocutor as enduring until the offender specifically remedies both injustices. This concern therefore speaks to matters regarding publicity, remedies, and standing considered later.

G. Categorical Regret

Several commentators claim that "regret or sorrow" is essential to an apology, and Tavuchis goes so far as to claim that "[w]hatever else is said or conveyed, an apology must express sorrow."[104] Yet because sorrow or regret can indicate sadness in response to any distant misfortune for which one accepts no blame, the relation between regret and apologetic meaning could benefit from some clarification. Regretting, much like being "sorry," can mean many things. Several of these meanings can be consistent with an outright refusal to apologize. Whereas regret typically expresses a sentiment that I wish things could be otherwise, this does not necessarily entail that I believe that I have done anything wrong. I might regret, for instance, that you have taken offense at my refusal to convert to your religion. Or I might find my host's dismay over my breaches of etiquette regrettable. In these cases I regret the acts of others, rather than my own, because I believe the fault lies with them. I might also regret a state of affairs without being able to attribute blame to anyone, such as the regret I might experience in response to the suffering resulting from a natural disaster.

The colloquial use of "regret" can also refer to displeasure for harm that I intend. A judge can regret sentencing a parent to a prison term even if she believes this is the right decision. If she determines that the convict deserves to serve time and that the sentence is just and beneficial for the community, the judge may continue to find it terribly unfortunate that the offender will spend a portion of her life incarcerated and will be separated from her child. Although incarceration provides the best option among unfortunate choices, the judge may nonetheless describe the outcome as "a shame." The judge's regret longs for a world in which things "didn't have to be this way" even though she continues to endorse her decision. In this respect, noncategorical regret could be more than an expression of sympathy or compassion. If the judge takes care to explain her regret, she draws attention to the costs of even what she believes is the right choice. In doing so, she may explicitly explain the importance of her choice and why she endorses the underlying principle despite its high price. She might also comment on the many other conditions – such as poverty, racism, and a failing educational system – that place far too many of these choices before her.

In this light we can make sense of the lack of categorical regret in Zina-dine Zidane's apology for his intentional head butting of an opponent during the 2006 World Cup final. "I apologize, to all the children," Zidane stated, explaining that the opponent provoked him by repeatedly insulting his family and that he "would rather have taken a punch in the jaw than have heard that." "My act is not forgivable," he admitted, "but they must also punish the true guilty party, and the guilty party is the one who provokes." Zidane then spoke as if he were a judge channeling divine retribution on the pitch: "If things happened this way, it's because somewhere up there it was decided that way. . . . I don't regret anything that happened, I accept it."[105] Zidane may frame his remarks as an apology, but he explicitly claims a higher power guided his actions and thus he should not regret them. Unlike Agamemnon's vilification of the Homeric gods for meddling with his affairs, Zidane embraces the will of the football gods. From his statements we may also infer that he might find himself justified if he responds violently to similar provocations in the future. Rather than believing that he has made an error that he wishes could be undone, he effectively continues to endorse his actions.

Likewise, a patient may find it regrettable that others cannot afford an expensive life-saving surgery while she can, but this does not necessarily indicate that she regrets her choice to exercise her advantage. Instead, she regrets that others cannot enjoy the same benefit, just as she might regret the suffering of others caused by a natural disaster. Similarly, when an employer explains to an employee that she "regrets that it has come down to this" and proceeds to fire the employee, the supervisor stands behind her decision but regrets that she must undertake the unpleasant task and cause hardship for the employee. This notion of regret also surfaces when a partner ends a romantic relationship, as she might "regret that the relationship has failed" while walking out the door. Such use of regret can parallel expressions of sympathy described earlier in that both do not accept blame for the harm.

I use the notion of "categorical regret" to refer to an offender's recognition that her actions, which caused the harm at issue, constitute a moral failure. In this sense, an offender wishes that the transgression could be undone. She explains that she regrets what she has done because it is wrong, she wishes she had done otherwise, and in accordance with this realization she commits to not making the same mistake again. In other words, the offender's recognition that her actions were wrong leads to a belief that she should have done otherwise and a motivation that she will do otherwise in the future. As I consider in the context of offering the apology to the appropriate person, notice that one can express this kind of regret without categorically apologizing, for instance if the offender expresses the regret to someone other than the victim.

Suppose I am faced with a choice of whether or not to rescue a stray dog by adopting her. I do not rescue the dog because my landlord does not allow pets and I am unwilling to look for a new apartment. I later learn that animal control captured and euthanized the dog. Now I realize that the inconvenience of finding a new apartment is superficial compared to the well-being of the animal and the companionship we would have shared. I wish I could turn back time and rescue the dog. I made a mistake and I regret it. Notice that rather than merely expressing disappointment *that* I had to choose between the apartment and the dog, I wish I had chosen differently. In the context of apologizing, categorical regret as I use it refers specifically to recognition of a mistake rather than an expression of sorrow over missed opportunity. This nuance invokes problems of incommensurability. When choosing between incommensurable goods such as rescuing a dog and remaining in my apartment, I will suffer a loss either way. I may interpret my feelings regarding this loss as regret. Unless I believe I should have chosen otherwise, however, sorrow over the recognition of what was lost rather than categorical regret best captures my sentiment. Again, merely choosing between incommensurables cannot cause categorical regret unless I believe I made the wrong choice, and I cannot apologize fully if I would again make the same choice however difficult or tragic it may be. We find a source of confusion in this regard in invitations asking for "regrets only"; on my account, we cannot categorically regret something we have yet to do while continuing to endorse it. As with "sorry," the conflation of these distinct senses of regret causes the moral force of categorical regret to bleed into other uses of the term. When commentators call for regret to accompany apologies, we should differentiate these meanings or we risk reducing the full moral meaning of categorical apologies to expressions of sympathy or disappointment.

My characterization of categorical regret as central to apologetic meaning appears to be a minority position in apology scholarship. Lazare implies that he does not find regret to be a necessary element of apologies, as he provides three consecutive examples of what he considers "successful" apologies: a lawyer expressing shame for not sending an important letter, a parishioner admitting embarrassment for her delay in returning a book, and a driver gesturing contritely to a pedestrian after nearly colliding with her.[106] In each case we have no way of knowing if the offender would commit the offense again given similar circumstances. Unable to gauge the nature of the offender's regret, the apology's meaning remains ambiguous. Similarly, Louis Kort claims that an apology can be "full-fledged" even if it successfully fakes any of the forms of regret mentioned earlier, including those that do not recognize wrongdoing.[107] Richard Joyce believes an apology only requires "adequately convincing affectation."[108]

Notice, however, the stark distinctions between an apology declaring the offender's transgression as wrong and wishing it could be undone and an apology that does not do so. If the *Enola Gay* bombardier offers an apology for dropping the bomb on Hiroshima but continues to endorse his actions

as the best option given the geo-political situation and his personal circumstances, then he would appear – like the judge who regrets that she must
imprison a mother – to regret only that this justified action carried such
costs. Richard Nixon's resignation speech famously invokes to this concern:
"I regret deeply any injuries that may have been done in the course of events
that have led to this decision [to resign]. I would say only that if some of
my judgments were wrong, and some were wrong, they were made in what
I believed at the time to be in the best interests of the nation."[109] In addition
to refusing to corroborate the historical record by referring to "injuries that
may have been done" and not identifying which of his decisions were wrong,
Nixon implies that his actions may not have been wrong given the choices he
faced. Confronted with similar circumstances, he might still have believed
those decisions were "in the best interests of the nation." Under Nixon's
ambiguous logic, morally abject acts such as lying to the public could be in
the nation's interests. Such a position parallels the common disclaimer "I am
sorry but I must."

Jana Thompson has noted in this regard what she calls the "Apology
Paradox."[110] If apologizing commits the apologizer to wishing that the deeds
in question could be undone, for some harms this might entail the apologizer
suggesting that she should not exist. Following Derek Parfit's notion of the
contingency of persons, our existence is predicated upon a great number of
interrelated events in the past. If we wish that a major historical event like
African slavery could be undone, we effectively wish for the elimination of
the conditions required for our existence. Because we presumably prefer to
exist, regretting the events that led to our existence (and thus our ability
to apologize) presents a paradox or at least a rather awkward claim. Given
that the existence of the contemporary African Americans who would be the
recipients of an apology for slavery also depends upon the abduction of their
ancestors, categorically regretting slavery might also suggest that the world
would be more just if they did not exist. Interpretations of this sort can add
further concerns to the considerable list of problems confronting collective
apologies addressed later.

Considering how many unfortunate events result from uncertainties, this
also raises the question of the relationship between regret and risk assessment. Suppose I regret driving while intoxicated only because a police officer
apprehended me. If I regret driving drunk because I underestimated the likelihood of being caught, my regret would attach to the miscalculation rather
than the moral error of driving drunk. I might do it again if the odds were
more in my favor, and we should be especially attuned to this distinction
when evaluating the apologies of convicts: do they now believe that their
actions were wrong as such or do they only regret being caught? We can
consider such questions regarding the probabilities of costs and benefits to
my choice to rescue the stray dog. Perhaps another family rescues the dog
soon after I decided not to adopt her and she lives an idyllic life on their

farm. Suppose I do rescue the dog, take a large financial loss moving to a new apartment, and she attacks my new neighbor soon thereafter and must be euthanized. Such circumstances might lead me to question my judgment, but I could continue to believe that I had made the right choice given the information available to me and the priority of my values. My response to the next stray dog I come across would test my evaluations of risks and benefits. As I discuss later, such questions often arise in collective apologies offered by corporations or governments because institutional policy often must take calculated risks in order to manage multiple objectives.

Politicians from across the ideological spectrum face these issues, and U.S. Senator Hillary Clinton's refusal to apologize for her vote authorizing the use of force in Iraq invokes several of the concerns that span the preceding chapters. Perhaps even more than her husband, Hillary Clinton has a reputation as a lightning rod for criticism from conservative commentators. The attention drawn to her in this case, however, resulted from challenges issued by fellow Democrat John Edwards. Edwards and Clinton both voted for the Authorization for Use of Military Force Against Iraq Resolution of 2002. As rivals for the 2008 Democratic presidential nomination, both sought to distance themselves from the increasingly unpopular war. Edwards repeatedly offered apologetic gestures for his vote, titling one editorial "I Was Wrong" and stating that he "should not have given the president this authority." "Had I known," Edwards explained, that the information "I was being given by our intelligence wasn't the whole story . . . I never would have voted for this war."[111] He later expanded on *Meet the Press*: "It wasn't just the weapons of mass destruction I was wrong about." "It's become absolutely clear – and I'm very critical of myself for this – become absolutely clear, looking back, that I should not have given the president this authority." Having said this, Edwards challenged Clinton: "anybody who wants to be president of the United States has got to be honest and open, be willing to admit when they've done things wrong."[112]

As Stanley Fish pointed out in coming to Clinton's defense, Edwards seems to be manipulating an overly simplistic conception of apologies. Although he admits that he was "wrong," he effectively says that he was wrong because the Bush administration lied to him. He admits that he was factually wrong – like the child who is wrong in answering an arithmetic problem – but he does not explicitly shoulder blame for that wrong because he implies that those who provided misleading intelligence proximately caused his vote.[113] Thus what looks *prima facie* like an apology can be read as a means of deflecting blame. We might specifically blame Edwards, for instance, for failing in his duty to treat the intelligence presented by the president more critically. Perhaps he *should have known* that the intelligence provided "wasn't the whole story." And although one would not ordinarily think of an apology as opportunistic, in this light Edwards' statements appear to exploit the public's desire for a president whose style of leadership contrasts with the Bush administration's stubbornness and refusal to admit its mistakes. Edwards' emphasis on how he is "very critical" of himself contributes to the impression that he might have chosen his words to achieve this end. As I discuss later, suspicions that political ambition rather than moral principles motivate an apology can cause the gesture to backfire.

Fish agreed with Clinton's refusal to apologize, reminding us of the content of her 2002 statement on the Senate floor: "A vote for [the resolution] is not a vote to rush to war; it is a vote that puts awesome responsibility in the hands of our president and we say to him – Use these powers wisely and as a last resort." Because Bush did not use the powers wisely or as a last resort, Fish believes that Clinton is not morally responsible for the situation in Iraq. Fish suggests that Clinton may deserve blame for trusting Bush, but this differs from holding her accountable for the war. Fish claims that "the appropriate response to that mistake is not an apology – 'I apologize for thinking better of you than I should have' doesn't quite sound right – but a resolution not to do it again."[114]

We can say a bit more about this situation. First, I think the issue of categorical regret and risk management is paramount. If U.S. forces had marched into Baghdad, discovered stockpiles of nuclear and biological weapons, quickly vanquished Saddam Hussein and his military, and successfully oversaw the transition to a flourishing democracy, then I doubt that either Edwards or Clinton would be backpedaling from their votes. Instead, we might expect them to congratulate themselves for their bipartisanship and strengths in matters of foreign policy and national security. Both faced a choice. As is usually the case for all of us, they made their choices without the benefit of perfect information. Do either regret their vote to authorize the war, or do they rather find the outcome unfortunate? Did they make the wrong choice considering what they knew at the time, which would amount to a personal and professional failure? Should they have known more and known better? In future matters, how will they ensure that they act on legitimate and sufficient intelligence? Or do they regret how poorly the campaign was executed, which shifts the blame for the failures in Iraq to others but does not necessarily reject the need for invasion? How would they respond differently as president? Such distinctions may prove crucial not only to future voters, but also in foreign relations as other nations gauge the United States' diplomatic tendencies by such comments from leading Democrats.

Second, Fish may underestimate the seriousness of their failure of judgment. At the time of the vote, the evidence that Iraq possessed weapons of mass destruction seemed quite weak and the purported connection between Saddam Hussein and the attacks of September 11, 2001, were even more suspect. It also appeared that the Bush administration was fishing for justifications to invade and that they might do so without the support of the United Nations. In addition, if Clinton claims that she does not deserve blame for the war because Bush did not satisfy the conditions that he use the powers granted wisely or as a last resort, we can still judge her for trusting that he would satisfy these prerequisites. Congress could have required Bush to return for its authorization once he had satisfied its conditions, and she could have voted against a resolution without such precautions.[115] Even if the intelligence was incomplete and misleading, twenty-three other senators saw enough to reject the resolution. This makes us wonder what those twenty-one Democrats, one Independent, and one Republican senator (along with 133 members of Congress) saw that Edwards and Clinton did not. What principles separate those who supported the resolution from those who opposed it? I, for one, would like to know more about what Edwards and Clinton were thinking when they cast their votes. Did either allow their political ambitions to influence their judgment? Did they place their fortunes with the majority on that issue, but retrospectively hedge those bets once they lost? Honest answers to those questions would be illuminating.

A categorical apology from Clinton and Edwards might share their portion of the blame for the war in any of these senses. In doing so they could improve our understanding of the factual record surrounding the lead-up to the war, including providing a more transparent picture of how they analyzed the issues. If we could see the questions as they saw them at the time, perhaps we would better understand, sympathize with, or support their decisions. A categorical apology from Clinton and Edwards could also accept their portion of blame for the war, explain why and how they were wrong, endorse the values they breached, and acknowledge those they harmed. They could also express the sort of categorical regret that commits them to reforming and providing redress. All of this could be quite fortifying for contemporary politics. It also would demonstrate the importance of apologies providing rather detailed accounts of the salient historical record because seemingly minor details about the offender's knowledge and mental states may fundamentally transform judgments regarding the offense and the apology.

Instead, we hear binary sound bites: Edwards apologized and Clinton did not. If we learn anything from the war in Iraq, it is that recent U.S. politics have been allergic to nuance. The conflation of the threats posed by al-Qaeda and Iraq or President Bush's declaration that one is either "for him or against him" in the fight against terrorism are but the most obvious examples. John Kerry's attempt to account for basic distinctions regarding his votes on the war may have cost him the presidency. Some portion of the electorate seemed moved by drumbeats from conservative analysts that only unpatriotic, flip-flopping metrosexuals need subtlety to explain themselves in a time of war. Here again we should hear Adrienne Rich: "Lies are usually attempts to make everything simpler – for the liar – than it really is, or ought to be."[116]

And I do not refer to the "metrosexual charge" lightly. Just as Kerry's opposition attempted to emasculate the decorated veteran, Clinton's gender is obviously in play. Deborah Tannen describes at least one bind Clinton faces: "To the extent she's a woman and has to prove she's tough, standing her ground is the best thing to do. And to the extent she's a woman and people don't tolerate toughness in women, she's going to be faulted for that."[117] If she apologizes, she will be criticized as a feminine flip-flopper. If she does not apologize from fear of such accusations, she drifts closer to the leadership style of President Bush.[118] Yet then again, perhaps Bush's "black and white" view of the world is a response to Bill Clinton's bad faith parsing of terms like "sexual relations."

H. Performance of the Apology

We have seen that stating the words "I am sorry" may signify but a fraction of possible apologetic meaning. Uttering that phrase may begin the process of apologizing, but without more we are unable to clarify the many ambiguities within the gesture. This attention to other dimensions of apologizing should not cause us to overlook the importance of the act of uttering apologetic sentiments. We often hear, for example, an offender claim that she "owes X an apology" but then leaves it at that. The lone recognition that the victim deserves an apology seems to stop short of providing at least a portion of what the offender owes. Just as my recognition that I owe you some money differs from repaying my debt, the recognition that I owe you an apology differs from providing that apology. The recognition itself may convey considerable apologetic meaning in that it can be a form of admission of wrongdoing and acceptance of blame, but the statement "I owe you an apology" is too bare to determine what sorts of meaning the offender wishes to convey. For what do you owe me an apology? Why do you owe it? For what do you accept blame? What value did you breach, and are you committed to that value? What redress will you provide?

These questions may remain unanswered when an offender offers nothing beyond symbolic apologetic gestures. Consider Pope John Paul II's visit to Jerusalem's Western Wall in March of 2000, where he placed a piece of paper in the wall of the Temple on which the following was written:

> God of our fathers,
> You chose Abraham and his descendants
> to bring your Name to the Nations:
> we are deeply saddened
> by the behavior of those
> who in the course of history
> have caused these children of yours to suffer,
> and asking your forgiveness
> we wish to commit ourselves
> to genuine brotherhood
> with the people of the Covenant.[119]

Although this is typically described as an apology, we can readily notice multiple ambiguities in the statement: 1) the Pope expresses sadness for the suffering of Jews but does not explicitly accept blame – either personally or as a representative of the Catholic Church – for those harms; 2) he does not name any wrong in particular, leaving us to wonder for which of the many offenses against the Jews, by Catholics and others, he expresses sadness; 3) the value he endorses appears to be a "brotherhood with the people of the Covenant," but the relation between this value and the transgressions to which he refers remains vague; 4) this leaves unclear how the Catholic Church intends to reform its behavior and provide redress for its (yet to be specified) offenses against the Jews; 5) given the long history of Catholic offenses against the Jews, we wonder if the Pope has standing to speak for offenders across the ages; and 6) without these issues clarified we cannot be sure for what the pope seeks forgiveness or if he and the Church deserve such forgiveness. According to Lazare, the Pope's actions would be an effective apology "even without the note."[120] Apparently for Lazare the Pope's very presence and contrite physical postures at the holy site convey all of the essential meaning of an apology. I would be more cautious here. The meaning remains cryptic even with the Pope's written statement, but without the explanatory note his gestures would be even more inscrutable. Like German Chancellor Willy Brandt's gesture of kneeling before the monument to victims of the Warsaw Ghetto Uprising, the Pope's visit undoubtedly holds profound symbolic value. The absence of an explanation of the gestures leaves us without a window onto the mental states directly relevant to apologetic meaning. Perhaps in light of our desire to receive satisfying apologies, we may read more meaning into opaque gestures of contrition than they warrant.

Even if the offender articulates apologetic utterances, it matters to whom she apologizes. An offender's internal monologue regarding her responsibility and regret for the transgression will bear meaning for her, but until she offers those thoughts to her victims they cannot become significant for them. It matters not only that I speak the words, but to whom I speak them. If I only denounce my sins to a priest in confession or in prayer to my god, the victim may never learn of my contrition. I also may continue to fail to treat my victim as a moral interlocutor if I do not engage her in a conversation recognizing her right to be free from my trespass. In some cases offenders awkwardly direct their statements to a general audience without acknowledging the victims specifically. A spokesperson for *Weekly World News*, which listed an Arizona police officer who suffered severe burns over his face, arms, and upper body as one of the world's "Top Ten Ugliest People," offered the following statement: "We feel terrible about this. It was a mistake on the editor's part, which won't happen again."[121] Acknowledgment of the victim appears conspicuously absent in the statement, as if the spokesperson was apologizing to the subscribers boycotting the tabloid rather than to the officer.

Another question arises regarding the audience for an apology: how meaningful can an apology be if it never reaches its victim? In contrast to cases in which the offender does not intend to address the apology to the victim but rather to a priest, a judge, or some third party, suppose that the apologizer attempts in good faith to reach the victim but fails. Imagine that the offender offers what we might consider a full apology but the victim does not hear her, or perhaps she mails a written apology but the victim never receives it. Or suppose the victim is dead by the time the offender apologizes.

Some might be surprised to learn that Kant argued for apologies to the dead. He provides this example in *Metaphysical Elements of Justice*:

> If someone spreads a rumor about a dead person's crime that when alive would have made him dishonorable or at least despicable, anyone who can provide evidence that this accusation is intentionally false and a lie can then openly declare that he who cast aspersions on the dead man's character is a calumniator, which [in turn] makes [that person] himself dishonorable. He [the defender of the dead man] would be unable to do all of this if he did not rightfully assume that the dead man was insulted thereby, even though he was dead, and then he [the dead man] was owed an apology from him [the rumor monger], even if he no longer exists.[122]

If one takes a deontological view of apologies, the death of your victim does not discharge you from your duty to apologize. We can also appreciate how utilitarians and virtue ethicists would find value in such apologies for the offender and community. Even if an apology to the dead cannot achieve certain kinds of meaning, others are not only possible but also quite important.

Such apologies may hold great significance for the offender and the community even if they do not reach the victim, as they can – among other things – create a historical record, attribute blame, endorse the breached value, promote reform, and provide various forms of redress. In this respect, apologies for genocide retain considerable significance even if the victims will never experience this meaning. Yet we should not fail to notice what is absent. Categorical apologies require dialogue between victims and offenders as they agree on the factual record of events, attribute blame, identify shared moral principles breached between the offender and victim, provide relief to the victim, and transform the relationship between the offender and the victim. Presumably within secular accounts, even a categorical apology cannot coax forgiveness from the dead. Without the victim's participation in these processes, certain forms of meaning are lost. We can imagine an offender who had long wished to reconcile with a recently deceased family member offering an apology at her funeral. Here the loss of the opportunity to apologize, forgive, and reconcile would compound the grief over loss of life. Under extraordinary circumstances one might enter into a dialogue with the victim's account of a transgression after her death. If a Holocaust survivor made explicit in her memoirs who wronged her, how she wronged her, and why it was wrong, then the offender could corroborate and agree with the account and enter into a dialogue with the dead in this sense. Some forms of meaning would remain precluded, but we might generate meaning in unforeseeable ways with some creativity and persistence. In the absence of certain beliefs regarding the afterlife, however, the death of the victim or offender causes the opportunity for some types of meaning to be lost forever. This becomes quite evident in cases of collective apologies for harms in the distant past, which I discuss later.

Whereas death may present an absolute bar to some forms of meaning, other questions regarding the timing of apologies require more subtlety. According to some etiquette guides and dispute resolution manuals, an apology should follow immediately after the offense.[123] Immediate apologies prevent the victim from suffering an unacknowledged indignity for longer than necessary and allow the parties to work toward reconciliation as quickly as possible, but this may not be appropriate or possible in cases of serious injuries. If I accidentally harm you, I may instantaneously explain my lack of intention and take measures to minimize your injury. If I intentionally harm you, it may take years for me to understand my wrongdoing as such. If I decide to rob you, presumably at the time of the attack I feel justified in some sense or believe my actions require no justification. I may need to undergo considerable moral reflection and transformation before I regret my actions and see a need to apologize. As several religious traditions discussed later accept, this can take some time. Thus if I decide to apologize for the robbery years after the attack without coercion from a penal system – imagine that I admit the offense and apologize even though it seems that I will never be caught for the crime – this could signify a decisive development in my moral growth. This might apply not only in cases where the victim and offender are strangers, but also between enduring friends. If I apologize to a close friend for mistreating her many years ago, the time between the harm and the apology may indicate that I have given the matter serious reflection. I did not forget what I did, and now I find the value I breached so important that I return to it even though she may have long forgotten my transgression and our relationship may be quite strong even without an apology. Such an occasion can renew our commitment to shared values that perhaps we have allowed to lapse over the years, and we can see how such an apology could be extraordinarily significant within an intimate relationship. Sometimes in cases of collective apologies, such as the Pope John Paul II's for the Crusades, the duration between the injury and the apology can be hundreds of years. Such situations may also reflect an institutional moral transformation as representatives of a collective come to understand that moral standards have evolved and members now believe that it is incumbent upon them to denounce the old ways while stating their new standard. For some this may be too little too late, but others may find it better late than never.

We can also notice a further concern related to the timing of an apology: Does the offender deliver the apology only after the victim has requested (or an authority has commanded) an apology? Or does she volunteer the apology before experiencing pressure to do so? If a parent commands a child to apologize or even suggests that the child should consider whether she should apologize, the parent initiates the reflective process. If a child apologizes before the parent brings attention to the potential need to apologize, this can signal a significant development in the child's moral education because it suggests that she has internalized the norms at issue and has engaged in something like autonomous moral deliberation. Without prompting, the offender realizes that she has breached a value that she endorses and thus finds internal motivation for engaging in apologetic behavior. We can say the same of the robber who appears years later to apologize: we are more likely to view her gestures as indicative of a genuine moral transformation if she freely recognizes the wrongness of her actions and offers an apology. In this sense, issues regarding whether acts of contrition occur before or after requests for apologies speaks to the intentions of the apologizer as noted later.

We can draw distinctions not only between who receives an apology and when she receives it, but also between how and where the apology comes to them. First, we can consider the medium of the apology. Tavuchis and Aviva Orenstein both emphasize that we should attempt to provide apologetic declarations "face to face" instead of in writing.[124] I do not question the importance of the parties engaging each other in a direct conversation about the offense, but we should note the benefits of committing the apology to writing. Although standing before the victim and pronouncing the apology creates emotional and ceremonial meaning that I consider separately later, a written apology may be more likely to attend to the elements of a categorical apology. As we have seen, an apology can be a potentially technical undertaking as it corroborates a record, identifies norms, parses causal moral responsibility, and commits to certain kinds of reform and redress. A written version of the apology allows the offender to construct a precise statement attending to these details. Oral apologies often occur in emotional fits and starts with garbled content. In a written statement, the offender may be likely to consider her words more carefully. Rather than attempt to identify the contents of the apology amidst an emotional and highly nuanced conversation, the victim can benefit from scrutinizing a stable written statement in order to identify the sorts of meaning the offender may or may not have offered. In addition, a written apology provides a physical record of the statement that she may share with others or produce as evidence in legal proceedings.

Working through an apology in writing also may increase the offender's ability to engage the victim in a dialogue regarding its content. We might offer the victim a draft of our proposed apology and allow her to suggest revisions. Offenders might learn a great deal about the nature and consequences of their wrongdoing through this process, and victims will have an additional opportunity to voice their views and develop their relationship with the offender. Such exchanges could prove quite beneficial for the reconciliation process.[125]

Where we find an apology will also alter its meaning, as potential contexts present an infinite source of symbolic and instrumental value. Even if otherwise identical in content and form, an apology from Clinton for the Lewinsky scandal takes on different significance if offered in a televised news conference from the Oval Office than if spoken to Hillary Clinton in their private home or in the office of their marriage counselor. This leads us to consider the private or public nature of apologies. Although philosophers debate the nature and boundaries of the public and private spheres, some distinctions bear obvious relevance for apologies. In some situations a victim may prefer that an offender not pronounce the apology to a general audience. If the perpetrator of a sexual assault wishes to apologize, publicizing the offense through an apology may increase the harm to the victim. We can imagine other scenarios where disclosing the contents of an apology to anyone other than the victim could cause her various forms of discomfort or humiliation. If a former romantic partner apologized to me for being unfaithful, I would probably not enjoy my colleagues, friends, and family reading about it in the *New York Times*. Occasionally we should be wary of the intentions behind an urge to publicize an apology. The desire to broadcast one's contrition may bespeak moral grandstanding, attempts to improve one's image before voters or consumers, or even an intention to disgrace the victim.

In most cases, however, I suspect that attempts to limit an apology's audience arise from the offender's interests in minimizing the exposure of her wrongdoing. Suppose a surgeon accepts blame for killing a child through an act of gross medical negligence and privately apologizes to the parents, yet she refuses to admit her wrongdoing to anyone except for the parents and hires attorneys to deny her wrongdoing aggressively in protracted litigation. Behind closed doors, the surgeon may explain precisely what went wrong, accept causal and moral responsibility for the death, identify and commit to the breached underlying value, express categorical regret with genuine intentions and emotions, and even confidentially provide compensation beyond what she stands to lose in the worst possible legal determinations against her. If the surgeon publicly denies all of this, we will lack certain meanings. As the "safe apology" legislation discussed earlier provides, the surgeon can express sympathy for the parent without admitting any wrongdoing. Although the parent may have learned how her child died, the broader community will not. History will record the cause of the child's death as a contested matter. In such a case, information regarding the cause of death will be especially important for the community served by this doctor in order to evaluate her competence, and indeed the doctor's desire to protect her reputation may be her primary motivation for her public denials. This accounts for the conditions within many settlement agreements that provide that the victim must not publicly disclose the terms of the agreement, often including whether the alleged offender provided an apology or the content of such an apology. Such conditions, like the apologies designed primarily as a means of achieving legal advantage that I discuss at length in subsequent work, should lead us to question the intentions of the apologizer. Although the surgeon may identify and commit to the breached underlying value in private discussions with the parent, her public defense will likely cause her to deny that she has indeed breached the value. She might privately claim, for instance, that she finds inadequate medical care resulting from overworked surgeons performing too many procedures to constitute a moral crisis. Although she refuses to admit publicly that her practice suffers from this failure, in private conversations with the parent she blames the death on just these conditions. Such a position could seriously impede efforts to reform the surgeon's practice as well as those of the broader profession. Refusing to address her offense publicly against the grieving parent can also fail to honor her status as a moral interlocutor before the community. Failing to honor her dignity publicly in this way also conveys the sentiment that the surgeon's reasons for denying the apology trump the parent's justifications for publicizing the apology, which can continue to view the parent as a mere means to the doctor's ends. We should also not forget that the surgeon's denial would constitute a lie. In addition to the contempt we might hold for lying, such behavior may also lead us to question how the doctor's intentions, emotions, and character relate to the meaning of her apology, as considered later.

I. Reform and Redress

For many of us, a promise never to repeat the offense often constitutes the most important aspect of an apology.[126] Above all else, we may simply desire for the offender to forbear from reoffending. This may require her to reform a suite of related behaviors, or we may be able to isolate the transgressive act as anomalous. Whether motivated by a moral recognition of the wrongness of the act or social pressure to cease behaving in the proscribed manner, we want assurance that the offender will not do it again. Perhaps most basically, we want an apology that provides security against further harm.

This renders the dissonance in Eric Harris' apologetic statement prior to the Columbine massacre especially chilling. "I just wanted to apologize to you guys for any crap," he stated. "To everyone I love, I'm really sorry about all of this. I know my mom and dad will be just [expletive] shocked beyond belief."[127] We know that Harris did not refrain from killing, and the victims should not have taken any security from his apology. Indeed, in this same monologue he indicated that he hoped to kill 250 of his classmates. We might read his "pre-apology" not as denouncing the ensuing massacre, but as regretting that those who he did care for – he expresses sympathy for his parents and some friends – would suffer from their association with him or from his post-rampage suicide. We might think that he regrets not the murders but the collateral damage to those who are not the primary objects of his wrath. Yet while he sympathizes with them, this does not prevent his offense. Like those who send regrets when they cannot attend a dinner party,

Harris *regrets that* unintentional victims will suffer. All told, he continues to endorse his actions and his apology should not be interpreted as indicative of reform. Harris does not believe he is about to make a mistake.

As discussed earlier, categorical regret views the past action as an error and thus vows to refrain from committing the same error again. Without this, the offender could engage in a continual cycle of transgressing and apologizing. Because of this worry we meet apologies of serial offenders and apologizers with skepticism until the offender consistently avoids temptations to repeat the offense. Otherwise, as Amitai Etzioni puts it, "a person could sin all week, show remorse on Sunday morning, do his or her repentance by citing a prayer fifty times, and start all over again."[128] Even if the offender relapses after apologizing due to a weakness of will rather than disingenuous intentions, this distinction may hold some meaning for the victim in that the offender recognizes the immorality of her act. It will not, however, provide the victim with security that the offender will not harm her again.

The ultimate meaning of apologies – like the meaning of promises – depends on future behavior and therefore we cannot conclusively judge them at the moment they are spoken. Here we can appreciate the wisdom of Maimonides, who explained that we should only consider repentance complete if the offender confronts and resists similar temptations that led to her sin. Without abstinence in the face of temptation, Maimonides is unwilling to judge the meaning of the offender's words. In addition, one act of abstinence does not close the record on the value of an apology. We often judge an offender's commitment to reform and forbearance over their lifetime, and any regression can diminish an apology's significance. If we view a categorical apology as a promise to reform kept over a lifetime, violating the conditions of reform or redress vitiates its meaning. An apology gains credibility as time passes without a relapse, and for this reason we can only finally judge the offender's commitment to reform over the duration of her life. Some might find this overdemanding. If I apologize for stepping on someone's toe, for example, it may seem excessive to claim that repeating the offense years later devalues the initial apology. Yet if I have apologized for intentionally stepping on someone's foot – perhaps I have done this on a few occasions when expressing anger with someone and I do it with enough force to cause an injury – repeating the offense would indeed call into question my commitment to reform. In cases of marital infidelity, the importance of never betraying a spouse again would be paramount. I see no satisfying means of identifying a point prior to death when the promise to reform can expire without compromising the meaning of the apology. If I only express sympathy for the offense, however, then we cannot necessarily presume that I am committed to not reoffending. I am reminded here of Tolstoy's caricature: "I sit on a man's back, choking him and making him carry me, and yet assure myself and others that I am very sorry for him and wish to ease his lot by all possible means – except by getting off his back."[129]

Denouncing my wrong and fulfilling my promise to reform typically constitute only the initial stages of responding to an injury. We often seek a kind of penance from the offender and we can describe this by any number of terms: reparations, remuneration, restitution, recompense, compensation, damages, amends, restoration, redress, or others. Our use of these terms can be misleading. Consider common usage of "reparation." Whereas restitution refers specifically to returning something taken wrongfully, we often use reparation to describe a form of recompense for less tangible losses. Derived from the Latin for repair, reparation implies that such responses return victims to something like their pre-injury state. Similar notions such as redress, amends, and restitution are often said to make a victim "whole" by returning what the offense has taken away. Theoretical treatments of apologies speak in these terms, explaining how remedies "repair" or "correct" the injured, "restore" the victim to her state before the injury, or reestablish a "moral equilibrium."[130]

Quantifying the values of apologies can generate additional confusions. A numerical model may suggest that if the offender can transfer X quantity of an apology to the victim, then she will have balanced the scales of transgression and contrition. As Montaigne describes it, "if repentance were laid on one dish of the scales it would outweigh the sin."[131] We find this view reflected in retributive calls for an "eye for eye" and characterizations of an apology as "owed" as if discharging a debt to a bank. Yet unless one commits to the most reductive forms of utilitarianism such as those forwarded by some advocates of the Law and Economics movement, there exists no economy of apology wherein the offender can simply repay a debt to clear her moral account. Circumstances may arise when transferring a defined amount of money to replace a fungible commodity clearly addresses an aspect of a wrong, for instance if I pay the repair bill for your property after I damage it. Apologies, however, are very rarely "just about the money." Money often supplants other elements of an apology, and paying the repair bill may lead me to believe that I have satisfied my debt without offering any other apologetic meaning. Because I can pay the bill without identifying or endorsing the wrong at issue, promising to refrain from such behavior in the future, or addressing many of the other considerations discussed herein, the economic exchange risks replacing all of the other elements of an apology. As we often find in legal settlements, I can throw money at the problem without admitting that I have done anything wrong.

Although acutely critical of one-dimensional metrics of punishment, the "Restorative Justice" movement also risks unwittingly reinforcing conceptions of a one-dimensional moral universe in which we can neatly weigh all harms according to a single calculus. An apology cannot "restore a relationship" as one restores a piece of furniture. Nor do apologies necessarily "clean the slate" because moral transgressions often leave indelible marks.[132] We can respond to injuries with an infinite number of remedies, and each response will transform the relationship between the victim and offender in distinct and often unpredictable ways. Our figures of speech may distort our perceptions if we believe that we can erase our mistakes from our relationships. As Benjamin Disraeli has said, "[a]pologies only account for that which they do not alter."[133] Every injury creates particular suffering and loss in the lives of individuals. Nothing can unscramble those eggs. Even after a robust apology, the relationship moves forward forever in the shadow of the injury rather than backward to a time before the trespass occurred.[134] "Apologies may restore some dignity," writes Martha Minnow, "but not the lives as they existed before the violations."[135] Our moral language often masks the utter obviousness of the simple fact that moral injuries create an unrecoverable loss regardless of what remedy might follow. If an assailant apologizes for robbing me and devotes her life to reforming her behavior and providing me with various forms of compensation, her apology may hold great meaning and accomplish many social objectives. It seems far too simple, however, to believe that her actions are equivalent to the harm done. Although a proper discussion of the problems of moral incommensurability is beyond the scope of this work, at a minimum we should be aware of how such ontological and metaphysical presumptions orient understandings of apologies.

As I consider subsequently in relation to binary notions of forgiveness, these observations expose the potentially misleading characterizations of apologies and attendant remedies as providing "closure."[136] The attempt to make narrative sense of our lives and overcome wrongs against us renders the idea of definitive closure quite appealing. As will be especially noticeable in cases of grievous injuries or collective atrocities, no remedy can provide a "tidy ending" to suffering.[137] This creates numerous difficulties for our moral sensibilities, and we often prefer to act as if moral debts have been fully paid even when we recognize an irreducible balance. This unpleasant truth occasionally appears in socially destructive forms, such as in the tendency to continue to brand criminal offenders who have served their sentence as "convicts." When the fact that no compensation or punishment can undo a crime becomes undeniable, some offenders live out their lives continually reminded of the impossibility of closure.

If no remedy can definitively account for an injury, this does not render payment and other forms of apologetic compensation meaningless. For Glen Pettigrove, "while an apology absent reparation may be an apology in form, it is not one in substance."[138] Yet how do we determine what constitutes an appropriate remedy? History offers numerous attempts to formalize answers to this question. Examples from antiquity include the Sumerian Code of Ur-Nammu, which provided economic compensation even for violent offenses, and the Babylonian Code of Hammurabi.[139] The *Roman Law of the Twelve Tables* penalized thieves twice the value of the goods they stole, and early Germanic tribal laws codified under the *Lex Salica* provided a restitution schedule for both grievous and petty crimes. Ethelbert of Kent promulgated laws assigning precise values to body parts, even differentiating between the worth of the various types of teeth in one's mouth. Contemporary attorneys' manuals such as *What's it Worth?* and *Stein on Personal Injury Damages* categorize the human body and the pain it can suffer, organizing injuries under headings such as *Amputations, Brain Cancer, Burns, Buttocks, Comatose State, Eyes, Eyelids, Face, Finger, Genitalia and Reproduction, Heart, Leg, Lung, Liver, Miscarriage, Skull, Sexual Assault,* and *Wrongful Death*. As if leafing through a department store catalogue, one can browse the inventory of injuries, read a few sentences about the litigants' misfortunes, and find the price of the loss.

This returns us to the issues described in the introduction that led me to consider the possibility of apologies providing a form of remedy beyond economic compensation. Three related points arise here. First, we appreciate that no remedy can erase the past. Second, we sense that economic compensation – while often valuable in many respects – can be an obtuse, incomplete, and even offensive remedy. If I send my friend some money as restitution without further comment after inexcusably breaking our dinner appointment, I risk further offending her by implying that I can reduce her time and our relationship to an economic transaction. My offense may have cost her some money, but the economic loss does not constitute the moral core of the injury. She may construe suggestions otherwise as an affront to her dignity, as Kant famously claimed: "In the realm of ends, everything has either a *price* or a *dignity*. Whatever has a price can be replaced by something else as its equivalent; on the other hand, whatever is above all price, and therefore admits of no equivalent, has a dignity."[140] This would be still more evident if rather than missing a meal I committed a serious offense – such as rendering her child paraplegic – and responded by cutting her a check after consulting the valuation estimates in *What's it Worth?* Although the money may be valuable and indeed essential to pay for the child's medical bills and future care, the check alone would likely seem insufficient and even insulting because it fails to address the non-economic aspects of the loss. The U.S. Supreme Court indicated that "[r]estitution is an effective rehabilitative penalty because it forces the defendant to confront, in concrete terms, the harms his actions have caused," but if I am ultra-rich and the payment for severely injuring the child is inconsequential for me – as may be the case in many corporate offenses – the remedy would seem transparently inadequate and unjust because it would cast moral and financial value into stark relief.[141] Money, to put it differently, would not cost enough. Restitution provides commensurate financial compensation, but other spheres of value remain ignored. Wagatsuma and Rosett find this oversight endemic to the U.S. legal system because of its "historic pre-occupation with reducing all losses to economic terms that can be awarded in a money judgment and its related tendency either not to compensate at all or to award extravagant damages for injuries that are not easily reducible to quantifiable economic losses."[142] In this context apologies risk becoming "transactional," seeking to supplant designations of guilt with the morally equivocal language of costs and benefits.[143]

Third, how should we account for those nonpecuniary lexicons of value within the remedial aspects of apologies?[144] Instead of conceiving of apologetic compensation as a retrospective *quid pro quo*, it can be helpful to understand remedial measures as oriented toward the future rather than the past when remedies cannot provide equivalent or even commensurable reimbursement. Rather than attempting to undo history or balance the scales of justice, we can think of remedial action as taking *practical responsibility* for the harm caused by the offender. Taking practical responsibility must often go well beyond legal and economic consequences, and again such needs can take an infinite variety of forms. How should a victim and an offender determine appropriate expiation? Shared conceptions of fairness should guide the parties. Because categorical apologies convey a shared commitment to an underlying moral value, the victim and offender may share a concomitant conception of how to respond to an offense of the norm. A shared commitment to the underlying value, however, does not necessarily entail a shared view of the appropriate remedy for breaching that value. Offenders' expectations for satisfying such responsibility will differ according to injury and context, and we can notice how it will be necessary to parse blame before determining how to best attend to those responsibilities. We can imagine, for example, that if I accept moral responsibility for crippling a friend's child that – beyond paying the bills for her treatment – I might personally care for her and share the various kinds of work required of parents in such a situation. Persistent devotion of my time to the child would address aspects of apologetic meaning beyond the usual reach of a financial settlement.

Situations arise where offenders cause harms exceeding their resources. If an impoverished person causes expensive property damage, she may be incapable of ever paying restitution even if she agrees that she should repay the debt. Is an apology then beyond her means? Although she cannot provide a certain sort of meaning if she cannot relieve me of the burden of paying my related bills, that may be insignificant when compared with other efforts she can make. As a testament to the offender's dedication to honoring the breached value, a small amount of hard-earned money provided to a victim may convey more meaning than a large check from a billionaire because money possesses differential moral value depending on the situation of the debtor. A small amount from someone without vast financial wealth (consider a child offering a year's allowance) may not pay the bills she has caused, but it can provide considerable meaning within non-economic spheres. Moreover, if we need not think of the costs of injuries in strictly economic terms, an offender's offer to personally care for me or provide some other valuable deeds while I am injured could be much more mean-ingful than a sum of money. As mentioned earlier with regard to thinking of reparations as discharging our moral debts, none of us can really ever pay off our victims for their injuries. We can only do our best to reform and try to help those we have injured when we make moral errors. Neither the rich nor the poor can erase the past. We will return to these issues in the context of collective apologies for harms across generations, for instance where families or nations may have benefited from the spoils of slavery so fundamentally that liquidating all of their wealth would not suffice to repay even the economic dimensions of their debt.

Beyond poverty, another obstacle may prevent an offender from provid-ing remedies even if she agrees that her reform is necessary and the proposed remedy is appropriate: offenders may die before providing redress. We rec-ognize the difference between an offender's agreement to complete a certain remedial recourse and her actual fulfillment of those responsibilities, and we appreciate that innumerable challenges may confront even the most sin-cere efforts to provide remedies. Nevertheless, although we can consider the degree to which an offender satisfies our expectations of how she should take practical responsibility for her actions, her death can be an absolute bar to remedial action. If the offender dies without fulfilling her promises to reform and take practical responsibility, the apology's meaning will not have the occasion to bloom. For these reasons, deathbed apologies should be suspect because the promise to reform will never be tested and death will foreclose most forms of redress. Regardless of how sincere an apology may appear at the moment it is given, death denies the possibility that it will be corroborated by actual and continuous reform and therefore its meaning will remain forever limited. If a mother apologizes with her dying breath to her child for a lifetime of verbal abuse, this may offer a profound moment in the relationship. Yet we will never know if, had she lived another day, the par-ent would have immediately returned to her abusive ways. The parent might alter her will to provide restitution from beyond the grave, but this cannot corroborate a change of heart in the same manner as enjoying a relationship with her as a person who recognizes her error, reforms her behavior, resists enticements to regress, and takes appropriate remedial actions for subjecting her daughter to a lifetime of degradation. Hence Maimonides requires us to demonstrate our reform by forbearing in the presence of temptation before we can consider repentance complete.

I review the stance of various religions on deathbed apologies later, but we can immediately notice their importance. If I can enjoy a life of sin and denounce my behavior as my last act in an attempt to curry favor in the next world, theologists might want to close this doctrinal loophole. We can also notice here the dynamic of apologies within suicide notes where the deceased recognizes the wrongness of some act – such as her commission of a corporate scandal – that leads to her suicide. By killing herself she may convey that she would rather die than suffer through providing the remedy, which might include public humiliation, destruction of her personal finances, or a prison sentence.

Notice here the continued relevance of standing considerations. The very idea of reform loses much of its meaning if I can delegate it to another. Just as I will not enjoy the health benefits if someone else exercises for me, only I can undergo my own moral reform. One cannot delegate self-improvement. Likewise, we can appreciate the importance of the offender undertaking remedial activities herself. If I cause harm and my mother pays the bill, this differs considerably from compensating the victim with earnings from my own labor. Unlike many fungible commodities within capitalist markets, the origin of the goods offered as redress bears great significance. This would seem still more apparent if the redress took the form of services rather than money. If a wealthy offender can pay nurses to tend to her victim, this would fundamentally differ in spirit from the offender providing the care personally.

Situations will arise where the offender and the victim or community disagree about the appropriate remedy. The offender may believe that she must reform and undertake some remedial action but find the request for compensation excessive. If I apologize for breaking your window and you demand that I buy you a new house, I would find your proposed remedy disproportionate to the offense. I intend this example to emphasize how disagreements regarding appropriate remedies do not always result from the offender balking at legitimate remedial demands. Victims may knowingly make unreasonable demands to test the waters and determine just "how much an apology is worth." The victim as well as the offender may exploit apologies to her advantage. If an attorney who stands to gain one-third of a settlement mediates between the victim and offender, she has considerable economic incentive to exploit the apologizer's vulnerability and guilt and negotiate for the highest possible award. A victim's abuse of an offender in this way can constitute an offense in its own right. As is often the case in personal, legal, and political conflicts, the giving and receiving of apologies can become a thinly veiled power struggle divorced from the moral harm that occasioned the exchange. As I consider later, this was evident in the aftermath of the emergency landing of a U.S. spy plane on a Chinese military airfield after it had collided with a Chinese fighter jet and killed its pilot in 2001. Although Chinese and American officials performed elaborate apology rituals, it became clear that both parties used the apology as a pretext to negotiate their purely instrumental pursuit of their respective political ends.

Apologetic offenders may find various kinds of informal redress justified but legal remedies excessive. This can create difficulties. If I privately apologize for punching you but then deny that I did so in criminal proceedings and refuse to accept legal consequences of assault charges, then I trigger the earlier concerns regarding the public functions of an apology. Lee Taft appears to believe that a full apology requires an offender to accept any legal sanctions regardless of their proportionality: "When an offender says, 'I'm sorry,' he must be willing to accept all of the consequences – legal and otherwise – that flow from his violation." He continues to argue that if "a person is truly repentant, he will not seek to distance himself from the consequences that attach to his action; rather, he will accept them as a part of the performance of a moral act and the authentic expression of contrition."[145]

We can distinguish, however, between cases where an offender simply wishes to avoid legal consequence and one who finds the legal sanction unfairly excessive. In the case of the Lewinsky scandal, we can imagine that Clinton may have wished to offer a categorical apology for both the affair and his perjury. As events unfolded it became clear that his enemies had leveraged these offenses in such a way that admissions from Clinton would result in severe – and what some, including Clinton, might think unjustifiable – legal consequences. Even if we stipulate that Clinton categorically regretted his actions and wished to accept practical responsibility for the harm he caused, he probably believed that impeachment constituted an unjust consequence. He might accept various forms of personal and political blame while rejecting the argument that he should be impeached. A parent who wishes to apologize to her children for using narcotics only once could face a similar problem: although she wishes to apologize, she may believe the jail term she would face for admitting her deed in court is unfair.

Distinct from questions regarding the legitimacy of legal sanctions, there may be uncertainty regarding the extent of the victim's suffering. Because the apologetic offender shares the commitment to the breached moral principle underlying the harm, she will find it reasonable if the victim takes offense. But how much offense is justified? If she has offended an "eggshell victim," a term used in tort law to describe a particularly sensitive party, must she take remedial responsibility for all of the suffering or only for what an ordinary person would have suffered? In the previous example of killing my spouse's tomato plant, suppose the plant held deep symbolic value for her and its destruction triggered profound remorse. Minor incidents often bring about major conflicts because of the serious moral issues beneath the surface of what may appear to be a superficial injury. The damaged tomato plant may come to symbolize my disrespect for my wife, and I would recognize that considerable anguish is an appropriate response to such an affront because I share the breached value with her. Yet suppose that she grieves for years over the loss, and I come to learn that her older sibling intentionally crushed her tomato plants every year during her adolescence and my act has caused her psychological trauma that was unforeseeable to me at the time of my act. Here the question of whether I proximately caused the deeper injury would be like the case of the friend who is attacked while waiting for me after I fail to meet her for dinner as we had planned: I did something wrong, but another's actions may supervene upon mine. The proximity of causation in these cases may be difficult to untangle, but such determinations haunt many questions regarding our remedial responsibilities to others.

Some offenders may resort to a familiar strategy when they find a victim's requests for remedy excessive, engaging in self-castigation in order to immunize themselves from further responsibility for their offense. As Oscar Wilde quipped, "[w]hen we blame ourselves we feel that no one else has the right to blame us."[146] An offender may preemptively blame herself before the victim can participate in the assignment of responsibility, thus allowing the offender to assert control over and frame the apologetic discourse. She may then attempt to make quick work of apologizing. If this does not satisfy the victim, the offender may assert something to the effect of "I *said* I am sorry" with the emphasis on the past tense of the act to remind the victim that the work of apologizing has already been completed. In addition to the numerous ambiguous meanings of the word "sorry" that allow the offender to eschew a more explicit moral conversation regarding her offense, the offender attempts to use the very utterance of language of contrition as a shield against accepting further remedial responsibilities. Some use this tactic aggressively, perhaps believing that the best defense is a good offense.

Consider conservative pundit Bill O'Reilly. In advance of the 2003 invasion of Iraq, O'Reilly claimed that Saddam Hussein's acquisition of weapons of mass destruction justified Operation Iraqi Freedom. O'Reilly promised the following if no such weapons were found: "I will apologize to the nation and I will not trust the Bush administration again."[147] Operatives found no such weapons and the following exchanges unfolded between O'Reilly, Charles Gibson, and Robin Roberts on *Good Morning America* on February 10, 2004:

O'REILLY: "Well, my analysis was wrong and I'm sorry. Absolutely. You know. And I'm not pleased about it."

GIBSON (OFF CAMERA): "Camera's right there."

O'REILLY: "Yeah, I just said it. What do you want me to do? Go over and kiss the camera? All right. I was wrong. I'm not pleased about it at all. And I think all Americans should be concerned about this."

ROBERTS (OFF CAMERA): "It's not the apology that I care about. That's truthful. You did say in there, though, if he's clean, if there's nothing, I will never trust the Bush administration again."

O'REILLY: "I am much more skeptical of the Bush administration now than I, I was at that time. Absolutely. And I'll tell you why. I understand from reading the Kay report how it all happened because I believe Kay. All right? I don't think Bush lied, but I don't think Bush was, and his people, were nearly skeptical enough about George Tenet and his guys bringing him in this stuff. I think they cherry-picked what they wanted to remove Saddam Hussein."[148]

By several measures, O'Reilly offers a rather meaningful apology. He admits wrongdoing, he explains why he was wrong, and he expresses his increased distrust of the Bush administration. Surely many would have liked more from him, for instance a recognition that his error contributed to public support for the war given his status at the time as a leading news analyst. If he accepted blame for this, then appropriate remedial action from him might include more than uttering apologetic words. Depending on the contours of a causal analysis, some might even claim that O'Reilly's remedial responsibilities include accounting for the blood on his hands.

I am primarily interested in what some might consider an inconsequential remark: "What do you want me to do? Go over and kiss the camera?" O'Reilly implies that he has met his promise to apologize as soon as the word "sorry" crosses his lips. Demanding anything more of him, he suggests, not only overreaches but also constitutes an offense against him. In his opinion he has apologized and lingering on his mistake causes him to suffer an unnecessary indignity, as he insinuates with his "kiss the camera" comment. He might have asked if he should "drop down, kiss their feet, and say 'I'm sorry,'" as did Olympic sprinter Ben Johnson after being repeatedly asked about the steroid use that caused him to be stripped of a gold medal.[149] In O'Reilly's case he may be justified in this counterclaim, as Gibson's "Camera's right there" comment seems to revel in O'Reilly's comeuppance. In less nuanced instances we often find the offender arguing that because she expressed some degree of contrition or took some remedial action that the matter should be put to rest. One might find this strategy at work in a case of unfaithfulness in a romantic relationship where the cheater uses the "I *said I am sorry*" charge to assert that forgiveness is warranted before the victim is satisfied with the offender's redress. If I offer some amends, I might claim that the matter no longer merits discussion or further action and accuse the victim of opening wounds that should have already healed. I might even turn the tables, asserting that in light of my actions I *deserve* to be forgiven and the victim's continued harping on the matter holds hostage a moral status that rightfully belongs to me.

In contrast to these scenarios where the offender claims that the victim demands too much of her, we might find an apologetic offender performing excessive redress for her wrongdoing. Consider if someone devotes her entire life to apologizing for the suffering she caused. In some cases this might become obsessive and even unwelcome for the victim. If someone seriously injures my child, I may not welcome her daily apologetic presence in my life as she continues to remind me of my suffering when I prefer to direct my attentions elsewhere. At this stage we might sense how the offender's actions do not serve my family's remedial needs but rather attempt to assuage the offender's own guilt and torment. Nevertheless, in some cases a life of devotion to the offended may be appropriate and welcome. If the offender renders the victim disabled, taking practical responsibility for that injury by caring for the victim may amount to a full-time occupation. Inflicting an injury and apologizing for it could also provoke a life-transforming awakening in the offender such that she crusades against similar wrongs and her life's work becomes entwined with and an extended response to her initial wrongdoing. Yet because we typically believe that an offender can only accept blame for the harm she proximately caused, at some point it may no longer seem entirely appropriate to characterize her actions as redressing the initial wrong because they have so obviously surpassed typical expectations for remedial actions. As I indicated earlier, however, it is rarely a simple matter to determine when someone has discharged her debt to the offender. Indeed, thinking in such an economic manner belies the incommensurability of injuries and remedies. Suppose I apologize to my spouse for a sexist act and I immerse myself in studying sexism to demonstrate my commitment to the underlying value. This then spurs me to devote the remainder of my career to teaching classes in sexism, publishing on topics in sexism, and advocating in various forums for the eradication of sexism. In this example, it would be impossible to discern precisely where my actions have satisfied my debt to her and become non-apologetic in nature. In light of my resistance to binary conceptions of forgiveness discussed later, it would be especially difficult to identify the apologetic tipping point where I have cleared my moral account and should be rewarded with her forgiveness.

J. Intentions for Apologizing

Having previously examined concerns regarding the apologizer's *mental states at the time of the alleged offense*, which often take the form of assertions that the accused "did not intend" the harm and thus describe it as accidental, we now turn to the offender's *intentions for apologizing*. Even if an offender attends to all of the previous elements of a categorical apology, it still matters *why* she apologizes. Although many of the previous discussions speak to the offender's intentions to some degree, we should be careful not to underestimate the significance of the offender's motivations and mental states. If an unfaithful spouse offered what appeared to be a categorical apology not because she believed that she had committed a moral error but because she sought a strategic advantage in divorce proceedings, this would dramatically alter the meanings of the gesture. Similarly, if I knew that my boss would fire me if I did not provide what appeared to be a categorical apology for insubordination, the apology would be considerably less meaningful to both of us if she knew that I only went through the motions of apologizing while continuing to believe that my actions were justified. The apology would be less meaningful in both cases even if the offender completed the requested remedial tasks and did not reoffend or otherwise degrade the apology.

We might be tempted to think of this as a "sincerity condition," but doing so may miss potential subtleties at work. Even if we confine ourselves to the most common definition of sincerity as an absence of deceit, hypocrisy, or impurity, various possible uses of sincerity in this context may signify material distinctions in apologetic meaning.[150] I might sincerely feel sympathy for the injured. I might sincerely regret that you have taken offense to my justified act. I may not share the value at issue, but I sincerely commit to never breaching it again because I understand that doing so would jeopardize my employment, my social standing, or my freedom from incarceration. I might sincerely believe I have made a moral error for which I must atone. It also seems possible that I could believe that I sincerely apologize although I am actually quite confused about an element of an apology. I might assert that I sincerely apologize, for instance, even though I do not wish to accept blame for the harm. I might believe at the time that I sincerely apologize, but then come to believe that what I intended was not an apology at all according to my revised views. We can compare this to an adolescent sincerely believing that she loves her first romantic partner, but later in life recognizing the relationship did not meet her mature standards of love. We would not think of her as insincere or dishonest when she told her adolescent companion of her love because she later came to change her understanding. In these senses it matters to which aspect of my apology the sincerity attaches and therefore general assertions or judgments regarding an apology's sincerity can overlook crucial distinctions in meaning.

Categorical apologies entail a commitment to a shared value, which speaks not only to the prospect of a future free from harms caused by breaches of the shared principle but also to a relationship that may include a shared sense of goodness, justice, or even the meaning of life. An apology motivated by a commitment to one's principles and relationships will hold meaning beyond the ultimate consequences of an apology even if an act of contrition produces disastrous results. We need not commit to a form of Kantianism to see why intentions of this sort matter to apologies. If, while under hypnosis, the offender is directed to execute a categorical apology and conditioned to reform and provide redress for the remainder of her life, then we would see her words and acts in a different light. Although such mind control might be an effective means of ensuring that the offender will not repeat the injury and that the victim will benefit from the offender's clockwork remedial activity, something will seem absent because an autonomous reflective commitment to the value does not motivate her efforts. In most instances we want an apology from a person who consciously agrees with our sense of right and wrong, not from a machine mimicking moral agency. If my spouse apologizes for being unfaithful, it would be essential for me to know whether she – as my life partner – freely shares the breached commitment to marital fidelity, secretly scoffs at my puritanical monogamous values, or has been coerced or conditioned into behaving as if we are of the same mind regarding this core value. Understanding the intentions behind an apology not only provide predictive power into the offender's future behavior but also provide insight into the nature of our relationships. Categorical apologies serve many functions, and we can advance some of these objectives without regard to intentions. The uses of apologies, however, account for only some of their meanings. In this sense, apologies may speak to the offender's character rather than merely to her ability to navigate a maze of social expectations.

Here we can contrast Lazare's largely instrumental account of apologies. Lazare does not consider "strategic apologies" – which he understands as "motivated by the offenders' attempt to change how others perceive them or keep their relationships intact or enhance their social stature" – to be "somehow less truthful" than apologies motivated by deontological or other-directed concerns. He suggests this position "even if the offenders do not exhibit shame, guilt, or empathy."[151] Inquiring into the mental states behind the appearances of apologies seems imprudent for Lazare because doing so risks questioning their worth, and in light of this Lazare asks: "How can we argue against social harmony among individuals, families, and nations?"[152] "To believe that a 'pragmatic' apology is somehow less truthful or less effective than a more impassioned one," he continues, "is to value style over substance, as if we believe that the manner in which an apology is delivered is more important than the goals it seeks to achieve."[153] However manipulative or malicious an offender's intentions may be when apologizing, Lazare implies that ignorance is bliss for a victim and we should not interfere with her illusion: "As long as an apology meets important psychological needs of the offended...we should not diminish its effectiveness by becoming critics."[154] Philosopher Richard Joyce shares Lazare's opinion that we may occasionally reduce the value of an apology to a cost-benefit analysis, with social utility occasionally trumping veracity. "For my money," Joyce claims, "if there are important beneficial consequences that can be attained if that individual 'says sorry,' and little in the way of costs, then I would prefer to see him do so...rather than see him retreat behind a defensive wall of 'I didn't do it.'"[155] Thus, if you believe that you have not done anything wrong and feign your way through apologetic gestures in order to advance some social objective, these theories have difficulty accounting for the radical shifts in meaning between such a performance and a soul-rendering act of contrition.

I do not deny that even the most deceptive and disingenuous apologies serve important social functions, but surely they do not provide certain forms of meaning. If the injured party learned of the deception, for example, this would drain the purely strategic apology of much of its value because it would be a less convincing indicator of the future performance, it would cast attributions of blame into question, and it would destabilize the supposedly shared value at stake. The victim might also consider her injury compounded because, in addition to the original harm, now she has been deceived regarding the offender's apologetic intentions. Even without a deontological commitment to the wrongness of lying, many will consider a falsehood told to them in the guise of an intimate apologetic gesture as a particularly insidious affront. The illusion of a categorical apology may indeed salvage a marriage or a friendship, but I would not find it rhetorically excessive to claim that lies hold together such relationships. Indeed, it seems that many of our most commonsense criticisms of apologies arise from an intuition that they perpetrate some form of a lie, as we so often hear unsatisfactory apologies described as false, disingenuous, deceptive, or pretextual.

Apologies occasionally appear empty because they transparently seek only to manipulate others. Less odious intentions drive many apologies, but with some the motivations appear obviously and exclusively self-serving. We can be moved to apologize not only because we want to win favor with others but also because we sense that we need to apologize for our own well-being. If wracked by shame, guilt, or self-loathing, apologizing may offer the only means to exorcise these demons. In such cases of apologizing for what Lazare helpfully describes as "internal" motivations, we can remain oblivious to the remedial needs of the victim.[156] When I apologize in order to silence my conscience, I undertake the act to satisfy my own desire. If a victim asked me why I was apologizing and I answered that my psychologist advised me that doing so would help me sleep better at night, she would realize that the apology primarily concerns my needs rather than hers. I might fashion my apology to meet my objectives, and perhaps uttering the word "sorry" without engaging in a moral dialogue regarding my wrongdoing would suffice for my purpose. The victim might remain a mere means for me, and this might justifiably strike her as suffering from a continued lack of sympathy and respect for her and the value breached.

In particular, some offenders may view apologies as the most efficient tool for gaining the forgiveness that they desire. Consider these words from Cathleen Crowell Webb, who falsely accused Gary Dotson of raping her, resulting in Dotson serving six years in prison: "I'm so sorry for what I did to you and your family, especially Gary and his name and how I took six years away from him, and I really want your forgiveness, especially Gary's forgiveness."[157] If the longing for forgiveness motivates Webb, then her apology seems oriented toward her needs rather than Dotson's. Although she has caused Dotson to suffer a detestable injustice, Webb speaks as if her own redemption presents the primary moral concern.

Analyzing apologies for transgressions in the distant past can help demonstrate how the internal motivation of seeking forgiveness can move offenders to rather awkward displays of contrition. Imagine a long-forgotten friend contacting you to convey that, previously unbeknownst to you, she lied to you about something and now wishes to apologize for it. That period of your life is a distant blur to you, you remember very little about the relationship or this person, and you feel no injury when learning of the offense. She then asks if you can ever forgive her. In such a case we suspect that we represent a check on the offender's moral housekeeping ledger, and perhaps she seeks peace with herself or her god as she approaches death. We may play along even if the apology holds little meaning for us because we sense that it serves a purpose in the offender's self-understanding. Steps eight through ten of the Alcoholics Anonymous program, for instance, require the individual to list those whom she has wronged, to "make direct amends to such people," and to continue to admit when she is wrong.[158] We may find an offender's dredging of the past unwelcome if, for her own benefit, she revisits an injury she caused without regard for pain she produces in us when recollecting the offense. The Alcoholics Anonymous program recognizes that insensitivity in this respect can amount to a distinct injury and thus wisely requires offenders to make amends "wherever possible, except when to do so would injure them or others."[159]

Jeffrie Murphy points to a related issue. "We normally consider granting mercy or pardon when someone begs or petitions for it," Murphy writes, yet a "truly repentant person ... would normally see his suffering punishment as proper and might ... even seek it out." Why, then, does the offender plead for a reduction in punishment? "Is the fact that he wants us to reduce his punishments," Murphy asks, "perhaps evidence that he is not repentant and are we then faced with the problem that the only persons who are truly eligible for mercy on grounds of repentance will almost never get it because their repentance will cause them not to ask for it?"[160] I plan take up this conundrum at length in future works with respect to criminal punishment, but we can notice here how questions regarding the apologizer's motivations can fundamentally alter our perception of acts of contrition.

Jay Rayner lampoons apologies motivated by desires internal to the offender in his novel *Eating Crow*. I discuss this entertaining story later in the context of collective apologies, but Rayner's protagonist provides illuminating examples of how perverse some motivations for apologies seem. At the outset of the book, Marc Bassett works as a London restaurant critic who gains notoriety for his acerbic reviews. A chef kills himself in his own oven after Bassett lambastes him in his column and Bassett subsequently apologizes to the deceased's family. Bassett finds the experience of delivering the apology so gratifying that he becomes addicted to the ritual and seeks out everyone in his past that he has wronged so that he can again ride the "high" of expressing contrition.[161] He describes the feeling as a "buzz," with some apologies reaching a full catharsis and others providing but "an espresso of apology" helping him to "start the day on a little high."[162] As Bassett comes to understand apologies as a means of "getting things off of your chest," "closing up an aged wound," and being able to claim that a "matter had been dealt with," his peers realize that his actions have little more meaning than his "enjoying the purging of guilt."[163] He apologizes primarily because he likes the way it feels, and his targets refuse to indulge him once they understand that he apologizes merely as a means of pleasing himself. Although this fictional example presents an extreme case, it helps to isolate the importance of intentions to the meaning of apologies. If the offender's intentions do not correspond to the victim's or the community's expectations, this can seriously damage the significance of the apology.

If intentions play such a role in determining the significance of an apology, how can we read the offender's mental states? Even if she makes her intentions explicit, a degree of skepticism seems prudent when interacting with an offender who has recently wronged you and stands to gain from convincing you of her sincerity. In the context of religious repentance, Montaigne doubted we could have much success measuring the souls of the contrite. "They give us to believe that they feel great inward grief and remorse: but of amendment and correction, or of ceasing sin, they show us no sign." "I know of no quality so easy to counterfeit as godliness, when the life and morals do not conform to it," he continues, its "essence is abstruse and secret; its externals are easy and ostentatious."[164] Despite such skepticism, however, we regularly judge the mental states of others and our notion of *mens rea* in criminal law depends on this ability.[165] An offender's emotions provide one such measure of her mental states.

K. Emotions

In light of the entwinement of the apologizer's intentions and her emotions, many identify certain "feelings" as a prominent feature of an appropriate apology. This contributes to the common conception of "I am sorry" – which we can read as a declaration that I am experiencing the emotion of sorrow – as the primary indicator of apologetic meaning. A closer look at the role of emotions in apologies presents many important and perhaps intractable questions. Consider but a few: What sorts of emotions must accompany an apology? We think of guilt, shame, remorse, and sorrow as typically apologetic emotions but might others also qualify? Can we expect the typical apologizer to self-consciously experience each of these emotions and the recipient of the apology to discern their presence? Even researchers in the field of emotions have difficulty not only defining guilt, shame, and remorse but also disagree regarding the boundaries between these often interrelated "feelings." Unless the apologizer specializes in the phenomenology of moral sentiments, how will we know when her feelings move between the subtleties distinguishing sorrow, shame, and guilt? Do all apologies require the offender to experience the same suite of emotions or do different offenses warrant different emotions? To what degree must the apologizer feel the appropriate emotions? Do more serious offenses require more intense emotions? How would we measure not only the presence of an emotion, but its intensity? For what duration must the apologizer experience the emotion? Must she only feel the emotion when articulating the apology, or must she experience it prior to apologizing and while she undertakes any form of redress? Should the intensity differ at various stages of apologizing? At what rate should the emotions dissipate? Must her emotions, rather than some external value, motivate her to apologize? On the contrary, if the offender's desire to alleviate her feelings of remorse, guilt, or shame drives her actions, does this render the apology a selfish action undertaken primarily for the apologizer's mental health rather than from a duty to the victim? If apologizing for harm in the distant past, do the same emotional expectations apply? Does it suffice for the apologizer to feel an emotion, or must she express these feelings to the offended or the broader community? Must she express these emotions in a certain manner, for instance with the proper tone and gestures? Does the relation between apologies and emotions differ with cultural or gender expectations? If some of us lack typical emotional capabilities, for example due to brain injury or mood-altering medication, will this hinder our ability to apologize?

I am afraid that philosophers of emotion only compound these difficulties, as they notoriously dispute the nature of emotions and their role in moral life. For Aristotle, learning to experience the proper emotions in the proper circumstances constituted a central aim to living well, but one might also manipulate emotions for questionable rhetorical ends. Numerous medieval, early modern, and modern philosophers debated the worth of emotions, with Augustine, Aquinas, Descartes, Pascal, Locke, Hobbes, Spinoza, Shaftesbury, Malebranche, and others weighing in on the growing debate. Whereas Hume argued that "reason is, and ought to be, the slave of the passions," Kant influentially followed the Stoics' conceptions of emotions as irrational judgments and considered emotions a form of impulsive inclination that could impair rationality and tempt us to stray from our duties.[166] The romantic tradition elevated the emotions to the apex of human experience, and Nietzsche extolled passion generally while he denounced some emotions akin to resentment as driving the slave morality.[167] Figures as diverse as Rousseau, Schopenhauer, and Adam Smith believed that emotions should play a role in the development of moral sentiments.[168] Disparate treatments of emotions continued into the twentieth century, and philosophers from diverse methodological perspectives seem increasingly interested in the topic.[169]

Given the breadth of phenomena considered under the rubric of emotions, we should not be surprised that contemporary philosophers and scientists have reached little consensus on the subject. Even the seemingly simple ontological question of what emotions exactly are offers numerous competing answers. Common sense may indicate that sadness is a sort of "feeling," but what provides the source of that sensation? Is it a bare physiological process, a secondary experience of physiological processes, a social-psychological construction, a kind of normative judgment, or something else? What even qualifies as an emotion? Martha Nussbaum lists "grief, fear, love, joy, hope, anger, gratitude, hatred, envy, jealousy, pity, [and] guilt" as standard examples.[170] However, can we draw clear distinctions between emotions and moods? Nussbaum distinguishes between two forms of depression, one an objectless mood and the other an emotion.[171] How precisely can we draw these boundaries? Does melancholy, anxiety, or fear in response to my death – even a death in the distant future – constitute a mood, an emotion, or something otherwise? We can envision debates regarding whether various characteristics potentially relevant to apologetic meaning qualify as an emotion, for example humility, courage, honor, generosity, hope, integrity, loyalty, prudence, respectfulness, self-respect, and so on.

Thankfully, I can leave the bulk of these thorny questions to those conducting excellent and interesting work in this area and focus here on why we tend to value certain emotions most commonly associated with aspects of apologies.[172] Most intuitively, emotional displays help us read the offender's mental states and gauge her seriousness and sincerity. A display of sadness provides the offended with some observable physiological evidence – tears, a red face, or sweaty palms – to evaluate the appropriateness of the offender's mental state. Although a determined offender could stage all of these external indicators of her mental states, it may be a bit more difficult to fake one's emotions than to simply lie about one's feelings. In this way emotions also contribute to a sense of decorum associated with apologies, conveying the seriousness of the act. According to my account, however, other elements of an apology probably provide more reliable indicators of the offender's seriousness. An apologizer's clear articulation of her appreciation for the wrongness of her actions, consistent forbearance, and performance of remedial activities probably offer better measures. Emotions may corroborate sincerity, express an appreciation for the extent of an injury, or convey how deeply one prizes the value at stake, but they offer only one of many angles from which to assess the act.

Beyond their capacity as evidence for the offender's inner life, Aristotle's insight that a person who recognizes that she has done something wrong and harmed another *should* feel certain emotions rings true. If someone smiled and giggled while delivering an apology for a serious harm, this would surely strike us as odd or even offensive. If the offender appears giddy while apologizing, she would seem to suffer from a sort of moral failure in that she appears to take a kind of pleasure in my pain. Perhaps she fundamentally misunderstands the nature of the suffering that she caused me. One's values and emotional experiences should correspond in certain ways, and when they do not we question the individual's character. This speaks not only to "controlling" one's emotions, for example in suppressing the hatred a racist feels against a racial minority or in masking the pleasure felt by a misogynist when witnessing the degradation of a woman. Regardless of our ability to control outward manifestations of our emotions, we can identify moral impropriety in simply feeling certain emotions in certain contexts. If I, as an advocate for the rights of animals, were overwhelmed with feelings of happiness when watching a video depicting the torture of dogs in research labs, then I would feel a strong dissonance within myself. My emotions would be alienated from my values. As Gabriele Taylor and Martha Nussbaum have argued, emotions can be wrong in this sense and others.[173] If a child felt emotions discordant with her values (or the values she was in the process of internalizing), her parents and teachers would hopefully attempt to cultivate more appropriate feelings in her. If our child plays on a sports team and begins to experience feelings of hate for her competitors, we would take extensive measures to correct these feelings.

Bernard Williams has likewise noted the tight relationship between moral and emotional concepts. We consider some emotions, such as wrath, nearly synonymous with vices. We think of others, such as love, as virtues.[174] In this sense it can be difficult to untangle the specifically emotional meaning of an apology given its interrelation with the other elements. If the offender appreciates that she has wrongly caused someone else to suffer, this moves her to accept blame for the injury, and she then cares for the victim, it seems that sorrow is already embedded within these activities. As Nussbaum explains, an "emotion such as grief is not simply a mindless surge of painful affect: it involves a way of seeing an object, an appraisal of that object as important, and the belief that the object is lost."[175] This builds the judgments of other aspects of apologizing into the "feeling." Given our vague and contested understandings of what specifically constitutes the emotion of sorrow and the dialectical relationship among belief, cognition, action, and emotion, we can see the difficulty in isolating a specific emotional component of apologetic meaning. If someone laughed while apologizing for a serious harm, I would suspect that this emotional inappropriateness would signify only the beginning of the problems. The embodiment of emotions further complicates matters, as I might explain an especially emotional apologetic gesture not only by reference to my values and beliefs but also to my physical state. I might feel particularly emotional today because of a lack of sleep, back pain, or the drugs I have ingested. These factors may not directly relate to my contrition – though in some circumstances they might, for instance if my restlessness resulted from anxiety over my offense – yet they trigger an emotional outburst when I apologize.

With these concerns in mind, we can draw out the relationship between the emotions most commonly associated with apologies.[176] In light of my earlier efforts to distinguish between expressions of empathy or sympathy with an acceptance of blame, I return to these emotions first. Empathy typically refers to one's ability to recognize, understand, and feel another's emotions. The better we can comprehend another's beliefs, desires, and life situations through empathic understanding, the more likely we can ascertain and relate to her emotional states.[177] Sympathy relates more closely to compassion, wherein we perceive a subject suffering or in an otherwise undesirable state and wish for the alleviation of the negative condition. We can think of sympathy as "feeling sorry for," not necessarily in the sense of having pity but rather in hoping that another will be relieved from hardship or offering our companionship while she endures a negative experience. Whereas empathy understands one's mental states but may not evaluate whether they are appropriate or justified, sympathy judges those states and hopes for their alleviation. We often use compassion to entail not only the passive sympathetic wish for relief, but also an active effort to provide such relief. Stephen Darwall stresses the perspectival shift between empathy and sympathy. In empathy we may adopt a clinical stance on the subject's viewpoint and imagine how she must feel. "Sympathy for someone," Darwall distinguishes, "is felt, not as from her standpoint, but as from the perspective of someone (anyone) caring for her."[178] Philosophers debate the relationship between empathy and sympathy, for instance with Stocker and Hegeman resisting Nussbaum's suggestion that empathy leads to sympathy. Yet we can imagine scenarios where one might be empathetic but not sympathetic (I understand your feelings but believe you deserve to suffer) or even sympathetic but not empathetic (I want to help you although I have no idea what bothers you, why, or even if anything is wrong).[179]

Given these usages, why do we associate empathy and sympathy with apologies? A 1996 letter to the *New York Times* in response to an essay by Deborah Tannen captures one reader's opinion: "One of the reasons that my ex-husband is my ex is because he found it easy to say, 'I was wrong,' but next to impossible to say, 'I'm sorry.' The former is an intellectual acknowledgment of error, but the latter shows remorse and empathy for a fellow human being."[180] We will turn to remorse shortly, but her distinction between empathy and other apologetic meaning resonates. Although I previously drew our attention to the common avoidance of the phrase "I was wrong" when apologizing because of its stark admission of wrongdoing and acceptance of blame, I risk overemphasizing the importance of this cognitive component to the exclusion of empathic meaning. Explaining that "I was wrong" may identify my offense, affirm the breached underlying value, and accept blame for the harm. To the victim all of this may seem abstract, distant, or cold. Empathy snaps into focus the suffering of a particular person by bringing us to understand "how she feels." Rather than simply sharing rules, we share feelings. We connect emotionally as well as intellectually. *Prima facie* this may sound like an imprecise platitude, but we should not underestimate the significance of appreciating the relevance of the mental state of the victim to an apology. Without empathy, the apology risks becoming so concerned with the violated principle, the offender's failures, or the process of the offender's redemption that the victim's felt suffering becomes incidental. The apology may appear to be *about* and *for* the offender and the value at issue rather than taking its orientation from the victim and her lived experiences. In this light we can imagine the alienated husband of the *Times* contributor paying more attention to the rectitude of his actions than to the feelings of his wife.

Empathy and sympathy also speak to an apologizer's recognition of her wrongdoing as such as well as her motivation for redressing the harm. When I empathize with the offended, I better appreciate the consequences of my acts because I am attuned to what it feels like to suffer such harm. If I cause you to incur medical expenses, for instance, empathy provides an understanding of the less visible and noneconomic damages. If I understand that you also experience considerable physical pain, anger, and increased anxiety and fear, I may be more likely to appreciate why my actions were unjustifiable. Hume and Schopenhauer found sentiments essential to moral judgment for these reasons. If we can relate to a victim's mental states and recognize them as undesirable, this triggers a sympathetic desire to ameliorate such suffering. Thus sympathy can provide motivation for an apologizer to undertake remedial actions.

Shame, guilt, embarrassment, remorse, and regret also commonly appear in apologetic contexts. As with empathy and sympathy, drawing sharp distinctions between these interrelated and often concomitant emotions proves challenging given the contested definitions of each phenomena. Philosophers have paid considerable attention to distinguishing shame and guilt, with Rawls' analysis in *A Theory of Justice* exerting some influence over the field.[181] According to Rawls, "shame is the emotion evoked by shocks to our self-respect"[182] but we feel guilt when we "act[ ] contrary to [our] sense of right and justice."[183] Both involve our sense of morality, but in guilt "we focus on the infringement of just claims of others and the injury we have done to them, and on their probable resentment and indignation should they discover our deed."[184] In shame we feel "struck by the loss to our self-esteem and our inability to carry out our aims: we sense the diminishment of self from our anxiety about the lesser respect that others may have for us and from our disappointment with ourself for failing to live up to our ideals."[185] A single wrongdoing might provoke feelings of both shame and guilt, but the primary distinction involves the emphasis on either my disappointment with myself (shame) or my concern for the victims and norms I have transgressed (guilt). Bernard Williams and Rawls agree that guilt and shame produce different worries and desires in the offender. Both describe shame as eliciting contempt – as opposed to anger – from others.[186] Whereas guilt may result in anger against the guilty, one can typically ameliorate the emotion by taking remedial actions. Shame can produce remedial paralysis, and according to Williams shame results in "not just the desire to hide, or to hide my face, but the desire to disappear, to not be there."[187] Nussbaum provides a similar distinction. Unlike shame, guilt does not "sully the entirety of one's being."[188] Because it can be eliminated by correcting one's actions, guilt "is a dignified emotion compatible with optimism about one's prospects."[189] In light of these distinctions some have made broad claims about the moral structures of "guilt cultures" versus "shame cultures,"[190] and I will later consider Sandra Bartky's feminist phenomenology of shame and guilt as it relates to potential gender difference in apologetic meaning.

A few further distinctions may prove helpful. Embarrassment suggests a lesser degree of control and culpability, as I might feel embarrassed rather than ashamed for accidentally bumping into you – the accident bespeaks a bit of bad luck rather than a moral failure or flaw in my character. We might also experience embarrassment as a kind of bashfulness or uneasiness when we have done no wrong, as when someone publicly lavishes praise upon us. Remorse tends to indicate an intense regret for one's wrongdoing, and its Latin roots suggest "biting again" as if the memory of the transgression gnaws at our conscience. I considered the various notions of regret in some detail earlier, but notice that my account there hardly characterizes regret as an emotion.[191]

How does each of these broadly distinguished emotions relate to apologetic meaning? Perhaps Kantian moral theories would view such emotions as largely irrelevant or even potentially distracting impulses that duty-bound agents should override. A complete disregard for the significance of apologetic emotions, however, is surely a minority position. Understood in accordance with the earlier description, guilt would seem like an appropriate emotional component of an apology because it accompanies the recognition of wrongdoing as such. When we identify and share a commitment to the value underlying a transgression, guilt would appear to designate the corresponding emotion. As an undesirable emotion, guilt also spurs us to undertake the reform and redress likely to free us from its clutches. Notice how the Kantian objection resonates here: we should not be motivated by a desire to alleviate the ill effects of our own negative emotions but rather by our responsibilities to the transgressed values. In some respects it seems that the wish to improve the well-being of the other, rather than the inclination to assuage our own guilt, should motivate us to apologize and provide redress. For Kant, however, proper motivation would arise not from the desire to relieve the suffering of either the offended or the offender but rather from a duty to the universal law. One might also object that if the bare "feeling" of guilt provides the catalyst for apologizing, the apology might suffer from being "undertheorized" in that the offender might skip the work of making the breached underlying value explicit. Whether the feeling of guilt leads to the cognitive appreciation of the wrongdoing or vice versa presents still another consideration.

In emphasizing the offense against self-regard, shame relates more closely to the failure to achieve my own objectives than to the violation of shared values so central to apologies. If an offender experiences the remedial paralysis symptomatic of shame with sufficient intensity, she may feel so forlorn that she lacks the hope or will to provide redress or expend the effort to transform her behavior. If Williams' description of shame as a desire to disappear is accurate, it will be difficult for an offender suffering this effect to come before her victim and community, accept blame for her wrongdoing, and set out to redress the injury.

In a general sense we can also notice the role apologies play in transferring emotions from the victim to the offender, as an offender's acceptance of blame may lighten the victim's emotional load. Victims may feel guilt and shame for their suffering, as cases of domestic violence often demonstrate. If a transgressor comes to bear the emotional responsibility for the harm and justifies the victim's sense of injustice, then the victim may come to feel less burdened by the guilt or shame arising from her unwarranted feelings of complicity in her own abuse.

In future work I will consider the relation between apologies and the recent revival in shame as punishment, for example in the work of John Braithwaite, but the punitive role of emotions in apologies presents some interesting and disconcerting issues. Negative emotions can have a deterrent value in that potential offenders may resist urges to commit offenses if they wish to avoid the unpleasant feelings of guilt or shame that may accompany their deed. Negative emotions may also serve rehabilitative objectives because an experience of guilt may move an offender to reform her behavior. Shame, guilt, sympathy, and empathy all play a role in reintegrating the offender into her community and sensitizing her to the consequences of her actions. Emotions may also incapacitate offenders, leaving them so embarrassed or ashamed that they lose their will to deviate.

Beyond these utilitarian functions, might emotions also serve a retributive role within apologies? Might we want an offender to feel negative emotions when she apologizes because we believe that she *deserves to suffer* from the emotions? In some circumstances, Kant explicitly claims that courts should command offenders to apologize in order to cause them to suffer public humiliation and thus pain commensurate with the harm they caused. Like requiring the offender to kiss the hand of the victim, a forced apology serves retributive ends because such "humiliation will compensate for the offense as like for like."[192] Watching the offender bear the weight of a heavy heart may sate our retributive desires, and therefore we might find that an offender who offers an otherwise robust apology "gets off too easy" if she does not serve her emotional sentence. Several social scientists imply that apologies mitigate a victim's "anger and aggression"[193] and social psychologist Ken-ichi Ohbuchi claims that apologies provide "aggression-inhibitory effects."[194] Results of one of Ohbuchi's studies indicate that "when the harm-doers apologized, as opposed to when they did not, the victim-subjects refrained from severe aggression against them." "The more severe the harm," Ohbuchi found, "the more extensive of an apology may be needed to alleviate the victim's anger and aggression."[195] This suggests that victims may harbor retributive sentiments when injured. The scales of justice can be corrected on this view either by the victim inflicting harm upon the offender or by the offender inflicting harm upon herself by apologizing. The greater the harm, the greater the aggression or apology needed to recoup its cost.[196]

Might finding inherent value in the suffering of the apologizer be motivated by less than deontological beliefs? Might we desire the apologizer to feel shame, guilt, remorse, humiliation, or other negative emotions because we take pleasure from her suffering? Do we desire the offender not only to provide the appropriate emotional accompaniment to wrongdoing, but also to debase herself through various forms of groveling? Perhaps apologies offer occasions for vengeance and we enjoy watching offenders buckle under our reestablished authority over them. Perhaps Nietzsche, more so than Kant or Bentham, illuminates our motivations by explaining our interest in the emotional pain of the apologizer – like the pain of the punished criminal – as an expression of resentment and a kind of power cheaply attained.[197] This may help to explain the cultural obsession with apologies of the famous, in that some might take particular delight in witnessing the powerful submit to, suffer from, and internalize the values of the herd. Some might even take pride in the apologizer's humiliation: I may feel a surge of strength as I watch a celebrity reduced to tears because of her failure to honor my values. Matters become still more perverse if we think of shame or guilt as emotions of self-punishment, potentially rendering the emotional content of apologies masochistic as well as sadistic.

Emotions present still further complications for apologetic meaning. First, I might experience multiple conflicting emotions while apologizing. I cannot begin to unravel the many possible webs of concurrent and contradictory emotions, but some examples should help to demonstrate the potential issues. Suppose I hear a hilarious joke the moment before I apologize. I quickly attempt to reorient my emotions from amusement to guilt, but I cannot help but think of the punch line and a giggle interrupts my somber gestures of contrition. Likewise, apologies for offenses in the distant past may not arouse emotions with equal intensity as will those for fresh injuries. Perhaps I experience concurrent emotions in a proportion that the victim deems inappropriate, for instance if, instead of being primarily filled with empathy and sympathy for my wife as I apologize to her, I am overcome with anxiety at the prospect of being abandoned by her. Although Sartre argued that we must take responsibility for our emotions and Aristotle believed proper emotions indicated a good upbringing, they seem to be at least in part involuntary and thus it would be odd to require an offender to manufacture the proper type and degree of emotions before we would take her apology seriously.[198] It also seems possible that providing an apology could be uplifting for the offender in that she could feel pride rather than guilt on the occasion of becoming a person who takes responsibility for her actions. In this sense we might think of the apologizer's pride in her moral progress overriding her guilt for past wrongdoing. Notice, however, the difficulty of identifying when the apologizer reaches the tipping point on the scale of self-respect from positive to negative emotions.

Emotions can also interfere with other aspects of apologetic meaning. Emotional outbursts can cloud an apology as we try to discern the meanings conveyed in a garble of fits and starts that may hinder gestures of contrition from a distraught offender. Offenders may also rely on maudlin displays to disguise deficiencies in an apology, but no amount of tears will provide the sort of significance, for example, resulting from a clearly articulated acceptance of blame. Similarly, offenders may use emotional intensifiers as substitutes for other forms of meaning, for instance explaining that they are "really, really sorry" for your injury. Without further explanation, such statements suffer from the ambiguities addressed earlier with respect to statements of sympathy that do not accept blame. Apologizers can also use emotions offensively in a campaign to win forgiveness, as a weeping offender can leave the victim so uncomfortable that she offers exculpation simply to bring the spectacle to an end.

We also should not fail to notice how the diverse role of emotions in various cultures inflects apologetic meanings. Some communities discourage emotional displays altogether. Others celebrate emotions. Whereas some emotions, like fear in the face of danger, have an obvious evolutionary function, others undergo social cultivation or suppression.[199] In some contexts an emotion may be glorified – consider the idolized wrath of Achilles – while in others the same emotion would be considered barbaric.[200] We also learn what sorts of things warrant emotional expenditure within given contexts. In this era I might find an insult to my penmanship from a superior colleague amusing, but one hundred years ago I might have been humiliated by such a judgment and suffer from the anxiety that poor handwriting may cost me my livelihood. Such insights motivate J. S. Mill and Catherine MacKinnon's respective studies of the construction of emotions as experienced by women within unjust conditions. This also informs the work on the distinctions between guilt and shame cultures referenced earlier.[201] Any discussion of the role of emotions within apologies, therefore, must remain mindful of the complex nexus of beliefs and values in which we find acts of contrition.

Having noted these complexities presented by the relation between emotions and apologetic meaning, let us consider one last example: Antonio Damasio's neurological studies of subjects who have suffered injuries to the prefrontal and somatosensory cortices of their brains.[202] These individuals lack the ordinary ability to experience emotions, and we can wonder how we might understand an apology from them without this capacity. Damasio claims that the emotional deficiency impairs a subject's ability to make practical judgments, and the extent to which this is true may prevent such an offender from seeing a need to apologize. One might expect, as Damasio's research suggests, that an offender would be considerably less likely to provide an otherwise categorical apology if she does not experience the requisite emotions because emotions spur us to apologize and help us navigate the complex interpersonal acts. I suspect that this is correct but little more than speculation without further empirical evidence. Nevertheless, suppose one of Damasio's subjects provides an otherwise exemplary apology for a serious offense. She accepts blame for the harm, she never reoffends despite facing temptations to do so, she affirms her commitment to the underlying value, and she completes a generous remedial program. Her apology is earnest and motivated by a desire to honor the breached value and increase the well-being of the victim. Yet she does not *feel bad* when doing all of this. If we believe that such an apology continues to suffer from a deficiency, we would need to identify meaning inherent to the emotion rather than instrumental to other kinds of apologetic significance already achieved by other means. What might this be? We might return to the punitive functions of apologetic emotions, but the deterrent, rehabilitative, and incapacitative aims will have presumably been met. This leaves retributive justifications: we want the offender to suffer emotionally, and if she does not then she evades her just desserts. According to this view, she has caused the victim to feel negative emotions and she must in turn suffer those emotions. Yet what if, instead of experiencing emotions such as shame or remorse, a migraine headache afflicts the offender whenever she thinks of her deed? Could non-emotional pain fulfill this retributive gap usually filled by emotional suffering? If so, would inflicting such headaches upon her be a legitimate form of punishment to compensate for her emotional insensitivity? I will leave those questions for retributivists and philosophers of mind and emotions, but we can see how multifaceted and delicate such matters become. Such concerns present some practical relevance if we broaden the example by including others who might similarly have atypical relations to emotions, for instance a Stoic who extirpates various emotions from her life, a psychopath or someone suffering from antisocial personality disorder with limited ability to experience remorse, or even someone scoring within the autism spectrum who exhibits abnormal empathic abilities.[203]

The complexity and importance of these questions regarding emotions and apologetic meaning, like those earlier regarding intention, reinforce my dissatisfaction with analyses offered by philosophers and social scientists who understand apologies as speech acts that either "fire" or "misfire." Just as a broken promise is still a promise, Richard Joyce argues that an apology still occurs when the offender delivers it without sincerity or any intention of changing her behavior. Such an all-or-nothing stance, when combined with his low threshold for what constitutes an apology, leads Joyce to disregard the multiplicity and complexity of purposes served by our complex practice of apologizing. Similarly, Lazare's aforementioned lack of concern for offenders who "do not exhibit shame, guilt, or empathy" because such matters "value style over substance" and do not influence an apology's veracity or effectiveness seems to overlook fundamental sources of meaning.[204] I have tried to show how matters are considerably more complicated. In one sense it seems clear that a categorical apology must satisfy some emotional expectations, yet it seems equally evident that I cannot establish a standard for the qualitative and quantitative emotional thresholds for categorical apologies. I am certainly unprepared and unwilling to claim that a categorical apology requires the offender to experience X emotion with Y intensity at time Z. Such a theory could not account for the range and subtlety of meaning possible within apologies, and such complexities only lead to further equally perplexing questions.

I do not foresee future technologies resolving these problems. Imagine that neurological devices allow us to measure the precise kind and degree of emotions experienced by an offender when she apologizes. Data from such tests would prove useful as a kind of advanced emotional lie detector that could expose insincerity. It would not be able, however, to tell us what kinds and quantity of emotions an apologizer should experience before we can consider her gesture to qualify as a proper apology.

CHAPTER THREE

Apologies and Gender

We often presume that women apologize more than men do. In this spirit John Wayne once advised the men of his generation: "Never apologize. It's a sign of weakness."[1] Comedian Jim Belushi offered similar advice in 2006, titling his book on relationships *Real Men Don't Apologize.*[2] Beyond these macho clichés, what role does gender play in the sorts of apologetic meanings I outline here? Does gender correlate to one's tendency to apologize? Do women and men emphasize different aspects of apologies or exhibit tendencies to apologize for different classes of harms? Or are these practices so entwined with culturally specific gender dynamics that speaking in generalizations would only reinforce patriarchal stereotypes and biases? Social scientists are better equipped to answer this question than I am, but my approach may offer some insight into how other disciplines theorize questions of apologies and gender.

Before going further, I want to emphasize an obvious point. In order to determine whether women apologize more than men do, we need to answer two questions. First, what do we mean by "apologize"? As I have shown, this takes some work. Do we refer only to categorical apologies? Expressions of sympathy? The utterance of the word "sorry"? Once we stipulate this, we would need to conduct methodologically compelling studies designed to answer such empirical questions. Notice that this applies to all questions of this sort: Who apologizes more, liberals or conservatives? Theists or atheists? The rich or the poor? Children or the elderly? Japanese or U.S. citizens?

At first glance, evidence seems to suggest that women do indeed apologize more than men do. Some read the social scientific literature to advance claims that women are more inclined to apologize than men if doing so repairs a relationship, but men may overcome this disinclination if they believe apologizing allows them to resume control over a situation.[3] Lazare confidently claims that "women, in contrast to men, apologize more frequently, are more comfortable in admitting culpability, and are more apt to use apology to decrease interpersonal tension."[4] Many academic and popular articles reiterate this belief, and like Lazare they cite the work of linguist Deborah Tannen.[5]

Tannen consistently claims that women apologize more frequently than men, but she relies on what appears to be limited and often anecdotal evidence to support this position. In *The Argument Culture*, for example, she claims that "[i]n our culture men are more likely than women to avoid apologizing" but she offers no citations to document this claim.[6] Women apologize more than men do, Tannen believes, because apologizing "is seen as a sign of weakness." Considering that "most boys learn early on that their peers will take advantage of them if they appear weak" but "[g]irls...tend to reward other girls who talk in ways that show they don't think they're better than their peers," Tannen concludes that many women apologize as a kind of verbal reflex. For the preponderance of women, Tannen claims, apologizing is thus like "an automatic tip of the verbal hat to acknowledge that something regrettable happened."[7] Tannen further claims in *You Just Don't Understand* that "many women seem to apologize all the time" and "women may be more likely to apologize because they do not instinctively balk at risking a one-down position."[8] Tannen also speculates that women *appear* to apologize more often than men because "women are heard as apologizing when they did not intend to do so [because they] frequently say 'I'm sorry' to express sympathy and concern, not apology."[9] As a result, she believes that women's "ritual way of restoring balance to a conversation" is often taken too "literally."[10] Tannen also worries that misconstruing women's expressions of sympathy for apologies causes women to bear a disproportionate amount of blame when they are not causally responsible for harm.[11] Tannen's theory seems intuitively compelling and I am quite sympathetic to her claims. I would prefer, however, more evidence and a more nuanced account of what she means by an apology before asserting with conviction – as much academic and popular writing does – that women do indeed apologize more than men.

The work of Janet Holmes provides Tannen's primary social scientific evidence, but this also seems rather inconclusive for our purposes.[12] As a linguist contributing to the "politeness" literature, Holmes defines an apology as "a speech act addressed to B's face needs and intended to remedy an offense for which A takes responsibility, and thus to restore equilibrium between A and B (where A is the apologizer, and B is the person offended)."[13] Holmes makes some provocative empirical claims, for instance asserting that in her studies "[w]omen gave 75 per cent of all apologies and received 73 per cent of them."[14] Holmes also concludes that while women "use significantly more apologies than men," they also "use more to each other than to men, and they use more to each other than men do to each other."[15] According to Holmes, both genders apologize to women more frequently than they do to men, regardless of the differential in social status between the parties.[16] Women apologize most often to female friends, but men apologize most often to socially distant females.[17] Women's apologies tend to "recognize the claims of the person offended and focus on the harmony of the relationship," while men "tend more than women to use strategies which focus on the apologizer's loss of face and the resulting status imbalance."[18] She claims that women's "apologies are predominantly directed to light offenses, whereas men use more apologies than women for more serious offenses."[19] Holmes also finds that women tend to apologize for breaches in conversational etiquette, while men "pay particular attention to" offenses against another's time and property.[20] When men do apologize, they use more formal language then women.[21] Holmes also found that men reject proportionately more apologies than women do,[22] and women respond to an apology with a counter-apology more often than men do.[23]

Although profoundly suggestive, we should be careful to note the numerous limitations of Holmes' studies. First, Holmes draws these conclusions from what appears to be a very small and local sample of 183 "naturally occurring remedial interchanges" predominantly between adult men and women New Zealanders of European descent.[24] Although I do not wish to diminish the importance of Holmes' findings, I am reluctant to generalize such a limited study into definitive – and stereotypical, as Sara Mills notes – assertions regarding gender behavior.[25] I am especially uncomfortable generalizing this study without critically evaluating how race, cultural, and class bisect these claims. Considering how widely Tannen is cited for the unqualified proposition that women apologize more than men and that Tannen draws this conclusion primarily from Holmes' very limited study, we should pause before accepting this generally held belief.

Even if Holmes provided more comprehensive data, her findings would likely remain inconclusive. Holmes notes in her own study that "the number of apologies between women and men is remarkably evenly distributed."[26] Mills argues that Holmes' statistics "do not back up her original hypothesis that women apologize more than men, and the raw data suggest there is no real difference between men and women except that which you would expect through randomness."[27] Furthermore, Bruce Fraser's study came to the following conclusion:

Contrary to popular stereotype, we did not find women offering more apologies than men. In all the variations of situations we recorded – formal and informal, alien and familiar, trivial and severe, social and personal – we found that both men and women sometimes apologize, sometimes not, with no apparent systematic or predictable frequency. The fact that we have one case of a woman apologizing to a tree stump which she just tripped over is surely offset by the case of a man apologizing to his reflection in a glass door.... In short, we found that there are those that apologize and those that do not, and this does not seem to lie with one sex over the other.[28]

Fraser does not include precise figures or methodological information that would be helpful for evaluating these assertions, but his findings suggest that we should question the presumption that women apologize more than men. Further studies have not settled the issues; one corroborates Fraser's finding and another supports Holmes' and Tannen's theses.[29]

We can also note the complexity of performing any empirical study of this kind. I have emphasized the difficulties of categorizing speech acts neatly into the binary senses of either being an apology or not because of the number of variables at play in apologetic meaning. Research measuring whether women or men apologize "more" would need to be refined enough to differentiate between the various kinds of meaning an apologetic gesture might hold. Holmes does note four varieties of apologies – explicit expression of apology, explanations or accounts, acknowledgments of responsibility, and promises of forbearance – but we have seen that matters are considerably more nuanced.[30] Holmes notes in her study, for example, that "there is little overall difference in the likelihood that women rather than men will acknowledge responsibility for the offense."[31] If we consider accepting blame central to apologetic meaning, then it would be misleading to say that women apologize more than men even according to Holmes' findings. Mills also notes the multitude of ways that women in various cultures use words like "sorry" without conveying anything that we would typically consider to fall within the broadest spectrum of apologetic meaning.[32] Tallying these as instances of women apologizing would further skew the totals. We can also imagine the difficulty of quantifying several of the elements discussed earlier, for example trying to convert the apologizer's emotional tenor or the appropriateness of her intentions into a quantity. The importance of mental states when considering the meaning of apologies may also tempt researchers to attribute stereotypical motivations and responses to the parties they study.[33] We might expect that men would be the recipients of most apologies given the power differential endemic to patriarchal culture, but according to Holmes "men apologize twice as often to women as they did to men, regardless of the women's position in relation to the apologizer."[34] If we view apologies as indicators of power where the subordinated humbles herself before the entitled hierarchy – think of Lazare's example of an abused woman pleading "I'm sorry. Please don't hurt me!" – then accounting for Holmes' statistic that men apologize more to women than to other men would require considerable (and surely contested) cultural analysis.[35] This could make for a complex discussion if apologies are at times expressions of weakness and submission, at times expressions of strength and courage, and at times both simultaneously with respect to distinct aspects of character and culture.[36]

In addition, much of an apology's meaning arises out of a dialectical interchange between parties where each may contribute different aspects of apologetic meaning. As Tannen notes, victims will often respond to an apologetic offering by searching for a fault of their own for which they provide similarly apologetic language. Victims might engage in this self-deprecation not because they believe that they share moral culpability for the offense, but because they wish to extend the courtesy of helping the offender shoulder the blame and not place her in a subordinated social position.[37] For this reason Tannen goes so far as to claim that "accepting an apology is arguably quite rude"[38] and one "might even make up a fault to admit" to diffuse the hierarchy, implying that it may be better to lie than to directly confront the moral status of the offender's wrongdoing.[39]

Each of these concerns increases the difficulty of isolating and tallying individual utterances and attributing the apology to one person in order to collect statistics on which gender "apologizes more often."[40] I do not mean to imply that more comprehensive and nuanced statistics regarding gender and apologies data would not be very useful if we could obtain them. If we found that women express sympathy more often than men and that legal systems often mistake these sympathetic gestures for admissions of guilt, measures could be taken to remedy this injustice disproportionately affecting women.[41] Likewise, one study claims that male physicians are three times more likely to be sued for malpractice than female physicians.[42] Perhaps an analysis of the difference between expressions of contrition from male and female doctors would be revealing here. On the other hand, one study suggests that women understand the nuances of apologies better than men, enabling them to distinguish between different sorts of apologetic meaning and act accordingly. Such practical wisdom may confer many benefits.[43] In light of the inconclusiveness of studies in this area, however, I am afraid that I must join others who find the current state of the argument that women apologize more than men inconclusive.[44] To help myself to the refrain of the social sciences: more research is required.

As we continue to think about gender and apologies, it may prove productive to move away from the question of whether men or women "apologize more." Beyond difficulties arising from the binary presumptions typically built into such a question, organizing our thoughts around such a theme suggests that empirical studies provide the prevailing method of understanding the relationship between apologies and gender. Although they may not help in quantifying the incidence of apologies between genders, phenomenological accounts of gendered apologies would surely offer insight. Sandra Bartky's phenomenology of gendered emotions offers an enticing model. Bartky's argument that women disproportionately experience shame, which she defines as a "species of psychic distress occasioned by a self or a state of the self apprehended as inferior, defective, or in some way diminished," would have certain application to gendered apologies.[45] In Bartky's sense, women do not merely suffer more episodes of shame than men do. Within a sexist society that constructs a vulgar and anemic view of women's bodies, sexuality, and interior lives, Bartky claims that for women shame may become a "pervasive affective attunement...a profound mode of disclosure of self and situation."[46] Although men may also feel ashamed, shame has a "different meaning in relation to [women's] total psychic situation and general location than has a similar emotion when experienced by men."[47] Such emotions may arise from a misogynistic "internalized audience" and therefore shame can haunt a woman in her most private life.[48] Bartky holds similar views of guilt as "a moral-existential predicament" that does not apply equally between genders or cultures.[49] If we find her accounts of these emotions persuasive, patriarchal culture may stain a woman's entire mode of being within any given apologetic context. As well as her emotional states, this might include her perception of events surrounding an injury, her views on causation and moral responsibility, her deepest moral values, her willingness to maintain unpopular views, her ability to express public contrition, her sense of remedial justice and capacity to undergo reform and complete reparations, and her likelihood to seek or grant forgiveness. For Bartky and other select feminists, gender may color every aspect of apologetic meaning.

Although this might seem overstated to some, we can imagine a situation in a transparently sexist culture where a woman fails to perceive her husband's sexual assault against her as nonconsensual (her perception of events), believes that she was responsible for the assault because she resisted (her views of moral causation), thinks that her body belongs to her husband and that she has thus failed in her familial duties by resisting (her deepest moral values), and so on. Gender inequalities would entirely transform the meaning of an apology from or to a woman in such circumstances. The extent to which this might apply to less blatantly sexist communities remains an open question that I hope more qualified scholars might take up.

CHAPTER FOUR

Apologies in Diverse Religious and Cultural Traditions

We can trace much of the meaning attributed to apologies in modern life to archaic religious and cultural practices associated with repentance. Consider Jeffrie Murphy's definition of repentance as the "remorseful acceptance of responsibility for one's wrongful and harmful actions, the repudiation of the aspects of one's character that generated the actions, the resolve to do one's best to extirpate those aspects of one's character, and the resolve to atone or make amends for the harm that one has done."[1] Indeed, this might well serve as an abbreviated definition of a robust apology. I can thankfully leave the detailed work of analyzing these traditions to others, but we can notice here how the broad contours of several of the major traditions of repentance share features with each other and how contemporary secular notions of apologies map onto these beliefs. We can also observe where these conventions resist translation into pluralistic discourse and create dissonance between those operating with opposing belief systems. The dilution of repentance into apology may partially account for our sense of the weakness of so many gestures of contrition.

Before discussing the specific traditions, several general observations seem noteworthy. First, religious rituals of repentance are explicitly moral acts. We commonly understand repentance not as a mere social necessity, but rather as an act of faith and form of communion with one's god. Within religious traditions, repentance affirms the sinner's ultimate values and invokes her basic understanding of the meaning and purpose of life. Whereas repentance requires some degree of soul-searching, apologies in secular culture can seem comparatively superficial when they function as little more than social commodities with primarily instrumental value.

Second, apologies between members of the same religion will likely benefit from the fact that victims and offenders share the moral code endorsed by that tradition and will be familiar with the customary repentance rituals. This shared underlying framework should facilitate the interaction and remove some of the obstacles to apologetic meaning present in pluralistic societies.

In addition, apologies in religious contexts typically emphasize repentance to a god for a sin committed against divine law. Offenders are often concerned with apologizing to god rather than to the human victims. This seems prudent given that many faiths believe that only their gods hold the ultimate power to forgive the sinner and distribute punishment or benefits accordingly. Some traditions therefore view reconciliation with other humans as a welcome but incidental by-product of reconciliation with their god.

Considering that the repentant offer their gestures to an omniscient god who would know the absolute truth regarding the historical record and chain of moral causation, the offender's mental state at the time of the deeds, her intentions in offering an apology, the degree of her remorse, and perhaps even the extent to which she will reform and take practical responsibility for her harms, there may be less likelihood that the offender will seek to deceive her god or use repentance as a ruse for personal gain. This did not prevent skeptics like Montaigne from doubting the hearts of the repentant.[2]

We should also be mindful that the sorts of voluntaristic beliefs commonly held in the West today enjoy less prevalence in other cultures. Conceptions of causal and moral responsibility would obviously differ within predeterministic religious frameworks, as repentance would take on a different meaning if my god chose that I would sin. Even those belief systems that afford humans moral choice may have understood freedom in less absolute terms than commonly used today.

Religious traditions also usually judge repentance according to binary standards: Either you have successfully repented or not, and one's eternal status may depend on whether she passes the test in the eyes of her god. This may account, in part, for the binary notions of apologies prevalent in modern secular theories. It seems fair to assert that apologies were somewhat simpler in the premodern world and that their moral meanings could be heard with less cultural interference. Although this has led Amitai Etzioni to argue that "we should adopt the religious concept of repentance into our civic culture," I certainly do not mean to advocate for this.[3]

In addition, religious traditions have played an important role in defining the sorts of persons to whom duties are owed. Beliefs regarding whether infidels, women, untouchables, or nonhumans deserve recognition as moral interlocutors often rest on a tradition of religious metaphysics, and the need for and nature of apologies to such beings will be understood accordingly. One need only consider the various Native American traditions of expressing gratitude to animals and vegetation to appreciate how our metaphysical beliefs define the scope of our moral communities and obligations.[4]

Finally, although we can find many differences among the variety of religious and cultural protocols of repentance, the meanings and rituals of repentances are often disputed *within* traditions. One need only consider the role of indulgences in the Protestant Reformation to appreciate the deep divisions within Christianity regarding the true nature and path to penitence. I will now note some particularly interesting aspects of repentance and apologies within various religious and cultural traditions.

Judaism offers an extensive and refined tradition of repentance, referred to as הבושת (*teshuvah*) and derived from the root for "return" – as in a return to God after a time of estrangement.[5] Repentance provides a central pillar in Judaic theology and culture, with the Hebrew Bible repeatedly emphasizing the necessity of repentance for salvation and the high holidays of Rosh Hashanah and Yom Kippur marking stages in atonement rituals.[6] God will not pardon humans unless they repent, and repentance is said to be so fundamental that it preceded creation itself.[7] Moses Maimonides (1135–1204) provides the primary text of *Teshuvah* through an exegesis of passages from the Torah in his *Hilchot Teshuvah* (*The Laws of Repentance*). Along with outlining how a repentant offender must cease her transgressions, resolve to abstain from further offense, regret her wrongdoing, confess, and provide compensation for sins against fellow humans, Maimonides demonstrates an acute sense of the meanings underlying these conventions. In addition to grading sins according to severity, Maimonides also distinguishes protocols applicable to repentance for sins committed by humans against god and for offenses between humans.[8] He also warns that those who confess publicly may lack shame.[9]

Recognizing the importance of the mental states accompanying repentance, Maimonides explains that one cannot judge repentance solely by the extent of the sacrifice, compensation, or punishment.[10] Even execution does not necessarily entail successful repentance unless undergone with the appropriate state of mind. He warns with a colorful analogy that merely speaking penitent words also will not suffice: "Anyone who verbalizes his confession without resolving in his heart to abandon [sin] can be compared to [a person] who immerses himself [in a ritual bath] while [holding a dead] lizard in his hand. His immersion will not be of avail until he casts away the lizard."[11]

In order to achieve "complete Teshuvah," Maimonides requires the offender to overcome the temptation to commit the offense again. According to earlier accounts, one should only be considered truly penitent after resisting similar temptation twice: "With the same woman, at the same time, in the same place."[12] For Maimonides, only a "person who confronts the same situation in which he sinned when he has the potential to commit [the sin again], and, nevertheless, abstains and does not commit it because of his Teshuvah alone and not because of fear or a lack of strength" will have properly repented.[13] The offender must remain faithful, in other words, not because the opportunity or ability to sin has passed or the benefits of sinning are no longer as desirable but strictly out of a desire to honor god's law.[14] One commentator distinguishes between these attitudes as either coerced repentance – as when you have no opportunity and thus no choice to reoffend – and deliberative repentance in which you freely choose forbearance. According to this account, incarceration typically leads only to the former.[15] Nor can offenders believe god licenses them to sin if they simply repent thereafter.[16] This nicely captures, in theological language, the test of categorical regret discussed earlier.

Continuing to emphasize the importance of intentions, Maimonides explains that sinners should not repent "in order to receive all the blessings which are contained within [the Torah] or in order to merit the life of the world to come." Nor should individuals resist sin to "be saved from all the curses contained in the Torah or so that [their soul] will not be cut off from the life of the world to come." The truly faithful walk "in the paths of wisdom for no ulterior motive: not because of fear that evil will occur, nor in order to acquire benefit." "Rather, he does whatever is true because it is true."[17] Notice how Kantian sensibilities parallel these views in their emphasis on the importance of an individual's intentions to act from a recognition of truth and duty rather than from self-interested or otherwise instrumental motivations. Also notice that Maimonides advises such dispositions only for pious men, while women and children should be taught "to serve out of fear and in order to receive a reward."[18] Unlike Kant, Maimonides also judges the quality of acts of repentance by their emotional tenor.[19] Maimonides also considers the timing of repentance, warning that a "person should always view himself as leaning toward death, with the possibility that he might die at any time." With this in mind, "one should always repent from his sins immediately and should not say: 'When I grow older, I will repent,' for perhaps he will die before he grows older."[20] Other commentators establish a temporal hierarchy of repentance, with the quality of the act declining if not provided immediately after the sin. Sincere deathbed repentance, however, remains valued to a lesser degree.[21]

The middle chapters of the *Hilchot Teshuvah* offer an excursus on human freedom, providing the necessary framework for moral responsibility:

Free will is granted to all men. If one desires to turn himself to the path of good and be righteous, the choice is his. Should he desire to turn to the path of evil and be wicked, the choice is his.... A person should not entertain the thesis held by the fools among the gentiles and the majority of the undeveloped among Israel that, at the time of man's creation, God decrees whether he will be righteous or wicked.[22]

Such freedom only became possible, according to Maimonides, because god "desired that man have free choice and be responsible for his deeds, without being pulled or forced."[23] Indeed, repentance occupies such a central role in Judaism that Maimonides elevates the sinner who has become a *Baalei Teshuvah* (master of repentance) over those who have never sinned.[24] Repentant sinner Aaron appears as the first high priest mentioned in the Bible, and King David successfully repented for acts of adultery and murder.[25]

Hilchot Teshuvah counsels victims and their communities as well as sinners. One must not, for instance, taunt or remind the repentant of his transgressions.[26] Maimonides advises that, in contrast to "the insensitive gentile" whose "wrath is preserved forever," Judaism requires that when "the person who wronged him asks for forgiveness, he should forgive him with a complete heart and a willing spirit."[27] An aggrieved human should forgive the repentant even in cases of severe harm.[28] In the context of the president of the Stockholm Jewish Community's rejection of a professor's rather thorough apology for earlier anti-Semitic remarks, prominent Bard College Professor of Judaic Studies Jacob Neusner offers an interesting account of how "ethnic Jewishness"[29] struggles to honor this "most compelling and insistent teaching of the Torah."[30] This refusal to forgive resonated for Neusner: "Here, for the first time in my life, I came face to face with the results of the total secularization of the Jews; . . . their absolute total refusal to behave in a concrete circumstance in accord with the morality of teshuvah that forms the foundation of our relationship with God."[31] Here Neusner personally experienced the slippage between traditional conceptions of repentance and their modern legacies. Abraham Kook offers an alternative modern perspective, providing a kabbalistic and collective theory of repentance wherein the repentance of each individual Jew strengthens the soul of Israel itself.[32]

Sophisticated traditions of repentance also appear in Islamicate culture, drawing comparisons among the writings of Al-Ghazzali, Ibn Paquda, and Maimonides on the subject.[33] As in Judaism, there is no savior in Islam and repentance and divine forgiveness therefore become especially axiomatic to the faiths and cultures.[34] Like *teshuvah*, the Arabic term *"tawbah"* translates as "to return" to the ways of god and its various derivatives occur eighty-seven times in the Quran.[35] Commentators agree on the central elements of repentance in Islam: awe for the divine, recognition of sin, genuine remorse and contrition, resolve to right one's actions, and the completion of restitution or "blood money."[36] Muslims must repent before the Day of Judgment, and therefore Muhammad (like Maimonides) advised frequent repentance in order to reduce the possibility of dying with moral debts outstanding: "O people, seek repentance from Allah. Verily, I seek repentance from Him a hundred times a day."[37]

Muhammad tells of god's love for repentance in an often-repeated comparison:

Allah is more pleased with the repentance of His believing servant than a man who loses his riding beast carrying food and drink. He sleeps (being disappointed of its recovery) and then gets up and goes in search for that, until he felt thirsty, then comes back to the place where he had been before and goes to sleep completely exhausted placing his head upon his hands and waiting for death. And when he gets up, lo there is before him his riding beast carrying his provision of food and drink. Allah is more pleased with the repentance of His servant than the recovery of his riding beast.[38]

Again similar to Judaism, Islam regards the experience of repentance as so fundamental that Muhammad is said to have explained that if "you were not to commit sin, Allah would sweep you out of existence and He would replace [you with] people committing sins seeking forgiveness from Allah, and He would pardon them."[39] As a quotidian ritual of faith, Fredrick Denny explains that repentance differs from "conversion" and thus it is "usually believers who are called to repentance and not outsiders."[40] Only Allah may forgive sins, but certain sins require public repentance and outward expressions of contrition.[41] The Quran and various *hadiths* (traditions attributed to Muhammad) repeatedly characterize Allah as "most merciful" and even willing to forgive repeat offenders, but Allah only confers such mercy upon the "truly" repentant.[42] The repentant's mental states will determine her ultimate fate, as she must adopt "an intentional posture which through positive acts seeks to keep [the sinner] on the straight and narrow."[43] God sees into the heart of the repentant and will not reward pretensions of internal piety.[44] While marveling in Allah's mercy, even the truly repentant remains fearful that she may not receive the gift of atonement because the Quran preserves Allah's discretion to grant mercy: "Turn to God with sincere repentance, that *perhaps* your Lord may expiate you."[45]

Islam generally divides penitents into four classes: 1) the prophets living in a state of perpetual and "perfect" repentance; 2) those who unintentionally commit minor sins and live continuously in remorse; 3) those who are slow to repent for repeated sins; and 4) "the persisters in evil" who fail to repent.[46] One who persists in sin after repenting "is like one who mocks his lord,"[47] and it appears that forgiveness is denied for those who repent on their deathbeds.[48] As with other religions, Islamic jurists debate the relationship among repentance, punishment, and forgiveness. If the offender is truly repentant, should we still punish her? If she serves her sentence on Earth, does this gain the criminal forgiveness in the next world? Should an offender always remember her sins or attempt to forget them? Such questions remain contested within the many forms of Islamic religions and cultural practices.[49]

Although we commonly associate *mea culpa* – the Latin phrase found in the Confiteor penitential prayer – with contrition in Christianity, the New Testament derives its notion of repentance from the Greek term μετάνοια (*metanoia*).[50] We might think of the most literal translation of *metanoia* as "afterthought," as in something after and incidental to a decision or process.[51] According to Kittel's *Theological Dictionary of the New Testament*, the Hellenistic philosophers used *metanoia* primarily in an intellectual sense, as the verb μετανοέω meant simply "to note later," "to change one's mind," or "to adopt another view."[52] A very different conception of *metanoia* appears repeatedly and prominently in the teachings of Christ, for example in his entreaty beginning the Gospel of Mark: "The time is fulfilled, and the kingdom of God is at hand: repent ye, and believe the Gospel."[53] From John the Baptist's proclamation to "Repent, for the kingdom of heaven is near"[54] to the final references to the unrepentant hordes in

Revelation, *metanoia* came to mean much more within Christian doctrine than the Greek sense of "changing one's mind."[55] Within the New Testament, *metanoia* signifies not merely a revision of beliefs but a "stirring of the whole consciousness" which leads to spiritual rebirth.[56] Now understood as a "conversion,"[57] for Christians repentance "affects the whole man, first and basically the centre of personal life, then logically his conduct at all times and in all situations, his thoughts, words, and acts."[58] Freedman's *Dictionary of the Bible* attempts to bridge the gap between the Christian notion of *metanoia* as a complete spiritual transformation and its etymological origins as an afterthought, arguing that for the Greeks μετανοέω meant "to understand something differently after thinking it over," which "necessarily leads to changed actions, in keeping with the Greek view that the mind (*nous*) controlled the body."[59] Although such "subsequent knowledge" might provoke a change in mood or course of action, Kittel argues that for the ancients "*metanoia* never suggests an alteration in the total moral attitude, a profound change in life's direction, [or] a conversion which affects the whole of conduct."[60] Therefore, Kittel claims, "one searches the Greek world in vain for the origin of the [New Testament's] understanding of μετανοέω or μετάνοια."[61]

Numerous commentators have divided Christian repentance into its constitutive elements, with Harvey Cox arguing for four essential components: remorse, resolution, restitution, and restoration.[62] Others, including Anselm, considered how the centrality of repentance presents a conundrum for Christianity.[63] If Christ was sacrificed for the sins of humans, then it would seem that he accomplished much of the work of repentance for us. Why, then, must we undergo the labor of atonement?[64] As Etzioni notes, "The more a theology relies on the redeemer to attain repentance, the less room there is for free will, individual actions, and personal responsibility."[65] Oliver North helped himself to this interpretation with respect to his role in the Iran-Contra affair: "Am I forgiven? Yes. Maybe not by the Washington Post, but I know where I'm going, and it's not because of anything that I've done. . . . It's all because God cared enough to send his Son to die for me. . . . I know that I am forgiven."[66]

Despite these questions, the often gruesome spectacle of penitential rituals evolved with Christianity into merits and indulgences that in part led to the Protestant Reformation. The 1546 Council of Trent differentiated between imperfect contrition motivated by fear of eternal damnation and perfect contrition oriented by love of god.[67] Presumably because God can perceive our mental states, perfect contrition is possible even for an offender on the verge of death. The story of the "good thief" on the cross beside Christ is often cited to demonstrate this possibility.[68] Pascal and Leibniz both spoke of the moral benefits of Christian practices of penance and confession. Following Hebrews 6:4–6, Augustine warned that the notion of *metanoia* as a definitive "changing of one's mind" implies that any backsliding into sin may signify an irredeemable failure: "Wherefore dost thou once more spare this man who after a first penance has again bound himself in the fetters of sin?"[69]

The Catholic Sacrament of Penance and Reconciliation, often referred to as "confession," emphasizes particular features of repentance.[70] Unlike the notion of *confessio* as a public statement or defense of one's faith such as those found in the writings of St. Patrick and St. Augustine, the Sacrament of Penance and Reconciliation is notably private as an act between the penitent, the clergy, and god. The Seal of the Confessional enforces the inviolable confidentiality of statements made by the penitent during the sacrament, even for grave criminal offenses or matters endangering others.[71] Whereas Catholic penance primarily directs the sinner to express her remorse to god, other biblical passages recognize the importance of confessing faults to human victims.[72] Augustine advocated for the public performance of penance for grievous offenses causing "scandal" to others.[73] The 1911 *Catholic Encyclopedia* also emphasizes that confession constitutes more than merely recounting one's sins and performing the prescribed penance: "Without sincere sorrow and purpose of amendment, confession avails nothing, the pronouncement of absolution is of no effect, and the guilt of the sinner is greater than before."[74] Despite this elaborate tradition, there is general agreement that repentance no longer holds the place it once did within Christian culture.[75] We also should note that recent scandals in the Catholic Church have unfortunately demonstrated that some Christian institutions appear to suffer from many of the same confusions as secular establishments regarding the meanings of repentance and apologies.

Hindu traditions of repentance predate most others, with some tracing their origins to the seventh millennium B.C.E.[76] Early Hindu culture conceptualized moral transgressions as a debt (*rina*) to the gods to be paid with acts of purification such as fasting and performing acts of charity.[77] Debts for the five major sins were too great to repay in one lifetime, leading to the intergenerational spiritual destitution found in the caste system.[78] The schedule of cosmic reparations set forth in the Dharma-Sutras of the classical period gave rise to the early Hindu laws of the castes and the ancient Indian criminal code.[79] The belief that physical or even intellectual contact could spread sin further worsened the conditions of the outcasts.[80] Repentance could expiate less serious sins, such as killing a person of a low caste.[81] As with other religious traditions, the *Manu-Samhita* emphasizes the significance of the penitent's mental state:

An evil-doer is freed from his evil by declaring (the act), by remorse, by recitation (of the Weda), and, in extremity, by giving gifts. The more a man of his own accord declares the wrong that he has done, the more he is freed from that wrong, like a snake from its skin. The more his mind-and-heart despises the evil action that he has committed, the more his body is freed from that wrong. For a man who has done evil and felt remorse is set free from that evil, but he is purified by ceasing (to do it, with the resolution), I will not do that again.[82]

This requirement to "despise" one's sins has contributed to a tradition of repentance poems expressing extreme self-deprecation.[83]

One might think that the absence of a judging god would make repentance less significant in Buddhism than in other religions, but the practice has played an important role in Buddhist life.[84] Repentance functions as an occasion to meditate on the nature of one's actions, to purify the mind, and to fortify one's discipline, rendering even confessions to the community primarily contemplative acts.[85] Theravada monks recite the monastic code on the days of the new and full moon and must confess and apologize for transgressions of the precepts. Serious offenses may result in ostracism for the monk, and lesser infractions may result in the suspension of privileges for six days during which the offender must also repeatedly recount the offense to fellow monks.[86] Although some assert that repentance in Buddhism avoids an appeal to divine sanction, Malcolm David Eckel questions this, for example by referring to Buddha's command to the murderer Angulimala: "If you do not stop now, you will be stopped in hell."[87] Thus even within Buddhism repentance may serve punitive ends.

These religious heritages contribute to diverse understandings of apologies within secular cultures as well, and we can note a few broad themes that make certain forms of apologies more common and appropriate in some contexts than others. First, the disintegration of religious beliefs and value systems may render traditional notions of repentance obsolete. The resulting transition to secular practices of apologies can be awkward. If we expect an apology to provide a complete spiritual transformation, we will often find ourselves disappointed. As noted earlier, victims and offenders may suffer from a basic moral disorientation without the underlying values shared by members of a faith community. Conflicts between religious and secular conceptions of apologies can also produce friction, leaving some alienated by a reference to an underlying religious value and others offended by an absence of such a grounding. This often leads public figures to use ambiguous phrasing to mollify various constituencies.

As I consider in more detail later, the prevailing social, political, and economic cultures will also influence how a population views apologies. Societies with a more collectivist sense of identity, for instance, will view apologies differently from those endorsing radical individualism.[88] Collectivists may be more sensitive to the importance of reestablishing shared moral values and may also attribute responsibility more widely given the tightness of their social networks. This would influence their conceptions of standing to apologize and increase the significance of apologies from community leaders, even if they are causally remote from the harm. Communal societies may also consider an injury against one of its members as an offense against all, which further complicates the dialectical exchange between victims and offenders. Individualist cultures tend to respond to injuries with adversarial means of dispute resolution such as legal proceedings rather than informal forms like apologies. In addition, religious views often inform cultural perceptions of gender, age, race, caste, and other characteristics. It might be very rare – and particularly meaningful – for an elder to apologize to a child or for a member of the ethnic majority to seek forgiveness from those historically oppressed. All of this makes for highly nuanced interactions, and we can appreciate the daunting prospect of apologizing between cultures. Such concerns present considerable social obstacles for non-native speakers of a language, as noted earlier.

The often-discussed distinctions between apologetic customs in the United States and Asian cultures should therefore not surprise us.[89] Consider the demand from Chinese officials that the United States apologize for the Hainan Island incident in April 2001 in which a U.S. surveillance aircraft and a Chinese jet collided, killing the Chinese pilot and requiring the U.S. plane and crew to make an unauthorized emergency landing in Chinese territory. After U.S. representatives initially refused to apologize because they argued that the fault for the accident belonged to the Chinese pilot, U.S. Ambassador Joseph Prueher eventually issued to Chinese Foreign Minister Tang Jiaxuan what has come to be known as the "letter of the two sorries."[90] The letter stated, in part:

President Bush and Secretary of State Powell have expressed their sincere regret over your missing pilot and aircraft. Please convey to the Chinese people and to the family of the pilot Wang Wei that we are very sorry for their loss. Although the full picture of what transpired is still unclear, according to our information, our severely crippled aircraft made an emergency landing after following international emergency procedures. We are very sorry the entering of China's airspace and the landing did not have verbal clearance, but very pleased the crew landed safely. We appreciate China's efforts to see to the well-being of our crew.

The letter also proposed a meeting between U.S. and Chinese officials, and the "meeting agenda would include discussion of the cause of the incident, possible recommendations whereby such collisions could be avoided in the future, development of a plan for prompt return of the EP-3 aircraft, and other related issues." Upon receiving this statement, Chinese officials allowed the twenty-four U.S. crew members and their disassembled aircraft to return to Hawaii. At this point President Bush added the following: "I know the American people join me in expressing sorrow for the loss of life of a Chinese pilot. Our prayers are with his wife and his child."

Notice the diplomatic wrangling at work here. Setting aside questions regarding standing and collective apologies, the carefully crafted statements convey just enough diplomacy for both parties to save face. Although expressing sympathy by stating that they were "very sorry for the death," noting their "sincere regret" over the missing pilot and aircraft, and indicating that they were "very sorry" that the Chinese did not provide clearance for entering their airspace for the emergency landing, U.S. officials did not accept blame for any aspect of the accident. They note the aircraft landed after following "international emergency procedures," suggesting that they should not be faulted for entering Chinese airspace and implying that China should have granted clearance. Nor did they admit that conducting reconnaissance missions off the coast of China was improper. Even though the apology was already ambiguous in significant respects, according to some accounts the United States intentionally did not translate the statement into Chinese languages because doing so would have required U.S. officials to navigate more precise apologetic terminology. Translation would force U.S. officials to make the meaning of their statements explicit and thus take a position on their responsibility for the incident. They instead left the statement in English, allowing them to mask the limited meaning of their statements while affording Chinese officials the benefit of translating it into the meaning they desired.

The culture of apologies in Japan has received considerable critical attention, and I take this up in later work with respect to the role of apologies in Japanese criminal justice systems. Although I am reluctant to speak in such generalities, research suggests that mediation practices are deeply embedded within Japanese cultural values and everyday interpersonal relations. Incidents that would be likely to produce denials or excuses in the United States are more likely to elicit an apology – or at a minimum an expression of sympathy – in Japan.[91] Japanese offenders commonly apologize and provide nominal gifts even when they clearly do not face legal liability, and studies suggest that Japanese customs cast apologies as honorable acts of humility that restore social harmony and consider resorting to legal action as an interpersonal failure and a source of defeat, submission, and shame.[92] We can contrast this with the United States, where many perceive apologizing as an expression of weakness and consider prevailing in adversarial proceedings as the vindication of one disputant over another. This resonates with findings in one study indicating that Japanese respondents favored responses to criminal behavior that reintegrated offenders into the community whereas U.S. respondents preferred sanctions tending to remove offenders from the community.[93]

Florian Coulmas offers an interesting explanation for the distinctiveness of apologetic culture in Japan. Coulmas notices the close relation between apologies and gratitude. If I am late for a meeting, I might either apologize for my tardiness or express thanks to my colleagues for their patience. Although subtly different, we can appreciate how both statements flag the trouble that I caused. According to Coulmas, the "link between object of gratitude and object of regret is the concept of indebtedness."[94] Whereas for Westerners "the distinction between shame and gratefulness is clearly marked," Coulmas claims that "this is not so in Japanese culture."[95] For the Japanese, he claims, "the boundary between apologies and thanks is blurred" and apologies are appropriate along the entire spectrum of indebtedness.[96]

In light of this, apologies express gratitude as well as debt. In "Japan the smallest favor makes the receiver a debtor" and interpersonal "relations can be regarded, to a large extent, as forming a reticulum of mutual responsibilities and debts."[97] He claims that the Japanese practices of gift giving and generosity emphasize "the trouble they have caused the benefactor rather than the aspects which are pleasing to the recipient."[98] This causes recipients to apologize for their imposition upon the giver. "The reverse side of the benefit of a favor is the strain that it cost the benefactor to carry out," he explains, and "for this strain the one who benefited is held responsible."[99] As a result, rather than thanking you for hosting me at your home I might apologize to you for my intrusion upon your home. We therefore might find apologetic language where we do not perceive any offense, and apologies might resound throughout the most generous and festive occasions. Here we can appreciate the significant difference between a practice aimed at returning the apologizer to good standing with one in which even the innocent seeks to restore communal order and communicate how sensitive she is to the complex allowances required for social life.

I have only superficially considered a few of the many religious and cultural traditions that shape notions of repentance and apology, and one could fill many volumes with detailed discussions of these practices. My point is not to catalogue such customs but to invite appreciation of their influence over modern acts of contrition. Even the most secular contemporary apologies descend from ancient rituals attempting to reunite with the divine.

CHAPTER FIVE

Unusual Cases: Apologizing to Animals, Infants, Machines, the Deceased, and Yourself

Most of the previous discussions consider apologies between typical adult humans, but we sometimes find people apologizing to animals, plants, machines, infants, deceased humans, and even themselves or their god. We might think that people who apologize to themselves or to their pets suffer from a kind of delusion brought on by dissociative identity disorder or an anthropomorphizing imagination, but I am inclined to attribute more meaning to these acts than first impressions might lead us to believe. These marginal cases cast into relief the different forms of apologetic meaning and seem worthy of some attention.

Suppose I do not fill my dog's water bowl one afternoon and intentionally ignore his requests for a drink because I do not want to interrupt my work. Upon rising from my desk several hours later, I see him lying by an empty bowl and panting heavily. I now believe that I made a moral mistake. I immediately give him water and say the following with genuine emotion while petting him: "I was wrong to not fill your bowl and then ignore your pleas. I value your companionship and I unjustifiably caused you to suffer from thirst. I am so sorry and I will be more considerate and responsive to your needs in the future." I then give him a treat as a kind of reparation. From that day forward I vigilantly attend to his needs and I never make the same mistake again. Have I apologized to my dog? As should be clear at this stage in the argument, I want to resist the binary question of whether or not I have apologized and instead consider what kinds of meanings my words and actions would have in this case. How significant is this apology? I have accepted blame for his suffering. I admit that what I did was wrong, explain why it is wrong, clarify values that we presumably share at some level, and commit to those values. I fulfill a promise not to repeat the offense, and I provide an appropriate form of redress. I categorically regret my mistake, I intend nothing disingenuous, and I genuinely feel emotionally distressed. What, then, does my apology to my dog lack?

From my perspective, the apology looks very similar to a categorical apology that I might offer another human and it would have meaning *for me* in many of the usual respects. It might also be meaningful for other humans. If my disregard for the dog is a source of conflict in my marriage, for my wife this apology may signify a fundamental change in my attitudes and behavior. Yet because apologies can provide meaning for the victim as well as the offender and the community, much of its significance in this case depends on the mental states of the dog. Even if the apology is so monumental for me that it transforms my relationship to all animals and spurs me to devote my life to caring for them, all of this could take place without the dog registering much of this significance. For him, my revelatory monologue could hold little more meaning than the usual bowl of water and affection. What, then, does the apology mean to the dog?

Although I will not speculate about the minds of canines here, we can appreciate the relevance of such questions. The meaning of an apology to an animal depends, in part, on what the animal understands and values. These abilities will differ according to the behaviors and mental capacities of various species. The dog may understand after my apology that I did not intentionally cause him to suffer, just as he would be able to make various distinctions about the meaning of my accidentally tripping over him as opposed to intentionally kicking him. He might also judge the value of my apologetic gestures based on my past and future actions. If I often deny him water and undergo such ritual of contrition regularly, then he will likely come to find me less reliable and attribute meaning to my repeated apologetic gestures accordingly. In this sense, apologies to animals can be flawed in the same ways as those to humans and more sophisticated animals will discern some of the nuances. If a caretaker regularly said to Koko the gorilla that she is "sorry that you live in a cage" (presuming that this communication is possible at Koko's level of proficiency in American Sign Language), then I suspect that the statement would have limited meaning not only for the human but also for Koko. Koko would probably realize that the gesture might earn her a sympathetic treat, but not freedom.

One form of meaning is especially rare between humans and nonhuman animals. As suggested earlier, for many humans the act of restoring their dignity and status as beings who cannot be treated as mere means constitutes a core element of a meaningful apology. When one person apologizes to another and explains why her actions were unjustified, she engages the victim as an ethical subject and interlocutor rather than a mere thing in the world. Such powerful moments are rare at best between humans and animals. Although I might find apologizing to an animal to be a deontologically meaningful act because I have a duty to care for it and honor my beliefs regarding the well-being of animals, this is not to say that I am willing to consider my dog a full moral agent. My apology to him probably does not recognize his dignity and autonomy, particularly in the Kantian sense. I do not allow him, after all, to go outside at will or without a leash, thereby denying his autonomy in the most obvious respect. My dog and

I may agree in some sense that he should have adequate food and drink, but does he understand this in abstract moral terms? Whereas a Kantian may refuse the possibility that my dog and I share an autonomous commitment to the violated moral principles and therefore reserve some sorts of meanings exclusively for apologies between humans, a behaviorist may understand the normative lives of humans and animals as differing only in degree. For this reason, apologies between the species might not look that different to a behaviorist. Beyond the unlikelihood that I would recognize my dog as a moral agent, it is unclear that he would care about such a thing even if I did. Dogs, I think it is safe to say, are less concerned with whether they are perceived as moral agents. They are surely, however, concerned with the benefits that come with such recognitions. A dog, in other words, may by some accounts understand the instrumental value of the apology as well as a human but be less likely to comprehend or value its deontological aspects.

Such examples emphasize the dialectical meanings of apologies – the more meaning the apology has for the victim, the more it is likely to have for the offender and vice versa. If the injured person finds great value in being respected by the offender, the offender can find further meaning in this apology than if the victim is unresponsive. Just as one may find her charitable act more meaningful if she learns that the recipients cherish her gift, an apology will be more meaningful to both the offender and the victim if they share an appreciation of its full importance. We might call this "feedback" meaning. If a nonhuman animal cannot appreciate whether she is being respected as a moral agent, this will impact the meaning of the apology for both the animal and the human. Although I can learn a great deal from my dog and I share certain profound bonds with him, I doubt we can experience a fellowship in moral discourse in the same sense that I can with my human companions. I should not overinflate the importance of this difference or fail to note that I only rarely experience such an explicit "fellowship in moral discourse" with my human companions, even if it implicitly pervades much of my existence. Yet if we review many of the examples of apologies in this book, we might fairly conclude that my apology to my dog for denying him water conveys considerably more moral meaning than those that often pass for apologies between humans.

The notion of dialectical meaning may also help to make some sense of the idea of apologizing to oneself. Setting aside those suffering from something akin to multiple personality disorders, we can imagine someone of sound mental health providing an apology to herself for behavior that interfered with her own well-being. If I am required to restrict my diet because of a heart condition, I might apologize to myself after a weekend of binge eating. If it was a frenzy of consumption, I might first compile a list of everything I ate to create a factual record of the events. I could also accept that I did this to myself, rather than blame a relative for forcing food on me. I could make explicit precisely which values I breached and why I am committed to those values. I may be genuinely disappointed with my actions, feel that I have "let myself down," reform my behavior, and increase my exercise regimen. The desire to care for and respect myself, as well as a wish to remain alive and fulfill my duties to my family, motivates the apology. I post the apology on the refrigerator, and I remain faithful to it for the rest of my long life. Although this may bring to mind Al Franken's lampooning of self-help programs with his Stuart Smalley character on *Saturday Night Live*, such a self-apology could signify a breakthrough in my process of self-understanding. The primary distinction between such a monological apology and dialogical forms would be the difficulty of making sense of feedback meaning without cleaving the self into the "good victim" and the "bad offender." As discussed earlier with respect to Goffman, splitting personal identity in this way could be a means of deflecting blame for the act into a previous self. We can notice here how an apology to one's god would also be monological – presuming that one's god does not speak to the offender – and would therefore share features with an apology to oneself. This is also true of apologies offered to the dead, and in each of these cases the primary meaning of the apology concerns the offender and her community.

Given their cognitive and emotional immaturity, apologies to and from children have a similar structure as apologies to animals and will face similar limitations. Indeed, it seems more likely that my German Shepherd will understand more of the meaning of an apology than a newborn. One important difference, however, is the child's potential to come to appreciate the apology more richly than my dog. Imagine that a parent injures a newborn in a drunken stupor and then provides an exacting apology both orally and in writing. The incident spurs the parent to a life of abstaining from alcohol and she regularly shares the written apology with the child as she grows into an adult. Such an apology could be deeply meaningful for both the parent and the child in ways that the dog would not understand.

Likewise, apologies from young children may initially convey little more meaning than a conciliatory gesture from my dog. A child's apology can be very different from a dog's however, in relation to her moral development and how the recipient perceives and appreciates that growth. Apologies to and from children seem crucial for their moral development in that apologies provide a context for children to think about and internalize the moral concepts discussed throughout this text, including notions of responsibility, self-control, and redress. As with adults, apologizing requires children to consider the values at stake in a conflict and endorse those principles as members of a normative community. Because of this importance for moral education, I worry that children who regularly experience superficial apologies like many of the examples I cite may risk not only of failing to learn how to give and receive rich apologies. They may also suffer generally from impaired moral development. I cringe whenever a revered public figure provides a transparently hollow apology, in part because I wonder if somewhere a child will model her own moral interactions on these examples.

Apologies to inanimate objects raise similar issues. According to most modern perspectives, an apology to a rock would be like an apology to an animal with no mental life whatsoever. Imagine a sculptor renewing her aesthetic values by apologizing to a block of marble for mishandling it. Such an apology would bear meaning for her, but presumably not for the rock unless we invoke a form of animism or panpsychism. We can again notice how underlying metaphysical beliefs can make even an apology to a rock a significant ritual. If I understand the world as an interrelated web of kinship between humans and nature, as many Native Americans do, I might give thanks to killed prey by blowing tobacco smoke into its nostrils or ask forgiveness from a tree for harvesting its bark.[1] Because such a worldview considers a broad scope of beings within its moral horizons, it extends opportunities for gratitude and contrition beyond most other traditions that strictly delimit the class of moral interlocutors deserving of apologies.

We should also remain mindful that the distinctions between animate and inanimate or among human, animal, and machine are imprecise and porous boundaries. Because meaning is tied to mental and emotional capacities enabling one to understand the interaction, we can see how varying degrees of abilities among individuals within the different categories complicates matters. A sophisticated computer of the future, for example, may be more capable of understanding the meaning of an apology than a dog, a human infant, or perhaps even an adult human. Although researchers disagree about how to create robots capable of fully participating in complex social activities, we can immediately sense how the ability of a computer or robot to give and receive meaningful apologies would depend on its emotional capacities as well as its computational abilities.[2]

Similarly, many beings change their moral status over their existence. Just as an apology to a child differs from an apology to an adult, apologies from the dead differ from apologies to the comatose or to the living. Kant suggested earlier that we are required to fulfill our responsibilities to apologize to the dead, and we can appreciate how such concerns operate across a spectrum rather than only between fully functioning moral agents. Whether apologizing to the dead, the cognitively disabled, the young, the unborn, the animal, the rock, or anything else that we find within our sphere of moral considerations, I suspect that a close review of the various kinds of meaning in such exchanges will provide more insight than simply asking whether such instances should count as apologies. Considering not only the range of contexts but also the varying degrees of sophistication of those who give, receive, and contemplate apologies, the nuances in meaning are innumerable but we can begin to outline the forms of meaning that matter to many of us. Defining the limits of such meaning presents a complex set of issues that will vary depending on one's conceptions of not only the mental abilities and moral status of beings and things but also the very nature of existence.

CHAPTER SIX

The Relationship Between Apologies and Forgiveness

We often understand forgiveness as synonymous with "accepting an apology," which naturally leads discussions of apologies to examinations of the nature and meanings of forgiveness. Forgiveness has thankfully received far more attention than apologies within various Western philosophical traditions, including discourses from Seneca, Bishop Butler, Hegel, Nietzsche, Arendt, Derrida, and others.[1] Many accomplished contemporary philosophers from diverse perspectives continue to contribute to this already rich field, including work by J. M. Bernstein, Cheshire Calhoun, Trudy Govier, Charles Griswold, Jean Hampton, Julia Kristeva, Martha Minow, Jeffrie Murphy, Martha Nussbaum, Kelly Oliver, Robert Solomon, Margaret Urban Walker, and others.[2] Rather than offering a comprehensive account of forgiveness here – which would easily double the length of this book because the meanings of forgiveness seem as complex as those of apologies – I will instead note how some features of my theory of apologies might relate to forgiveness scholarship.

Most generally, I expect that just as binary views of apologies prove too coarse to appreciate the intricacies of apologetic meanings, binary views of forgiveness also oversimplify the range of meanings and functions of the practice. I find it misleading to claim that one day I experience negative attitudes and opinions toward an offender but the next day I am able to entirely overcome these emotions and reverse judgments. Even if someone who harms me offers a categorical apology and comports herself to my highest expectations, I still wonder if it might be too simplistic to claim without qualification that I forgive her. It is not only that we should understand forgiving as a process that takes some time to undergo, or even that it would be difficult to identify the precise moment on a timeline when we can say that forgiveness is complete. Rather, I suspect that thinking of forgiveness as an act that we can definitively complete misleads us in many cases. The offense may fade in our memory, our pain may be assuaged or even disappear, and we may enter into valued and intimate relations with the offender. Certain kinds of damage and judgments may nevertheless linger indefinitely.

Although you might tell an unfaithful lover that you have forgiven her and trust her once again in order to restore a sense of security to the relationship, you may still experience nagging doubt, occasional bouts of anger, or even painful memories many years after reconciling. If we experience any of these thoughts or feelings to any degree, do we void our forgiveness? This seems like a rather ham-fisted question given the terribly complex moral and psychological issues it raises.

I doubt that any set of criteria or scale of forgiveness that provides the "necessary conditions of forgiveness" will settle matters. Take, for instance, Norvin Richards' claim that forgiveness requires eliminating "all negative feelings toward this person, of whatever kind, insofar as such feelings are based on the episode in question."[3] John Wilson claims that "'genuine forgiveness'... must involve reconciliation and a fresh start, with no debts outstanding and nothing still held against the wrongdoer."[4] The temptation to discover the definitive account of forgiveness is strong. Even Derrida, who you would least expect, appears to work with a binary conception when he distinguishes "genuine," "absolute," or "strict senses" of forgiveness from lesser forms.[5] Others parse different kinds of forgiveness, with Kelly Oliver and Mary Beth Mader helpfully contrasting four kinds of forgiveness according to Hegelian and psychoanalytic accounts.[6] Glen Pettigrove follows Austin and Searle to differentiate between three possible meanings of the illocutionary act "I forgive you": "(1) to disclose an emotional condition, (2) to declare a debt canceled, or (3) to commit ourselves to a future course of action."[7] Pettigrove argues that in practice "we seek" a hybrid account providing a unitary theory of paradigmatic forgiveness.[8] For Hegel, we only become individuated subjects within a community through the process of forgiveness.[9] Along with promising, Arendt describes forgiveness as a pillar that upholds "in an ocean of uncertainty, which the future is by definition, islands of security without which not even community, let alone durability of any kind, would be possible in the relations between men."[10] Without the possibility of forgiveness, Arendt writes, "our capacity to act would...be confined to one single deed from which we could never recover; we would remain the victims of its consequences forever."[11] The wound of separation from our community would never heal. Others emphasize that forgiveness requires a change of perception of the offender.[12] Psychologists offer several competing models of and programs for forgiveness, and medical researchers even advocate for forgiveness because of its apparent cardiovascular benefits.[13]

Return to the example of missing the dinner with my friend discussed earlier. My friend may eventually say that she "forgives" me and may be willing to schedule another meeting, yet she may still wonder if I will keep my word given that I once disappointed her. If she harbors even the slightest residue of doubt, is her forgiveness somehow inauthentic? If my friend experiences a pang of worry when I am a minute late for our appointment because she remembers my previous offense, does this mean that I am unforgiven even if she finds these feelings inconsequential for our relationship? That general question seems unavailing and too obtuse an understanding of our relationship. Similarly, I might believe on moral grounds that someone deserves my forgiveness, yet I cannot suppress my occasional sense of disappointment and anger years after I have reconciled with her. Does this mean that I have not forgiven her? I suspect a more nuanced account would make better sense of the situation.

Like apologies, notions of forgiveness seem to identify a loose constellation of interrelated meanings among various beliefs, judgments, emotions, and actions. This might include overcoming pain, anger, or resentment, renewing trust, compassion, or love, or withholding punishment, penalties, or the desire for retribution.[14] In specific circumstances it might be all of these things or it might be only one of these things. Perhaps I forgive you by canceling a debt you owe, or perhaps I require you to pay the money but I no longer have "hard feelings." A certain kind of forgiveness occurs in either case. Forgiveness might take root between lovers, murderers, and widows, parents and children, bureaucrats, warring nations, or nameless passersby. On one occasion forgiveness might be expressed through a pageant of dignitaries, but sometimes we find it in a smile, nod of the head, or wave of the hand. The basic self-worth of the victim and the offender may depend upon forgiveness, and forgiveness between groups can have the power to prevent the most heinous moral offenses. Alternatively, forgiveness can simply be a reflex of etiquette to diffuse an awkward social moment. Thus forgiveness might mean any number of things.

My point is that – again like apologies – we may value and emphasize different aspects of forgiveness in different contexts. A compelling theory of forgiveness would account for these distinctions in meaning. As with apologies, one might parse the various elements of forgiveness and consider paradigmatic instances satisfying each criterion in appropriate degrees to constitute something like "Categorical Forgiveness." We experience many instances in which only a few aspects of forgiveness matter to us, and it does not seem particularly helpful to claim that any act that does not satisfy all of the criteria fails as an act of forgiveness.

Just as cultures emphasize different aspects of apologies, diverse traditions may value forgiveness for distinct reasons. When Achilles declares with respect to Agamemnon's taking of Briseis that "our feud is at an end" and "we must let bygones be bygones, for all our resentment, and curb our hearts perforce," this may sound tepid to our ears. Yet it served its purpose at a moment of reconciliation between an ancient Greek king and his finest warrior.[15] Buddhism emphasizes the role of forgiveness in preventing harmful emotions from destroying one's peace and presence of mind.[16] Whereas only Allah, as "The Most Forgiving," can provide ultimate expiation, the Quran teaches that Allah will reward those who practice interpersonal forgiveness.[17] Christianity extols the virtue of forgiveness, and as in Islam, the ultimate fate of a Christian depends on her ability to forgive others.[18] Arendt goes so far as to claim that the "discoverer of the role of forgiveness in the realm of human affairs was Jesus of Nazareth" and then models her conception of forgiveness between humans upon the forgiveness of God for humans.[19] The Book of Matthew suggests that Christians should set no limits to their ability to forgive: "Peter came to Jesus and asked, 'Lord, how many times shall I forgive my brother when he sins against me? Up to seven times?' Jesus answered, 'I tell you, not seven times, but seventy-seven times (or seventy times seven).'"[20] Although this passage suggests that Christians should forgive even the unrepentant repeat offender, Judaism requires forgiveness only if the offender properly repents.[21] Some traditions may even view forgiveness as a vice because it suggests that the forgiver lacks self-respect, is incapable of exacting revenge, or generally suffers from a lack of power. In light of these differences, cultures will surely emphasize and find diverse kinds of meaning in the practices and rituals of forgiveness.

Some debates in the forgiveness literature will look a bit different from my perspective. Theorists often consider, for example, whether someone who has forgiven another must refrain from administering punishment against her. In my view, we could find certain elements of forgiveness present even if the victim pursues punishment, for instance because of her commitment to Kantian principles of justice that arguably require officials to punish regardless of the offender's contrition or a judge's inclination to exercise mercy.[22] We could also imagine someone entering into a close and trustful relationship with a person who has harmed her while continuing to believe that the offender deserves punishment for the harm or should be required to redress the injury. Truth and reconciliation tribunals often take forgiveness as an orienting principle while simultaneously minding a range of objectives including administering retributive justice, deterring future atrocities, granting amnesty in order to maximize stability, and creating a historical record to preserve the memory of the harm. These potentially conflicting goals do not render forgiveness impossible but rather require close consideration of the relative values and meanings of the different elements of forgiveness.[23]

Some argue that instead of forgiveness requiring that we suspend our right to punish, it entails a promise not to retaliate or demand compensation. Pettigrove claims that when "I utter 'I forgive you,' I commit myself to doing not unto the other what that other has done unto me," and Desmond Tutu believes that forgiving "means abandoning your right to pay back the perpetrator in his own coin. . . ."[24] Yet the lines among retaliation, punishment, and compensation often blur. Suppose the friend whom I previously stranded at the restaurant sees a colleague on her way to another dinner appointment with me. They strike up a conversation, and my friend realizes that she risks being a few minutes late for her meeting with me. She thinks to herself that I am usually behind schedule anyhow, so she can linger for a moment in conversation. Meanwhile, I wait for her at the restaurant. Is she retaliating? Is this a form of "payback," noting the linguistic similarity between retaliation and compensation? Is this her subtle means of punishing me or does she simply make a prudent judgment about the likelihood of my punctuality? She arrives for dinner fifteen minutes late, her tardiness passes without comment, and we enjoy each other's friendship throughout the evening. Cast the interaction in the following light: She remembers my harm against her, this memory orients some of her interactions with me, and in some sense I suffer harm (waiting) because of her continued negative attitudes against me and my questionable reliability. Understood in that way, has she forgiven me or not? I find such a question not especially illuminating because failing to satisfy one of the potential elements within an account of forgiveness does not drain the meaning from all of the other interrelated forms of meaning.[25] Just as some apologies will clearly name the underlying breached moral value and some may not be as explicit, some acts of forgiveness are best understood as absolution for a clearly named transgression whereas others will minimize the wrongfulness of the act in order to emphasize reconciliation between the parties. Rather than rule out the latter as unworthy of classification as an act of forgiveness, we can consider both "I forgive you for your sin" and "Please don't give it another thought" as offering distinct kinds of meaning relevant to the social practice.

This approach may help to make some sense of the notion of the "unforgivable."[26] Perhaps describing an offense as unforgivable can be understood as a belief that one element of forgiveness will never be met, for instance that the victim will – or must, as many argue in the case of the Holocaust – never forget the offense or "recover" from its consequences.[27] I can surely remember an event and the pain it caused while enjoying a close and friendly relationship with the person who injured me long ago. One might reconcile in various ways with a former lover who once betrayed her – including overcoming all anger and entering into a friendly relationship – but never again trust the offender in a romantic relationship. She might forgive in some respects, but not in others. Thus when we describe an act as unforgivable, it might prove useful to unpack the many possible meanings behind this assertion because doing so could have serious personal and political ramifications. If I claim that someone's offense against me is unforgivable, this risks estranging us entirely and ending all attempts to work toward some imperfect relationship. If a student plagiarized in my course, I might fail her for that class and never allow her to take it again with me for credit. That possibility for our relationship, I might maintain, is over. Under certain circumstances, however, I might happily allow her to audit the course and I might take great value in discussing philosophy with her. In one sense I might find her actions unforgivable, but this does not necessarily entail that we cannot enter into an otherwise fulfilling relationship. If an offender describes her own acts as unforgivable – as Nazi architect Albert Speer claimed that "no apologies are possible" in his case – this may fundamentally structure her attitude toward her crime. Such an attitude might lead an offender to view reconciliation as futile and provide an excuse to resign from all remedial efforts.[28]

Viewing forgiveness in this way may clarify not only who or what is unforgivable but also who or what is forgivable. Philosophers from both Analytic and Continental traditions claim that forgiveness and mercy are only morally justifiable after the offender has apologized and repented. Levinas, for example, argues that no "person can forgive if forgiveness has not been asked of him by the offender, if the guilty party has not tried to appease the offended."[29] Aurel Kolnai claims that forgiveness without repentance can lead to complicity in the wrongdoing, Murphy worries that prematurely forgiving the unrepentant may bespeak servility and a lack of self-respect, and Novits warns that those who forgive too readily "underestimate their own worth and fail to take their projects and entitlements seriously enough."[30] My account of the meanings of apologies seems to complicate matters because we have seen that it can be misleading to judge in binary terms whether someone has apologized or not. It is more likely that they provide some kinds of apologetic meaning with some degree of intensity, and thus any claims that apologies are necessary conditions for forgiveness would need to argue for which sorts of meaning the apology must convey in order to justify forgiveness. Such an analysis would need to explain how the various kinds of apologetic meaning link up with the conditions for forgiveness. Contextual intricacies informing the interchange would further complicate considerations of the relationship between any particular apology and act of forgiveness.

Further questions arise when we ask whether apologies are not only necessary conditions for forgiveness but also sufficient conditions, raising the possibility that an apology from an offender creates a moral duty for the victim to forgive her.[31] Might, in other words, the victim *owe* the offender forgiveness if she apologizes properly? Can the offender justifiably demand for the victim to forgive her in such circumstances, as if the tables in the moral economy have turned and the victim must now discharge her debt to the offender by conferring forgiveness? Should we understand forgiveness as a gift or supererogatory act of forbearance rather than as a means of cashing in on the work of apologizing? We can also restate this in terms of when we should "accept" an apology and whether we should think of accepting an apology as synonymous with forgiveness. Before we can begin to respond to this issue, we face the recurring problem of what sort of apology creates conditions for what sort of forgiveness. Achieving conceptual tidiness in such an analysis seems like an onerous project, and cases of collective apology and collective forgiveness would surely compound the difficulty of such work.

Some attempt to sever the dialectic between apologies and forgiveness, arguing that forgiveness is most virtuous when granted freely and without regard to the offender's repentance. According to this view, the act of forgiveness bespeaks the moral fortitude of the victim who possesses the strength to overcome feelings of resentment and cravings for revenge. Bishop Butler and Martin Luther King, Jr. are often cited for this position, as both invoke the teachings cited earlier from the Gospels of Matthew and Christ's words from the cross: "Forgive them Father, for they know not what they do."[32] Although forgiveness without repentance might suggest condoning the offense or bespeak the victim's lack of self-respect, we can imagine how a desire to maintain moral purity, offer a magnanimous gift of mercy, or provide an example to others of a life of peace, forbearance, and freedom from resentment might motivate such a gesture. This speaks to differing opinions regarding whether forgiveness primarily serves the forgiver or the person being forgiven. For some, like Arendt, forgiveness constitutes an "affair in which *what* was done is forgiven for the sake of *who* did it."[33] This perspective may conceptualize forgiveness as a "gift of grace," given freely without expectation of return. For others, forgiveness advances one's own moral character, offers therapeutic benefits, or even provides physiological health benefits.[34] We need not rule on which orientation provides the true meaning of forgiveness but rather can evaluate each act with these possibilities in mind.

Thinking of forgiveness in this way also illuminates other questions. Can I forgive someone if I am indifferent to the offense?[35] Presumably such a gesture may have limited meaning for me, but the forgiven may take great meaning in expressing her belief that she has breached her own value and knowing that her actions did not alienate her from me. Likewise, can we forgive the dead? Such an act might offer profound value to the forgiver and the descendants of the forgiven without generating any meaning for the deceased. I might cancel a debt inherited by the children of the deceased without changing my sentiments toward what I continue to perceive as the wrongdoing of their parent. Can those who are on their deathbeds fully forgive their killers, as Mahatma Gandhi attempted? Such acts may convey some forms of meaning but not others. We will never know, for instance, what sort of relationship Gandhi and his assassin might have experienced or how Gandhi's feelings toward this deed would have evolved. In this sense the meanings of forgiveness, like the meaning of apologies, can be judged over lifetimes. This would be relevant not only in deathbed cases but to all acts of forgiveness. We could imagine those who once claimed to have forgiven relapsing into resentment and disdain or those who once viewed a harm as unforgivable overcoming their previous barriers to certain kinds of forgiveness. Can I forgive myself? Arendt thinks not; Julia Kristeva thinks so.[36] Again, this would mirror the possibilities of apologizing to myself in that it might make sense to speak of forgiving myself in some senses but not others. I may, for example, no longer experience self-loathing for previous mistakes, but it seems awkward to speak of restoring a relationship with a self from twenty years ago. These questions become even more difficult when considering the intricacies of collective and institutional forgiveness, and I expect that we can map many of the discussions of collective apologies in subsequent chapters onto problems of standing and collective forgiveness. As Levinas has advised: "No one, not even God, can substitute himself for the victim."[37]

Such concerns present us with one question regarding the meaning of apologies that I have not yet considered: how does forgiveness or acceptance of an apology change the meaning of that apology? Regardless of the content or sincerity of an apology, its reception surely alters its meaning. I referred to this earlier as a kind of dialectical or "feedback" meaning. Victims might reject even the most thorough apologies, and this would have serious consequences for an apology's meaning. If a victim of my actions refuses to hear my words of apology or returns my attempts at restitution, some potential meaning will go unrealized. We will probably not enjoy, for instance, the renewal of our friendly relationship. Thus while my apology may provide transformative meaning for me, it may fall on deaf ears in a manner similar to an apology to the deceased. A victim's refusal to forgive may also amplify certain forms of meaning for me, such as my regret. A rebuff may also affirm the sanctity or inviolability of the breached value for the victim. By contrast, a victim has the ability to extend and compound its meaning if she gratefully receives the apology. If an apology results in a form of forgiveness that saves a marriage, we can view its meaning as extending indefinitely through the relationship. As we find with apologies, responses to acts of forgiveness may seem unclear: our interlocutor may reply with a counter-apology, an expression of counter-forgiveness, a gesture of thanks, or some series of moves to diffuse the awkwardness common in such exchanges. This underscores how many of the meanings of both apologies and forgiveness bear significance for the offender as well as the victim.

CHAPTER SEVEN

Varieties of Apologies

As the preceding discussions suggest, apologies can seem like confounding social exchanges. The considerable variability of apologies across time and cultures can further complicate matters. As I understand apologies, we can think of them as presenting a loose constellation of interrelated meanings. Having isolated and scrutinized the prominent stars in this constellation, we may find it useful to reconfigure them into a more intelligible horizon of meaning. I now suggest grouping a few different arrangements of apologetic meanings into more easily identifiable varieties. If I have been deconstructing the meanings of apologies, we might think of what follows as my attempt at a bit of reconstruction.

On my account, apologies present a potentially infinite variety of particular meanings. Classifying each variation would not be possible. Instead, I name a few of the more commonly occurring varieties in the hope of synthesizing some of the considerations previously discussed into a more manageable nomenclature. I hope that these terms will prove helpful and this convenience warrants the simplifications required.

The Categorical Apology

We can begin with the Categorical Apology, which I consider the most robust, painstaking, and formal of the varieties. We can understand a categorical apology as conveying certain kinds of prescriptively stipulated meanings. With the requisite disclaimers and without attending to all of the possible nuances distinguishing between particular categorical apologies, I suggest the following general outlines:

1. Corroborated Factual Record: A categorical apology will corroborate a detailed factual record of the events salient to the injury, reaching agreement among the victim, offender, and sometimes the community regarding what transpired. The parties will also agree regarding what amounts to such salient events, leading them to share an understanding of the relevant aspects of the context in which the injury occurs. Rather

than providing general and vague descriptions of the events ("I acted badly"), the record will render transparent all facts material to judging the transgressions. Such a record will often include honest accounts of the mental states of the apologizer at the time of the offense when such information would prove relevant, for example by describing the offender's intentions when committing the transgression.

2. Acceptance of Blame: In accordance with notions of proximate causation, the offender accepts causal moral responsibility and blame for the harm at issue. We can distinguish this from expressing sympathy for the injury or describing the injury as accidental or unintentional.

3. Possession of Appropriate Standing: The categorical apologizer will possess the requisite standing to accept blame for the wrongdoing. The offender can and does accept proximate responsibility for the harm and she – rather than a proxy or other third party – undertakes the work of apologizing described herein.

4. Identification of Each Harm: The offender will identify each harm, taking care not to conflate several harms into one general harm or apologize for only a lesser offense or the "wrong wrong."

5. Identification of the Moral Principles Underlying Each Harm: The offender will identify the moral principles underlying these harms with an appropriate degree of specificity, thus making explicit the values at stake in the interaction.

6. Shared Commitment to Moral Principles Underlying Each Harm: The offender will commit to the moral principles underlying these harms (again with an appropriate degree of specificity), vindicating the value at issue and finding the victim's offense at the apologizer's breach of this value justified. Here the phrase "I was wrong" will better convey this meaning than the traditionally favored "I am sorry," as the former accepts personal blame for wrongdoing while the latter may provide no more than an expression of sympathy or a displeasure with a state of affairs.

7. Recognition of Victim as Moral Interlocutor: Through this process the offender comes to recognize and treat the victim as a moral interlocutor. With this, the offender treats the victim as a moral agent worthy of engaging in moral discourse and abandons the belief that she can disregard the victim's dignity, humanity, or worth in pursuit of her own objectives.

8. Categorical Regret: The offender categorically regrets the actions in question, meaning she believes that she has made a mistake that she wishes could be undone. We can distinguish this from continuing to endorse one's decisions but expressing sympathy regarding what the offender perceives as the justifiable consequences of her actions.

9. Performance of the Apology: The offender expresses the apology to the victim rather than keeping her thoughts of contrition to herself or

sharing them only with a third party such as a judge or member of the clergy. She addresses the apology to the victim as a moral interlocutor. She expresses the content required of a categorical apology explicitly. The apology reaches the victim. The victim may exercise reasonable discretion regarding whether the offender must present the apology only to the victim or also to a broader community. The determination whether the apology must be committed to writing and conferred to her also lies within the victim's reasonable discretion.

10. Reform and Redress: The apologizer will reform and forbear from reoffending over her lifetime and will repeatedly demonstrate this commitment by resisting opportunities and temptations to reoffend. Thus a categorical apology allows the victim to isolate the cause of her suffering, apportion blame for her injury, and take some security in the offender's pledge never to repeat the offense. The apologizer accepts sanctions for her wrongs, though she may protest penalties that she finds unjustifiable or disproportionate to her offense. The offender takes practical responsibility for the harm she causes, providing commensurate remedies and other incommensurable forms of redress to the best of her ability. The offender provides a proportional amount of redress, but she need not meet excessive demands from victims with unreasonable or inappropriate expectations. I leave questions regarding what constitutes unreasonable or excessive demands to be determined in consideration of cultural practices, and I appreciate that such deliberations will often be contentious.

11. Intentions for Apologizing: The categorical apology also requires certain mental states. Rather than promoting the apologizer's purely self-serving objectives, the offender intends the apology to advance the victim's well-being and affirm the breached value.

12. Emotions: As a result of her wrongdoing, the apologizer will experience an appropriate degree and duration of sorrow and guilt as well as empathy and sympathy for the victim. I leave further questions regarding what constitutes the appropriate qualitative and quantitative emotional components of categorical apologies to be determined in consideration of cultural practices and individual expectations.

I offer this as a kind of benchmark for apologetic meaning. I could have adjusted the standards up or down, but I find that these criteria capture what we might think of in Iris Murdoch's terms as a "highest manifestation" of the practice as opposed to a "lowest common denominator" between anything that might arguably be classified as an apology.[1] Conceived as such, categorical apologies are demanding ethical acts indicating a kind of transformation that resonates with thick conceptions of repentance within religious traditions. We should recognize when apologies fall short of this standard and pursue their full meaning or understand them as less than categorical. This is not to say that all apologies must be categorical or that all noncategorical apologies are meaningless. As we have seen throughout, there are many kinds of apologetic meaning. The categorical apology offers but one possible arrangement of such meanings.

In one sense, where we set the standard for categorical apologies is less important than simply having a standard. With a standard in place, we can measure particular examples against it. Not all injuries call for categorical apologies, and we can seek more or less apologetic meaning depending on the circumstances. The elements of categorical apologies involve multiple and sometimes discrete meanings, and occasionally we will be interested in only or primarily one of the meanings. If someone steps on my toe, I may be satisfied with any expression that simply conveys that the harm was not intentional. If someone dents my car, I may seek little more than a fulfilled promise to pay for repairs. This also applies to culturally divergent conceptions of apologies. Some groups emphasize different aspects of apologies, for instance deeming an apology satisfactory even if the offender feigns remorse or does not accept fault for the harm. I am not primarily concerned whether such interactions should be properly understood as an apology or some translation of the term, but I do wish to decipher how such statements convey meaning or omit certain potentially significant content. I hope that such a fine-grained conception of apologies helps us to make sense of the range of possible meaning that a categorical apology can convey. We can then better compare the apologies we receive with the apologetic meaning we desire.

Recall the example of Pope Benedict XVI's statements after his controversial address at the University of Regensburg. Many interpreted his statements as disparaging to Islam and vowed to continue a campaign of violence against Christians until he apologized. The Vatican and the Pope offered statements akin to apologies. Some were satisfied with these apologies. Others were not. Some who were at one point satisfied changed their minds, deciding that the Pope's statements were not a proper apology. Potentially useful questions went unasked: What sort of apology did those offended seek? Were the offended of one mind about the kind of apology they desired? What sort of apology did the Pope offer? Did the Pope provide too little of an apology, or did Muslim leaders ask for too much? Confusion fed the violence. A dialogue might have unfolded more productively if any of the parties could have pointed to some standard for apologies. The relevant players might then clarify events, attribute blame, debate or affirm values, or recommend changes. Perhaps the Pope would have refused to provide a categorical apology because he did not believe he had morally erred. Perhaps certain Muslim leaders would have requested something other than a categorical apology. Perhaps some would not have been satisfied until the Pope converted to Islam. Until they speak a common language of apologies, however, the conversation may never move beyond the juvenile exchange of one party saying "I'm sorry" and the other claiming "No you're not." However imprecise, this prescriptively stipulated notion of a categorical apology at least provides a common language in which to hold such discussions.

Having said this, we can make a few further observations about categorical apologies. Given their rigor, categorical apologies may prove most suitable in formal contexts or in response to serious harms. Parties can make adjustments to produce a better fit with informal interactions, and individuals are always able to tailor the standards to suit their objectives. The previous description of categorical apologies leaves open many questions raised earlier. Note, for instance, three such questions: How much emotion is required, what is the necessary intensity and duration of those emotions, and how might we measure such quantities? Just as I do not provide restitution schedules for every possible sort of injury, I leave parties to negotiate such potentially intractable questions in accordance with their customs and sensibilities. Also notice that we could not categorically apologize for an accident unless we could consistently accept blame for the harm. Disagreements about the worth of the underlying breached value also block categorical apologies. Unless we consider them moral interlocutors, we cannot categorically apologize to children, animals, or inanimate objects. For the reasons discussed earlier, the death of the victim or the offender forecloses the possibility of a categorical apology in all but the most exceptional cases. Deathbed apologies will likely prevent the offender from demonstrating reform or completing redress.

Because forbearance, reform, and redress present an ongoing task for the offender, we cannot conclusively measure her contrition against the standard of the categorical apology at the moment she offers it but rather will judge it over the course of her lifetime. This presents something of a problem in that we cannot immediately declare a gesture or ceremony to have "categorically apologized" because so much work remains. We can consider apologies at this declarative stage as a kind of promise. A categorical apology keeps its promises, and therefore we might describe the gesture before the offender has completed reform and redress as a "promissory categorical apology." If the offender breaks her promise to reform and provide redress over her lifetime, her gesture would not rise to the level of a categorical apology. Because categorical apologies are usually works in progress, in the strict sense we should refer to even the most exemplary apologies between the living as promissory categorical apologies. Some may find this inability to definitively judge an apology at the moment it is offered to be a nuisance. Although we may desire instant and conclusive gratification from a gesture of contrition, categorical apologies require patience from both the offender and the victim. We should meet urges to prematurely judge apologies with suspicion and scrutinize the motivations behind such haste. We should be especially wary of offenders who attempt to simplify the exchange so that they can "put it behind them."

In addition, although promissory categorical apologies may increase the likelihood of victims responding with certain forms of forgiveness (remembering that forgiveness also comes in numerous forms), receiving such an apology does not necessarily require the victim to forgive the offender. According to Maimonides, however, it seems that an observant Jew who received even a promissory categorical apology corroborated by acts of forbearance should forgive the offender. Some Christians hold similar beliefs.

Parties could agree to depart from the standards provided by the categorical apology, adjusting the apologetic meaning they seek to their situation and desires. Indeed, we might worry that a gesture that followed my script for a categorical apology might appear too rehearsed. If an offender appears to provide a paint-by-numbers apology, we might question her intentions and the depth of her understanding of the gesture she enacts. In some cases, diverging from the script could prove especially important. If an offender has extreme difficulties expressing emotions, for example, the victim might appreciate this idiosyncrasy and be entirely satisfied with something other than a categorical apology. Again, the point is not that every expression of apologetic meaning must satisfy the elements of a categorical apology. Nor do I mean to make the best the enemy of the good or imply that "imperfect" apologies are necessarily flawed in some way. Instead, we should interpret the categorical apology as providing a touchstone against which we can interpret and compare all apologetic expressions.

The Ambiguous Apology

Some noncategorical apologies will provide clear and significant meaning; others might seem like utter nonsense. I will classify a few additional kinds of noncategorical apologies for ease of reference. We can name what seems to be the most commonly occurring form the Ambiguous Apology. Here I have in mind isolated statements like "I apologize," "I am sorry," or various abbreviated versions of these. In these cases the meaning of the apology may remain almost entirely inscrutable for the victim – she simply does not know what the speaker means by her words. Imagine that the Pope had issued a three-word statement sometime after the Regensburg address: "I am sorry." He leaves us to guess at the meaning. Is he admitting wrongdoing? If so, for what exactly? And why is that wrong? Is he even referring to the disputed passages? Perhaps he apologizes only for what he perceives as a poor translation of his address and continues to endorse his assertions. Is he "sorry" that his remarks – which he continues to find justified – have been misinterpreted by people he views as illiterate zealots, thus rendering his statement akin to an insult of the form "I am sorry that they are so ignorant and violent"? Does he plan to refrain from making similar statements in the future, and does he intend to redress the situation? We would not know the answers to these and numerous other questions bearing on the meaning of his words. Occasionally we face extensive ambiguities such as these, but often only a few of these sorts of unanswered questions suffice to render the meaning of the apology indeterminate on central issues. I offer scores of examples of this sort throughout the book. As I consider later, ambiguous apologies have their place. Political leadership, for example, may occasionally require ambiguity in apologies as a tactful means of forging consensus or mobilizing citizens without alienating the ambivalent. Once we recognize their ambiguity, however, their value is likely to decline.

The Expression of Sympathy

Next we can describe what we might call an Expression of Sympathy, distinguishing between an Expression of Sympathy without Causal Moral Responsibility and an Expression of Sympathy with Justification. An expression of sympathy of either type admits no wrongdoing, but instead offers condolences or sympathy. Notice that I do not describe this as a "sympathy apology" because I hope to discourage the conflation of sympathy, causal responsibility, and blameworthiness discussed at length earlier.

Expressions of sympathy without causal moral responsibility, like "I am sorry to hear that your grandmother passed away," offer condolences without suggesting that the speaker bears any causal moral responsibility for the harm. The speaker does not admit causing the harm at issue. Other examples of this sort express sympathy for accidental injuries involving the speakers, for instance if two people are involved in a faultless car accident and wish to console each other for their injuries. Such an example demonstrates the need to distinguish between a claim that I caused damage by *accidentally* crashing into you and one that accepts causal moral responsibility for the damage by indicating that I deserve *blame* for the event. In addition to expressing sympathy, the words "I am sorry" in such a situation may also serve the important function of explaining to the injured party that I did not intend to harm her.

Expressions of sympathy with justification convey sympathy to the victim and take some causal responsibility for that harm but maintain they were justified in doing so. Think here of a judge explaining that she is sorry for having to incarcerate a parent despite her continued belief that the convict deserves the sentence: The judge takes some responsibility for the decision to incarcerate and continues to stand by the decision but offers sympathy to the convict as a recognition of her humanity and misfortune. Given its ambiguity with respect to whether the speaker believes her actions are justified, notice how we might understand a statement like "I am so sorry that my actions caused you such pain" as an expression of sympathy with justification.

Expressions of sympathy of either sort can be prospective or retrospective. I might express my sympathy for what I am about to do to you ("I am sorry that I am about to bump your car accidentally but I cannot stop" or "I am sorry I must sentence you to this penalty") or what I have already done to you ("I am sorry for having bumped into you accidentally" or "I am sorry that I dropped an atomic bomb on your country but it was the best available option"). Neither kind of expression of sympathy necessarily commits the speaker to any redress or reform. I might offer a grieving grandchild gifts of mourning such as flowers and the judge might send the convict away with a few of her favorite books to help her pass the time productively, but we ordinarily think of such gestures as a kind of gift rather than a form of compensation. We do not consider a debt owed. Likewise, I have no reason to reform if I have done nothing wrong. For this reason, we should take little security from either kind of expression of sympathy. In the case of categorical apologies, we know that the offender caused our injury and has committed to forbear from reoffending. We can then identify the cause of our suffering and have some assurance that the offender will not do it again. If I am sorry that your grandmother passed away, her killer may still be at large. If I only sympathize with you after bombing your country, I do not commit myself to not repeating the act. An expression of sympathy alone offers little justification for restoring trust between the victim and offender if it has been breached.

We should also note that the different kinds of expressions of sympathy actually do require the apologizer to experience some sympathy for the harmed person. Even if I believe that your injury is not my fault or that your suffering is justified (as in the example of the sentencing judge), I offer my compassion and assistance. I previously noted the potential difficulties of testing for sympathy in others or even identifying its presence within oneself, and I purposely avoid indicating "how much" sympathy would suffice in these cases. Instead, I want to emphasize the presence of a degree of some emotion akin to sympathy as a distinctive feature of this sort of exchange.

A subclass of Minor Expressions of Sympathy may be useful to describe a very common gesture. Here I have in mind informal expressions uttered when causing someone an inconsequential harm or inconvenience, for example by saying "sorry" when brushing against someone in a crowded restaurant or arriving a few moments late for a meeting. Such gestures casually acknowledge another's presence, convey to her my recognition that I may cause her annoyance, and indicate that I do not intend to harm her. Minor expressions of sympathy are often quite ambiguous. If the person I bump was standing in the aisles or otherwise being inconsiderate of passersby, I may still express minor sympathy but to some extent blame the contact on her. Much of the content of such gestures will be implicit, and intonation can be revealing. I might believe that the minor harm I cause is justified, for instance if I am a doctor and offer a few "sorrys" when administering a slightly uncomfortable vaccination shot. The difference between minor and major expressions of sympathy is primarily a matter of degree and formality, and there is no clear boundary between them. Thus a doctor might offer a minor expression of sympathy for a vaccination shot, but a more solemn and ceremonial expression of sympathy if she must amputate a patient's limb. In the same respect, a quick "sorry about that" without further condolence and emotional resonance would seem like a callous response when learning that a friend's relative has died.

The Value-Declaring Apology

The Value-Declaring Apology primarily serves to announce the values of the speaker (or denounce the acts of others) and to commit her to honoring those principles. The apologizer does not accept personal blame for the past wrongdoing but instead proclaims that actions committed by others were somehow wrong and vows not to commit similar offenses. Recall the Internet petition where Australians can "apologize" for the government's forcible removal of aboriginal people. The signatories were encouraged to think that this apology says: "This should not have happened; this should never happen again." "It doesn't," they advise, "say 'I was there and let it happen; I am guilty.'"[2] In other words, the apology states a position on the past actions of others and an opinion about the preferred direction of future policy. I could say "this should not have happened; this should never happen again" about any action I disagree with, including those from the distant past for which I obviously cannot be blamed. In instances such as the Pope's apology for the Crusades, a declarative apology serves the important functions of confronting the Church's history, recognizing its past failures, and pledging never to commit those same mistakes even if questions of standing prove intractable.

Difficult questions may arise regarding whether those issuing a declarative apology should indeed accept blame for the transgression at issue. Clinton's actions during the Rwandan genocide and his subsequent statements discussed earlier come to mind here. Occasionally those accused of wrongdoing may refuse to admit their own guilt but still wish to affirm the value they allegedly breached. A value-declaring apology may serve an important role in such situations while parties debate accountability. In this sense, I could promise not to do something in the future without admitting that I accept blame for doing it in the past. Although not understood as compensation for harms committed by the benefactor, a party may provide various sorts of redress to accompany her declarative apology in order to provide support for the value endorsed or combat the wrong denounced. Any number of emotions may accompany declarative apologies and they may share characteristics with expressions of sympathy without blame. I should emphasize that the value-declaring apology, like the categorical apology, promises to forbear from committing the offense in question and we can evaluate it accordingly.

The Conciliatory Apology

In the Conciliatory Apology, parties continue to disagree about an underlying value but the apologizer makes gestures to regain the goodwill of the person she disagrees with. I may vociferously argue with a colleague about her political beliefs, and our exchange might become uncomfortably intense. For a time it may be unclear if our relationship has been damaged by the exchange. A conciliatory apology would allow me to express my appreciation for our relationship without relinquishing my beliefs about the value in question. We establish that our relationship does not require us to share this value. We agree to disagree and my gestures diffuse lingering animosity. A conciliatory apology might also serve an important function as interlocutors find themselves in the midst of working through the consequences of injuries and disagreements.

We should take care to distinguish conciliatory apologies from categorical apologies for breaches of values related to how we speak to each other. If I crossed a moral boundary while arguing about politics with my colleague, for example by raising my voice or insulting her, I could categorically apologize for those failures while continuing to hold my political views. In my experience, we often fail to appreciate this subtlety and instead offer only conciliatory gestures when perhaps we should accept blame for our breaches of conversational norms.

The Compensatory Apology

The Compensatory Apology accepts no causal responsibility, admits no wrongdoing, and expresses no opinion regarding the underlying value. It does, however, disburse goods to the injured party. Apologetic language may accompany such exchanges, but it will typically commit to little more than expressing sympathy. We find quintessential examples in settlement agreements that provide injured parties with cash sums while admitting no wrongdoing and otherwise remaining silent or even barring the parties from speaking further about the issues or disclosing the terms of the settlement. Compensatory apologies often appear as ambiguous apologies plus some redistribution of resources. I hesitate to describe these as compensatory apologies rather something like "resource-conferring apologies" because the party conferring the resources may not describe such funds as a direct response to the injury. Indeed, the paying party may take measures to create the appearance that the injury and award are unrelated: she may contend that she does not *owe* the injured party anything but instead describe the conveyance of resources as a gesture of goodwill or a means of dispensing with what she perceives as a meritless legal claim against her.

The Purely Instrumental Apology

The Purely Instrumental Apology views apologetic meaning strictly as a means to the apologizer's ends. By outward appearances, the purely instrumental apology can provide all of the meanings of categorical apologies. The instrumental apologizer, however, understands her apology merely as a means of manipulating social conventions to her advantage and thus the apologizer's intentions provide the distinguishing feature of purely instrumental apologies. Depending on what the victim requires from an apology, the instrumental apologizer will comport herself accordingly to achieve her objectives. She may maintain the appearance of honoring the underlying values, feign concern for the well-being of the injured, or stage emotional displays. Purely instrumental apologizers need not be moral skeptics or sociopaths, as they might be capable of detaching their personal values from those required in a given context or as they occupy an institutional role.

We might understand Agamemnon's apology to Achilles as an instrumental apology. Agamemnon tellingly describes the gifts he will offer as a "ransom" while initially strategizing with his counselors and he seems to offer these gestures only in order to return Achilles to the battlefield. He does not consider himself responsible for the offense because the gods controlled his will, we remain uncertain about his position on the underlying value, and he seems to construct his apology to offer just enough meaning to Achilles.[3] Homer even appears to have some fun with Agamemnon in this respect. At this stage in the narrative, Achilles only wants to immediately spring into battle to avenge the death of Patroclus – so much so that he wishes to forgo even a meal before fighting – but Agamemnon's apology rambles on about the power of the gods who deceived him. Agamemnon may have achieved the objective toward which his instrumental apology aimed more quickly without his address wasting the warrior's time.

The Coerced Apology

Without attending to the many debates within moral philosophy regarding the notion of coercion, the Coerced Apology mirrors the purely instrumental apology but another party with power over the would-be apologizer dictates the objectives of the apology and threatens to harm her seriously if she does not comply.[4] The state, parents of minor children, and violent agents are typically thought to possess such authority. A judge might require a convict to apologize to her victim or she will add years to her sentence. A parent might demand that her child apologize or else suffer corporal punishment. During the time of the Cultural Revolution, Maoists demanded expressions of regret from those straying from approved doctrines. In many cases coerced apologies will serve as a kind of punishment, though we may often question the legitimacy of such measures. The alleged offender may simply do as she is told and go through the motions of apologizing until she satisfies the person or institution threatening her.

If an estranged spouse threatens to kill her former husband unless he apologizes, the case for describing an ensuing apology as coerced would seem clear if he apologizes only to save his life. Other cases will be less obvious. What if my wife threatens to divorce me if I do not apologize? What if she merely threatens to be very angry with me? What if the consequences are unclear, as in the previously discussed case of Veronica Berlusconi? The risk of unpleasant consequences for not apologizing does not seem sufficient to describe a subsequent apology as coerced. What if opposing counsel claims that she will reduce the amount I must pay in a personal injury settlement agreement by millions of dollars if I apologize? Could such an offer, as opposed to a threat, be coercive?[5] Rather than offer a systematic theory of coercion here, we can think of coerced apologies as those offered in circumstances where a threat or offer significantly compromises someone's ability to choose not to apologize. An ultimatum from someone with power over her, rather than the apologizer's recognition of her blameworthiness or desire to increase the well-being of the victim, drives her decision to apologize. This would not include cases where the alleged offender risks only disapproval from others who wish for her to apologize but who lack the desire or ability to cause her serious harm. Otherwise, we might view all disagreements as potentially coercive for apologizers.

Although we typically void contracts entered into under coercive conditions and discount coerced confessions, coerced apologies may provide various forms of meaning even if only to demonstrate the power of the coercing parties or their commitment to the breached value. Coerced apologies can also provide the vehicle for the authority to establish a version of the record, assign blame, identify harms, affirm values, acknowledge victims as worthy of moral recognition, create a spectacle of apologetic performance, and ensure reform and redress (perhaps through incapacitation or forced labor programs). They can also serve punitive, retributive, vengeful, or humiliating ends, for example by requiring the accused to publicly renounce her deepest value or accept blame for a crime of which she is innocent.

The Proxy Apology

In the Proxy Apology, an individual or group apologizes for the wrongdoing of others. The proxy may personally be entirely detached from the injury, the offender, the victim, and the values at work in the apology. The proxy claims to have some authority to represent the responsible parties. The clearest examples of proxy apologies are those offered by attorneys on behalf of their clients or by private firms – such as the Tianjin Apology and Gift Center – that will provide "emissaries of regret" to apologize for those unable or unwilling to apologize themselves.[6] Apologies via proxy can provide a wide range of apologetic meanings, as they face many of the complexities discussed with regard to apologies generally. Proxy apologies, however, cannot be categorical because of their failure to satisfy requirements of standing. I consider these issues in detail with respect to collective apologies in the following chapters.

The preceding discussions of the vast range of apologetic meanings, some of which point in opposite directions, can render the subject so tangled that we may feel lost among the possibilities. The previous classifications mark but a few of an infinite variety of possible paths through apologetic meaning, and even these suggestions intersect in ways that make them increasingly difficult to discern. I hope these signposts will prove to be useful markers pointing toward the diverse kinds of meaning we may seek from any particular apology in our private and public lives. If we desire assurance that the offender will refrain from reoffending, a mere expression of sympathy will probably not suffice. A promise to refrain from reoffending will not be enough if we want the offender to pay for the damage she caused. If we seek an ethically rich gesture of contrition, I hope that my notion of the categorical apology provides a reliable guide. After pausing at this vantage point to survey the ever-shifting terrain of apologetic meaning and identify some landmarks that may help guide us, we now head into the thicket of collective apologies.

PART TWO

Collective Apologies

CHAPTER EIGHT

The Collective Categorical Apology

I should warn readers who would prefer an account that treated apologies as a black and white matter that collective apologies only lay on a few more coats of gray. Corporations, governments, religions, sports teams, families, and various collections of people issue what they describe as "apologies."[1] Whereas most of the preceding arguments concerned apologies from individuals to individuals, we also find apologies from individuals to collectives, collectives to individuals, and collectives to collectives. Each variety presents distinct issues for consideration. From the outset, I want to make clear that I do not doubt that groups of people can categorically apologize. I do believe, however, that collective categorical apologies are even more uncommon than individual categorical apologies.

We can begin by considering a relatively simple case. Recall the previous example of my failure to meet a friend for dinner because I decided at the last moment that I preferred to see a film. Now suppose that I was not alone in this transgression but that my wife and I jointly decided that we would leave our friend waiting. We later come to regret our decision and realize that we should apologize to her. We can individually satisfy each element of a categorical apology and issue it as a collective, perhaps by collaboratively drafting a letter that we both sign and discuss with our friend. Yet in order to issue a categorical apology together we must *individually* satisfy each required element, agreeing on the factual record, admitting shared culpability, identifying and committing to the same moral principles, finding the victim's suffering legitimate and proportionate, expressing categorical regret, undergoing parallel reform, providing commensurate redress, and so on. This presumes that we have identical standing and are in perfect agreement about all salient aspects of the apology. We might fashion the shared apology to account for some differences in our culpability. If I was primarily responsible for the initial decision but my spouse compounded the offense by lying about our excuse for missing dinner, our collective apology could reflect this. We would apologize for different harms, but because of their interrelation we address them together. Although such a joint apology might be a complex matter requiring substantial discussion, it seems possible in principle for us to apologize categorically together.

We can also notice how easily we might drain such a collective apology of much of its meaning. If I continue to believe that we made the correct choice in avoiding the dinner because I wanted to exact retribution against the friend for the time she left me waiting at the train station, any apology that my wife would give on "our" behalf would lack a considerable portion of its possible meaning. If my wife goes to great lengths to repair the relationship with her friend while I flaunt my refusal to reform, this would render the status of our apology as genuinely collective increasingly suspect. If my wife insisted to her friend that "we apologized," the friend would be justified to correct her and explain that I did not seem apologetic at all.

In the case of two people, we should wonder why we would bother issuing a collective categorical apology rather than each of us apologizing for ourselves. We might think that expediency would drive us to apologize together and such concerns regarding economy of scale would become increasingly relevant as the contrite group becomes larger, but properly coordinating our apologies seems to generate more work than it saves. A shared commitment to apologizing provides various additional potential meanings considered later – for instance renewing the marital bond on the relevant value in this case – but I suspect that individuals often opt for collective apologies as a spurious substitute for individual categorical apologies. The following chapters examine that suspicion.

I could imagine a medium-sized group – such as the twelve faculty members of the philosophy department to which I belong – undertaking the process of apologizing collectively. Imagine that we wronged our students by failing to address their concerns about gender inequalities in the department and we then realized that we were all insensitive to their legitimate complaints. We could work together to draft a formal statement precisely articulating our mistakes. If we each met the required elements of a categorical apology, memorialized these commitments in a letter signed by each of us, and follow through with the promised reforms and reparations, then our students will have received a collective categorical apology from us. The practicalities might present serious difficulties, but in theory this possibility of a categorical apology from a collective seems fairly unproblematic. In this case, good reasons support apologizing collectively rather than individually. Our solidarity expresses unity in our opinions and intentions to undertake personal as well as institutional transformation.

Matters become much more complicated as the group asserting an apology increases in size, represents a wide range of responsibilities for the harm, or stretches over generations. Can Germany categorically apologize for the Holocaust, Japan for the "Rape of Nanking," the United States for slavery, or the Catholic Church for the Crusades? How might "the international community," in Bill Clinton's terms, apologize for the Rwandan genocide? Could a defunct corporation like Enron categorically apologize for its misdeeds? Would it make much sense to speak of men, as a collective, apologizing to women for the historical and contemporary harms resulting from patriarchy?

Readers will anticipate the daunting range of issues that these questions present. Who performs the apology for a group, and what authorizes them to do so? What should we make of a collective apology if significant factions within the group refuse to apologize or undermine the meaning of the apology, for instance by disseminating competing accounts of the historical record or continuing to engage in the denounced activity? Can we attribute blame to collectives as such? Does assigning culpability to the collective diminish the personal accountability of individuals within the group? Events like the Crusades and African slavery defined periods of history and their legacies continue to structure modern life. It seems difficult, therefore, to imagine a single apology addressing the multitude of wrongs committed within these campaigns with adequate specificity. Further, how might we understand collectives to experience apologetic emotions or intentions? Who undergoes reform? Who takes practical and economic responsibility for the damage? Collective apologies from large groups often address similarly sized groups of victims, for instance entire racial groups, economic classes, or nations. Do collective apologies recognize each victim as a moral interlocutor, or only the moral standing of the group as some sort of abstraction? Victims in these situations may have died long ago, and those still living may hold divergent views regarding the possibility or desirability of forgiving the offenders. Can a collective apology lead to collective forgiveness? In light of the relation between secular apologies and religious conceptions of repentance, does extending the analogy to collectives strain it too far if corporate bodies have no soul or conscience? How do the institutional structures within a given group influence each of these questions?

These are obvious yet immensely complex issues. I suspect that most groups cannot clear the high bar for categorical apologies, yet these shortcomings often go unnoticed. Both offenders and victims have reasons to overlook obstacles confronting collective apologies, and noncategorical collective apologies may serve numerous valuable social functions. Although I appreciate the potential meanings of noncategorical apologies, I hope to draw attention to how many political, corporate, and other group declarations stretch the notion of apology so thin that it lacks most of the moral force characteristic of categorical apologies. I first consider the problem of consensus, which seems to trigger concerns at every stage of group apologies. I then work back through each of the previously discussed aspects of apologetic meaning and flag concerns specific to collective apologies.

Much of the subsequent analysis treats collective apologies with a healthy skepticism, but before proceeding I want to assure readers that I am not cynical about their importance. Instead, I raise these concerns so that we can identify the weaknesses of our current practices and invigorate them with the rich moral meaning I believe they can convey when considered more carefully.

CHAPTER NINE

The Problem of Consensus

Return to the example of twelve members of my philosophy department apologizing for our insensitivity to gender issues in our curriculum. I should emphasize that although we have had many discussions regarding gender in our curriculum, I intend this as a fictional example and do not mean to suggest that my colleagues would respond as I imagine in this hypothetical situation. My experiences as a departmental administrator, however, have offered some insight into the complexities of deliberation within even this small and, in many respects, homogenous group. It would make sense within this example for us to express contrition jointly if we all shared culpability, regret, a commitment to fix the problem, and a desire to apologize. If we reach a consensus on all relevant issues, then a collective apology seems appropriate. We could evaluate such an apology according to the considerations discussed throughout this book.

Alternatively, imagine if only four members of the department strongly feel that an apology is necessary. Each of the four has slightly different reasons for taking this position, but in the end they draft an apology that all four of them support. Suppose that two senior professors within the department openly refuse to apologize, one of whom supports his position by claiming that "there are no women philosophers worth reading" and we should not pander to "political correctness" by apologizing. This professor is the most prominent researcher among us. The other senior professor who refuses to apologize holds the department chair. Two others believe that the department is generally rather progressive on gender-related issues but think that we could try harder and therefore offering an apology seems like a good idea. Irritated by the strong statements from the two senior professors opposing an apology, they agree in principle to support an apology but only if they review and approve its language. I will include myself in that group. Another does not want to apologize because she believes that she, personally, is entirely conscientious about these issues. She believes all of the blame should fall on the two senior professors who she believes are sexists. Still another believes an apology is an empty gesture and we should stop wasting our time arguing about it. Instead, she insists that we should concentrate our efforts on reforming the department curriculum to address the concerns. One professor sees merit in each of the positions, even reluctantly suggesting that women may under-achieve in philosophy because of patriarchal social conditioning, and it is not clear whether she supports an apology. The untenured member of the department remains silent, fearing that aligning herself with one of these positions could offend her superiors and adversely affect her prospects for promotion. We have many conversations about the issues, some in depart-mental meetings and others less formally.

Frustrated with the discussions, seeking to provide an immediate state-ment, and without any official departmental vote on the issue, the four pub-lish the apology in the university newspaper "on behalf of the Department of Philosophy." The apology states:

The Department of Philosophy recognizes the injustices experienced by our female students and faculty members. We take responsibility for these wrongs and we now publicly apologize for failing to honor core principles of gender equity. Philosophy has historically been a "boy's club" and we have not done enough to prevent these patriarchal, sexist, and misogynist values from infecting our own curriculum, peda-gogy, and environment. We are committed to rectifying these moral failures.

The four authors struggled with the language in the apology, but after sev-eral drafts they found that they could all agree to this general statement. The two others who agreed to the apology in principle expressed dismay that the four did not wait for a departmental vote or allow them to contribute to the process of drafting the apology. Yet as the issues further polarized the department, these two generally and passively appeared to support the apology and its authors. After the statement was published, little happened. Some in the department continued to plug away at attempts to address the issues, but with every step forward they took a step back given the lack of consensus and collective will. The dean denied funding for our most promis-ing initiative. Unrelated projects increasingly occupied us: Some of us shifted our attention to our children, others were on sabbatical working on books, and a few devoted considerable energy to initiatives supporting racial diver-sity on campus. Within a year, two of the original drafters left the department for more prestigious positions at other universities. Both senior professors resisting the apology retired within five years.

Given all of this, what would such an apology mean? Before we go any further, notice just how much dialogue would be necessary to achieve a clear sense of where each member of the collective stood with respect to the apol-ogy. The majority of those reading the statement in the newspaper would not be aware of the internal divisions regarding the apology. Also set aside the numerous substantive ambiguities within the apology even if the department were to offer it with perfect consensus on all salient issues: for what precisely are we apologizing, how did the department fail, what will we do about it, and so on? Focus strictly on the very serious problems created by the lack of consensus. Anyone learning of the "Philosophy Department's apology" would require considerably more information before she could make sense of its meaning. Suppose a student does not learn of the struggle over this apology, infers consensus among the faculty, and decides to major in philosophy rather than Women's Studies because of our department's apparently progressive stance on gender. This would be terribly misleading, and she would be in for a surprise if we assigned one of the sexist professors as her advisor.

However unlikely, imagine that all of the deliberations leading to the printed apology also become public information and the record captures all the details that I provided in the preceding paragraphs. Even such a record would lack important information. We would not know, for example, what the drafters of the apology disagreed upon that led them to this language. Do they agree on the significance of "taking responsibility" for the wrong, or did they intentionally leave this ambiguous because some refused to accept blame and preferred to speak of "taking responsibility" in the sense of honoring a duty to address an injury that they did not cause? The views of at least two of the professors would remain inscrutable. Once the community reviewed the record, a debate might ensue regarding whether the department had apologized or not. If cast without reference to some prescriptively stipulated standard, I imagine that such an exchange would prove unsatisfying. Given what we know, all the information conveyed here would inflect the clearest possible understanding of the apology. Perhaps even this would be insufficient, and students might want to interview faculty members to learn more about their beliefs, principles, intentions, emotions, and so on. Perhaps we cannot evaluate the apology's significance until we judge the extent of the remedial activity undertaken by each professor. Taking all of this into consideration, we might have a clearer sense for what the apology is: It is a vague statement arguably accepting blame for unnamed gender-related harms occurring within the department that some of the faculty support, some resist for various opposing reasons, and that generally provides a tangle of meaning requiring a good bit of interpretation.

As convoluted as that example seemed, I am afraid matters only become more complex as we expand the size and interests of the collective. Consider what is often described as Clinton's apology for the Rwandan genocide. Clinton could apologize categorically for his own personal failures with respect to this atrocity, and we will consider this possibility next. Nevertheless, let us first examine the statement Clinton delivered on the Tarmac of the Kigali airport in March of 1998:

The international community, together with nations in Africa, must bear its share of responsibility for this tragedy, as well. We did not act quickly enough after the killing began. We should not have allowed the refugee camps to become safe havens for the killers. We did not immediately call these crimes by their rightful name: genocide. We cannot change the past. But we can and must do everything in our power to help you build a future without fear, and full of hope. . . . We owe to all the people in the world our best efforts to organize ourselves so that we can maximize the chances of preventing these events. And where they cannot be prevented, we can move more quickly to minimize the horror.[1]

Notice at the outset that Clinton speaks not for the United States, his administration, or himself but rather for the "international community," thus diluting culpability for the genocide and enlarging the collective to include everyone that might be considered within this very broad classification. Although much of the world finds the Rwandan genocide appalling, surely Clinton does not speak from a consensus of the entire international community. After considering the difficulties facing the twelve philosophers, we can appreciate the likelihood of reaching global consensus on culpability for such a geopolitical event. Even if Clinton limited his statement to representing the sentiments of the citizens of United States, he clearly does not speak from a mandate derived from a unanimous consensus of Americans. A substantial number of isolationists and political realists continue to argue that more rigorous American intervention would have been erroneous. Clinton does not speak, in any literal sense, for them. Surely the president speaks for the people in some institutional sense, but allowing this to override all of the respects in which our leaders do not represent our opinions, values, and commitments oversimplifies and misleads. Given that Clinton calculated his decision not to intervene in light of the events in Mogadishu and his domestic unpopularity at the time, we cannot even be certain that he categorically regrets the choices made. Would he act differently if he could turn back time? How intensively would he intervene? What would have been the appropriate actions? How will the future be different? We do not know even Clinton's personal answers to these questions, let alone the beliefs, values, and commitments of the "international community" as a whole. What is Belgium's position? What do the Hutus think of Clinton's statement? Did Clinton consult representatives from these groups before offering this gesture? Are any of these collectives of one mind on the issues?

I expect that this example is, unfortunately, utterly typical. Clinton waxes eloquent about the horrors suffered and expresses vague policy commitments to prevent future genocide. Media sources then characterize the ambiguous declaration as an apology and attribute this weak statement to a vast collective: The World Apologizes to the Rwandan Genocide Victims. Yet surely Tutsis have not received a categorical apology from the international community, the United States, or even Bill Clinton. Imagine if Tutsis – or any similarly persecuted group such as refugees from Darfur – took Clinton's words to mean that all Americans regretted our failures and then planned their future around an assurance that the United States would take every possible measure to prevent future genocide. This could be a grave misconception.

I do not mean to suggest that Clinton's words are meaningless. Even if he deflects blame away from the United States, he does recognize that the international community failed to classify the conflict as genocide and that this impeded relief efforts. Perhaps an American president publicly calling attention to this issue will trigger some reform in the application of international human rights law. In that sense we might think that Clinton offered a value-declarative apology, but we have some reason to remain skeptical that the United States and the international community will honor the stated values. I consider other aspects of Clinton's statement later, but here I wish to emphasize the difficulties presented by the fact that the collective he claims to represent has reached nothing like a consensus in support of his statements, even given their ambiguities.

A fictional example may help isolate issues related to consensus within a large-scale collective. Suppose a Democratic anti-war candidate won the 2008 U.S. presidential election by the narrowest of margins. As her first act as president, she states:

The United States apologizes to the people of Iraq for an unjust war. I cannot begin to catalogue the depth and breadth of our failures here because the previous administration hid many of the most morally repugnant actions from us. It will require considerable effort and political will to untangle the web of deception, wrongdoing, and incompetence. I can begin today by denouncing our actions as motivated by callous self-interest and executed with disregard for human life. Let there be no doubt: we are to blame for the unjustified devastation wrought by our actions. Our profound regret and our reflection on our core values as a democratic nation have transformed us. We hereby subject all U.S. officials to the jurisdictions of international criminal courts and we will cooperate with all fact-finding efforts undertaken by these courts. History will judge our war by the account given by these international bodies. We will accept all punishments determined just by these courts and we will complete all remedial efforts ordered by these courts. We understand that we cannot undo the damage we have caused. Nor can we give life to those who unjustly died at our hands. We will, however, immediately withdraw our troops and begin the long process of taking practical responsibility for the damage we have caused. We pledge never to make these mistakes again. For as long as we exist as a nation, all people of the world will judge the integrity of citizens and leaders of the United States by our faithfulness to these promises.

The statement sparks a firestorm of responses. Members of the Bush administration refuse to recognize the apology and issue statements defending the moral justifications for the war. Former President G. W. Bush reasserts his belief that history will understand the war as "the great and noble liberation of the Iraqi people from an evil dictator." Politicians from the slight Republican minority adamantly protest the apology, reiterating Bush's description of the war. Some Democrats who voted for the new president believe her apology went too far – just as some who voted for Bush came to believe he overreached – and polls show that less than half of the country supports the apology.

In such a case we can appreciate how distorting it could be to claim without qualification that "the United States apologizes to Iraq." Although the president's statement would become a landmark in the history of collective apologies, an Iraqi would want to appreciate the political fragility of its sentiments and commitments. Even this strongly worded apology leaves numerous substantive ambiguities. Which international courts will she grant jurisdiction? Does the president have authority to subject officials to these tribunals retroactively? Which offenses do the apology address? Does she intend to include the Gulf War, the subsequent sanctions against Iraq, all of the prewar affronts against the United Nations and the international community, and any wrongdoing that may occur during the withdrawal and thereafter? What are our "core values as a democratic nation"? Precisely which mistakes will we never make again? How far up and down the chain of command will she allow the courts to trace causal responsibility? Might the tribunals prosecute individual soldiers?

We could continue to ask such clarifying questions, but focus for a moment on the issues of consensus. If less than half of Americans support this apology, political tides may change and the United States could soon return to Iraq to "finish the job." Of those who do not support the apology, with which aspects do they disagree most strongly? Do they agree with everything except subjecting U.S. officials to international criminal courts? Which percentage agrees with which assertions? The future well-being of individual Iraqis could hang in the balance of how these percentages relate to the likelihood of the United States withdrawing troops, stemming sectarian violence, rebuilding infrastructure, and providing financial redress. A binary determination regarding whether the president did or did not apologize would be of little use in these respects.

Similar dynamics complicate corporate apologies. Most often, a corporate executive officer or spokesperson expresses contrition to the media in some form. Who do they represent? Does the spokesperson convey the beliefs and sentiments of the accountants who manipulated the books and the financiers who distanced themselves from the company just before the scandal broke? Has the board of trustees undergone a moral transformation or does it remain committed to pursuing profits at the expense of all other values? Just as an Iraqi would want to know more about the apology provided by the president before building her future in Baghdad, potential investors and customers would be well advised to gauge the future of a corporation by more than the apologetic promises of an executive who may be leading another company within a few months.

Notice the difficulty of attempting to assign a specific percentage of support that would somehow tip a scale toward a definitive determination that a political or corporate leader apologized for the collective she represents. We might be tempted to claim that any amount over half will do, but the previous examples illustrate the arbitrariness of this. Even if everyone in the nation supported the new president's apology except for Donald Rumsfeld, Dick Cheney, and George W. Bush, we should account for these three dissenting opinions in our understanding of the apology. As I consider later with respect to questions of standing and delegation, many Iraqis might welcome an apology from Bush's successor and the vast majority of American citizens but refuse to forgive the United States until those three architects of the war accept blame. Even if a nation deposes and repudiates the offending leaders, it may find that it cannot accomplish certain moral work without the cooperation of those from whom it wishes to dissociate.

Further issues arise regarding group membership. Who belongs within the collective apologizing? In our original example of two people providing a joint categorical apology, the size and scope of the collective is transparent. As the group increases in size, the boundaries become less obvious. In the case of the apology for the Iraq War, does the collective include children, the cognitively disabled, or those ignorant or apathetic about the war? Do U.S. soldiers who died in battle belong in this collective? Do we include those who worked in Iraq for U.S. defense contractors but were not U.S. citizens? Can the apologizer exclude members of the collective against their will, for example if an executive fires unrepentant colleagues before publicly apologizing for the corporation so that she can offer her apology with a mandate from a consensus of employees? Could a nation exile or otherwise purge those who refuse to apologize in order to achieve consensus? The latter strategy draws attention to the possibility that the meanings provided by some collective apologies might come at too high a price.

Members of an institution may also splinter off from that group in order to redefine their collective identity around shared opinions regarding the transgression at issue. Once they have narrowed the scope of their group to like-minded individuals, they can issue their apology on behalf of a consensus. Instead of the president apologizing for the United States, she might explicitly state that she speaks only on behalf of a consensus of the members of the Democratic Party. We could imagine certain members of the philosophy department taking a similar approach, perhaps describing themselves as "Philosophers for Gender Equity." Proceeding in this manner also calls attention to those not within this group, implying that those who are not signatories to the apology do not support gender equity. I will consider these issues further in discussions of standing later.

This leads to additional worries that the desire for consensus can be at odds with other forms of apologetic meaning. As noted earlier with respect to the apology of the philosophy department, reaching agreement on the terms and language of an apology can prove difficult. Couching the apology in abstract terms can unify individuals who may nonetheless maintain subtly diverse opinions. Although precise apologies face more difficulties generating consensus, broader language often increases ambiguities. Leaders may find themselves confronting choices in this regard, weighing the value of providing an unequivocal apology against the importance of forging solidarity around broader values or policies. In the case of apologizing for Iraq, should a Democratic president excoriate the previous administration and enumerate all of its failures, or should she exercise restraint by painting the failures in broad strokes and absorbing the blame into herself? Once again, such considerations emphasize how apologies bear meaning for the offenders and their communities as well as the victims. A general apology might serve the interests of the Democratic Party better than a more exacting and comprehensive apology because the latter runs the risk of alienating moderate voters. An apology calculated to appeal to the American voter, however, might leave Iraqis dissatisfied and questioning the intentions motivating the gesture. Indeed, one version of the apology might best reconcile the United States with Iraqis and the international community, and another might best mend domestic wounds.

Problems related to the consensus of the collective will reappear throughout the subsequent sections. I now work back through the framework for individual categorical apologies outlined earlier and draw attention to meanings and complications specific to collective apologies.

CHAPTER TEN

Issues Specific to Collective Apologies

A. Collectives Corroborating Factual Records

As with individual apologies, creating a record of the offense at issue is an important component of collective apologies. Tavuchis goes so far as to claim that the "principal function" of collective apologies "has little, if anything, to do with sorrow or sincerity but rather with putting things on the public record."[1] Tavuchis describes this recording function as "the ultimate source of [a collective apology's] power to remedy and conciliate," and he believes that "to demand more of the form is to mistake its task and logic."[2] I explain why I find this a bit of an overstatement – even if the "things" that a collective apology "puts on the record" refer to something more like the entire performance of the apology rather than only the details of the incident – but I agree that we should not underestimate the importance of creating an official, public, or otherwise authoritative record of facts salient to the offense.

Collective apologies typically multiply the difficulties of establishing a factual record faced by individual apologies. When apologizing for the actions of a legion of warriors, a loosely organized mob, an intricate corporate bureaucracy, or a market in human slaves, cataloging the wrongdoings will seem like a daunting task. If we return to the example of my philosophy department apologizing for what I described earlier as "failure to address concerns about gender equality," notice the importance of including more information on the record than this vague description offers. Suppose that additional details about the nature of the offenses are available. We learn that one member of the department consistently discourages female students from applying to graduate school in philosophy, telling them that only men are capable of advanced work in the discipline. Another has never included the writings of a female philosopher in his courses because, as he explains to his students at the beginning of each semester, "no female philosopher has ever written anything worth reading." Another admits that she opposed hiring a particular woman philosopher during our last search because she believed that her children would prevent her from completing serious research. Three others agree that they should include more feminist readings in their classes regardless of the course, for example including feminist critiques of beauty in their philosophy of art classes. The remaining colleagues feel that they have not personally done anything wrong but feel a duty to do even more to improve the educational experience of our female students. Any apology from us that described these transgressions as "failing to address concerns about gender equality" would distort the nature of our culpability and minimize the extent of our wrongdoing.

Interrelated concerns arise regarding both the amount of detail required and the difficulties in creating such a comprehensive account. Notice two extremes regarding the appropriate degree of specificity. Where would we begin chronicling African slavery? How much detail would we provide, and where would we end? By one measure, it seems like the entire history of the United States would belong on this record and therefore one might apologize most generally for "the history and legacy of slavery in the United States." Indeed, Clinton once noted that "we were wrong" in receiving "the fruits" of the slave trade "before we were even a nation."[3] On its face, such a statement says little to establish a record except to note that the United States has a history and prehistory of slavery. It offers no account of who exactly engaged in the slave trade, why they did so, and how this stain on our history continues to taint our nation. This, of course, would be a very long story in which many otherwise celebrated U.S. leaders would play less flattering roles.

Nor does it name in detail who suffered or how they suffered. The simple act of naming the victims of mass wrongs goes some way toward recognizing their suffering and establishing a record of the breadth of the harm. If the victim is alive, this gestures toward engaging her as a moral interlocutor rather than as merely an objectified statistic. Naming the victim differentiates her from the mass of unnamed sufferers, better enabling us to view her as an individual and sensitizing us to the particularity of the harm she endured. We can experience difficulty empathizing and sympathizing with a group of millions of refugees or thousands of civilian casualties, but when we learn the names and stories of each particular person the gravity of the loss exerts a greater pull on us. If our brutal history has desensitized us to the suffering of others, apologies can reawaken us to the horrors of mass violence. If the victim has died, naming her also increases the likelihood of drawing her successors into the moral discourse. This latter benefit could be especially important when distributing reparations owed to the deceased's heirs.[4]

For mass injuries in the distant past, any account we could provide would surely omit serious transgressions if only because of inadequate records. We can only estimate how many African slaves died without even their names finding their way into history, no less the details of their deaths that would allow us to fully judge their abductors. Events in the recent past may suffer from similar deficiencies for a variety of reasons. If a U.S. president wishes to apologize for the war in Iraq, how comprehensive and detailed should her account be? Again, some crucial information may never be available to her even after aggressive fact-finding inquiries. If members of the former administration go to their graves without revealing the true intentions motivating the war, an apology can only speculate about these most elementary facts. If they conceived the war to serve exclusively U.S. interests, then an apology should account for this. If they genuinely conceptualized the effort as a means of promoting the human rights of Iraqi citizens, then an apology focused on the execution of an otherwise morally justifiable campaign could reflect this. As I consider later, it seems that mental states play a role in collective apologies as they do in individual apologies.

Additionally, if individual U.S. soldiers conceal their offenses against Iraqis, this might also leave a gap in the record. If an Iraqi believes that a U.S. soldier wrongfully harmed her yet this offense does not appear on the president's record, this might lead her to believe that the United States does not find her suffering worth recognizing. The victim's status as a moral interlocutor may suffer further if those responsible never face prosecution. For every civilian casualty of the war, the family of the deceased would appear to have an equal right to learn the details of the death, including who provided the intelligence and who ordered the strike. For those whose relatives died in prisons or from subjection to the interrogation techniques similar to those made infamous at Abu Ghraib, further details could be profoundly important. Were the victims detained for legitimate reasons? How were they treated? Did they resist? Did they commit suicide, or die while being tortured? Such information allows victims or their friends and family to understand the transgression and judge those responsible for it while affording them the ability to memorialize this information in culturally appropriate ways. It would seem utterly arbitrary to assert that a general apology for the war need only explain and account for some injuries of this sort but not others. If some believe that such details are excessive or trivial for collective apologies, I ask them to consider whether such information would be meaningful to them if their child was killed in similar circumstances.

In light of these difficulties, legal and institutional fact-finding mechanisms take on special importance. I previously noted the significance of courts and international tribunals establishing historical records with the examples of the Nuremburg trials and the *coram nobis* opinion reconsidering the original *U.S. v. Korematsu*. Compiling such information into a coherent and comprehensive narrative may require an elaborate series of collaborations among international investigators, law enforcement officials, attorneys, legislators, judges, and others. Such work may also prove immensely expensive and beyond the resources of individuals. The audit of the fraudulent use of the accounts of Holocaust victims by Swiss banks cost $600 million, and the chairperson of the International Commission on Holocaust Era

Insurance Claims drew a salary of $360,000 yearly.[5] Such amounts often leave institutions better equipped than individuals to bear the costs of such undertakings.

Legal institutions may also hold the authority to investigate the actions of collectives even if the group genuinely believes in its innocence. Although she might not always admit it to others, an individual typically knows whether she is guilty. Misconduct can hide in the remote corners of collectives, and investigation may bring this to light. Swiss officials, for instance, initially found it unthinkable that their banks had improperly profited from Holocaust-related accounts.[6] Investigative commissions found otherwise. Thanks in part to a whistle-blowing security guard at Union Bank of Switzerland, these determinations include a $1.25 billion class action settlement in a United States District Court against Swiss banks.[7]

Although individuals may change their minds or offer conflicting explanations regarding underlying facts, collective apologies increase this risk. If the current president provides one account but the former president and those most directly involved in the wrongdoing contradict this story, the record remains contested. The South African Truth and Reconciliation Commissions repeatedly faced this problem when members of former President F. W. de Klerk's administration denied factual allegations against them and contradicted de Klerk's accounts.[8] Moreover, just as individuals revise their histories, a group or members of a group may retract or alter their previous accounts. A political party might document one history and apologize for it, only to have the opposing party rewrite history upon coming into power. After a 1993 apology from the Japanese government for its "undeniable" use of Korean sex slaves during World War II, in 2007 Japanese Prime Minister Shinzo Abe attempted to revise history by claiming that there was "no evidence to prove there was coercion" of the so-called "comfort women."[9] Without a coherent and consistent record established, the victim or community may struggle to evaluate the relative credibility of the competing accounts. Such confusion could make matters even more painful for a victim.

We can note several further considerations relevant to the meaning of a collective's corroboration of a factual record. With individual apologies, the victim, offender, and to some extent the community write the story of the underlying events. Collective apologies present further questions regarding which members of the group participate in this storytelling. How does a collective decide who speaks for it? Can it silence those who would offer competing accounts? Although I raised these concerns in relation to the consensus within the collective, I discuss these issues later with respect to standing. Also like individual apologies, how the facts of collective wrongdoing come to light influence their meaning. If my department decides to write a report on gender inequities in the curriculum only because students have complained to the dean and she commands us to report to her or suffer punishment, this will differ from an internally motivated searching of our collective soul. Although not always the case, large group apologies will also tend toward providing a public factual record. Unlike an apology following a domestic argument between two partners, an apology from a nation or corporation might seem suspicious if the institution prevents the victims from sharing it with others. This brings to mind settlement agreements mentioned earlier that provide an apology and redress on the condition that the victim does not disclose the terms of the agreement. Finally, recall the words of G. H. W. Bush: "I will never apologize for the United States of America, I don't care what the facts are."[10] Even if a spokesperson for a collective provides a comprehensive record of the events in question with the authorization of a full consensus, she may defiantly offer this as an historical testament to the collective's glory and achievements.

With these concerns in view, we can read the State of California's 2005 "Apology Act for the 1930s Mexican Repatriation Program."[11] As enacted, section 8721 of the legislation "finds and declares" the following:

(a) Beginning in 1929, government authorities and certain private sector entities in California and throughout the United States undertook an aggressive program to forcibly remove persons of Mexican ancestry from the United States.

(b) In California alone, approximately 400,000 American citizens and legal residents of Mexican ancestry were forced to go to Mexico.

(c) In total, it is estimated that two million people of Mexican ancestry were forcibly relocated to Mexico, approximately 1.2 million of whom had been born in the United States, including the State of California.

(d) Throughout California, massive raids were conducted on Mexican-American communities, resulting in the clandestine removal of thousands of people, many of whom were never able to return to the United States, their country of birth.

(e) These raids also had the effect of coercing thousands of people to leave the country in the face of threats and acts of violence.

(f) These raids targeted persons of Mexican ancestry, with authorities and others indiscriminately characterizing these persons as "illegal aliens" even when they were United States citizens or permanent legal residents.

(g) Authorities in California and other states instituted programs to wrongfully remove persons of Mexican ancestry and secure transportation arrangements with railroads, automobiles, ships, and airlines to effectuate the wholesale removal of persons out of the United States to Mexico.

(h) As a result of these illegal activities, families were forced to abandon, or were defrauded of, personal and real property, which often was sold by local authorities as "payment" for the transportation expenses incurred in their removal from the United States to Mexico.

(i) As a further result of these illegal activities, United States citizens and legal residents were separated from their families and country and were deprived of their livelihood and United States constitutional rights.

(j) As a further result of these illegal activities, United States citizens were deprived of the right to participate in the political process guaranteed to all citizens, thereby resulting in the tragic denial of due process and equal protection of the laws.

Section 8722 continues:

The State of California apologizes to those individuals described in Section 8721 for the fundamental violations of their basic civil liberties and constitutional rights committed during the period of illegal deportation and coerced emigration. The State of California regrets the suffering and hardship those individuals and their families endured as a direct result of the government-sponsored Repatriation Program of the 1930s.

Section 8723 sets forth the extent of the redress these individuals will receive beyond this official statement: "A plaque commemorating the individuals described in Section 8721 shall be installed and maintained by the Department of Parks and Recreation at an appropriate public place in Los Angeles."

Before noticing what this apology does not include in its record, I should be mindful not to make the good the enemy of the best. I imagine that many people first learned of Mexican Repatriation thanks to this legislation and the media coverage it produced. This racially motivated expulsion of over one million U.S. citizens receives little attention, especially when compared with the internment of approximately 120,000 Japanese Americans during the Second World War. California's legislative statement prevents history from expunging the injustice from its record.[12] A *National Public Radio* story on California's apology spurred me to learn more, and perhaps other politicians and academics will follow California's lead and take up the issue.[13] To this end, the act does provide some detail and avoids the temptation of offering one line simply declaring that the "The State of California apologizes for Mexican Repatriation." I do not wish to minimize the importance of these achievements.

Notice, however, what the legislature omits. We do not learn the name of a single victim, leaving history to remember the event as a faceless exodus. Subsection (a) blames "government authorities" and "certain private sector entities" for the program. Why does the apology not name President Hoover and the members of his Wickersham Commission responsible for this program at the highest levels? Members of the Hoover administration did, after all, publicly rally support for the program behind the slogan "American Jobs for Real Americans."[14] According to this program, U.S. citizens of Mexican heritage were not "real Americans." In addition, what justifies withholding the identities of the private entities behind the policies? Records indicate that the manager of the Los Angeles Chamber of Commerce's agriculture department found legal protections irrelevant to repatriation: "It is a question of pigment, not a question of citizenship or right."[15] Given the number of Mexicans and Mexican Americans working in Southern Californian agriculture, such a statement from the manager of this office certainly helps to understand the blatantly racist motivations driving the program. Likewise, subsection (e) mentions "threats and acts of violence" but does not indicate the source of these threats or the perpetrators of the violence. The apology casts blame upon no one in particular.

Subsections (h) and (i) mention how those repatriated "were defrauded of" property and livelihood. This use of the passive voice – notice how the legislation relies on passive construction throughout – is especially conspicuous. If officials of the State of California defrauded the victims, this would suggest that perhaps the state should now provide compensation for these wrongful takings. The apology's silence on the value of the extorted goods should also raise suspicions. Had the apology included values of the losses, the conversation regarding the possibility of redressing the injustices with something beyond a plaque might gain momentum. One might read the legislation a bit more critically in this respect if she knew that Governors Gray Davis and Arnold Schwarzenegger both vetoed bills seeking merely to create a commission to investigate the options for redressing the harm.[16] The apology also fails to mention the plight of those forcibly relocated once they found themselves in Mexico. Many had never set foot in Mexico, knew of no family there, and did not even speak the language. Many suffered through extreme poverty or death as a result.[17] The legislation mentions that the program began in 1929 but it provides no further context. Situating this program within broader Depression-era economic initiatives and the racial climate at the time would help make sense of the injustice. It would also draw attention to the possible parallels between the repatriation program and contemporary attempts at immigration reform.

Again, I do not wish to minimize the significance of the "Apology Act for the 1930s Mexican Repatriation Program." Contrasted with the controversies surrounding Turkey's refusal to recognize Armenian genocide as such, we can appreciate the accomplishments of such legislation. In my view, however, these concerns should lead us to question whether the passage of such legislation means that California has "officially apologized" for these injustices.[18] We also should not forget that the concerns raised here speak primarily to corroborating a factual record, which may be the most straightforward dimension of apologetic meaning. I now turn to one of the most complex: collective moral responsibility.

B. Collectives and Blame

1. Distinguishing from Collective Expressions of Sympathy

Like individual apologies, collective apologies often express sympathy rather than accept blame for wrongdoing. Suppose that instead of the apology I imagine earlier, the newly elected president offers the following statement: "I am sorry for the suffering endured by Iraqi citizens since the onset of the war." Such a statement could have several meanings. It might express sympathy for the hardships they have faced, rendering the statement parallel to an expression of condolences like "I am sorry that your grandmother passed away." It does not, however, explicitly accept blame for these hardships. The speaker might believe, for instance, that those who commit acts of sectarian violence are entirely responsible for the unfortunate situation. She *feels bad* about the situation, but does not believe that fault lies with the United States. From this perspective, we could understand the president as offering an expression of sympathy without causal responsibility. Alternatively, the president might believe that the United States did indeed cause all of the suffering, but that these are the growing pains of a fledgling democracy. Like a judge issuing a stern but fair sentence, the president stands by the war but offers her condolences to those who pay its fair price. We could consider this an expression of sympathy with justification. Neither meaning would provide a categorical apology, but either could convey significant meaning. Along with a statement of condolence, the president might recite the names of Iraqi police officers trained by coalition forces and killed in the line of duty, note their courage, and provide their families with medals and significant honoraria. Such gestures could play a modest role in recognizing the sacrifices made, but instead we often find expressions of sympathy offered as perfunctory attempts to appease critics. President Bush's reluctant remark that he was "sorry for the humiliations suffered by the Iraqi prisoners and the humiliations suffered by their families" comes to mind.[19]

Collective apologies present a few further nuances on these points worth mentioning. First, we should distinguish between cases in which the spokesperson for a collective refers to her own sympathy rather than that of the group. If the president says, "I am sorry for the suffering endured by Iraqi citizens," this differs from her stating that the "United States is sorry for the suffering endured by Iraqi citizens." Even if she utters these statements in her most official capacity, for instance in a televised broadcast from the Oval Office, it seems reasonable to assume that when she speaks of her personal feelings we should classify her statement as an individual expression of sympathy. Rather than a collective expression of sympathy, this seems like one person – albeit one very important person – expressing her thoughts and feelings. Victims may desire a gesture of contrition from the collective rather than from an individual spokesperson, as in the cases of Korean "comfort women" who refused to recognize the 1990 statements of Emperor Akihito or Prime Minister Miyazawa as anything more than their personal expressions of sorrow. Instead, they sought an apology from the Diet as a collective.[20]

If, however, the president refers to the sympathy felt by the United States, this also sounds odd: Can a nation *feel* sympathy? Similar concerns arise if an executive expresses sympathy on behalf of her corporation. Does it make sense to think of Enron experiencing emotional or cognitive states? I will consider the problem of collective intentions and emotions later, but we can already notice the awkwardness of translating language customary in apologies between individuals to collective apologies. As I attempted to explain earlier, expressions of sympathy generate a considerable degree of uncertainty in comparatively simple cases of expressions of contrition between two people. Collective expressions of sympathy – sometimes mediating between shifting populations of millions of people or over hundreds of years – exponentially compound the possibilities for confusion. We can appreciate the extent of the quandary if we add problems of consensus to this disarray. Not all citizens of the United States support a categorical apology to Iraqis harmed by the war, but we also have good reasons to doubt that they all even feel sympathy for them. The amount of sympathy experienced by individuals could also range immensely, with some so moved by their feelings that they devote years to relief work in Baghdad whereas others barely give the situation a second thought after feeling a pang of compassion upon seeing refugee children on television. Even if I did not expect a collective categorical apology from the United States, if I were an Iraqi I would like to know how broad and deep even such sympathy ran among Americans.

We can also recall significant meanings that collective expressions of sympathy may not provide. Because neither collective expressions of sympathy with blame nor collective expressions of sympathy with justification admit wrongdoing, they do not necessarily entail that the group will undertake reform or refrain from committing similarly justifiable acts in the future. Thus if the president expresses her sympathy with justification to the families of those lost in Iraq, this does not require her to limit the number of lives sacrificed in this campaign. An expression of sympathy with justification may in fact serve as a warning to others in the region that such costs do not erode the president's resolve when contrasted with the ultimate benefits of such conflicts. Collective expressions of sympathy also do not commit the collectives to providing redress of any kind, although they may offer various forms of charitable support for those with whom they sympathize.

2. Collective Causation and Collective Moral Responsibility
The Extent of the Issue
As we saw with respect to individual apologies, questions regarding moral causation can trigger significant disagreements regarding who bears blame for harms. Even within this minefield of metaphysical, ethical, social, and political issues, however, we can often attribute moral responsibility to individuals without much controversy. In most cases we can form judgments regarding who harmed us, hold them accountable, and expect an apology from them that accepts blame for the harm.

Matters become much more complicated when we attempt to attribute blame to collectives. Returning to the example of my philosophy department's apology for the harms resulting from gender bias within our classes and curriculum, should we trace responsibility for these failures to the department as a group or to the individuals belonging to the collective? Is the department itself – which I intentionally refer to as an "it" – somehow culpable for the harm beyond the sum of the blame attributable to its members? As a kind of "plural subject," does its culpability transcend that of its individual members? Alternatively, is collective responsibility entirely reducible and equivalent to the aggregation of the blame born by members of the group? If we can find collectives as such blameworthy, must groups apologize for harms even if all of their members apologize individually? If all blame falls on individuals, how should we understand an apology from the collective?

The stakes of these questions become more apparent when we attribute blame to large groups and expect an apology from the organization, often in lieu of apologies from all of its members. Consider the abuse of prisoners at Abu Ghraib. Not every member of the U.S. military is guilty of and responsible for these harms, or at least not in the same respect. Some U.S. troops were on the other side of the world at the time the abuses occurred and did not learn of the scandal until it reached the newspapers. Only a highly attenuated causal chain could link them to the acts, for example by citing their contribution to overall U.S. military force as enabling the invasion that in turn created the possibility for the torture. Because such abuses are a foreseeable consequence of war, we might argue, all members of the U.S. military deserve blame for the torture in some sense. Even if we find this controversial causal account compelling, surely the wrong committed remotely by these troops differs considerably from that of the guards who tortured detainees to death. Each individual seems responsible for a different offense, and apologies from members of the group should reflect such distinctions. We can draw further contrasts in type and degree of blame. Some knew of the abuse and tried to stop it at considerable personal and professional risk. Some knew of the abuse and attempted to conceal it. Some administrators wrote memos suggesting that torture may not be illegal against enemy combatants. Some supervisors appeared to encourage abuse by rewarding their subordinates for gathering intelligence by "breaking" detainees. Some soldiers tortured prisoners to death with their own hands. We could imagine categorical apologies from each individual in this case accounting for his or her specific role in the wrongdoing. Does this, however, render the "U.S. military" *as an organization* culpable for the harm? If so, is the institution capable of apologizing categorically for the actions of some portion of its members? Alternatively, is the U.S. military guilty in some specifically institutional sense, requiring an apology from the collective to account for this? If various groups demanded an apology for the abuses at Abu Ghraib, who or what should accept blame: the individuals, the institution, or both?

The few philosophers writing on apologies have found notions of group responsibility largely unproblematic, leading them to embrace the emerging trend of collective apologies. According to Richard Joyce's account of apologies, we should "assume" that collective responsibility and collective apologies make sense because doing so "is far more desirable than denying [them]." For Joyce, we only need to pay "attention to our language as it is ordinarily used" to realize that we commonly make such assumptions.[21] Like Joyce, Govier and Verwoerd claim in the context of collective apologies that it is "not a category mistake to think of an institution or collective as being responsible for wrongdoing" because a "collectivity can act, and be responsible for acts, without every individual in it being personally implicated."[22] Although I consider Harvey's helpful discussions of how organizational structures relate to the meanings of collective apologies later, Harvey concentrates on the role of individuals serving as "institutional agents" rather than on a sense of assigning responsibility to the collective as such.[23] Tavuchis and Lazare also leave the notion of collective responsibility largely unproblematic.

Previous discussions of collective apologies tend to pass over what I find to be lively and important debates on collective responsibility.[24] Collective moral responsibility has generated interest among philosophers in large part in response to concrete historical events. Whether considering the Holocaust or the recent spate of corporate scandals, it becomes evident that groups of people acting in concert can cause harm on a scale that exceeds that of even the most malevolent individuals. The ominous title of Manuel Velasquez's often cited essay – "Why Corporations are not Morally Responsible for Anything They Do" – helps to explain why some might be interested in defending collective responsibility.[25]

Prima facie, several sensible arguments favor attributing blame to collectives. As corporations come to wield increasing influence over modern life, we seek means of holding them responsible for their transgressions and we look to our traditional models of individual moral accountability to make sense of collective blame. Attention paid to gender, racial, and class justice feeds the debate as we evaluate whether men, whites, or the wealthy should be held morally responsible as groups for the privileges they perpetuate or inherit. As we come to appreciate the extent of wrongdoing in the world, we look for anyone and even anything to hold responsible. Collective wrongdoing often leaves massive amounts of suffering in its wake, and our prospects for redressing such injuries improve if we can find someone or something to bear this burden. Considering the resources available to corporations and nations, such kinds of "things" may be better situated than people to provide redress and institute reform. The U.S. military, for example, has much deeper pockets than does Sabrina Harman from which to compensate the family of Mandela al-Jamadi, with whom Harman appears in an infamous photo as she gives the "thumbs up" gesture over his corpse at Abu Ghraib. This provides a considerable incentive to bend the moral categories usually applied to individuals just enough so that we also attribute blame to collectives.

In addition to the practical consideration of casting blame as broadly and abstractly as possible to catch any possible source of compensation, others point to the "social facts" favoring collective responsibility: We regularly speak and act as if we believe in group agency. Just as our shared commitment to the status of certain kinds of pieces of paper as currency makes them valuable, we often speak of "the United States waging war" or "Enron misleading investors." As David Cooper explains, the "obvious point to be recognized ... is that responsibility is ascribed to collectives, as well as to individual persons. Blaming attitudes are held towards collectives as well as towards individuals."[26] The practice of speaking of institutional agents as moral agents in this sense effectively makes it so for us. We might state this more strongly, arguing that collective responsibility is not a merely contingent practice but is built into the "logical grammar" of our moral categories. Indeed, it is difficult to imagine human social life without speaking in terms of collective action and responsibility and it seems like a constant feature of our moral phenomenology.

Further, the membership of a collective often changes as individuals cycle through the group. Although no original members remain from Edison's founding of General Electric Company in 1860, General Electric lives on. The responsibilities of the institution transcend the aggregate responsibility of individual members of the group, leading commentators to view the moral accountability of the whole as greater than the sum of the responsibilities of its members.

I am sympathetic to all of these points favoring attributions of collective responsibility, but more needs to be said to explain the relationship between such arguments and the lives of collective apologies. Although a rigorous engagement of the issues raised in the emerging field of collective responsibility is well beyond the scope of this work, I would like to sketch the outlines of the arguments and note where they overlap with concerns regarding the meanings of collective apologies.

Theories of Collective Responsibility

Joel Feinberg influentially provides some precision to the debates over collective responsibility by identifying a few different models. Feinberg understands collective responsibility, like vicarious liability, as a form of strict liability. Strict liability covers cases in which we hold agents responsible for harm even though "the contributory fault condition is weakened or absent."[27] Some extremely hazardous commercial activities provide typical examples. Tort law stipulates that certain businesses engaging in dangerous activities will bear the costs of any harm resulting from their undertaking "no matter how carefully and faultlessly the activities are carried out."[28] If a company understands such potential liability as a cost of doing business, it will presumably take precautions to avoid such expenses. Although we can have strict liability even if no one is at fault according to Feinberg, vicarious liability occurs when we can ascribe fault to one party but shift liability to a different party.[29] The doctrine of *respondeat superior* follows this principle, allowing us to hold a superior responsible for the acts of her subordinate because we believe that she had a duty or ability to supervise the primary wrongdoer. For Feinberg, strict liability is only just if the party held liable "had some control over his own destiny" in the sense of having "some choice whether to take the risk assigned him by the law and some power to diminish the risk by his own care."[30] Vicarious liability therefore corresponds to the sensibilities motivating proximate causation. By asking where the costs for harm should land even if the direct causal chain leads elsewhere, doctrines of vicarious liability can assign responsibility according to social and political considerations. If an employer controls who she hires to undertake potentially dangerous work and can afford liability insurance as a cost of business, according to Feinberg it "may be unfair to make him pay for the accident that was not his fault, but it would impose an even greater hardship and injustice to put the burden on the equally faultless accident victim."[31] Rather than simple physical causation, considerations of justice guide strict and vicarious liability.

Feinberg then makes an often overlooked but crucial distinction for our purposes:

> There is an important point about all vicarious punishment: even when it is reasonable to separate liability from fault, it is only the liability that can be passed from one party to another. In particular, *there can be no such thing as vicarious guilt*. Guilt consists in the intentional transgression of a prohibition.... The root idea in guilt, then, is to be an appropriate person to make atonement, penance, or self-reproach, in virtue of having intentionally violated a commandment or prohibition.... Now when an innocent man is punished for what a guilty man has done, he is treated *as if* he were himself guilty. There may be a rational point, and perhaps even justice, in certain circumstances, in doing this. Yet even though criminal liability can transfer or extend vicariously from a guilty to an innocent party, it obviously cannot be literally true that the guilt transfers as well. For guilt to transfer literally, action and intention too must transfer literally. But to say of an innocent man that he bears another's guilt is to say that he had one (innocent) intention and yet another (guilty) one, a claim which upon analysis turns out to be contradictory.[32]

Even if prudence dictates in certain limited circumstances that we hold one person accountable for the moral debts of another, this does not entail that fault and guilt also transfer to the third party. If we apply this guilt-less notion of vicarious responsibility to a vicarious apology, a third party will be unable to assert that she harmed the victim. As a central assertion of a categorical apology that admits wrongdoing, the phrase "I was wrong" would be misplaced. I might declare that "she was wrong" and then explain that I will pay for damages resulting from her transgression without accepting any blame. In some circumstances, I might even resign my position as her superior. We should take care here to distinguish two sorts of wrongs often in play in these circumstances. First, we have the wrong committed by the subordinate, for example by a soldier who abuses a detainee. In cases of vicarious liability, the commanding officer may assume responsibility for the actions of the person under her command even if we find that the officer did everything within her power to prevent such offenses. The officer may be demoted, for instance, regardless of a finding that she improperly supervised the private. We might question the fairness of such a demotion but recognize that it serves institutional objectives. Second, the supervising officer may be found to contribute to the abuse in any number of ways, for instance by providing inadequate training, oversight, or enforcement of protocols. Although the two sorts of wrongs are often entwined, the accused party or institution may intentionally obfuscate their relation. In the case of Abu Ghraib, we still lack knowledge of who accepts guilt for which sort of wrong despite various forms of apologies at various levels in command. Apologetic statements from agents of the collective that are ambiguous regarding who accepts blame for which wrongdoings exploit the public's conflation of liability and guilt that Feinberg warns against.

Minding this distinction, Feinberg considers four different "collective-responsibility arrangements." He first describes collective liability without fault, wherein we hold whole groups responsible for the actions of only some members of the group. Here we hold even the faultless members of the group accountable. Feinberg finds this arrangement fair in criminal cases only if the group enjoys a high degree of solidarity, professional policing is unfeasible, the system of collective liability is an understood background condition of the group's existence, and those held vicariously liable "have some reasonable degree of control over those for whom they are made sureties."[33] For those who commit the primary offense in such situations, we would expect an individual apology. All of the concerns regarding apologies from offenders for their personal wrongdoing would apply. For the group as such, the preceding concerns regarding vicarious apologies apply, presuming that all members of the collective are indeed sureties of the offender.

Feinberg describes the second arrangement as liability with noncontributory fault, providing drunk drivers as an example. If a particular drunk driver causes an injury, then all other drunk drivers probably did not contribute to that specific harm in any direct sense. We might hold them all liable, however, because everyone who drives drunk is blameworthy in some respect. Only luck prevents some drunk drivers from causing harm, and this is not enough to distinguish their moral accountability from that of those who do cause harm.[34] We therefore might hold them all responsible, as a group, for any given accident even though only one of them was behind the wheel at the time. Thus they would be liable even though they did not contribute to the harm. Legal conceptions cut two ways here. On the one hand, collective responsibility in this respect runs against basic legal conceptions of fault. If the accident resulted in a conviction for vehicular manslaughter, the law would clearly individuate blame and punishment. All drunk drivers could not pool their legal liability, each agreeing to serve a few days of a life sentence against one of them. On the other hand, harsh punishments for driving while intoxicated recognize that even those who do not cause accidents share the blame and social costs of drunk drivers who do cause accidents. If you drive drunk and never cause an accident, you are guilty of a crime even if you did not directly cause harm to anyone. An individual apology from each drunk driver might accept blame for either 1) engaging in such hazardous activity and placing others at risk even if one does not cause an accident or 2) causing an accident and accepting blame for the resulting harm. In the former, we could imagine a group of drunk drivers reaching a consensus, accepting culpability for endangering others, and categorically apologizing as a collective.

In the latter case, we would find it more difficult to collectively accept blame and apologize for an injury caused by a single drunk driver. In liability with noncontributory fault, Feinberg has in mind those who are blameworthy in a sense that *does not contribute* to the particular harm. His example of drunk driving creates potential confusions because of the many ways that others do contribute to any particular accident. If a bartender continued to serve the driver after she was clearly intoxicated, we might hold the server responsible for contributing to the offense. A "culture" of drunk driving may also contribute to the accident. A society that simultaneously glamorizes automobiles and alcohol consumption while discouraging their combination will experience higher rates of drunk driving than societies without either alcohol or automobiles. We also might think of a culture in a more localized sense, for example if a group of teenage friends repeatedly encouraged each other to drive drunk and exerted considerable social pressure on each other to take turns driving each other home after weekly parties. This arrangement allows them to pool their risk, but not their punishment. Odds are that one of them would eventually cause an accident, and which one causes the accident is largely a matter of luck. In such an example, I imagine that their neighbors would want categorical apologies that accept blame for their share of the harm from each individual in the group of friends, even those who were not driving at the time of an accident. Legal concepts will draw sharp distinctions between the wrongs of participating in such an arrangement and being behind the wheel at the moment of impact, but our apologies can accommodate more subtle considerations than mere guilt or innocence. Apologies can account for the fact that we may be legally innocent yet entirely blameworthy, and I expect that the parents and neighbors would want apologies from the teenagers to mind this distinction.

Feinberg, however, intends for us to understand drunk driving as an example of liability with noncontributory fault in the sense of disconnected individuals who independently share a fault. If one person with this fault causes harm and the others do not contribute to this harm in any way – imagine all drunk drivers on opposite sides of the world with no morally relevant relationship to each other – according to the doctrine of liability with noncontributory fault we might still hold them all responsible not only for their faultiness in driving drunk but for a specific accident to which they have no "causal linkage."[35] While entertaining the possibility, Feinberg warns against such "extravagant hyperboles about universal responsibility." He instead advises us to attend to the various differences in degree and kind of blameworthiness between the agents. One may drive home on crowded highways every night completely soused and in a sadistic rage. Another may have offended only once when she was just over the legal limit in order to prevent a far more intoxicated friend from getting behind the wheel, but she has bad luck and seriously injures someone during this single lapse in judgment. An insufficiently precise collective apology risks minimizing the morally salient differences between the blameworthiness of individual agents in these sorts of cases.

In Feinberg's third arrangement, *contributory group fault: collective and distributive*, we aggregate the blameworthiness of each individual member of the group to determine the collective's total responsibility. After we add the contributory fault of each member, no additional fault remains to ascribe to the group as such. He uses the example of a bank robbery to emphasize that the fault of each member may vary in degree and kind: One sells the robbers the weapon illegally, one drives the car, one encourages the plan, two execute the plan, one congratulates them, one hides them from the police, and one looks the other way. Although Feinberg recognizes the difficulty of assessing the "various incommensurable dimensions of contribution" in such cases, criminal law has developed categories of offenses for just this purpose and our moral concepts allow for such distinctions. In this version of collective responsibility, the group may be loosely structured even as they cooperate or collude in some respects. The person who sells the guns, for example, may have no understanding that they will be used to rob a bank. Feinberg also uses an example of a random group of competent swimmers on a beach who fail to respond to a drowning person's calls for help. Here a group can be faulty in the sense of either cooperating to achieve a blameworthy objective or jointly failing to undertake a laudable end such as working together to save someone in distress.

Once again, I want to caution against conflating the various degrees and kinds of culpability of individual members of the collective into a general apology from the group that fails to differentiate on these grounds. In the bank robbery example, the individual moral agents have committed distinct offenses that call for accepting different kinds of blame and providing distinct sorts of redress. An apology for armed robbery should differ accordingly from an apology for harboring the robber. I worry not only that the collective apology will not properly individuate blame but also that it will minimize or ignore entire classes of offenses committed by members of the group, for instance by failing to address the full range of moral transgressions that contributed to the robbery. Having said that, we can also appreciate that an apology from a group of this sort may allow the victims and offenders to think together about how their individual faults combined to cause harm. In the case of Abu Ghraib, an outpouring of categorical apologies from every culpable individual might still lack a kind of synthesis that explained how the stream of responsibility of each fed into the confluence of wrongdoings that ultimately ended in torture. This "synthetic" work of collective apologies will be especially important in large-scale social harms like racism because individual apologies will often not suffice to reveal the institutional arrangements that require overhauling to adequately address structural ills. A collective apology, as a supplement to individual apologies, might be better positioned to provide such meaning. I suspect, however, that high-ranking officials could often include such synthetic meaning as part of the historical record included within a categorical apology for their personal culpability.

Feinberg describes his fourth arrangement, *contributory group fault: collective but not distributive,* as following from the principle that "there are some harms that are ascribable to group faults but not to every, or even any, individual member."[36] Here the responsibility of the group is not reducible to the responsibility of its members because the collective itself bears the fault. Feinberg and those following his analysis typically have in mind cohesive and enduring organizations with clear rules, traditions, and expectations that take on a life beyond the individuals belonging to the institution. On this account, we can view blameworthiness as a feature of the collective's culture or shared interests and needs. Peter French and other proponents of collective responsibility have developed a version of this conception in some detail.[37] French distinguishes between aggregate collectivity, which he describes as "merely a collection of people," and conglomerate collectivity.[38] According to French, a conglomerate collective is a group of people organized in a manner "such that its identity is not exhausted by the conjunction of the identities" of the individual members.[39] On French's account, conglomerate collectives can be understood as moral agents to which we can assign moral responsibility. Most dramatically, this leads French to claim that "corporations can be full-fledged moral persons and have whatever privileges, rights, and duties as are, in the normal course of affairs, accorded to moral persons."[40]

French's notion of an organization's internal decision structure (IDS) figures prominently in his account of "corporate intentionality."[41] An IDS has two primary features: "(1) an organizational or responsibility flowchart that delineates stations and levels within the corporate power structure and (2) corporate decision recognition rule(s) (usually embedded in something called 'corporation policy')."[42] With deliberation structures, power allocations, conduct standards, and general objectives made explicit, according to French an IDS "accomplishes a subordination and synthesis of the intentions and acts of various biological persons into a corporate decision."[43] Through their internal decision structures, French asserts that corporations have intentions, beliefs, values, and personalities that endure despite the continual turnover of their memberships. Because we cannot reduce the actions and mental states of the organization to those of its members, we should consider the corporation as such responsible. If the corporation radically alters its policies, French believes this constitutes a new entity.[44]

How might a theory like French's contribute to our understanding of the culpability in collective apologies? First, French makes clear that a finding of nonreducible collective responsibility does not render individual members of the institution blameless: If we blame an institution in some respect, this does not let individual members off the hook.[45] Distributing individual culpability for the harm caused by a group raises knotty issues, but generally we can look to the extent of an individual's role in the decision-making process, her knowledge of the wrongdoing, and her participation in the wrongdoing. Higher-ranking officials who have or should have more knowledge of and influence over institutional objectives will likely shoulder more blame. Given the importance of these distinctions even for French, I imagine he would also appreciate the importance of seeking apologies from each individual for her role in the collective harm. In this sense, both collectivists and individualists would share my concerns when an apology from a spokesperson for the collective supplants an apology from individual members who should accept blame for their personal contribution to the offense. Once we have apportioned individual blame, we can ask whether – in addition to the apologies from these members – the institution as such should apologize for its distinct and irreducible culpability. If French ascribes accountability to the collective over and beyond that of its members, how would we theorize an apology for this sort of group responsibility?

The work of French and others encourages us to think through how institutional structures relate to our assignments of blame and subsequent apologies. An IDS can be quite complex and its structure may be almost entirely opaque to victims: We know that the president is generally in charge, but we may understand almost nothing further about the inner workings of an organization. We also may lack access to pertinent information regarding who issued which orders. The Abu Ghraib example demonstrates a range of possible scenarios in these respects. Rather than a handful of renegade guards committing the offenses, we could imagine direct orders to torture detainees originating from the president and being implemented by administrators and troops who all explicitly agree that torture is proper and justifiable in these circumstances. Suppose the president cites a memo from the Attorney

General underscoring that the U.S. Constitution allows and even encourages such methods. In light of this reading of the Constitution, the military trains its soldiers not only how to torture but also to believe that such acts are legal and moral in every respect. In this scenario, we can understand the wrong as somehow embedded within the institutional structure and objectives of the United States, or what French might call the nation's IDS.

Here we could attribute aggregate (distinguished from conglomerate) blame to such a consensus of wrongdoers, but each would remain specifically responsible for her own contributions. An individual apology from the president would hold considerable meaning under these circumstances. He could explain how he was wrong, how his wrongs facilitated other wrongs, and how he accepts blame for the harm. He might admit that he made a poor choice in appointing the Attorney General and announce that the previous constitutional interpretation was incorrect. He might change course in Iraq and overhaul the military's detention policies. He might reform the nation's IDS. He might provide the synthetic meanings described earlier, for instance accounting for the institutional racism that contributed to these atrocities and undertaking related structural reform. Again, this individual apology from the president would not eliminate the need for each member of the collective to apologize for her specific contributions. If nothing else, we might still fault the soldiers who directly administered the beatings for not questioning the military's position on torture. Failing to question and resist the commands of one's superiors is a very different kind of failure from ordering an inferior to commit immoral acts, and I mean to emphasize here how an apology solely from the collective would risk conflating these distinctions.

Nevertheless, the question remains: What might an apology from the collective for its conglomerate responsibility – the blame of the group beyond that of its individual members – add in such a case? If the president apologizes for each of his personal failures and each individual responsible does the same, is any culpability unaccounted for and attributable to the collective as such? What if all of those responsible for creating the IDS – including not only the president but also legislators, members of the judiciary, and citizens – also apologize for their role in developing and administering these institutional features? Perhaps if we can trace blame for creating the IDS to the drafters of the Constitution and all of those who subsequently developed it, we can consider an apology from the collective as somehow metaphorically accepting blame for those who cannot because they are dead. This seems questionable for two reasons. First, the deceased presumably went to their graves unapologetic and without delegating their standing to apologize to the collective. Second, I worry that such a metaphorical understanding of the collective's culpability will supplant the literal blame that should be ascribed to living individuals. I will return to this later, but I want to underscore this concern that collective apologies often serve as poor substitutes for categorical apologies from individual members of the group even if they can provide important meanings as supplements to individual apologies.

At the other extreme, we could imagine that a few renegades who disregarded all training, supervision, and clear and unambiguous pronouncements that any abuse of the prisoners was unacceptable committed the tortures at Abu Ghraib. We could even imagine that the offenders tortured the prisoners and took photographs of the acts in an attempt to undermine the president's cause by drawing negative publicity, perhaps because they renounced their allegiance to the United States and intended to commit treason. If a few soldiers acted against direct orders and contrary to adequate training in humanistic detention and interrogation techniques, then it becomes increasingly difficult to attribute blame to the collective via its IDS. Although we might believe that the United States should not be conducting an offensive in Iraq, ascribing blame to the U.S. military for the acts of torture in such an example would allow group affiliations to override all notions of proximate moral causation. To be clear: We might think that once one nation invades another, its officials can expect that civilian casualties or breaches of detention protocols will result. Leaders cannot unleash hundreds of thousands of warriors and expect that none of them will ever cross the tenuous line between what their leaders describe as legitimate and illegitimate violence. Leaders may deserve some degree of blame in this respect. This does not, however, excuse individual soldiers for any offense they commit while at war. In this sense, we typically would not consider the United States culpable for the Oklahoma City bombing because Timothy McVeigh was a citizen and a decorated veteran. As both the U.S. government and McVeigh defined themselves, their objectives were fundamentally at odds. One might argue that the United States is responsible for McVeigh's actions in the sense that the U.S. military trained him, he claimed that witnessing carnage during his service in Kuwait fueled his anti-government beliefs, and he described the Oklahoma City bombing as revenge for the raids at Waco and Ruby Ridge.[46] Unless the United States is willing to accept blame in these more tenuous and contentious senses, a collective apology for the bombing or acts of torture would lack the meaning associated with accepting blame for the harm. Instead, collective renunciations of the acts, expressions of sympathy, and declarations of policy would seem like more appropriate responses.

These two situations – either everyone in the group is unanimously responsible or a few outlaws act independently to breach institutional values – throw into relief the various senses in which a collective can be considered responsible. Specific cases and institutional structures are rarely this obvious. Jean Harvey identifies four ways an institution can be understood as responsible for a wrongdoing even if it formally prohibits the wrong at issue.[47] First, if a high-ranking official commits an institutionally prohibited wrong, "it seems to reflect more on the institution as a whole than when someone with far less responsibility commits a wrong." Second, if the wrongdoing reflects a pattern of wrongs committed by members of the group, "an institution may eventually be charged with being generally corrupt." Third, an institution can be guilty of negligently supervising or policing its members. Fourth, it can be complicit with individuals violating its norms by ignoring evidence, suppressing violations, or retaliating against victims.[48] "The more institutional the wrong," Harvey claims, "the more appropriate it is for apologies to be offered to victims by an institutional representative."[49] I consider the notion of an "institutional representative" later with respect to issues of standing and delegation, but Harvey helps to identify the different ways institutional actors can contribute to harms. An apology from such institutional agents will serve many functions, including identifying just these sorts of contributory faults. Military officials could therefore differentiate between the culpability applicable for torture at Abu Ghraib with the kinds of accountability ascribable for the 2007 neglect scandal at Walter Reed Army Medical Center.[50] Given the institutional nature of the problems at Walter Reed, we can be fairly certain that some moral blame lies with at least midlevel administrators rather than isolated negligent individuals. Only the middle manager who committed moral errors only possible from her administrative post can categorically apologize for her role. Collective apologies typically overlook this, leading us to believe that the broad apology of a representative "covers" all of the specific misdeeds that add up to the aggregate, conclusive, or most publicized harm spoken of by the representative.

We should also keep in mind that the previous military examples present, in one respect, the strongest cases for collective blame. Even more than corporations, militaries tend to be tightly controlled hierarchies with clearly defined objectives. Militaries, in other words, are perhaps the most likely to operate with the sort of IDS that French believes can trigger collective responsibility. Notice how conglomerate responsibility becomes more tenuous if we assign it to a less clearly structured group, like a university, a racial group, a mob, or a random collection of individuals.[51] That list presents examples in which it becomes increasingly difficult to identify shared intentions, objectives, attitudes, group solidarity, decision-making structures, recognized representatives, choices to undertake coordinated actions, or even membership in the group.

For the most part, these theories attempt to extend Kantian notions of individual responsibility into a framework for group culpability. This typically entails understanding at least some groups to be like individuals in the respects salient to moral causation, for example in their ability to hold desires, make choices, and act. The Kantian tradition of assigning responsibility based on the choices of individual rational moral agents resonates with popular views, in part because it parallels fundamental beliefs in major religions. According to modern Judeo-Christian and Islamic doctrines, god judges each human on her own acts. Our conscience and deeds – rather than those of our siblings, political leaders, or employers – determine our eternal fates. As British Lord Chancellor Edward Thurlow remarked: "Corporations have neither bodies to be punished, nor souls to be condemned, they therefore do as they like."[52] It is not surprising, therefore, that arguments for collective responsibility face the numerous difficulties that I mention. Because our modern conceptions of apologies emerge from religious traditions of repentance designed to save individual souls, collective apologies cut against traditional moral practices.[53] Although ancient religions often allowed for collective responsibility – the Hebrew *people* are chosen, all Egyptians suffer under the plague, and original sin is undifferentiated – notions of tribal accountability lose currency in modernity, in part because of difficulties integrating such notions into liberal individualism and the ideologies driving capitalist markets.

Some defenders of collective responsibility have looked beyond Kant for more amenable moral concepts. A few take inspiration from Karl Jaspers' notion of "metaphysical guilt," according to which we are "each as responsible for every wrong and every injustice in the world."[54] Larry May turns to Sartre and the existentialist tradition, emphasizing how social relationships enable individuals to exceed their solitary powers. From this perspective, our affiliations and actions can be the by-product of "pre-reflective intentions" built into our relationships rather than originating in our individual mental states as Kantian frameworks require.[55] Intentions, in this sense, can be structural for May.[56] As Marion Smiley points out, May also suggests the utilitarian benefits of thinking in these terms.[57] Juha Raikka goes so far as to claim that we can blame individuals even if they cannot control the actions of the collective or if they dissent and attempt to distance themselves from the group.[58]

Arendt proves interesting in this respect as a theorist mindful of both Kantian and Marxist conceptions of freedom. She appreciates that social and economic circumstances can profoundly transform the choices of large groups of individuals, with the horrors of the Holocaust always punctuating her claims. On her account, "the chaotic economic conditions" prior to the war led the *paterfamilias* to "undertake any function, even that of hangman."[59] "It needed only the satanic genius of Himmler," she wrote, "to discover that after such degradation [the *paterfamilias*] was entirely prepared to do literally anything when the ante was raised and the bare existence of his family was threatened." In this most chilling sense, structural causation seems as real to her as it does to the most orthodox Marxists. Despite this, she distinguishes between structural or collective causation and collective guilt. Similar to the earlier distinction provided by Feinberg, Arendt claims that "guilt, unlike responsibility, always singles out; it is strictly personal."[60] She cites the following exchange between an American correspondent and a Nazi to dramatize the dangers of absorbing moral blame entirely into the collective:

Q: Did you kill people in the camp?
A: Yes.
Q: Did you bury them alive?
A: It sometimes happened.
Q: Were the victims picked up from all over Europe?
A: I suppose so.
Q: Did you personally help kill people?
A: Absolutely not. I was only the paymaster in the camp.
Q: What did you think of what was going on?
A: It was bad at first but we got used to it.
Q: Do you know the Russians will hang you?
A: (Bursting into tears) *Why should they? What have I done?*[61]

The offender here cleaves his identity into an individual who "out of sheer passion . . . would never do harm to a fly" and a servant of a collective that executes the Final Solution.[62] He identifies solely with the innocent self, in part because the structures of Nazism forced him to either kill or be killed. Resistance would have required heroism and martyrdom, a standard too high for the average worker. "When his occupation forces him to murder people," Arendt explains, "he does not regard himself as a murderer because he has not done it out of inclination but in his professional capacity."[63] In this context, individualist notions of personal responsibility make increasingly little sense, eventually eroding into an impossible dilemma for the administration of justice: "Where all are guilty, nobody in the last analysis can be judged."[64] Arendt thus walks a fine line, recognizing that our Kantian traditions always assign guilt to individuals yet finding our deepest solidarity in our shared vulnerabilities. Clear-thinking modern citizens will "not content themselves with the hypocritical confession, 'God be thanked, I am not like that,' in horror at the undreamed potentialities of the German national character." Even if we did not pull the trigger and are not guilty this time, we have "finally realized of what man is capable – and this indeed is the precondition of any modern political thinking."[65] For Arendt, the resulting "elemental shame, which many people of the most various nationalities share with one another today, is what is finally left of our international solidarity."[66]

Arendt leaves apologies in a bind: We feel shame for the condition of our humanity, yet for so many of us the source of this shame cannot be attributed to our own guilt and responsibility. Thus there seems to be so much to apologize for, yet so few who can accept blame for it.

Applying Criticisms of Collective Responsibility to Apologies
Ranging from Max Weber to Jan Narveson and others, theorists from diverse backgrounds express reservations about collective responsibility.[67]

H. D. Lewis' 1948 essay "Collective Responsibility" provides an influential set of challenges that have come to be known as the methodological and normative individualist critiques of group responsibility. Lewis attacks "the barbarous notion of collective or group responsibility," claiming that it revives notions of clan identity and guilt by association. For Lewis, the concept of collective responsibility results from a creative use of language gone awry. We use the notion of collective responsibility as a kind of shorthand in order to simplify discussions of the potentially vast complexities of situations where many individuals commit wrongs in some proximity to one another. Lewis reminds us that the concept of collective identity is metaphorical: "We hypostatize abstractions and make them bearers of value, forgetting that linguistic devices which make for succinctness of expression or poetic and rhetorical effect are not to be divested to their metaphorical and elliptical meanings, and taken as literal truth."[68] Instead of naming all of the individual agents responsible in the Abu Ghraib abuses each time we refer to the web of events, we refer to "U.S. military" or some similar abstraction for convenience. Although gathering individuals into groups simplifies conversation by saving us from the tedium of naming each individual wrongdoer every time we refer to the events, for Lewis we must not forget that "it is the individual who is the sole bearer of moral responsibility." The trend of "blaming the social 'structure'" for wrongdoing, Lewis believes, "is only meaningful in a figurative sense and as a rhetorical device when concern is to be aroused at distressful social conditions."[69] Any "literal sense" of collective responsibility will be misleading because "a 'structure' cannot be the bearer of moral responsibility; neither can society in general, for these are both abstractions which we must be careful not to hypostatize." Lewis sees a danger in anthropomorphizing these abstractions, particularly when we act as if this construction can bear the blame that individuals hiding behind it should accept. Govier and Verwoerd, for instance, claim that although no (or increasingly few) living Japanese citizens have exploited Korean comfort women as prostitutes during World War II, "Japan as a nation...did."[70] They imply that because the actual offenders died and can no longer apologize, "Japan as a nation" somehow absorbs their blame. Although Japanese people should take every measure to understand and respond to this horrific aspect of its history, from Lewis' perspective Japan is a political projection that cannot do anything without individuals acting on its behalf. Japan, like General Electric or the Ku Klux Klan, is a concept used as shorthand for the activities of its members. These concepts themselves cannot take responsibility or apologize, just as they cannot suffer or experience grief other than metaphorically. Only individuals, alone or together, can do these things.

For Lewis, instead of diffusing moral responsibility into a faceless collective, we should undertake the often-difficult work of identifying who hides behind the abstraction. Consider the case of an impoverished Indonesian person who steals food for sustenance. An excessively atomistic account might claim that the person made a choice to break the law and thus only she is responsible for her actions. Alternatively, an excessively structural account might claim that "the global capitalist market" is solely responsible for her condition and her theft. If we blame structures for the harm in this case, it would prove quite difficult to hold anyone in particular responsible for the economic injustice experienced by this individual. Rather than claim that social structures as such should be held morally responsible, on Lewis' account we should ask which individuals deserve blame for causing such poverty and who we should hold accountable for failing to assist those in need. Such analyses may find many if not all of us guilty of something, but we can imagine how we might distinguish between the responsibilities of any number of actors within a global economy. I might bear a certain kind of responsibility for buying merchandise produced in sweatshops, voting for leaders who institute unfair trade policies, not leading or participating in global economic reform, or not contributing enough to relief agencies. Corrupt officials in her community might be accountable for paying her inadequately or stealing the aid that she should have received. Nevertheless, each of us would be "responsible for this as individuals, and strictly in proportion to what each might have done, directly or indirectly."[71] The point is that we can attribute whatever is unjust – as opposed to unfortunate, as in cases where a natural disaster causes the harm – about the person's economic condition to the blameworthy actions of individuals. Assigning such blame requires some precision, and collective categories are often too broad for this work.

Lewis appreciates the difficulties of such a fine-grained perspective on moral responsibility, especially given that the "the normal working of our imagination presents us with a simplified picture in which the nation or group is personified, and, having been given a mind and will of its own, is set to act on the stage very much simpler than the actual stage of history."[72] Although prudence may on occasion dictate that we act "as if" the collective bears responsibility, we should make use of this fiction only in "exceptional cases" where "expediency requires proceedings to be taken against a group as if it were an individual entity."[73] Attempts to assign blame with some precision also confront the difficulty of tracing causal chains through complex bureaucracies, some of which lawyers designed specifically to obscure transparency. Our tendency to speak of collective responsibility may in part result from the frustration of repeated failures to make moral sense of organizational flowcharts. Like Adrienne Rich, Lewis justifiably harbors suspicion that such simplifications protect the guilty. As Arendt warned with respect to postwar Germany, "the cry 'We are all guilty' that at first hearing sounded so very noble and tempting has actually only served to exculpate to a considerable degree those who actually were guilty. Where all are guilty, nobody is."[74] Instead of speaking in euphemisms like "Enron was immoral," we should name names. We can then expect individual categorical apologies to track these more precise assignments of culpability. This is not to suggest that we need not consider social structures when addressing systemic problems or that "increased personal responsibility" is the solution to all societal ills. Instead, we can heighten our scrutiny of those behind such structures, hold them accountable, and expect apologies and the relevant structural reform accordingly.

Even if the presuppositions built into Lewis' sense of moral responsibility will be disagreeable to many readers, I want to draw attention to a consequence of his view for collective apologies that should be paramount for collectivists and individualists alike. Before we even begin to consider the ways in which we might attribute blame to a group as such, we can notice how over reliance on collective apologies allow individuals who should be held personally accountable for moral wrongdoing to deflect their own failures into a collective. Instead of apologizing for what I did, I allow the group to absorb my culpability. I then speak of how the group accepts accountability. In many instances, the individual making the apology for the collective has indisputable standing to apologize categorically for something she has personally done wrong.

In the case of Clinton's apology for the Rwandan genocide, he speaks for the "we" of the international community. This shields him from addressing his own failures and obscures his personal contribution to the genocide. As the president of the United States, Clinton made choices regarding this situation. We can sympathize with a politician who faced difficult decisions regarding the United States' role in preventing the massacre after the failed humanitarian campaigns in Somalia and during the nadir of his own domestic popularity. If he now believes those choices were wrong, however, then a categorical apology addressing his failures as a leader and an individual moral agent should convey this. Madeleine Albright, the U.S. Secretary of State at the time, also played a role. If she now believes that she made mistakes, then she can categorically apologize for those specific failures. Asserting simply that the United States, the United Nations, or "the international community" failed can obscure culpability too much, allowing those who deserve blame to hide their own wrongdoing within opaque bureaucracies. Individual agents decided for the United States what they and others would do and not do in the name of the United States. Clinton, Albright, and others each have the standing to state: "I was wrong. This is what I did and this is why I should not have done it. . . ." Instead, Clinton buries each of his individual failures under the generic "we." Here the collective becomes a kind of moral cipher and no one in particular takes personal accountability for her contribution to genocide. In a system designed to track political accountability through transparent decision-making procedures, this becomes an effective strategy for obfuscating lines of responsibility. Whether in the case of Rwanda or Abu Ghraib, institutional actors allow the collective to absorb all blame rather than accept the narrow culpability for their own misdeeds. To paraphrase Nietzsche, such individuals muddy the waters of responsibility to make them look deep. Although no one accepts blame, everyone enjoys the luxury of maintaining that *someone or something else* was wrong. If those who deserve some degree of fault abandon the organization, such as a leader who leaves for another post after causing a scandal, those remaining may be left holding the bag if we allow collective identity to eclipse personal responsibility.

In part, this deflection of blame into the collective left Clinton open to attacks from Republicans who claim that his apology for Rwandan genocide amounted to an attack on the United States.[75] Tom DeLay perceived Clinton's statements as a form of unpatriotic insurrection: "Here's a flower child with gray hairs doing exactly what he did back in the '60s: He's apologizing for the actions of the United States. . . . It just offends me that the president of the United States is, directly or indirectly, attacking his own country in a foreign land."[76] Pat Buchanan cast Clinton's statements as reducing the United States to "groveling and pandering."[77] To some, like George H. W. Bush, apologizing for the United States is comparable to desecrating the flag and it should never be done.[78] We could imagine, alternatively, that each individual who contributed to the genocide in any respect categorically apologized for his or her role in the atrocity rather than wait for Clinton to offer ill-defined gestures on her behalf. Indeed, this is difficult to imagine given the tenor of modern international relations.

Because the strategy of deflecting one's personal culpability into the collective can backfire within individualist cultures, some have developed an interesting variation on this technique. Public officials might announce, with all of the trappings of a confession, how they are personally responsible for some harm. They do not admit, however, that they have personally done anything wrong. They may even name, in the sentence following their declaration of personal responsibility, who really deserves blame. Consider Richard Clarke's March 2004 apology before the National Commission on Terrorist Attacks upon the United States. Referring to his service as chairperson of the United States National Security Council's Counter-Terrorism Security Group from 1992–2003, Clarke stated:

I also welcome the hearings because it is finally a forum where I can apologize to the loved ones of the victims of 9/11. To them who are here in the room, to those who are watching on television, your government failed you, those entrusted with protecting you failed you, and I failed you. We tried hard, but that doesn't matter because we failed. And for that failure, I would ask – once all the facts are out – for your understanding and for your forgiveness.

In addition to noting the failures of others responsible for national security, Clarke indicates that he takes personal responsibility for not preventing the September 11, 2001, attacks. As his testimony unfolds, it become less clear that Clarke believes he did anything wrong and more evident that according to his account the fault lies with those who failed to heed his warnings and enact his initiatives. He leaves us to wonder exactly what he finds blameworthy in his actions and why he is apologizing. If we accept his account, he may be one of the few people within the Bush administration who should not be apologizing for the security and intelligence failures. Yet by most media accounts, he is the only one who does apologize. This drew the ire of conservative commentators. Senator Bill Frist questioned Clarke's standing and intentions: "Mr. Clarke's theatrical apology on behalf of the nation was not his right, his privilege or his responsibility." Here Frist appears to conjure Maimonides' warning about public apologies grandstanding or lacking shame, claiming that Clarke's apology "was not an act of humility, but an act of supreme arrogance and manipulation."[79] William Kristol likewise claimed that Clarke's "pseudo-apology has cheapened the public discourse."[80] Some of these exchanges amount to little more than politically motivated attacks and counter-attacks: Clarke accuses the Bush administration of failing to prevent the attacks and the conservative respondents parry the charges by questioning Clarke's intentions and credibility. Once again, we can appreciate how offenders can use a nominal apology to convey the opposite of contrition. Indeed, Clarke seizes the platform to go on the offensive.

In this context we can also understand former Attorney General Janet Reno's statements in response to federal agents' deadly raid on the Branch Davidian compound in Waco, Texas: "I made the decision. I'm accountable. The buck stops with me."[81] Likewise, John F. Kennedy declared after the Bay of Pigs invasion: "I'm the responsible officer of the government."[82] In both cases, officials cut through the web of bureaucracy to announce their responsibility. We should wonder, however, what sorts of responsibility they accept. Do they believe they have done something wrong which proximately caused the harm? Do they accept blame? Do they continue to endorse the decisions, taking responsibility for their choices without categorical regret? Alternatively, do they only claim that because of their position they accept responsibility to remedy the situation, like a janitor who is responsible for cleaning up someone else's mess? Answers to such questions would allow us to determine what sorts of apologetic meaning such statements convey.

Many follow Lewis' skepticism toward collective responsibility, with some taking pains to trace what appears to be collective wrongdoing to the morally culpable acts of individuals. R. S. Downie, for example, claims attributions of collective responsibility rely on the ambiguities that I mentioned earlier and often fail to distinguish between causal and moral senses of responsibility. For Downie, blameworthiness requires a "morally faulty decision" made by an individual.[83] We might think, following Peter French, of the organizational structure and underlying beliefs of an organization as somehow transcending individuals. Downie disagrees: "The rules which constitute the collective have been created or accepted by the decisions of individuals, who therefore bear moral responsibility for their decisions."[84] We are too quick to think of institutional characteristics as somehow independent of human choices, as if national or corporate policies and procedures spontaneously appear and then somehow compel humans to execute their objectives. Institutional values and procedures do not make themselves. A more accurate and non-anthropomorphizing account would consider how the choices of individuals or groups of individuals form institutional structures. Such an account would include the rationale and choices of the founders of an institution as well as those who modify its structure throughout its history. We can judge the blameworthiness of each of these acts, including where individuals fail to change policies when they should. If the organizational principles and values of a group tend to produce morally repugnant or morally laudable behavior in its members – contrast the Ku Klux Klan with the Peace Corps – according to Downie, "this will be partly because the decisions of the individuals who created the collective are to be morally praised or blamed."[85] Just as we might take credit for instituting an effective reform when we apply for a promotion, we can take blame for supporting morally defective policies and apologize accordingly.

Return to the example of my department's apology for its gender insensitivity, and imagine that one of the charges against us is our failure to teach courses in feminist philosophy. Now suppose that we discussed the issue of whether to hire a feminist philosopher several years ago. Imagine that six of us preferred to hire a feminist, but seven preferred a logician and we hired according to the will of the majority despite vocal protests from the minority. Now the department's failure to teach feminism looks a bit different, and we can begin to track and individuate blame more precisely. We can better understand our policies as the result of our choices as well as the choices of our predecessors. From my personal experience, members of my own department often treat discussions of curricular objectives as immensely important. If we voted to change our policies, for example deciding whether to make feminism a required course for philosophy majors, I am fairly certain that the individual will and agency of each of us would be present in that discussion. Although an outsider might find us obsessive in the attention we pay to such procedures, we would appreciate that what might look like a small change actually signifies a tectonic shift in our values and mission. Given the importance of such a decision for us, we might also want our votes recorded in order to preserve our individual views for posterity. If we devote such energy to revising our procedures, we can appreciate the importance of altering a nation's operating procedures. If the electorate of the United States voted to amend the Constitution to ban same-sex marriage, I suspect that many would expend considerable energy exercising their agency and recording their position. Future generations can assign praise and blame duly and seek apologies from the guilty for their specific role in the wrongdoing.

Keeping in mind the usual caveats regarding the authenticity of one's freedom to join a collective (Have I freely joined the groups of white, male participants in capitalist markets?), we can also cast judgment on an individual's decisions regarding which organizations she joins.[86] If upon graduation one of my students decides to take an administrative position with the Klan rather than join the Peace Corps, I will judge her choice. I will simultaneously reflect on the structural power and ubiquity of racism in the contemporary United States, but this will not direct my attention away from the detestable behavior of all the individual racists who make this so. Likewise, we can appreciate how institutions can magnify wrongdoing without divesting individuals of agency. Uncritically executing the orders of your employer may generally constitute a moral failure, but the gravity of such a vice will differ considerably depending on for whom you work.

Other methodological individualists focus further on the metaphysical coherence of attributing intentions to groups. If actions – as opposed to mere behaviors – require intentions and if moral blameworthiness requires bad intentions, then defenders of group responsibility must explain how we can sensibly attribute such mental states to collectives beyond those held by individual members.[87] John Ladd compares organizations to machines in this respect.[88] Like even a complex machine, an organization as such only functions according to the rules its leaders have programmed individual agents to recognize. Just as we would not typically attribute culpability to machines because they are not morally responsible for their operating procedures, it is a mistake to think of organizations as moral agents if they cannot exhibit nonprogrammed behavior. Although this might resonate with excessively individualist arguments like those that claim that "guns don't kill people; people kill people," it can accommodate a much more sophisticated analysis: People manufacture guns, people profit from weapons sales, people fuel conflicts to increase weapons sales, people pander to gun lobbies, people fire guns, and so on. Moral agency lies not in the weapons, but in those who drive and participate in gun culture. Just as we do not punish guns, we do not expect guns to apologize.

Although methodological individualists believe that we can redescribe all of the morally salient characteristics that we are tempted to attribute to collectives as belonging to the individual members of those collectives, normative individualists worry about group responsibility offending conceptions of justice. Several distinct concerns arise here. If we consider collectives to be responsible for serious harms, should we then punish all members of the group? The notion of punishing a child for the transgressions of her parent, for example, offends our most basic notions of fairness. I suspect Lewis has such practices of group punishment in mind when he describes collective responsibility as "barbarous," but we should not fail to notice how often we resort to rather primitive beliefs regarding tribal punishment. When a nation levies economic sanctions or wages war against a nation in response to the offenses of its dictator, the most innocent members of the group may suffer the worst of the punishment. Yet if we do not distribute the punishment across the collective, how would we apportion blame and punishment without ultimately referring to individualist conceptions that allow us to trace degrees of wrongdoing to single moral agents?

Aside from those deontological issues, utilitarian problems also arise. If we administer punishment against collectives, will this reduce its deterrent effect because individual offenders will be less likely to suffer the full force of sanctions if they are spread across a group?[89] Alternatively, might it shift the emphasis to reforming institutional features in a manner that individual punishment alone might not? I discuss the possibility of collective emotions later, but here we can simply note that while executives may fear prison and stockholders may dread plummeting values, corporations do not fear at all. In addition, would thinking of groups as responsible for the transgressions of its members increase tensions between collectives? If we think of Group X harming Group Y, rather than Person A harming Person B, might this potentially lead to conflicts between masses of people rather than individuals? Collective retribution has had disastrous historical consequences. Still others worry about the repercussions of allowing notions of collective responsibility to grow roots in a culture. Contrary to communitarian hopes for cultivating solidarity, increased attention to nebulous notions of collective responsibility within traditions steeped in individualist conceptions of wrongdoing could result in a general deterioration of a population's sense of personal culpability.

If we worry that such critiques of collective responsibility produce a version of selfish egoism, Lewis explains that "we are all extensively 'responsible for' our fellows in the sense that we have duties towards them." Even the thickest conceptions of moral duties "may be fully allowed without affecting the principle that value belongs to the individual and that it is the individual who is the sole bearer of moral responsibility."[90] Lewis believes that his position "is not individualistic in any way which is incompatible with a true estimate of our essential social relationships" and thus it "is not 'atomic' in any objectionable sense."[91] Lewis concludes with the now standard response to structural determinism: "Anyone who holds that the individual is never free to choose his action in a way not determined by factors outside himself should surrender the idea of properly moral responsibility; the position cannot be saved by extending our responsibility to our environment, and the attempt to do so is *a reductio ad absurdum* of the view that morality is compatible with determinism."[92] Similarly, one might also take the Humean view and claim that the identities of individuals and collectives are not so different in that both are a kind of useful metaphor. Just as Lewis claims that collective responsibility is a convenient simplification, perhaps individual responsibility is not so different. If we are nothing other than a series of experiences irreducible to anything more permanent, our individual identity is an abstract simplification much in the same sense that collective identity gathers the mental states of its members. Indeed, Hume found the self and the republic similar in this respect.[93] Even if the self is a useful fiction like the collective, this points toward reducing the possible meanings of individual responsibility rather than increasing the significance of collective responsibility. If moral responsibility withers, so withers certain forms of apologetic meaning.

The various positions on collective responsibility invoke the range of competing theories of moral causation and accountability discussed earlier. How one conceptualizes moral responsibility will of course influence how one views collective moral responsibility. As we saw with respect to individual apologies, this range of beliefs regarding standards for moral blameworthiness generates considerable confusion. Collective apologies compound these difficulties, but I believe we can distill a few compelling insights for collective apologies from this contested field.

First, certain kinds of apologetic meaning make little sense without relying on a rather thick notion of personal responsibility. If I have done nothing wrong, an apology from me will lack the sorts of meaning discussed at length earlier. In the absence of blameworthy individuals, apologies drift toward expressions of sympathy or declarations of values. Our temptation to cast blame widely may serve numerous social functions, but if we erode the relation between proximate causation and moral responsibility then we risk losing a considerable portion of the possible meaning of apologies. Without some conception of blame predicated on individual moral responsibility, we might understand all injuries to be unintentional accidents or excusable consequences of structural coercion. Here we can recall the example of someone attempting to categorically apologize for being struck by a meteor that causes her to arrive late for an obligation. If she truly had no control over this accident, we have no reason to blame her. She does not deserve to be punished, nor must she reform her behavior. We also cannot be assured that it will not happen again. A categorical apology therefore seems misplaced. Similarly, if we assign blame to groups for metaphysical guilt or pre-reflective intentions, even though members have arguably no control over such traits, then the relevant harm begins to look increasingly accidental. Apologizing for my metaphysical guilt can express a variety of important meanings regarding my values and plans, but with respect to accepting culpability it would be like apologizing for being struck by a meteor. We might believe that even my metaphysical guilt results from my active or passive complicity in a wrongdoing for which I should apologize, but in such cases we would resort to some version of individualism to assign such blame to me. In this respect, some of the most robust meanings of categorical apologies make little sense without certain presuppositions regarding personal agency and moral causation. I am not claiming that we must necessarily analyze all moral questions solely in terms of individuals, but rather that many kinds of apologetic meaning require us to think in this normative vocabulary.

Second, I find many attempts to shift blame to a collective entirely suspect. Rather than cast blame widely to catch all of those who contributed to any harm, in practice many collective apologies allow wrongdoers to diffuse blame into the ether of institutional doublespeak. It seems that in modern life we often want to have it both ways. Our strongest, if not entirely dogmatic, opinions regarding individuated personal identity surface when it comes to accepting benefits: I deserve praise for my hard work, I should receive credit for that idea, I earned the highest grade in the class, or I merit consideration for a promotion. When things go wrong, we shift to collective notions of responsibility: We made mistakes, our policies failed us, market forces are unpredictable, or "we did not act quickly enough after the killing began." When accepting praise, we shorten causal chains. When deflecting blame, we extend them indefinitely and even question whether moral responsibility makes sense given any number of metaphysical conundrums. When we seek a raise, we emphasize freedom and responsibility. If faced with punishment, we invoke determinism. We thus tend to describe benefits as the work of free-willed agents, but harms as disproportionately accidental. We expect to be singled out when thanked, but prefer to be identified as a member of a group when blamed. Although one might object to such characterizations by citing star athletes or politicians who invoke "team speak" – "I'm just one player," "I couldn't do it alone," "our victory was a team effort" – we can appreciate how easily they jettison this language to emphasize their personal accomplishments during contract negotiations or election campaigns. The ability to "have it both ways" provides a boon to institutional actors within democratic capitalism because leaders and executives can maximize the benefits of individualism while minimizing personal risk. This should provoke our suspicions regarding the motivations for simplifying many individual offenses into one conglomerate wrong that a collective apology attempts to cover.

This brings us to my third, and perhaps strongest, worry: Offenders too frequently provide collective apologies *instead of* individual apologies. In addition to the range of possible meanings that a collective apology might offer, we should seek and receive the categorical apologies that individual wrongdoers should provide. We typically find the meatiest apologetic meaning in the contrition of individuals who accept personal blame for harming another. Any additional meaning provided by an apology from the collective to which this individual belongs is often gravy. What collectives often serve, however, is an unsatisfying dish of gravy without the meat. We may outthink ourselves in this respect, seeking complex apologies from the souls of institutions when the person within the institution who accepts that she made a mistake can often provide the most powerful meaning. Looking to collective apologies in lieu of individual apologies plays into the hands of those who prefer to allow their institutions to absorb their wrongdoing. In the vast majority of circumstances, apologies accepting collective responsibility should supplement – rather than replace – apologies from individuals for their personal wrongdoing. I suspect that even the strongest advocates for collective responsibility, including those who reject Kantian and other forms of individualism, would agree.

Fourth, sustaining some degree of precision in our attributions of moral causation provides one means of preventing collective apologies from supplanting individual apologies. We can often trace what may at first glance seem like collective wrongdoing to the culpable actions of individuals. Malefactors may hide within shadowy institutional structures, but with some investigation we can expose their misconduct and hold them accountable for it. Such research will require the fine-grained moral analysis that Lewis recommends, and we already have a sense of the sorts of transgressions that individuals tend to ascribe to institutional features. If one blames harm on institutional rules or policies, for instance, we can typically track how such features of organizations result from the choices of individual institutional agents. Institutional objectives and the structures designed to achieve them are not somehow prior to human choice but rather represent the sediment of individual agency. Just as executives and politicians take credit for their roles in an organization's progress, they can accept blame and apologize for how their decisions cause harm. If a senator votes in favor of waging a war, we can hold her responsible for the consequences of this vote rather than shift her share of the blame onto the legislation or the nation as a collective. Similarly, we can judge an individual's decision to join a collective with a morally suspect mission or her failure to reform an institution with dubious procedures. Even if an institution's stated policies appear morally sound, there are many ways that members of the group can be culpable for breaching or failing to enforce those rules. As we pay closer attention to how individuals behave and misbehave within collectives, we should become more skilled at connecting the dots between what initially appears to be collective wrongdoing and the actions of those whom we should hold accountable. We can then pair our expectations for apologies with the gestures of those most suited to give them. With these distinctions in mind we can watch for those who obfuscate lines of moral responsibility. Such subterfuge can take a variety of forms, including the most audacious tactic of declaring that one accepts all responsibility while transferring all blame to others.

In addition, failing to trace moral responsibility to individual wrongdoers leaves important gaps in the historical record. Speaking in generalities about the responsibility of the collective will likely fail to create a record of the multitude of faults that we should ascribe to individuals in cases of large-scale harm. Consider the variety of degrees and kinds of contributory responsibility for which individual members of the "international community" should apologize for the Rwandan genocide. Despite numerous obvious culprits, including himself, Clinton blamed no one in particular. If the history books only explain how the international community in general erred, they do not tell the story of how the actions and omissions of individuals aggregated to produce an atrocity. This fails to teach a crucial lesson regarding how seemingly minor offenses can compound and contribute to the commission of mass murder. In this respect, not individuating wrongdoing may also minimize the scale and breadth of wrongdoing. The assertion that the "international community failed" Rwanda seems both more innocent and more isolated than a detailed account of the many different ways in which thousands of political leaders and billions of global citizens share blame for genocide. The former description gives the impression that the policies of the United Nations would benefit from reform; the latter points toward the ubiquity of racism and indifference in our age. Racism and indifference can be understood in individual and institutional senses, and we can address these ills at both levels. Structural features of modernity make it likely that Western nations will respond similarly to future crises in Africa, as the Darfur conflict proves. If we blame only Clinton, Albright, and others for the failures in Rwanda, we will not understand or treat the institutional diseases that repeatedly produce such gruesome symptoms. Yet if we address only the institutional features, we fail to identify those who infect us or exacerbate our condition. Apologies can and should reflect these complexities.

Given my focus on the importance of individual moral agents to apologetic meanings, I should again emphasize that I do not intend my preceding comments to suggest that we should disregard structural causation. Indeed, I find structural considerations essential to understanding the social meanings of apologies. As I hope to have shown, we can hardly make any sense of apologies in contemporary life without placing them in the contexts of our religious traditions, legal cultures, and global markets. These structures can surely cause harm in some senses. Capitalism, for instance, causes many problems, leading economists and political philosophers to debate whether harms such as the material inequality inherent in free markets outweigh the benefits offered. Yet blaming capitalism, rather than capitalists, often disfigures many of the applicable moral concepts beyond recognition in the case of apologies. We can therefore make little sense of the idea of "capitalism apologizing." Instead, we give capitalism a face. We might first think of corporations as the face of capitalism, but the notion of Enron apologizing seems equally anthropomorphizing even if it is a "legal person." For reasons that I will discuss later, a cartoon featuring an apology from an animated Enron logo would probably prove unsatisfying. Eventually, we come to appreciate that only those individuals most directly morally responsible for the harms committed in the name of Enron can provide certain kinds of apologetic meaning. Here again we can emphasize the distinctions between *causal responsibility* and *moral responsibility*. Meteors can be causally responsible for injuries; a rock falling from space can cause damage. A meteor is not, however, morally blameworthy for the injuries that it causes and therefore the notion of punishing a rock seems deeply confused. This would be especially clear if a person intentionally threw a rock at another and then blamed any resultant harm on the rock. Just as a person would be misguided if she sought an apology from the rock rather than the person who threw it, we should ascribe blame to those who set corporations and governments into motion rather than on the institutional features at the point of impact. Optimally, our apologetic practices would remain mindful of structural causation while attributing individual moral culpability when appropriate. If we maintain a sense of personal responsibility while appreciating a degree of structural causation, we can appeal to normative frameworks that rely on individual agency while using those notions to reform unjust social conditions. I hope such a balance would seem sensible to both collectivists and individualists.

The fact that collective responsibility does not resonate especially well with some kinds of apologetic meaning, however, does not mean that we should abandon all notions of collective identity and causation. As Alasdair MacIntyre correctly argues, our collective identities drive our narrative understandings of ourselves and the world: "The story of my life is always embedded in the story of those communities from which I derive my identity." "I am born with a past," he continues, "and to try to cut myself off from that past, in the individualist mode, is to deform my present relationships."[94] Because of this, MacIntyre, claims, "I inherit from the past of my family, my city, my tribe, my nation, a variety of debts, inheritances, rightful expectations and obligations."[95] We can inherit debts and obligations, however, without being blameworthy. Just as I can inherit the wealth of an ancestor without being praiseworthy, I can inherit her debt without deserving blame. This applies to moral debts as well, for example if our predecessors leave us to redress the harms they cause. Thus regardless of whether you believe that all living Caucasians deserve blame for the slave trade, you can assert that all Caucasians have a collective duty to remedy the legacy of slavery. I may also be morally responsible for remedying a wrong even if neither my ancestors nor I caused it. I may have a moral duty to provide famine relief or help a stranded motorist even if I did nothing to cause the harm. In this respect, we can speak of moral duties applying to classes of people regardless of the blameworthiness of individuals within the group. We can therefore argue that all global citizens have a duty to address gender inequality, including those who are most innocent in this regard, without believing that all of them should categorically apologize for gender inequality (unless we further argue that each is personally guilty in some respect). We can also identify situations in which institutions have heightened obligations to those previously wronged. When an institution recognizes its mistreatment of a group in the past, its leaders may feel a special solicitude toward the interests or values of the victims and take exceptional care not to repeat offenses against the group.[96]

I would also like to note here several related issues that I will take up in more detail later but that relate to these concerns regarding collective responsibility. First, questions of collective responsibility raise a series of crucial issues regarding reform and redress. If the collective as such is blameworthy, who must undergo reform? Who, ultimately, bears the cost of remedial efforts? If categorical apologies have some punitive content, who or what will be punished? We can immediately sense the importance of such questions and the difficulties they pose, and I consider them in the section titled "Collectives Reforming and Providing Redress." Second, we typically consider the intentions and emotions of agents when assigning blame. Does it make sense to speak of the mental states of collectives in these senses? I raise these issues with respect to the emotional content of apologies from collectives and the intentions motivating a collective to apologize. Similarly, collective responsibility can present serious difficulties regarding defining the membership of a group. A nation, for instance, is a complex arrangement of overlapping organizations and individuals. Membership at all levels is in constant flux. How, then, do we identify who belongs within such a collective? I consider these questions in the section titled "Collectives, Standing, and Delegation."

Finally, what sorts of meaning do collective apologies provide beyond an aggregation of individual categorical apologies? If we should often think of collective apologies as the gravy on the ethical meat of individual apologies, what meaning do collective apologies add? Rarely, I argue, do collective apologies add significance with respect to groups accepting blameworthiness. Instead, collective apologies often serve as declarations of the values and intentions of members of a group. Such meaning can be momentous, but we can clearly distinguish between the ethical significance of categorical and value-declaring apologies. Likewise, I also mentioned previously that ambiguity within apologies occasionally serves important ends. Some ambiguity regarding distributing blame across a group might allow, for instance, a group to move forward with remedial efforts without undergoing the kinds of protracted causal analyses that fine-grained accounts of blameworthiness can require. Given the damage that such investigations and finger-pointing might cause to group solidarity, situations may arise wherein leaders would be well advised to forgo the sorts of meaning associated with findings of individual guilt. In some contexts, it may be wise to emphasize the prospective significance of apologies over the retrospective meanings. Although those administering truth and reconciliation tribunals often make this choice, I hope to have provided some sense of the costs and dangers of such strategies. Collective apologies can also, in certain circumstances, pave the way for individual members of the group to provide categorical apologies for their own wrongdoing. If a collective offers an apology, for example, individuals can worry less that they will shoulder all of the blame if they offer a personal apology or that their admissions will conflict with accounts provided by their superiors. Additionally, an apology from the institution is often best situated to provide the sorts of "synthetic" meanings that account for and attempt to reform a collective's structural failures. In some respects, this allows collective apologies to foster solidarity around the breached principles and mobilize remedial efforts.

I should also remind readers that collectives can, in principle, offer categorical apologies if they provide sufficiently detailed accounts of the aggregate responsibility of the members of the group. As my initial examples suggest, parsing moral responsibility in this respect becomes increasingly difficult as the size of the group expands or its membership spans over long periods. In general, however, I worry that it is far more common that collective apologies simply dodge questions of culpability in order to protect individual members from bearing the cost of their wrongdoing. Both collectivists and individualists should appreciate the moral price of such trends.

3. Collective Accidents and Denials of Intent

As I outlined earlier, intentions matter to apologies in at least two senses. First, an offender's mental states at the time of the transgression are often crucial for assigning blame because we judge those who accidentally injure us differently from those who harm us intentionally. For this reason, the offender's intentions can be a potentially crucial component of the historical record. Second, the intentions motivating an apology inflect its meaning. An apology begrudgingly provided only to avoid punishment will differ from one motivated by a sense of duty to the victim and the breached principle. I will discuss how intentions matter to collective apologies in the first respect in this section, but a few of these concerns apply to collective intentions for apologizing as well.

As we saw with respect to individuals, the mental states of offenders can be difficult to discern because we cannot see directly into the minds of others, especially if they do not want us to. Lie detectors and similar devices provide a glimpse into the consciousness of the accused, but they can hardly reconstruct the motivations of suspects. Those accused of wrongdoing often make matters still more difficult by claiming that even the most transparently malicious acts were accidental. Recall, for instance, the examples of public figures caught espousing venomously hateful ideas but then claiming that they had not intended to offend anyone. Likewise, those who apologize for purely self-interested or even deceptive reasons will often take every measure to appear as if the suffering of the victim or the gravity of moral reform motivates their contrition. Collective intentions compound these difficulties because we have so many more potentially uncooperative minds to read.

Beyond the difficulties of gauging the intentions of groups, we can wonder if it makes metaphysical or normative sense to speak of collectives possessing mental states. Did the U.S. military, as a collective, intend to commit acts of torture at Abu Ghraib prison? Even if we claim that only a handful of renegade guards committed the acts, did they intend to commit these acts as a group or as individuals? Recent research in collective intentionality often runs parallel to the questions I considered earlier with respect to collective responsibility, with nonsummative accounts like those advanced by John Searle and Michael Bratman arguing that collective intentions of the form "we intend to do x" are more than the sum of the independent intentions of individuals in the group.[97] Those who prefer nonsummative accounts emphasize how collective intentions allow us to plan and coordinate our actions, thereby contributing to an irreducible sense that "we intend" to work together toward some objective rather than independently directing our activities toward the same goal. Margaret Gilbert and others describe the normative aspects of group belief, explaining how collective intentions can generate joint commitments and obligations.[98] Due to spatial constraints I will not address the debates regarding collective intentionality to the extent that I considered collective responsibility other than to note the most salient concerns for apologies.

In one respect, the intentions of some tightly structured institutions may be more easily accessible than those of individuals. Perhaps with the exception of those who strictly observe religious doctrines, most of us do not orient our lives by a personal charter or constitution that renders our principles and intentions publicly transparent. Some groups, however, articulate their intentions in just this sense through legislation or other declarations of organizational objectives. Such statements can prove revealing of a group's intentions. If a law explicitly cites homophobic reasons for criminalizing sodomy, legislators will have difficulty later claiming that any discriminatory prosecution experienced by homosexuals was accidental because legislators merely intended for the law to generally promote abstinence. As Peter French explains regarding internal decision structures, the cohesiveness of a group will influence the extent to which we can attribute stated intentions to the group as such. Keeping these institutional features in view, we could imagine situations in which the intentions of members of a group align uniformly with institutional policies at the time of the offense and the group could apologize accordingly.

More commonly, however, the intentions of groups and their members prove even more difficult to discern than those of individual wrongdoers. We can first apply all of the previous concerns regarding consensus to the intentions of the group at the time of the offense. Multiple and even conflicting intentions may motivate even individual wrongdoers. In the example of leaving my friend waiting at our dinner appointment, many mental states may coexist within me. I may feel terrible about leaving her waiting but lack the courage to call to cancel our meeting. Some part of me may relish the idea of her waiting alone for me, perhaps as retribution for some similar harm that she caused me. Maybe I feel a bit of guilt initially, but then think that her friends regularly visit this restaurant and rationalize that she will be fine without me. My point here is that our intentions can be nuanced or even opaque to ourselves, but the complexities compound accordingly when we speak of the intentions of groups. Although we can attempt to gauge the intentions motivating Clinton's failure to intervene in the Rwandan genocide, how do we read the intentions of the international community? Or return to the Abu Ghraib example. What were the intentions of the United States there? What were the intentions of the U.S. military? What were the intentions of those who directly administered the torture? What if some intended to humiliate the prisoners for sadistic reasons, others were driven by racist hatred, some took no pleasure in the acts but believed that their actions served U.S. intelligence interests, and still others participated only because they feared disobeying their superiors? We can see in such circumstances how a general claim that the group intended to torture the prisoners would conflate morally distinct offenses that a categorical apology would reflect. An apology from either the individuals or the group would convey quite different meanings if they admitted racist intentions rather than simply misguided interrogation techniques.

Even if we adopt what Gilbert criticizes as a "summative account" of collective intentionality whereby we describe a group as holding an attitude if most of the members of the group individually hold the attitude, this can exclude crucial opinions of dissenters.[99] I suspect that the twenty-three senators who voted against The Use of Military Force Against Iraq Resolution of 2002 would like for the historical record accompanying any future collective apology from the United States for the war to reflect the distinctions between their mental states during that period and those of the majority. Some U.S. officials had no intention of invading Iraq, and recording such dissent preserves important information about the opinions, beliefs, and motivations of legislators at the time. By suggesting that the currents of political will were so strong that no U.S. politicians could resist them, failing to register these differences in intentions would also serve to minimize the agency and thus the culpability of those who voted for the resolution.

Not only might a general attribution of a certain intention to a group fail to provide the fine-grained distinctions discussed with respect to collective responsibility, but it would also multiply opportunities for individuals to deny that the harms caused by their actions were intentional. To recall an earlier example, if someone can claim that he did not intend any anti-Semitism when calling a woman a "stupid Jew bitch," then we can imagine the sorts of arguments that individuals within groups would conjure in order to describe the consequences of their actions as incidental. With some procedural distance between themselves and the blood they spill, offenders can bury their intentions within vast institutional depths. The institution would be described as wicked, somehow transforming the innocent intentions of its members into pernicious outcomes. The Nazi could claim that she did not intend genocide, the soldier that she did not intend civilian casualties, and the executive that she did not intend fraud.

As with collective responsibility, the temptation to deflect all blameworthy intentions into the faceless abstraction of a collective would be strong. If we claim that the will of the collective, rather than our own, was the primary force behind the wrongdoing then we might assert our innocence. The accused might even claim that they too are victims, having been swept up by forces beyond their control. Here one might assert that we should understand social structures and conditions as accidental, like intentionless natural disasters. As we saw when ascribing blame to members of collectives, with some effort we can trace institutional objectives and features to the actions – and intentions – of individuals. One might claim that the Democratic Party generally supported the war in 2002, but explain that the party held this position not because the majority of Democratic legislators personally supported the war but because party leaders believed that not supporting the war at that time amounted to political suicide and thus advised members to acquiesce to the president's initiatives. In my view, such circumstances make a degree of precision with respect to the mental states of group members even more important to apologetic meaning. In addition to rebuking the Democratic Party for its intentions, we should demand that individual Democrats answer for their self-serving motivations. This seems compatible with Raimo Tuomela's distinction between operative and non-operative members of a collective, with operative members determining the content of a group's intentions.[100] Corporate executives, for instance, set the agenda for the organization and lower-ranking employees internalize these collective intentions. If we differentiate culpability according to operative and non-operative members, we might expect apologies from leaders to account for their actions that instilled certain intentions within the group. We might simultaneously require the rank and file to apologize for tacitly assenting to and adopting blameworthy intentions. As we saw with collective responsibility, research in collective intentions sharpens our awareness of how individuals coordinate to produce large-scale harm. Something like a slave trade or an illegitimate war can require millions of individuals to internalize culpable intentions, and an apology that disregarded the distinct culpability of each of these mental states would lack meaning accordingly.

4. Collectives, Standing, and Delegation
Standing

I argued that an individual must have "standing" in order to apologize categorically. This important element ensures that I can only categorically apologize for injuries I cause and for which I can accept blame, and Pettigrove suggests that issues related to standing can render moot all other considerations regarding whether the U.S. Congress should apologize for slavery.[101]

The missing link between the injury and the apologizer can be obvious. If I state that "I apologize for the assassination of Abraham Lincoln," we immediately notice the limitations of the gesture because I did nothing wrong to cause his death. Similar deficiencies would be evident if I announced that "United States hereby categorically apologizes for its history of slavery." Not only did I not trade or own slaves, but I appear to lack authority to speak for slave traders or the United States. I certainly cannot speak for all Americans, the United States did not grant me authority to speak on its behalf, and I cannot make any claim that those responsible for slavery bequeathed their standing to apologize to me. I could categorically apologize for any unjust benefits I have received and continue to receive as a white man living in the legacy of racial oppression or for any personal failures related to remedying the legacy of slavery, but I would have standing only to make these narrowly tailored categorical apologies.[102] Such apologies from me could be quite meaningful in their own right, but they would be very different from the United States categorically apologizing for slavery. I therefore lack standing to apologize categorically for either Lincoln's assassination or the slave trade in two senses: 1) I cannot accept blame for causing the harm; and 2) those who did cause the harm did not delegate the authority to apologize to me in any obvious respect. To the extent possible, I would like to separate these issues when considering how they relate to collective apologies.

Before proceeding, I should not fail to appreciate the importance of the meanings that can be provided by third parties who cannot accept causal responsibility for the harm at issue. As explained with respect to individual apologies, third parties can corroborate the victim's account of the event, apportion blame, vindicate her moral principles, legitimate her suffering, and provide reparations. Both Tavuchis and Gill note, for example, that corroboration of the historical record of injuries by public officials who did not cause the harm can be deeply meaningful.[103] Such accounts confirm that the injuries are real, and this initial recognition of suffering can be especially important in cases of political conflict. Third-party accounts may help victims and their families understand what transpired in the chaos of war or behind opaque bureaucracies, enabling them to trace culpability for the harm. Injured parties sometimes want third parties to tell their stories so that the world can judge the offender. This can be the case not only for a victim subjected to torture but also in more pedestrian cases, for example if a consumer who has been mistreated by Wal-Mart requests that the Better Business Bureau investigate and publish her claim. In both instances, parties seek to have their stories legitimated and to remedy their personal problems but also to publicize the misdeeds so that the offenders cannot hide the transgressions from the court of public opinion. Third parties can also punish the offenders and care for the victims. Although declarations, court proceedings, and policy commitments from third parties can be meaningful in these respects, only an offender can provide much of an apology's meaning in the respects detailed earlier.

The distinctions between the meanings possible from an apology with standing and one without may clarify some confusion. For many, it generally seems that collectives should apologize for the sins of their predecessors in order to help reconcile rifts between groups: Germany should apologize for the Holocaust, the United States should apologize for slavery, and Australia should apologize for the Stolen Generation. Apologies appeal to a rudimentary sense of justice, if only to the barest intuition that we should somehow right wrongs. Arguing against such apologies appears, at some level, like arguing against reconciliation. Perhaps for this reason, many writing on apologies minimize the importance of standing.[104] Aviva Orenstein claims outright that apologies can be issued by a "moral predecessor-in-interest (such as a national leader apologizing for prior wrongs committed by her country or a parent apologizing for her child's behavior)."[105] Gill argues that to expect institutional apologies to meet the usual requirements of apologies is to hold them to an "impossibly high standard." "Holding groups to such a standard would," she reasons, have "prohibited the German government from offering an apology to surviving [Holocaust] victims."[106] Michael Cunningham eliminates the "need to establish a linkage between responsibility and apology" because an apology "has the potential to improve relations between groups."[107] In order to enable collective apologies, Govier and Verwoerd downplay the requirement that the apologizing party have any causal relationship to the injury, claiming that a spokesperson for the collective can apologize even if she "had little or nothing to do with the wrongful acts in question."[108] Jean Harvey prefers a sliding scale: "The more institutional the wrong, the more appropriate it is for apologies to be offered to the victims by an institutional representative, at some time later if necessary."[109]

Unlike those who minimize the importance of standing for collective apologies, I want to emphasize three points. First, certain kinds of apologetic meaning are only possible with standing. Considering all of the reasons why we value apologies, it would be deeply meaningful for the German nation to apologize categorically for the Holocaust. If we stretch our definition of apology too thin, however, it can no longer bear certain moral weight. Many Nazi henchmen went to their graves unrepentant, and the meaning of the apologies they never gave died with them. Gestures from contemporary German officials would be meaningful in their own right, but they are incommensurable with a survivor hearing the words "I was wrong" from those who once treated her as vermin unworthy of moral acknowledgment. There are no shortcuts or alternative routes to this particular sort of meaning, regardless of how strongly we may desire it. One victim of sexual abuse within the Canadian Roman Catholic Church made his search for meaning clear in this regard: "I don't want an apology from you [Archbishop Marcel Gervais]. I want an apology from the brothers that ruined my life. I want an apology from those two dogs – those two pedophiles."[110] In these respects, an apology from a third party is like your mother telling you that she loves you after your romantic partner abandons you – they are the right words, but from the wrong person.

We can also notice that these apologies for the wrongs of others come rather easily because the apologizer does not need to admit that she has done anything wrong. Instead of suffering the anguish of admitting that they were personally wrong and confronting uncertain responses from their victims, those who apologize for others enjoy a breezy walk on the moral high road explaining how others failed. C. S. Lewis shares my impression of this form of confession without culpability:

> Since, as penitents, we are not encouraged to be charitable to our own sins, nor to give ourselves the benefit of any doubt, a Government which is called "we" is ipso facto placed beyond the sphere of charity or even of justice. You can say anything you please about it. You can indulge in the popular vice of detraction without restraint, and yet feel all the time that you are practicing contrition. A group of such young penitents will say, "Let us repent our national sins"; what they mean is, "Let us attribute to our neighbor . . . in the Cabinet, whenever we disagree with him, every abominable motive that Satan can suggest to our fancy."[111]

Presidents have little difficulty apologizing for the sins of the prior administration of an opposing party, if only to emphasize that the inauguration severed chains of causal responsibility. We should therefore be especially suspicious of groups apologizing for their predecessors as a cheap means of currying favor by sacrificing the already dead.[112]

Third, we can achieve many of the social objectives cited for reducing the role of standing in collective apologies without providing anything that we would have considered an apology according to commonsense accounts. It is even possible, I believe, that reducing the importance of standing to collective apologies risks undermining their legitimacy and impeding transgenerational justice through means other than apologies. As we reflect on the role of moral causation in categorical apologies, it seems increasingly tenuous for individuals within modern institutions to confess to wrongdoing without standing. To a citizenry, the prospect of collectively apologizing for some historical injustice may come to seem entirely vacuous. If we are not accepting blame, what is the point of dredging up the past? For those who wish to deny any responsibility for past wrongdoing or shirk duties to provide redress, the public's disenchantment with collective apologies can be a boon. Unwilling to bear the cost associated with apologizing and providing compensation to victims of the Stolen Generation, conservative Prime Minister John Howard of Australia refused a "formal apology" because he argued that "Australians of this generation should not be required to accept guilt and blame for past actions and policies."[113] Camille Paglia has similarly argued that "an apology can be extended only by persons who committed the original offense," rendering an apology from the modern United States "illogical" and an "empty gesture."[114] If I need not accept blame, this argument claims, then I need not take responsibility.

Both Howard and Paglia conflate two notions of responsibility. Even if I did not cause an injury, I may still have a moral duty to remedy it. I may have a moral obligation to help victims of a natural disaster even if I did not cause the harm in any sense. Yet Howard and Paglia's conception of apology suggests that if I am not causally responsible for an injury, then I cannot apologize for it. If I have no standing to apologize, I have no obligation to repair. The notion of a categorical apology, however, helps us to understand how we can achieve some kinds of apologetic meaning without others. We might imagine, for instance, an African-American president of the United States who is also the descendant of slaves being asked to apologize for the nation's history of slavery. Here the previous distinctions regarding the sorts of meaning that a third party can provide would be sharp. The president might fill volumes with declarations documenting the history and future of U.S. racial policy and devote vast economic resources to providing reparations to all victims of slavery as defined in the broadest sense. She could accomplish all of this without describing her actions as an apology, and indeed she might take pains to explain that she herself is a victim rather than an offender. Here we can appreciate the significance that a collective apology can provide even in the absence of the sorts of apologetic meaning that are possible only when the apologizer can assert causal standing.

It may prove helpful to categorize the different ways that standing problems arise for collective apologies. Because I find that small groups provide the clearest sense of the contours of these matters, let us return to the example of my philosophy department apologizing for gender inequities. With this example in view, we can classify a few common forms of attempts to assert standing for collectives: 1) *standing for nonmembers of the collective*; 2) *standing for individual members of the collective without authority to represent the collective as such*; and 3) *standing for an individual as a member of collective with authority to represent the collective, including the various ways that delegation might endow an individual with such authority*.

In the case of *nonmembers* asserting standing, imagine that the Department of History (with which we share no faculty or courses) attempts to apologize for us. Given that the history department does not belong to the group that caused the injury in question, their gesture would be like my apology for assassinating Lincoln. Even if it appears obvious that the apologizer must at least belong to the group for which she apologizes, determining membership can be more problematic than one might think.

Jay Rayner manipulates our intuitions regarding group membership and standing to apologize and creates an amusing parody of collective apologies in his 2004 novel *Eating Crow*, discussed earlier in relation to intentions for apologizing. The book tells the story of Marc Basset, a vituperative restaurant critic who becomes addicted to apologizing after ruining the careers of numerous London chefs. Basset develops such skill in the theatrics of contrition that the United Nations enlists him as the "Chief Apologist" and sends him on an apology world tour in order to ease international relations. UN officials select him for this position not only because of his ability to deliver apologies but also because of his family's role in orchestrating so many atrocities. This, UN operatives believe, endows him with a sort of standing described as "plausible apologibility": "No apology can be made unless the apologizer is entitled to make it...[w]hich means that if somebody is to apologize for an event of great or even midrange antiquity, there must, on their family tree, be a person who was directly involved with that hurt."[115] UN officials found that Basset's ancestors "were deeply involved in the slave trade, obviously big in various colonial administrations, and were enthusiastic prosecutors of military campaigns throughout the 18th, 19th and 20th centuries." This keeps Basset busy earning his generous salary, which is laden with incentives based on the amount of money his apologies save the institutions he represents:

I flew to Drogheda to apologize to the Irish Taoiseach for Oliver Cromwell's bloody rampages through Ireland. In a moving celebration in Ho Chi Minh City, I apologized to a group of saffron-robed monks for America's ill-judged adventures in Vietnam. I headed south to Australia and a fading sunset at Ayer's rock. There I told the appalling story of my nineteenth-century ancestor Jeremiah Welton-Smith and his vicious treatment of the Aborigines who lived on his sheep station before offering a complete and unreserved apology to leaders of the community for the deprivations their people had suffered at the hands of white Europeans. On a frantic whistle-stop tour of the Indian subcontinent, I apologized in turn to India, Pakistan, and Bangladesh for the general mess the British had made of independence and partition, and then I went even further east to the city of Nanking, where I apologized on behalf of the British, Americans, and the French for the ruinous opium wars.[116]

I trust that readers immediately sense the folly in the United Nations' "Office of Apology and Reconciliation" hiring a performer to deliver moving apologies for such a range of failures across such a stretch of history.

One source of amusement results from Basset's failure to satisfy our expectations for standing. Distant family history seems insufficient to establish Basset's standing because his link to the culpability of his ancestors appears too tenuous to consider him a member of the group of wrongdoers. He may share their blood, but not their blame. As considered next, we might take his claim to standing more seriously if the historical offenders had selected Basset as their proxy, but they have not. Instead, a third party chooses him as a mouthpiece because of his flair for empathy and then spreads his "plausible apologibility" so thin that it becomes transparent. Basset's "Penitential Engagements" serve as valuable declarations of principles and policies endorsed by the United Nations, but framing them as apologies is something of a bait and switch: They promise moral depth but deliver superficial political instrumentality.[117] Basset did not cause the suffering, he will not accept blame for it, he will not explain how he was wrong, and he will not personally provide reparations for the harm. He is a political puppet performing an ethical dance.

After becoming a global celebrity and media darling, Basset unravels. An Israeli rebukes Basset for looking at his watch while in the throes of expressing his profound sorrow for the "dark stain on history" suffered by the apologee.[118] His vocation causes him to suffer from a lack of credibility in his closest relationships and his friends and lovers become skeptical of his apologies. Basset eventually resigns from his UN position to become a founding partner in a private apology firm. In the future, a confidant advises him, multinational corporations will have "sound economic reasons" for apologizing and they will need people with Basset's skills.[119] "Unless they're either unlucky or criminal," most of these corporations will find it "[f]ar better to outsource the work to professionals with serious credibility."[120] "Plausible apologibility" in these transactions would be established by "ownership of one, but only one, share in the corporation involved."[121] One stock, like one drop of blood, supposedly links the apologizer to the chain of responsibility. Here again, we sense that although buying one stock may technically induct Basset into the collective, this formulaic conception of membership does not confer substantive standing because it cannot include him within the group of those causally responsible for the harm. He is a member in name only and without the ties required to offer a categorical apology for the group.

If one agrees that one must be a member of the collective for her to possess standing to apologize for it, further questions arise regarding membership criteria. We may wonder precisely to which group the apologizer must belong in order to possess standing. Must she be a member of the group of wrongdoers, or only share membership in a broader group with them? If the latter, just how far can we expand the scope? If someone wishes to apologize for the sexism of the philosophy department, is it enough if she is not a member of the department but a professor in the same university? What if she teaches at a different university but she belongs to the American Philosophical Association or the American Association of University Professors, memberships she shares with everyone in our department?

What if the shared memberships are not only horizontal but also vertical, in that she not only belongs to the same groups as we do but also occupies a leadership position in these groups? Suppose that instead of the history department apologizing for the sexism of the philosophy department, the University's Board of Trustees "apologizes to all members of the University Community for the sexist behavior of the philosophy department." Contrast this with the statement of officials from the University of Colorado regarding Professor Ward Churchill's remarks comparing the office workers who perished during the collapse of the World Trade Center to the technocrats driving the Nazi genocide machine: "The Board of Regents agrees that Ward Churchill's post-9/11 comments have brought dishonor to the University . . . [and] apologizes to all Americans, especially those targeted in the 9/11 attacks and those serving in our armed forces, for the disgraceful comments of Professor Churchill."[122]

In the case of the history department apologizing for the philosophy department, the lack of standing seems obvious. The history department did not cause the harm at issue, just as they did not cause Lincoln's assassination. An apology from them for either wrong would seem odd. The cases of higher-ranking university officials apologizing for the members of the faculty, however, seem less misguided. Why is this? Surely the Trustees are not members of the philosophy department, and the Colorado Board of Regents does not speak for Churchill. Indeed, the Board of Regents apologizes for Churchill against his will. We might think that the fact that even if the officials are not members of the class most directly under scrutiny – the class of the philosophy department or professors named Ward Churchill – they share a broader collective with the wrongdoers as university citizens. Although the history department also shares this community, it does not stand in a position of authority over the wrongdoers. Thus we might attribute standing to officials through some kind of vicarious liability, as discussed earlier, or perhaps the officials could categorically apologize for approving Churchill's appointment to the faculty. Yet as standing becomes divorced from blameworthiness, the possibility for certain forms of meaning wanes in the respects described earlier. We can understand apologies from contemporary German officials for the Holocaust in this light. Just as the Colorado Board of Regents apologized for Churchill against his will, Nazi leaders did not confer standing to anyone to apologize for them. Hitler, for one, would probably have defied any apology offered by someone else for his actions.

I will soon say more about standing and rank, but in each of these cases we can read apologetic gestures from nonmembers not as attempts to assert membership in the group of wrongdoers but rather the opposite. Like the child who apologizes for her racist parents in order to explain to a guest that she does not share their hateful views even though they raised her, the earlier examples serve to distance the history department, the University Trustees, the Board of Regents, and modern Germans from wrongdoers who they otherwise might be associated with. Thus instead of such apologies asserting membership, they dissociate third parties from those who deserve blame.

Once we identify the group to which the apologizer should belong in order to satisfy standing requirements, we face questions regarding how we define the temporal existence of a collective. If we decide that the faculty of the University of New Hampshire's Department of Philosophy is the relevant institution, do we mean every professor who has ever taught in the program? Would this include those who left to teach elsewhere twenty years ago and those who taught as adjuncts for only one semester? Should we include only those who currently have tenure in the department, or perhaps only those continually affiliated with the program since we elected the current chair?

If answers to these questions do not appear obvious even after previous considerations regarding collective responsibility, notice how they become more problematic as the group becomes larger and membership more fluid. If we determine that the "United States President and Cabinet Members" is the collective to which one must belong in order to possess standing to apologize for certain acts, does this group exist continuously throughout the history of the United States? Perhaps we should deem each successive administration a distinct group, meaning that members of the Bush administration lack standing to apologize for the Clinton administration and vice versa. Should we consider the degree to which successive administrations share what French calls an internal decision structure, not only in their commitment to the U.S. Constitution generally but also with respect to their policies? If a vice president in the current administration is elected president in a subsequent administration, should we deem the successive administrations one continuous group? If we are too reluctant to draw moral boundaries between political bodies, we risk defining membership so broadly that any leader has standing to apologize for any other. Bill Clinton, for instance, asserted his standing to apologize for the harms caused by African slavery even before the United States existed: "Going back to the time before we were even a nation, European Americans received the fruits of the slave trade. And we were wrong in that."[123] If we extend standing any further, Clinton may apologize for the slaves kept by the ancient Egyptians as well. Although even this might express significant meaning as a denunciation of how the injustices of antiquity extend into modern life, we can appreciate just how far this meaning drifts from notions of apologies that require standing to express personal wrongdoing.

I would next like to consider *standing for individual members of the collective without authority to represent the collective as such*. Even if a person undoubtedly belongs to the group of wrongdoers and shares personal blame for some aspect of the harm, this is not necessarily a sufficient condition to grant her standing to speak for the collective. One may possess standing to apologize categorically for her own portion of the wrongdoing but not for the collective as such. We would not draw the conclusion that the Nazis had collectively apologized if one or two former midlevel Nazi officials apologized categorically for their wrongdoing. We would instead conclude that *one* or two Nazis had categorically apologized for certain acts. Membership within the group of wrongdoers does not grant the member standing to speak for the entire group. It seems that even members require some additional form of mandate from the collective to speak on behalf of the group, which leads me to the third form of attempts to assert standing within a collective: *standing for an individual as member of the collective with authority to represent the collective.* How does one earn such authority?

As has been unfortunately the case throughout this book, the simple answer may prove deceiving. Some argue that the apologizer must not only be a member of the offending institution but must also hold its highest office. According to what we can call the "membership with rank" theory, the highest-ranking current member of the institution will hold standing to apologize for any prior injuries committed by members of the institution. Any current U.S. president, therefore, can apologize for all of the injuries caused not only by U.S. presidents but also by any current or previous administration, official, or citizen. Such authority reaches across decades, political parties, and even the battle lines of civil war. Under this account, the United States is akin to one person throughout history and the succession of presidents creates something like a single evolving moral agent. Govier and Verwoerd make the following argument:

> Unlike [Tony] Blair, the government of the United Kingdom did exist in the nineteenth century, and its policies helped to bring about the famine that so severely affected the Irish people. Thus, the apology makes sense if understood as the initiative of a collective. The state and government persist; the existence, and persistence, of these collectives are not reducible to the existence, or persistence, of any of their individual members. As Prime Minister of the United Kingdom, presumably after consultation with his Cabinet colleagues, Blair can speak for the country's government. That government bore some responsibility for the nineteenth-century famine, and that government continues to exist. By issuing a public apology, the government can express sorrow and regret about its past policies, and disassociate itself from them.[124]

A few points may be helpful here. First, I share their belief that such a statement from Blair is meaningful as an expression of sorrow, denunciation of prior decisions, and a declaration of future policy. Blair could accomplish all of this without anything like a categorical apology. Blair could state: "Previous officials made grievous errors that caused great suffering. We do not share their values and will not make their mistakes." If the "officials" referred to here were Nazi officials, we would be more likely to classify Blair's statement as a condemnation rather than apology. Yet because of Blair's rank, we are tempted to endow his rather ordinary statement of policy with the rich meaning of a categorical apology from Britain as such. In the case of the philosophy department, we might think that the department chair automatically holds standing to speak for us. Not only is she a member of the department, but she holds its highest administrative post. Regardless of whether she has been a member of the department the longest or her research is the most respected, she outranks the rest of us in this respect. Despite this authority, however, she does not necessarily possess standing to speak for us on all matters. If the chair unilaterally issued a statement apologizing for the department's sexism, numerous concerns related to consensus discussed previously would return forcefully. Regardless of the chair's rank, colleagues might legitimately assert that they have not authorized her to speak on their behalf regarding such issues. Some might find the idea of the department apologizing ludicrous; others may believe that the chair's apology understates the problem. Legislators and citizens might raise the same concerns when a president apologizes on their behalf, as many Republicans made clear in their assertions that Bill Clinton did not speak for them.

Beyond holding membership and rank, the strongest candidates for standing to apologize for a collective will have undergone a process whereby a consensus of members of the group agree to delegate this authority to their leader to express the content and undertake the actions that are also consensually agreed upon by members. In some cases, we consensually delegate authority to speak for us while granting the appointee some degree of discretion. We agree that the chair represents us during meetings with other administrators in the college so long as she expresses views generally in line with our interests. If we cannot agree on our interests, then we appreciate that the chair often finds herself qualifying her statements with phrases like "most of my colleagues support X" or "my eleven colleagues have twenty-two different opinions about Y." If we have not granted her authority to speak for us about the issue in question, how might she earn this standing?

Delegation

If delegating authority to a proxy strengthens the agent's standing to apologize for a wrongdoer, this transfer of authority might occur in any number of arrangements: 1) an individual delegating to another individual; 2) an individual delegating to a collective; 3) a collective delegating to an individual; 4) a collective delegating to a collective; and 5) variations on these arrangements where members delegate to nonmembers or nonmembers delegate to members. I will not work through these possibilities in much detail, but a few examples may illustrate the distinctions between them.

Because they avoid problems of consensus, the simplest cases involve an individual wrongdoer delegating authority to another person to apologize for her. Richard Joyce imagines someone leaving instructions in his will for the executor to apologize "to Aunt Mabel for insulting her at the Christmas party all of those years ago."[125] Here we would have one person with standing delegating the work of apologizing to another, and therefore the offender unanimously conveys a consensus. "Aunt Mabel may find it a sign of cowardice that the apology was postponed in this manner," Joyce speculates, "but will accept that, in the end, she received her due apology." I warned earlier about the limited meaning of deathbed apologies because the victim will not be able to judge the offender's commitment to change, but perhaps the deceased's years of insult-free family gatherings satisfies Aunt Mabel that "he really meant it." Perhaps he also leaves her his life savings to pay for her therapy and to support the study of anger management. In addition, maybe he wrote the words read by the executor and they struck all of the right emotional notes for a categorical apology. It would be difficult to find a deficiency in this apology beyond the deceased's failure to engage the victim in a dialogue regarding the injury.

Yet the possibility that one individual could delegate such a meaningful apology to another does not guarantee that all successfully delegated apologies are equally meaningful. Suppose the offender's instructions to the executor were as follows: "My Aunt Mabel is upset about a comment I made a while back. I do not remember what I said and I feel no regret, but I do not want her to leave my children out of her will because she is angry with me. Frankly, I find her intolerable and I cannot apologize to her with a straight face." The offender adds: "I will add an extra thousand dollars to your bill if you apologize for me after I'm dead and my children deem that you performed the apology in a manner that appears genuine on my behalf." Despite the fact that the offender has successfully delegated the authority to apologize, here we sense the distinction between outsourcing the work of designing and delivering an apology and undergoing a moral transformation. The intentions for delegating are self-serving and deceptive, hollowing out much of its meaning. In the first example, the offender already accomplished much of the work of apologizing and then delegated little more than the act of delivering it. In the second example, the offender pays a proxy to appear as if she conveys rich apologetic meaning for him. He cannot delegate these aspects of the process of categorically apologizing because of their entwinement with the normative life and actions of the reformed offender. In the same respect, it would make sense for me to ask my spouse to "tell the children that I love them," but I could not sensibly ask my spouse or anyone else to undertake the work of loving my children for me. Only I can do that. This helps to explain why the concept of the Tianjin Apology and Gift Center – whose motto is "We Say Sorry for You" and will deliver a personal apology to the victim's home for a fee – strikes us as so odd. Some moral work cannot be outsourced.

If cases of one person directly delegating authority to another are open to such difficulties, we can anticipate some of the issues facing more complex transferals of authority. In the Ward Churchill example, a collective (the Board of Regents) asserts standing to apologize for an individual against his will. Churchill's defiance drains the Board's gesture of meaning beyond a denunciation of his actions. If a collective delegates standing to an individual, for instance if a president apologizes for the nation she leads, the serious problems regarding consensus discussed earlier may arise. Sometimes we find second order delegation, where the collective delegates authority to a leader who then delegates authority to a spokesperson. When a U.S. fighter jet recklessly severed cables to a ski lift in the Italian Alps and killed twenty passengers, U.S. Ambassador Thomas Foglietta stated: "On behalf of President Clinton and the American people, I wish to apologize."[126] Even if we can be certain that Clinton and not some other official delegated his authority to Foglietta, we wonder if this chain of delegation loses strength as it stretches from the pilots, to U.S. citizens, to Clinton, and to Foglietta. Also consider cases in which a collective delegates standing to another collective, for example if the U.S. Marines as a collective transfers its standing to apologize to the United States as a collective or if a massive corporation stands in for its slightly less massive subsidiary. If we imagine one collective delegating authority to another collective several generations in the future, we can appreciate the range of issues related to standing that would confront a contemporary apology from the United States for slavery.

When the wrongdoer delegates her standing to a person or group, an apology from the proxy will gain meaning in the respects I have noted. If the harm occurred in the distant past or by unrepentant individuals or groups, we face a fact that we might prefer to overlook: The dead rarely delegate. Although the deceased may transfer standing through a will or similar deed, I do not know of any cases in which the offenders from the distant past delegated the standing to apologize to a representative from a future generation. Hitler certainly did not confer any such authority to Willy Brandt or members of the current German government. If an offender underwent a transformation and came to believe an apology was necessary, she would typically apologize during her lifetime and there would be no need for delegation. This should make us question anyone who claims to apologize for the deceased, especially in cases of collective apologies from the dead.

In the absence of past generations delegating their standing to apologize to spokespersons from future generations, we may be satisfied with an apology from a member with rank but without delegated authority. It would be nice if the offenders had unanimously granted current spokespersons standing to apologize for them, but without this authorization an apology from a ranking member is better than no apology at all. Although I would caution that we should maintain an awareness of the loss of meaning resulting from such concessions, they do not render the subsequent gestures meaningless. Consider what commentators often describe as Pope John Paul II's apology for at least one atrocity committed during the Crusades: the sacking of Constantinople in 1204.[127] In a statement to bishops of the Greek Orthodox Church he stated:

For the occasions past and present, when sons and daughters of the Catholic Church have sinned by action or omission against their Orthodox brothers and sisters, may the Lord grant us the forgiveness we beg of him. Some memories are especially painful, and some events of the distant past have left deep wounds in the minds and hearts of people to this day. I am thinking of the disastrous sack of the imperial city of Constantinople, which was for so long the bastion of Christianity in the East. It is tragic that the assailants, who had set out to secure free access for Christians to the

Holy Land, turned against their own brothers in the faith. . . . To God alone belongs judgment, and therefore we entrust the heavy burden of the past to his endless mercy, imploring him to heal the wounds which still cause suffering to the spirit of the Greek people. Together we must work for this healing if the Europe now emerging is to be true to its identity, which is inseparable from the Christian humanism shared by East and West.[128]

Setting aside other concerns about the Pope's gesture, we can appreciate the difficulties of delegating authority to apologize for eight-hundred-year-old injuries. Despite this, his gesture conveys important meaning. For one, if we read the Pope as referring to the Church itself or its highest officials as the culpable parties – rather than some recreant "assailants" – then the Pope suggests that the Church can make and has committed moral errors. For an institution whose authority rests on a pillar of infallibility, such a shift signifies a potentially profound transformation of Catholic self-understanding. The statement also reaches out to non-Catholics, thereby advancing a vision of a more unified Christendom. The Pope can convey such meaning regardless of his standing to speak for those culpable for committing the atrocity long in the past.

In some cases, victims may be entirely uninterested in whether the apologizing party possesses standing to speak on behalf of the wrongdoers. If the victim is primarily concerned with an institution revising a policy or providing redress, a ranking member may be much better positioned to generate this meaning than those directly responsible for the harm. Even if the wrongdoers explicitly refuse to delegate their standing to a superior or successor, victims may be more interested in assuring their future well-being than in properly ascribing blame for the past. In these situations, the injured and those at risk of injury may prefer apologetic gestures from those with the highest rank and most power to control the future regardless of even their membership status in the culpable group. Any number of other circumstances might arise wherein victims prefer expressions of sympathy or declarative apologies from high-ranking officials to categorical apologies from the actual offenders. I may refuse to recognize a full apology from my assailant – perhaps because I have broken off relations with her entirely – yet take deep meaning from a judge who sympathizes with me and restores my status as a moral interlocutor worthy of dignity. For an Iraqi civilian maimed by a U.S. soldier in Baghdad, a categorical apology from the soldier to the victim might facilitate reconciliation between them; a value-declarative apology from the president of the United States in which she takes ownership of a problem she did not cause might bring peace. We can appreciate how the meaning of the categorical apology might seem comparatively inconsequential in such a context. We should not lose sight, however, of the relative costs and benefits of such preferences. For one, encouraging officials to apologize for institutional wrongs even when their standing to do so is questionable can result in overly broad conceptions of responsibility that collapse individual wrongdoings into the collective. This, as I discussed at length earlier, can prevent leaders from categorically apologizing for the harms they *do* directly cause. Thus political leaders are quick to denounce the failures of their countries – especially before *they* led the country – but slow to apologize for their own misdeeds.

Lastly, the issues considered here relate not only to the standing of collectives and those who apologize for them but also to the authority of collective victims as recipients of apologies. I mentioned several concerns regarding the standing of individual victims. Who is the proper subject of the gesture, and should the offender apologize to one's god or to the media rather than the victim? To whom should one provide redress? Who holds the power to forgive the offender? When an offender or group of offenders apologizes to a group of victims, the previously stated issues regarding the standing of collective offenders apply to collective victims. These questions regarding the standing of collective victims can prove even more contentious than those concerning collective offenders. Whereas we may welcome all who attempt to apologize and accept blame for some facet of Nazi genocide, we may be more discriminating when determining who speaks for Holocaust victims. Such issues could be quite divisive when deciding who deserves a portion of financial reparations intended for victims. If the pool of reparations is large, who determines how it will be spent? Should it go to individual survivors and their heirs or to international programs advancing Jewish causes? Who holds standing to represent the dead? Who speaks for Judaism, especially in the absence of consensus or delegation of standing?

Using the Norman invasion of 1066 as an example, Richard Joyce argues that "the question of whether an apology should take place depends partly on whether anyone cares."[129] Because he believes that the "social function of apologies is primarily one of reconciliation," Joyce claims that "if all parties are perfectly content with each other – regardless of what harms they have inflicted on each other in the past – then no act of reconciliation is called for."[130] Setting aside the many examples in which the living place transgressions from even the ancient past at the center of their religious or cultural narratives, if we believe that apologies convey deontological meaning then we might desire them regardless of whether any living person or group feels personally wronged. If the meanings of apologies exceed their instrumental value as a means to reconciliation, then who is the proper recipient of such gestures? Who represents justice itself? Recognizing that answers to these potentially important questions are far from obvious should help us to appreciate the many intricacies of collective apologies.

C. Collectives Identifying Each Harm

Categorical apologies from individuals require the offender to name each specific offense, identify the moral principle breached by each offense, and endorse this underlying principle. To recall an earlier example, if I destroy my wife's tomato plant and then blame it on our dog, I owe her apologies for both disrespecting her property and for lying. Because collective apologies often address a range of injuries spread throughout an institution and over a period of time, this presents a number of difficulties in these respects. As I suggested at several points already, covering the range of injuries related to some offenses can seem like a daunting task. I also noted with respect to corroborating historical records for large-scale injuries that these injustices can span across generations and continents. I emphasized in the context of collective responsibility that fine-grained causal analyses of institutional and institutionalized wrongdoing will trace blame to culpable actions of individuals deep within bureaucracies. If we take these requirements seriously, some collective apologies would need to identify catalogues full of harm.

We can sense how such problems would impede a collective apology for slavery in the United States. The slave trade in which the United States' citizens participated harmed and continues to harm hundreds of millions – perhaps billions – of people, all of whom suffer because of the acts of individual people as well as institutional structures. Slavery penetrated every moment of the victims' and offenders' lives. Some of the offenses would be specific to the highest-ranking profiteers from the slave trade and others would relate to the mistreatment of individual slaves by individual owners. An apology for slavery that accounted for all of its moral failures might document the entire lives of generations of people whose every thought and action degraded the enslaved.

Identifying harms in more recent and seemingly contained collective injuries can prove nearly as challenging. Clinton's apology in Rwanda names some offenses specifically: "We did not act quickly enough after the killing began. We should not have allowed the refugee camps to become safe havens for the killers. We did not immediately call these crimes by their rightful name: genocide."[131] This does not exhaust the wrongs committed by Bill Clinton, officials of the United States and the United Nations, and members of the "international community" against the Tutsi people. Clinton does not name the racism, the disregard for human life, the willingness to sacrifice victims for political and economic ends, the indifference of the international media, the continued failure to provide adequate aid and relief, or the lies perpetuated regarding our alleged unawareness of the extent of the butchery. This names but a few of the additional wrongs committed against the Tutsis, and many of these injustices result from an aggregation of still more banal offenses. Further, when Clinton claims that we "did not act quickly enough after the killing began," what exactly was the underlying wrong? What should we have done? Did we err in not allowing UN troops to engage the Hutus with military force, or was it simply that we did not name the genocide as such? We gloss over these complexities in order to assert that Clinton completed the work of apologizing, but this sloppiness leaves many moral injuries unaddressed. In other words, containing such a range of distinct wrongful acts and types of suffering within antiseptic humanitarian generalities misses much of the meaning sought by injured parties. In some instances, this may render the possibility of a collective categorical apology nearly impossible. Even among those of us who are categorically apologetic for our failure to act in Rwanda, our causal relationships to the atrocities are so distinct that it is difficult to imagine an apology that could cover with the required degree of specificity both my failures as an apathetic student at the time and Madeline Albright's as the Secretary of State.

This relates to a web of interrelated concerns regarding identifying the harms at issue in a collective apology. As we see in the Rwanda example, we can easily conflate multiple wrongs into one general apology without recognizing each offense. If we cast the primary failures of international governments as legalistic in nature, then we risk avoiding the multitude of distinct harms that contributed to the genocide. This would include, for instance, identifying any racism motivating the failure to intervene. Not only might a collective apology attempt to cover incommensurable harms with an umbrella apology, it may also allow leaders and wrongdoers at all levels to deflect their individual wrongdoings into the culpability of the collective. I considered this in some detail with respect to collective responsibility, but we can notice here how this tendency to transfer blame from the individual to the collective as such can impede our ability to identify each blameworthy act. As the strategy of shifting blame into the collective obscures our view of the many ways in which vast numbers of individuals harmed the victims, we also risk minimizing the scale of wrongdoing. Also notice how collective apologies increase the opportunities for addressing what I previously described as the "wrong wrong." With so many harms to identify, officials can choose which offenses to recognize based on any number of strategic considerations. If they wish to appease an audience without admitting to an offense for which they might be criminally liable, a collective might identify only moral failures while remaining silent regarding illegal activity. Corporate officials might explain that they "should have done more to advance the interests of investors and employees" without admitting to defrauding them. Regardless of instrumental concerns, collectives may be unwilling to identify the worst of their failures. I suspect that to most Rwandan survivors, the terminological issues regarding whether and when the international community should have named the atrocity "genocide" is of little interest. Even if this designation would have required the United States to intervene under the 1948 Convention on the Prevention and Punishment of the Crime of Genocide, these debates hide the substance of the wrong behind humanitarian legalese.[132] The harm – or at least one of the harms – to be identified in this case is the reprehensible failure of those who could have prevented the slaughter of one million Africans but did not.

D. Collectives Identifying the Moral Principles Underlying Each Harm

As we saw with individual apologies, pairing the harm identified with the abstract principles it violates allows us to understand the nature of the wrongdoing so that we can denounce it as such. Identifying the moral principle, in other words, helps to explain why the offense is offensive. We can then classify other violations of this principle as similarly offensive. As the scale of wrongdoing increases in cases of collective apologies, many moral principles may be in play. Choosing among these principles and deciding which to accentuate and which to disregard can significantly transform an apology's meaning.

Consider the apology of Frederik Willem de Klerk, the last State President of apartheid-era South Africa:

Let me place once and for all a renewed apology on record. Apartheid was wrong. I apologize in my capacity as leader of the National Party to millions of South Africans who suffered the wrenching disruption of forced removals in respect of their homes, businesses, and land. Who over the years suffered the shame of being arrested for pass law offenses. Who over the decades and indeed centuries suffered the indignities and humiliation of racial discrimination. Who for a long time were prevented from exercising their full democratic rights in the land of their birth. Who were unable to achieve their full potential because of job reservation. And who in any other way suffered as a result of discriminatory legislation and policies. This renewed apology is offered in a spirit of true repentance, in full knowledge of the tremendous harm that apartheid has done to millions of South Africans.[133]

Unlike Clinton's failure to mention the racism that many believe motivated the failure to intervene in Rwanda, de Klerk names racial discrimination as a root moral failure from which grew economic, legal, political, and psychological harms. He might have chosen to gather the wrongs of apartheid under a different principle – perhaps blaming colonialism or classism – but by identifying apartheid as a racial injustice, de Klerk describes the failures in a way that orients reforms toward a particular set of values.

An apology for slavery would face similar choices given that the practice violates so many moral principles. Would we cite racial discrimination, distributive injustice, coercion, exploitation, objectification, deception, greed, the denial of personal and sexual autonomy, the violation of the practical imperative, the infliction of pain, the degradation of god's children, or some other moral standard? Indeed, it proves difficult to name a credible moral principle that slavery did not violate. Depending on which principles we identify, subsequent reform might shift accordingly.

This also relates to the scope of the principles identified. Recall the earlier example: Should I apologize to my wife for killing this particular tomato plant because of its sentimental value or should I treat this as an instance of the broader offense of disrespecting her efforts? Does a corporation identify a narrow principle (one should not reduce the cost of mid-sized vehicles over $35,000 by installing inferior safety harnesses), an intermediate principle (the highest quality safety harnesses should be standard on all vehicles), or a broad principle (one should never compromise the safety of an automobile in order to maximize profit)? In the case of slavery, one might cite the exploitation of

Christian Africans as immoral while defending a trade in the unconverted. Hence we should pay close attention to the nature and scope of the values honored within collective apologies.

The sorts of principles identified in collective apologies may tend toward classes of harms that we find more frequently within group activity. These might include negligence, complicity, breaches of fiduciary duties, failures to adequately train or supervise, or refusal to use institutional resources to promote justice or prevent injustice. Given the tendency to believe that governments or corporations – even more so than individuals – should orient themselves according to strict self-interest, it may prove especially important in some cases for collectives to identify values other than bare assertions of power.

Similarly, citing deontological principles can change the basic assumptions regarding why collectives apologize. If members of a collective believe that they have a duty to honor a breached value, they might believe that someone is owed an apology of some kind even if insurmountable obstacles make a categorical apology impossible. Similar to Kant's earlier example of apologizing for defaming the dead, we might think that those who died on the slave ships *deserve* an apology even though they are long dead. We might believe they deserve an apology – as they would deserve a proper burial if we discovered their bones in a sunken ship – regardless of the instrumental value of such a gesture for modern race relations. In some cases, we might frame this as a recognition that an apology is owed even if we realize that such a moral debt cannot be fully discharged. It can be important to recognize publicly that some person or group is owed a categorical apology even though this debt can never be paid because the only people with the proper currency have defaulted in death. We should notice, however, that in Kant's example he refers to the actual offender apologizing to the dead rather than a third party fulfilling this duty for her. Just as Kant would not allow someone else to serve my sentence for me, I doubt he would favor a proxy apologizing for me given that he tends to equate the act with punishment.

E. Collectives Endorsing Moral Principles Underlying Each Harm

These discussions may run together in readers' minds, so I should pause for a moment to distinguish them. When I refer to collectives identifying each injury, I am primarily concerned that we give appropriate attention to each injury rather than conflate several distinct wrongs into one vague apology or emphasize only the lesser offense. As we identify the moral principles underlying each harm, we account for why the victim finds it wrong and we can then treat similar cases as such. Here I discuss the next stage, where collectives recognize the legitimacy of the values put forth and endorse them as their own. We should notice the difference, however, between endorsing a principle and honoring that principle. One might declare that she endorses a value yet repeatedly breach and thus fail to honor that value. Here we can think of Samantha Power's argument: The promise that genocide should "Never Again" occur is vitiated by the practices that allow it "Again and Again."[134] I later consider the gap between promises and actions with respect to collectives providing reform and redress.

When institutions endorse underlying moral principles with an apologetic gesture, this can serve as an explicit declaration of institutional policy. This may announce a fundamental shift in policy, for instance if an institution condemns its past actions and thereby announces that its values have evolved to align with contemporary norms.[135] Collectives may also use apologies to reaffirm members' commitments to values from which they have strayed, like a couple renewing their marriage vows. If the character of an institution comes into question, a declarative apology of this sort can provide one means of reestablishing integrity. The apologetic declaration may take legislative form, thus building the value directly into the institution's governing rules and enforcing those principles with its authority. Unlike the declarations of most individuals, institutions often record their policy announcements in public laws and charters and this provides an additional means of holding groups accountable for violations of their own values. Institutionalizing moral principles in this sense also notifies individuals of the expectations associated with membership and the penalties for transgressing those standards. If an institution declares its commitment to a principle and broadcasts this expectation, the collective and its members will have difficulty arguing in good faith that the value or the punishments for breaching it do not apply to them. Although the Nazis prosecuted at Nuremburg argued that the tribunal was illegitimate because it applied *ex post facto* laws, few modern governments could claim that a prohibition against genocide is not a fundamental principle recognized by most modern states. Given this declarative power of collective gestures of contrition, some even argue that state apologies provide a foundation for international human rights law.[136]

Yet if we conceive of collective apologies primarily as declarations of institutional values, several concerns arise. First, in some cases apologies may seem a redundant or even counterproductive means of endorsing a collective value. In "The United States Has Already Apologized for Racial Discrimination," Bernard Siegan argues that an apology for slavery would be "superfluous" because the United States "has already apologized for Jim Crow laws by adopting in recent years a multitude of statutes and judicial rules outlawing discriminatory policies and practices."[137] If "the American people have loudly and clearly expressed the deepest regret for past racial discrimination in their contemporary legislation and judicial decisions," why do we also need an apology? Do our actions not speak louder than words? In addition, Siegan notes, apologizing for slavery comes with costs. The debates may prove expensive, time-consuming, and may worsen racial relations by opening old wounds. Perhaps a better use of national resources would address forward-looking racial programs with palpable benefits.

In one respect, I am sympathetic to this argument. As we have seen throughout, the ritual and pageantry of collective apologies often serve as a superficial alternative to substantive reform. Instead of wringing our hands over the barbarity of our ancestors, perhaps we should roll up our sleeves and address the inhumane conditions that so many of the great grandchildren of slavery endure in our public schools and elsewhere. Yet of course we need not choose between apologies and reform, and I hope to have demonstrated their interrelation. In addition, failing to apologize can deny victims this symbolic effort to recognize their injuries. Even if a collective has an established record of honoring a principle, circumstances may arise when it proves especially important to restate that value. Although certain forms of racial discrimination have been illegal in the United States for some time, the racial dimensions of the domestic and foreign "War on Terror" warrant revitalization of the nation's commitment to human equality. Just as difficult times in a marriage may cause a couple to revisit their vows, politically turbulent periods warrant reminding ourselves of the values we hold.

Even if some within the collective recently endorsed the value at issue, it may be important for others to do so as well. If Congress passes legislation responding to racial injustice, we may like to hear the president express similar commitments. This leads to another concern that I took up with respect to standing and delegation. If some group of representatives declares its values through an apology, this does not necessarily commit its members' successors to the same principles. One administration may endorse a principle and the next may reject it. If we think of collective apologies primarily as declarations tied to shifting nodes of institutional authority, their meaning may become even more fugacious and difficult to enforce.

Finally, we can divorce the meanings of declarative apologies more easily from the apologizers' mental states. If we seek apologies to serve a declarative function, the intentions and emotions of the spokesperson will seem increasingly less important other than as a means of predicting the collective's future behavior. If a president apologizes for slavery merely to woo a portion of the voting population, her values may shift with future changes in demographics. Considerations regarding the integrity or emotions of a collective and its spokesperson may seem misplaced or even naïve, as I examine later. I also reserve for later the discussions of the differences between pledging to uphold a principle and actually keeping that promise.

F. Collectives Recognizing Victims as Moral Interlocutors

Apologizing can fundamentally transform the relationship between victims and offenders because they come to understand each as moral interlocutors as they engage in the normative discourse essential to a categorical apology. This means more than simply having a conversation about morality; it renders the offender and the offended equal in the most fundamental sense as together they struggle with life's ultimate values. In my most vulnerable moments I turn not to my allies but to my victims, now welcoming them as peers in the struggle for meaning and justice. In the Kantian sense, I honor their dignity as fellow moral agents. In the Hegelian sense, I recognize that my own dignity depends upon theirs.

These aspects of apologetic meaning can take on additional significance in collective apologies. For many historical injuries, an apology may recognize the status of an entire class of degraded people. Large-scale conflicts often deny the humanity of many victims, refusing to recognize the enemy as equal in moral worth. Demonizing the enemy is unfortunately not an antiquated practice: A 2006 study of U.S. soldiers serving in Iraq found that less than half believed that "all noncombatants should be treated with dignity and respect."[138] We can imagine how these soldiers view the moral standing of combatants if they face such difficulty respecting even noncombatants. Similarly, transcripts from Enron officials and employees document an utter disregard for those harmed by the California blackouts of 2000 and 2001. The dehumanization of slaves is even more obvious and would be especially important for an apology for slavery to engage victims as peers and moral interlocutors.

Noteworthy questions arise here. Must we engage every victim in such moral deliberation, or will a few representatives suffice? In the case of slavery, who would the apologizer recognize? Can we and should we at least name all of the victims? If the most direct victims died long ago, surely recognizing them now would be a bittersweet consolation. Considering that they presumably do not participate in the conversation, can we describe the dead as interlocutors?

Questions regarding who has standing to recognize victims as interlocutors may also generate debate. In some cases, victims may prefer that the highest-ranking official from the collective – rather than those most directly responsible for the harm – recognize their moral status. Indeed, victims may refuse to acknowledge offenders as interlocutors and prefer to engage with their superiors. As I mentioned with respect to individual apologies, those who claim to possess moral expertise may be particularly reluctant to recognize others as moral interlocutors. In case of collective apologies, this dynamic can create situations in which presidents or religious leaders genuflect before those previously held in contempt by considerable portions of a population. This emphasizes just how important it may be for a powerful figure to publicly recognize the moral standing of victims, as such an exchange can substantially improve the reception of oppressed people within a community.

Just as recognizing victims as moral interlocutors may bring groups together, failing to do so can drive them further apart. As with individual apologies, an offender's failure to acknowledge victims as worthy of an apology can be a more grievous injury than the underlying harm at issue. Members of a minority group may find that an action of their government inconveniences them in some trivial way, but then take serious offense to the fact that no one consulted them or thought to apologize. This, they may argue, demonstrates that offenders do not consider them full members of the community and leads to escalating in hostilities between groups. Such problems could also arise if offenders direct their apologies to someone other than the persons harmed. If Clinton apologized to officials from the Belgian government rather than to Rwandan citizens, Africans would have yet another reason to believe that the United States does not consider them full members of the international moral community.

G. Collectives and Categorical Regret

As I described it, categorical regret refers to an offender's recognition that her moral error caused an injury and she wishes the transgression could be undone. In light of her realization that she has morally erred, she commits to not repeating the offense. We can therefore distinguish categorical regret from the sorts of regret associated with mere expressions of disappointment in an outcome, feelings of sorrow over a missed opportunity, or gestures of sympathy for those who bear the burden of our justified actions. Returning to an earlier example, the United States may come to categorically regret dropping nuclear bombs on Hiroshima and Nagasaki if its leaders – or whoever ultimately has standing to make such judgments – come to believe that they should not have used such weapons and commit to not doing so again. Such regret would differ in kind from an expression that continued to endorse the bombing but conveyed regret that Japanese leaders did not surrender earlier and thus spare their citizens from such suffering. According to the latter, U.S. leaders continue to believe that they made the best choice given the circumstances and do not imply that they would choose differently in similar situations. Future enemies have no reason to feel secure that the United States would not take similar actions against them.

Especially when addressing large-scale wrongs, collectives face additional obstacles in arriving at categorical regret because their decisions to commit the offenses at issue often result from multivariable cost-benefit analyses or conflicting duties. Even more than individuals, a collective may pursue a course of action because it represents the best choice among imperfect options. Even hindsight can be blurry from this perspective. If multiple values and objectives compete, it can be increasingly difficult and controversial to recognize as morally regrettable what seemed like the best choice at the time. An administration may seek to balance directly competing worthy objectives, for example in seeking to both promote international humanitarianism and not risk the lives of its soldiers by deploying them into the war-torn regions where human rights violations often occur. Here we can return once again to the case of the Rwandan genocide. The recent death of U.S. soldiers in the battle of Mogadishu demonstrated the potential cost of interventions into African conflicts and thereby transformed U.S. foreign policy. This haunted the decision whether to intervene in Rwanda. Given these complications, does Clinton categorically regret his choice not to risk U.S. lives or does he mourn the cost of the best choice at the time? What if he had intervened more quickly, only to become embroiled in a protracted civil war that resulted in the deaths of hundreds of U.S. troops? Given such possibilities, does he believe he made the wrong choice? Or was he justified in making the difficult decision in light of these considerations?

Risk assessment of this sort often accompanies institutional decision making as it calculates dangers in order to manage multiple objectives. Officials at various levels, for instance, knew that New Orleans faced a risk of catastrophic flooding. In the aftermath of Hurricane Katrina, we learned that political entities did not take certain precautionary measures – like fortifying crucial levies – for economic reasons. As details of these choices become publicized, we should listen first to hear if anyone accepts blame for those decisions. If someone does come forward, do they apologize and express regret for those choices or do they justify them by claiming that the hurricane was unpredictably destructive and thus the risks were warranted? The Bush administration's initial response that the hurricane presented unforeseeable problems points toward the latter.

Instead of categorical regret, we often find collectives invoking countervailing objectives to justify what some might perceive as moral failures. Occasionally leaders preface an admission of wrongdoing with evidence of the competing objectives in order to *not quite* justify the action but instead to provide the context so that victims will better understand why the collective acted as it did. Due to the organizational structures and multiple objectives driving institutions, many excuses and justifications present themselves. A midlevel official, for instance, might claim that she was only following orders and did not appreciate the consequences of her acts.

The Cold War served as a catchall extenuating circumstance for some time. On a 1998 trip to Uganda, Clinton opened his remarks by invoking the Soviet Union. Although it "is as well not to dwell too much on the past," Clinton found it "worth pointing out that the United States has not always done the right thing by Africa."[139] This understatement serves not to remind us of the slave trade, which he refers to in the following paragraph, but to call our attention to the fact that the Cold War shaped recent U.S. policies on Africa. "We were so concerned about being in competition with the Soviet Union," Clinton explained, that "we dealt with countries in Africa and in other parts of the world based more on how they stood in the struggle between the United States and the Soviet Union than how they stood in the struggle for their own people's aspirations to live up to the fullest of their God-given abilities."[140] We should temper criticism of U.S. policy in Africa, Clinton suggests, by an appreciation of how these actions helped to defeat the "Evil Empire." Clinton took a similar approach in Athens in 1999 when addressing U.S. support for the colonels' junta from 1967–74: "When the junta took over . . . the United States allowed its interests in prosecuting the Cold War to prevail over its interests – I should say its obligation – to support democracy, which was, after all, the cause for which we fought the Cold War."[141] One commentator attributes Clinton's gesture to the decreasing geopolitical cost of apologizing: "The Soviet Union no longer has an enormous propaganda apparatus trained against us" and therefore "the nations of the West can admit wrongdoing without the fear that they are giving ammunition to the enemies of freedom."[142]

Instead of thinking of Clinton as disingenuously shifting onto communism blame for morally questionable U.S. policies, a more generous reading of his inclusion of these references to the Cold War would understand him to be identifying the precise nature of the moral wrong breached and expressing categorical regret for that failure: The United States should not have placed its interests above its moral obligations and regrets doing so. Does Clinton mean to suggest, however, that humanitarian obligations – including what he describes as the moral obligation to support democracy – now trump all others in U.S. foreign policy? This would be extraordinary.

We could ask similar questions regarding Clinton's statements in Uganda. If the U.S. could not have won independence and economic supremacy without African slave labor, then I doubt Clinton would go so far as to claim that the existence of the United States and its current power were founded on injustices that he wishes to reverse. Instead, I suspect he regrets that U.S. wealth and power came at such a moral price. As Jana Thompson describes in the context of the "apology paradox," when individuals benefit from injustices for which they have no causal responsibility, they typically do not regret that they enjoy such benefits "but that they came to have them in the way they did." "Our preference," Thompson explains, "is for a possible world in which our existence did not depend on these deeds."[143] We wish, in other words, for the benefits of slavery without their moral costs.

Occasionally we find collectives regretting not their policies but only their unintended consequences. Former South African President F. W. de Klerk provides an example that demonstrates just how self-delusional collectives can be in this respect as they underestimate the likelihood that policies that benefit their members will not harm others. Claiming that "it was not our intention to deprive people of their rights and to cause misery, but eventually apartheid led to just that," de Klerk attempted to mitigate his culpability for the suffering resulting from apartheid by claiming that he did not intend it. By this extraordinary account, the suffering was accidental. He then expressed his regret and paused to consider its meaning: "Deep regret goes much further than saying you are sorry. . . . Deep regret says that if I could turn the clock back, and if I could do anything about it, I would have liked to have avoided it."[144] How should we interpret this? If he could turn back the clock he would *like* to avoid the suffering – perhaps as the judge would *like* to avoid sentencing the convict – but this does not necessarily mean that he would have done anything differently when faced with the same choices. Perhaps he would have endorsed a form of apartheid that he believed would be less likely to cause such accidental suffering. His statements suggest that he does not believe that the deprivation of rights is intrinsic to apartheid, and therefore he implies that he does not categorically regret the policy but instead finds it unfortunate that suffering resulted from it.

Categorical regret, and thus an important kind of apologetic meaning, does not apply when collectives continue to believe that they made the best possible choice regarding the issue in question. A nation would not express categorical regret for what it continues to believe was sound foreign policy.[145] We can compare Nelson Mandela's refusal to apologize for the African National Congress' alliance with Iran, Cuba, and Libya, which the United States condemned as rogue states and sponsors of terrorism. "Our moral authority," Mandela insisted, "dictates that we should not abandon those who helped us in the darkest hour of the history of this country."[146] By the time of this 1998 statement, Mandela surely realized that maintaining such allegiances was contrary to South Africa's interests. He made choices, he continues to stand behind them, and thus he appreciates that an apology that expressed categorical regret would be inappropriate.

H. Collectives Performing Apologies

Having already addressed the majority of my concerns here in the context of individual apologies, I can be brief and underscore the most pertinent issues. First, many collective apologies suffer from serious timing problems. If it is best to apologize promptly after an offense, some of our examples of collective apologies were hundreds of years in the making. Although such delays create problems specific to timing, they also exacerbate worries. The longer an institution waits before apologizing, the greater the likelihood that problems will arise with respect to standing because both offenders and victims may have left the collective or passed away. If an apology never reaches the victims because of such delays, its meaning is obviously compromised. Timing also relates to the intentions of the collective for apologizing, which I note later. If a collective offers an apology only after victims have requested it or authorities have commanded it, this differs considerably from a group volunteering an apology before being prompted to do so. Even if long periods separate the injury and the apology, we can appreciate the importance of a collective offering an apology as a result of internal reflection on its values rather than in response to the threat of a lawsuit or other sanction.

In addition, I claimed earlier that written versions of apologies better allow parties to reflect upon and provide the sort of precision required of a categorical apology. Because a categorical apology can be a technical undertaking, I suggested that the emotional fits that often accompany apologies might benefit from the structure that a written version could impose on the gesture. The scope of collective apologies magnifies the importance of this, as some harms span generations of victims and an array of moral principles. Indeed, apologies for some historical injustices could fill volumes.

The distinctions between public and private apologies also become more pronounced in cases of collective acts of contrition. Not only can public apologies raise the status of entire classes of historically subordinated victims, but they can also generally contribute to public debate in significant ways. Whether creating a record of offenses, assigning blame for injustice, or bringing breached values to the foreground of public discourse, collective apologies can have considerable restorative power over a culture's moral, social, and political health. Whereas we can easily imagine cases in which victims might prefer individual apologies to remain private affairs, I suspect that the desire to shield wrongdoers from public scrutiny motivates many attempts to suppress collective apologies. Settlement agreements in which collectives provide apologies to individual claimants on the condition that the terms of the apology not be disclosed strike me as especially questionable in this regard. I take up this issue in detail in future work on apologies in law.

I. Collectives Reforming and Providing Redress

Collective Reform

A declaration promising to reform behavior and redress injuries obviously differs from one that actually honors such promises, and I elaborated this in the distinction between categorical apologies and promissory categorical apologies. Whereas individual apologies often fail to fulfill their own covenants, collectives face additional obstacles to reforming and providing redress. Like every other aspect of apologetic meaning, the stakes and complexities increase as we move from individual to collective reform and redress. A victim of an interpersonal conflict may seek assurance that the offender will not wrong her again, but in cases of collective apologies the security of entire populations may depend on whether a group of aggressors honors their commitment to uphold peace. We can imagine how such promises could lay the cornerstone of a new life for survivors of mass atrocities, with the entirety of their well-being conditioned upon the strength of this commitment.

Beginning with collectives undergoing reform, we can first ask precisely who or what must make these changes. With individual apologies, we expect that the offender will undertake the personal transformation required to prevent similar harms from occurring in the future. To invoke problems of standing once again, I cannot delegate my promise to reform to my attorney or to my mother and have it retain the same moral meaning. When a collective promises to reform, the relationship between offender and forbearance is more convoluted. If we believe that the collective as such bears responsibility for an injury, then we risk thinking that no particular individuals are guilty. If no particular members of the collective did anything wrong, why would they personally need to reform? This, in part, led me to underscore the importance of tracing blame and moral duty to individuals to the extent possible.

As I described them, categorical apologies are promises to reform kept over a lifetime and therefore we can only finally judge the offender's commitment to reform over the duration of her existence. How would this apply to a collective? When, for instance, does a corporation die? In some respects we can think of General Electric as a continuous entity since its inception and we could expect it to honor its promises to reform for the duration of its existence. Nevertheless, notice how easily this continuity can be broken by mergers, acquisitions, and revolving-door leadership. If one corporation absorbs another, does it also take in its promises to reform? Did those commitments die in the shuffling of assets and personnel? In this respect, recall the earlier discussion of deathbed apologies. If someone apologizes with her last breaths, she leaves us to wonder if she would have reoffended if only she had the opportunity. If Enron promised to reform its accounting practices shortly before it filed for bankruptcy and its executives fled the company or were indicted, it would never have the opportunity to fulfill its promise to reform. Enron might not reoffend after its dismantling, but its former executives who now lead other firms might not feel bound by the promises of their previous employer. I worry that attributing too much blame to the collective as such allows for this sort of moral afterlife where individuals apologize in the death twitches of one institutional position only to be reborn into another corporation liberated from prior commitments.

Institutions can also play the game of moral free agency with the opposite strategy. Instead of absorbing blame into the collective, they can condense it all into one person. Once they identify a scapegoat who carries the guilt for the entire collective, they can assert that only she must undertake reform. They can then cut ties with her, dissociating the collective from the scapegoat as she corrects her personal problems. Only a sufficiently precise tracking of moral causation protects against these worries by identifying wrongdoers – including those responsible for objectionable policies – and expecting them to undergo the appropriate reform. Supplementing appropriately individuated blame in this sense with structural reform appears to provide the most promising method of sustaining institutional change.

I would like to raise two further issues regarding collectives and reform. First, we can typically determine whether individuals have breached their promise to reform without too much difficulty even if we may occasionally wonder whether some action rises to the level of the prohibited activity. With collectives, however, situations arise where individual members of the group violate the collective's pact. We might encounter this, for instance, if warring nations apologize for past aggressions by vowing to never again attempt to resolve their differences with violence. If a conflict arises on the border between them and one soldier fires a shot, some might interpret this lone act as voiding the entirety of the apology from the collective. In this respect, a single reoffending member can set back the reform of even very large groups. Small groups face similar difficulties: A sexist remark from one member of the philosophy department could vitiate the efforts of all other members of the department to improve our behavior in accordance with our collective apology discussed earlier. The varying membership of groups compounds these difficulties, as individuals with different levels of commitments to reform may cycle through group membership and exhibit varying degrees of compliance with the efforts to reform. A group especially committed to honoring the promises of its collective apology may even build them into membership criteria, for instance by requiring members to take an oath pledging to uphold the apology and expelling those who do not.

Collectives also seem especially likely to apply their principles selectively and refrain from reoffending only when it proves convenient or advantageous. Closely related to the question of the scope of the principle endorsed by an apology, I have in mind situations wherein a group promises not to make the same mistakes again but employs justification of questionable merit to distinguish between past and present infractions. Thus, the United States might assert that it will "never again" allow genocide to occur, but then parse humanitarian terms when lacking the political will to undertake the dangerous and expensive work required to prevent a similar atrocity in a region with minimal strategic value.

Having mentioned these concerns, I do not mean to discount the importance of collective apologies for initiating structural reform, cultivating shared commitment to the values motivating the institutional changes, and encouraging individual members to personally accept their share of blame.

Collective Redress

Even if limited to economic damages, the size of the losses resulting from collective wrongdoing can be massive. One 2005 report from the Israeli government, for instance, claims that the Holocaust caused between $297 billion and $409 billion in material damages to the Jewish people.[147] Administration costs alone for determining and distributing such amounts can be staggering; I mentioned earlier that the audit of the misappropriated accounts of Holocaust victims by Swiss banks cost approximately $600 million. One can imagine the bottom line of full economic compensation for the African slave trade, a sum that might be large enough to shift the balance of global power from the northern to the southern hemisphere.

In one sense, collectives are often far better situated to redress such damages. The German government and German corporations have much deeper pockets than individual Nazis, and survivors of the Tuskegee experiments and the Japanese-American internment stood a better chance of collecting from the U.S. government than from the individuals who most directly caused these damages. This is especially evident for harms in the distant past where all offenders are long deceased and their fortunes are dispersed among many generations of heirs. As noted previously, this ability to maximize the likelihood that victims will be compensated for their losses appears to provide a powerful reason for attributing culpability to collectives. Even if the collective lacks sufficient resources to provide anything beyond nominal compensation, as will often be the case in governments of war-torn and economically depressed regions, the group may control more resources than any of its individual members.

A closer look returns us to the aforementioned problems. If we allow individuals to deflect their personal wrongdoing into collectives, it can prove exceedingly difficult to hold any particular person or group of persons responsible for providing redress. If the "international community" failed Rwanda, then who exactly should finance rebuilding the ravaged nation? Clinton offered $2 million from the United States for the Genocide Survivors' funds, or about a third of the cost of one of the Black Hawk helicopters downed in Mogadishu. If Clinton had promised "full economic compensation," would he commit the international community to paying this amount? Does he saddle subsequent U.S. administrations with such debt, and can future leaders renege on his promise?

Collectives experience more difficulty speaking with one voice when it comes time to pay the bills than they do when they express their condolences at no cost. Offenders are quick to sign on when contrition does not cost them anything, or, as in the case of California's apology for Mexican repatriation, it comes at the bargain price of a commemorative plaque. As we raise the stakes of redemption, fewer buy in. If we realize that collective responsibility will cost us, rather than insulate us from personal accountability, we revert to more individualist and liberal conceptions of responsibility. A U.S. taxpayer might support the nation in apologizing for slavery or Rwandan genocide only if it does not cost her anything because, after all, she will claim that she did not own slaves or slaughter Tutsis. If the income taxes contributed by descendants of slaves fund the pool from which the U.S. government pays reparations to these very individuals, we can appreciate how failing to track moral causation with some degree of specificity can result in compensatory circularity.

Again, we confront the hypocrisy of some applications of collective responsibility: We conceive of responsibility broadly when this works to our benefit, but our theories of moral causation become narrower when we wish to distance ourselves from blame and accountability. Here we can also notice how claims to group membership shift based on the advantages or disadvantages of associating with the collective. If we take pride in our national accomplishments, we emphasize collectivity. If we feel shame, we parse responsibility and blame some collective to which we do not belong, such as the opposing political party. While current administrations blame former administrations, interest accumulates on our moral debts.

Collective redress also creates opportunities for victims to manipulate questions of causation and standing to their advantage. Although one might deny membership if doing so requires her to pay into the reparations pool, she will be more likely to claim membership if this status entitles her to a portion of the pool. Criteria for distributing the proceeds flowing from a collective apology can prove as contentious as the criteria for determining who pays. Who are the proper recipients of such funds? Should we divide the pool only between the survivors, or can we extend the benefits to their heirs? If we look beyond compensating only those most directly harmed – such as those who survived Nazi camps and now seek damages for their losses – how do we determine who belongs to the class of extended victims? Should we look to race, ethnicity, citizenship, social and economic status, biology, self-identification, or some other indicia to determine membership in the class of victims? Consider how contentious such issues have become for defining Native American identity.[148] Once we determine membership, do we provide all recipients with equal amounts, or do we somehow weigh the relative suffering of each victim and compensate them accordingly? Do we adjust payments based on cost of living, providing victims living in Manhattan with larger sums than those in regions where an equivalent monetary award would buy them much more? Who controls the process of distributing the funds? These questions help us to appreciate how questions of standing and moral causation permeate not only who bears the costs of redress, but also who receives the benefits.

Even if we can determine who pays and who receives payment resulting from a collective apology, in many respects money is the simplest and most morally obtuse remedy. For all of the reasons mentioned with respect to individual apologies, economic compensation often provides only one sort of meaning and we risk further injustice if we believe that we can discharge moral debts with money alone. The incommensurability between money and justice becomes even more obvious in cases of collective wrongdoing, leading Martha Minow to reflect on the "incompleteness and inescapable inadequacy of each possible response to collective atrocities."[149] Although nothing can unscramble the eggs of collective wrongdoing, I suggested in cases of individual apologies that we should think of an offender's remedial activities as assuming practical responsibility for the she they caused beyond economic damages. Efforts to accept practical responsibility might take any variety of forms, but they would typically involve the offender somehow personally caring for and tending to the needs of her victim.

If they express a commitment to assuming practical responsibility, collective apologies face an additional set of difficulties that are somewhat less imposing for individual apologies. Once again, the sheer volume of severe injuries can render the prospect of caring for all of the victims daunting. Leaving aside how we might care for the dead and their relatives, the task of caring for even the survivors of the Rwandan genocide or the nuclear bombing of Hiroshima seems so overwhelming that the temptation to walk away and send a check instead would be strong.[150] Even if money is a poor substitute as a universal common denominator of value, it can seem like the only remedial medium of an appropriate scale to respond to such massive suffering. Moreover, many possibilities for taking responsibility have passed because collective apologies often respond to events from so long ago. If the victim has been dead for hundreds of years, we would need to be especially imaginative to take practical responsibility for her suffering. If collectives tend to reduce responsibility to a cash amount for these and related reasons, they will be less likely to provide the sorts of interpersonal meaning often desired by victims. Despite this, we should not fail to notice that contemporary victims often consider economic compensation the measure of sincerity for apologies, even for injuries of an apparently nonpecuniary nature. Although we may be suspicious of governments, corporations, and other collectives, there is a certain social gravity to money that can make its meaning seem more real than any others.

By some accounts, we should understand the reform and redress accompanying collective apologies as punitive in nature. I will reserve my analysis of collective apologies and collective punishment for my future work on apologies in law, but we can briefly note a few issues that will require attention. First, normative individualists raise a number of serious concerns regarding collective punishment generally, including deontological criticisms of punishing innocent individuals merely because of their associations with true wrongdoers and utilitarian worries that group responsibility reduces the deterrent effects of penalties. On the former point we can appreciate the potential injustice of a descendant of slaves being taxed to provide reparations for slavery. Others express concerns that collective punishment could have grave social consequences as it erodes our basic notions of moral agency. Although some doubt the efficacy of certain forms of collective punishment because groups "have neither bodies to be punished, nor souls to be condemned," others propose novel methods of disciplining institutions.[151] If economic sanctions, for instance, do not sufficiently deter corporations because they can build the price of their transgressions into their cost-benefit analyses, perhaps their apologies should provide some form of redress that would cause them genuine pain. This might include requiring corporations to transform their internal structures, submitting their operational decisions to external reviewers, or maximizing the damage to their reputations through public shaming.[152] I hope to address the role courts can play in fashioning and enforcing such features of collective apologies in some detail in future work.

J. Collective Intentions for Apologizing

However briefly, I already noted the debates regarding collective intention-ality in the context of collective responsibility and collectives denying that they intended to commit an offense. Rather than revisiting these issues here, I note how the intentions motivating a collective's apology can fundamentally alter its meanings. Lazare notices that if collective apologies serve primarily as "acknowledgments that a social or moral contract was violated," they can achieve this meaning "regardless of sincerity." He offers the example of "a company apologizing for racially prejudicial policies even when it is well known that the president of the organization is a racial bigot."[153] Although Lazare believes that even such statements "are usually enough to restore the offender to 'good standing' in society," I wonder what meaning would be conveyed by a defiant apology from an unrepentant racist who spits out words of contrition because she thinks they will boost her earnings. Beyond its potentially retributive features, the prevailing lesson of such a gesture might be its demonstration of the market's ability to coerce a semblance of moral compliance.

To return to the example of my philosophy department apologizing for its history of sexism, some of us may apologize out of a lifelong commitment to feminism. Others may have undergone a moral transformation and for the first time wish to advocate for our female students. Still others may apologize only because they fear being ostracized or denied promotion if they do not acquiesce to the will of the majority of the group. Even if the department reached consensus about the content of the apology, an understanding of the diverse and potentially conflicting intentions among the group would cast the apology in a different light. If our students learned that we only apologized because the dean threatened to reduce our budget if we did not, viewing our apology in that context would afford the students a more accu-rate understanding of our gesture.

Although reading the mental states of individuals can prove difficult because apologizers often hide self-serving motivations, the intentions of collectives can be not only opaque but also varied and opposed. Beyond concerns regarding standing and consensus, we experience additional dif-ficulties discerning the motivations driving collective offenders because we may not even have an opportunity to gauge their sincerity by looking into their faces. When a group speaks through a spokesperson, its members can obscure any emotional cues that might reveal their mental states. We under-stand that a spokesperson completes this work as a service to her employers and that her primary intention, like that of most employees, is probably to earn a living by emoting as directed.

We find a similar disposition orienting many forms of collective apolo-gies. Perhaps more than any other reason, we are skeptical of the meaning of collective apologies because we doubt the intentions motivating them. Cor-porate apologies, no matter how beloved the company or the spokesperson, immediately strike many as disingenuous. We understand that corporations seek to maximize profits and we suspect that apologies are but a calculated means to this end. We understand a corporation's moral reputation as an economic asset to some degree, and we expect executives to say and do whatever will increase the value of that asset. We have legitimate reasons to expect that behind the appearance of morally rich corporate apologies we will find pure economic instrumentality. We are only slightly less dubious of collective political apologies, which trade in political as well as economic capital. In an age of political focus groups and incessant polling, we understand that candidates must play the game of strategic contrition to maximize their appeal to voters and allies. Thus we have healthy skepticism for corporate and political apologies.

As with individual apologies, we also worry that many groups structure their apologies to mitigate payments or punishment. If an apology can save individuals from expensive litigation or shave years off their sentences, a well-crafted gesture of contrition could be even more valuable in cases of collective wrongdoing where reparations can cost billions of dollars. Rayner lampoons this dimension of collective apologies in *Eating Crow*. Chief Apologist Basset negotiates with Lewis Jeffries III, the prominent African American chosen to be the recipient of the United States' apology for slavery. Jeffries understands that Basset's apology precedes the federal government's "compensation package" for slavery, and he breaks the illusion that noble intentions motivate the apology: "Everybody knows that the whole point of [Basset's apology] is that it should result in reduced compensation payments, which means everybody has already made assumptions about the scale of the cash settlements that will result." Jeffries then makes his position clear: "The African-American community will not be settling for a twenty-three percent reduced payment simply for hearing the word 'sorry' from your lips, however finely said. We'll be going the whole nine yards. Only suckers will settle for less."[154]

Such honesty captures what many of us think: Collective apologies are often a pretense of moral etiquette preceding merciless legal and economic dealings. It is noteworthy in this regard that collective apologies can increase or decrease liability depending on the context and their content. Whereas some apologies may appease victims and judges as expressions of remorse and transformation, others may be interpreted as admissions of guilt that embolden those demanding the most severe penalties.[155]

K. Collective Emotions

The emotional content of individual apologies raises confounding questions that demonstrate, perhaps more than any other aspect of apologetic meaning, the difficulties of drawing bright lines between authentic and inauthentic apologies. We sense that emotions are an integral component of apologies, but beyond that matters become increasingly nebulous. Which emotions, for example, must the offender experience? Does each injury, context, and culture require the apologizer to experience a different suite of emotions? In what intensity and duration should she experience them? Should the same emotions accompany every stage of the apology or should different emotions attach to each element, for example the initial recognition of wrongdoing and the final payment of redress? Are emotions a morally edifying component of apologizing or an irrational distraction that increases opportunities for confusion and manipulation? Given the fine distinctions between some emotions, how will the offender or victim identify the presence and quantity of such "feelings"? If some of us are emotionally obtuse or impaired, might this render all of our apologies deficient? How, we can now ask, do these issues map onto collective apologies?

Even more than collective responsibilities or intentions, collective emotions may strike us as especially implausible. Even the strictest methodological individualist appreciates that policy considerations can require us to speak as if institutions are moral persons, but the argument that collectives as such can experience emotions seems to anthropomorphize too far. Individual employees experience pain, joy, temptation, or regret, but corporations as such do not. Despite popular representations of a bald eagle shedding a tear over the collapsing World Trade Center, the United States does not experience pain in a sense irreducible to that felt by individuals who associate with the United States. The notions of the interior lives of institutions as such serve as useful and occasionally powerful metaphors, but collective emotions stretch phenomenological credibility. When French claims that we should understand certain collectives as "full-fledged moral persons," such an assertion seems increasingly suspect if we include emotional states as features of moral personhood. If it seems comical if not ghoulish to think of the United States romantically loving General Electric, why would we speak so comfortably of General Electric feeling remorse, guilt, or sympathy for its victims?

We can approach this question through a slightly different intuition if we imagine a nation or corporation apologizing via an animated logo or an electronic voice message. Even if a cartoon or computer articulated an otherwise exemplary apology and mimicked the appropriate emotional states, these would not provide an indication that any of the offenders – or even the electronic spokesperson – is actually experiencing the requisite emotions. If no one actually *feels bad*, this creates a conspicuous gap in meaning. We can imagine executives and leaders enjoying themselves far from the spectacles of contrition as proxies grovel for them. This inability of a collective as such to experience guilt, for instance, leads Joel Bakan to describe corporations as structurally pathological.[156]

Until we have more sophisticated machines, human spokespersons will perform the work of expressing apologetic emotions for institutions. How do these emotional proxies differ from electronic avatars? For one, we feel more comfortable attributing emotional states to humans. Even if we believe that the spokesperson stages the emotions, at least she might come to experience pangs of sympathy or empathy for the victims. Human spokespersons also better fulfill our expectations regarding the relationship between apologies and repentance, as the religious and existential emotions associated with confession would seem particularly ill suited for a soulless machine. Because the emotions of a high-ranking member speaking for the collective may resonate more deeply for victims than histrionics from a third party, questions of standing and delegation also appear relevant here. Even if the emotions are entirely programmed, an automated response from a president or executive will resonate more than one from a machine if only because of the meaning we take from the illusion that a powerful person suffers as a consequence of harming us. Yet how far off is the day when a simulated Walt Disney, Thomas Edison, or George Washington returns to apologize for the transgressions of their institutions?

Beyond requiring a spokesperson to experience emotions for the collective, we might think of group emotions in two different respects.[157] First, we might understand the emotional component of collective apologies not as a phenomenological locus of experience but rather as certain institutional features that tend to encourage desired emotional experiences in its membership. Just as a nation may promote campaigns demonizing the enemy during wartime in order to reduce potential empathy and sympathy for the adversary, institutional leaders could take measures to cultivate appropriately apologetic emotions in members. Merely documenting the suffering of the victims, rather than suppressing such records, could prove emotionally transformative for members in many cases. Institutions may also take more aggressive measures to enforce emotional compliance, for example by punishing hate speech, hate crimes, and other acts driven by malicious feelings.[158]

Perhaps the least controversial sense of collective emotions takes an aggregate view: We can say that a collective experiences certain emotions if some portion of its membership feels them.[159] This parallels the discussion of collective responsibility as a shorthand description of the combination of the accountability of some individual members of the group. It also returns us to the problem of attributing properties of group members to the whole: What percentage of the group must feel the emotion in order to describe it as collectively experienced? If only a few in a group of millions feel guilt and sympathy for a victim, then it seems disingenuous to speak of the emotion collectively experienced. On the other hand, if only a few in a group of millions do not experience guilt and sympathy, it would seem problematic not to describe the emotion as collectively felt. As we saw with all questions of consensus, drawing bright lines in these respects can obscure more than illuminate. If 49 percent of U.S. citizens not only did not feel guilt for the invasion of Iraq but also felt contempt for those who did have such feelings, it would be quite misleading to believe "the United States experiences guilt for the war in Iraq." Temporal concerns may further skew these numbers, as some might have experienced only a moment of guilt before returning to ambivalence or apathy. I mentioned with respect to individual apologies that an offender might experience multiple and occasionally conflicting emotions – such as feeling shame at having wronged but pride in taking responsibility for the failure – and the possibilities for this increase substantially as the collective grows larger.

Considering that emotions play an important but nebulous role in individual apologies, we should not be surprised that collective emotions confuse matters further. I see several consequences of this. Many noncategorical individual apologies do offer expressions of sympathy, but collective apologies will face serious challenges expressing even this meaning in light of the limited ability of groups to experience emotions like sympathy. If I tell you that "I am sorry for your pain," at a minimum you are safe to assume that I experience – or at least I could experience – some negative emotions in response to your suffering. A president's claim that the "nation sympathizes with your pain" is dubious even in that respect.

In addition, we will often find emotions less reliable as evidence to help us gauge a collective's sincerity than we might in individual apologies where we can attempt to measure a person's mental states by her emotional displays. Whether speaking on behalf of an individual or a collective, a spokesperson's reports of her own apologetic emotions do not stand in for those of the wrongdoers. No one can feel for the offender, which returns us to the punitive dimensions of emotions. Beginning with retributive justifications, victims may find that certain kinds of collective apologies offend their sense of justice because the group or its members do not suffer negative emotions as much as they should. If a corporation humiliates a retributivist, she may believe that the corporation deserves to be humiliated in return. Yet if a collective as such cannot experience emotions, this may be like squeezing blood from a rock. Collectives, in other words, are in some respects structurally pardoned from emotional sentences. This may seem especially infuriating for those seeking vengeance against the world's most powerful institutions only to find them shameless emotional ciphers. Similarly, negative emotions may lose some degree of their deterrent and rehabilitative value if a collective or its members do not feel the consequences of their actions. If collectives do not suffer the unpleasant feelings of guilt, shame, or remorse, then they need not fear them or alter their behavior to avoid them. The absence of such emotions may also inhibit a collective's drive to reform and reintegrate. Such considerations underscore the importance of not allowing collective apologies to supplant individual apologies.

The limited emotional lives of collectives may produce some benefits for apologetic meaning. Although emotions may not motivate collectives in the same manner as individuals, for some this may increase the likelihood that a deontological commitment to a principle – rather than a selfish desire to eliminate their emotional suffering – motivates the apology. As I noted earlier, emotions can interfere with other kinds of apologetic meaning. Offenders often mask other shortcomings, such as a failure to admit wrongdoing or a refusal to reform, with emotional outbursts or excessive displays of sympathy. For this reason, Tavuchis claims that "sorrow or sincerity" have little place in collective apologies. Arguing that "putting things on record" is the primary function of collective apologies, Tavuchis believes that such work is best undertaken without interference from emotions: "After the heady emotional displays, celebrations, and exuberance surrounding the exchange, the indelible remains in the collective record are the apology and its announcement." "To demand more" of an apology, Tavuchis claims, "is to mistake its task and logic."[160] Govier and Verwoerd further recognize that a collective can, through spokespersons, acknowledge its wrongdoing and undertake reform even regardless of whether it "can in any sense feel sorrow or regret."[161] I should add that these observations are especially applicable to apologies for injuries in the distant past, where the emotional links between the offenders and the harms may be quite remote. Yet even if collectives can corroborate factual records, denounce wrongdoing, and provide redress without the sorts of emotional content expected of individuals, I do not want to lose sight of how such functions differ from the sorts of meaning possible in a collective categorical apology. I now hope to bring a bit more structure to these distinct meanings.

CHAPTER ELEVEN

Varieties of Collective Apologies

Some of the issues central to the meanings of collective apologies invoke significant debates within contemporary philosophy, and the preceding discussions raise far more questions than they answer. Despite the many nuances of my account of individual apologies, collective apologies add layers of complexity to nearly every facet of apologetic meaning. They also tend to traffic in large-scale and high-stakes injuries, adding multiple loathsome offenders, scores of seriously injured victims, and a range of ultimate values to an already intricate analysis. To complicate matters further, we find many of these exchanges within ever-confounding corporate and political contexts. All of this may leave some readers feeling more confused than when they began. When a UN report on the Rwandan genocide stated that the "United Nations as an organization, but also its Member States, should have apologized more clearly, more frankly, and much earlier," we might have initially viewed this as a laudable and unproblematic assertion.[1] Yet as we noticed in the introduction with respect to demands that the Pope apologize for his Regensburg address, we need some standard against which to measure such gestures. When we demand that a collective apologize, what do we mean?

Of all the issues raised regarding collective apologies, here I would like to highlight those that I consider most important. If apologies present loose constellations of interrelated meanings, these are the questions I ask first when scanning the horizons of collective apologies. We stand a better chance of finding the meanings we seek from collective apologies with these issues guiding our attempts to navigate the disorienting social landscapes. These questions should help to organize the thoughts of those who want an apology from a collective as well as those members of collectives who attempt to apologize.

First, we should not discount the possibility of a collective providing a categorical apology. Although rare and most likely to occur in small groups bound by considerable solidarity, each member of the group could individually satisfy the elements of a categorical apology and perform the gesture communally. The group would speak and act from a consensus regarding all relevant elements, and it would clearly define the group's membership. In essence, a collective categorical apology would be an aggregation of coordinated individual categorical apologies supplemented by the various sorts of synergies mentioned previously. We can appreciate the full range of obstacles that may prevent collective apologies from reaching the status of "categorical," but I want to reiterate that such meaning is not only possible but also highly desirable in many cases.

If a collective apology is not categorical, we can ask if and to what extent it serves as a poor substitute for categorical apologies from individual members of the group. Does the collective offer a noncategorical apology instead of the categorical apologies that the individuals most directly accountable for the harm should provide? Do individuals who should apologize for their personal wrongdoings conceal their culpability in the collective and allow it to shoulder the blame that they should bear? Do leaders and spokespersons invoke individualist conceptions of responsibility when accepting praise but shift to collective theories and speak in the passive voice when deflecting blame?

Precision in our analyses of moral causation provides guidance when we attempt to answer these questions. If we trace accountability to the intentional actions of moral agents within the collective, have these individuals offered suitable apologies for their roles in the offense? We can also scrutinize collective apologies that attribute harms solely to structural features of institutions. If a representative blames a rule, policy, practice, or tradition, we can inquire into the origins and maintenance of such features of the collective. More often than not, we can trace these structural characteristics to the choices of individual agents and assign blame accordingly. When tempted to cast an institution as evil, we will typically gain a better understanding of its blameworthiness if we judge those who set its objectives and those who advance or do not reform them. In general, our moral radar can become more sensitive and equipped to track accountability into institutional depths. This increased precision should also help us to detect the range of smaller offenses that compound to cause large-scale injuries. It may have the additional benefit of decreasing the tendency within liberalism to believe that finding one person within an institution guilty exonerates all others. Bureaucratic structures may impede efforts to untangle causal chains or obscure our view of decision-making structures, but informal research or even legally compelled discovery proceedings may elucidate where blame should fall. Democratic principles favor transparent voting procedures for these very reasons. The concerns drive what I have repeatedly described as a healthy skepticism for collective apologies, but critical evaluation need not lapse into a cynical disregard for collective acts of contrition. Collective apologies can provide distinctly meaningful and indispensable supplements to individual apologies, especially in their ability to mobilize structural reform. If I have appeared overzealous in finding faults with collective apologies, I attribute this to my frustration with so many occasions where institutions squander opportunities to enrich public discourse with morally reflective acts of contrition.

In many cases, we should understand collective acts of contrition as what I described as value-declaring rather than categorical apologies. Instead of accepting blame for past wrongdoing, a value-declaring collective apology announces or renews its commitment to a policy. A group can endorse a principle in this sense without admitting wrongdoing. It can also avoid attributing blame to its individual members or to the collective in an aggregate or conglomerate sense. The group can use the gesture to denounce the acts of others or even as a means of parrying an accusation against it by insisting on its unwavering commitment to the principle. We can even find value-declaring apologies insisting that someone else or some other group should categorically apologize. When victims and communities worry less about apportioning blame for the past but instead primarily seek an assurance that a group will not commit an offense in the future, value-declaring apologies may suffice.[2]

Yet even if we do not expect a collective categorical apology, we can still ask questions to determine if a collective value-declaring apology provides the meanings we seek. Consensus issues again provide crucial insights. Does every member of the collective, a slight majority, or only a powerful minority vow to uphold the value? The proportion of the group endorsing the principle speaks to the likelihood that the collective will keep its promise not to offend, but a declaration from a few with power to strictly enforce the commitment will also serve this end. Notice here how a declaration for a corporate president or an authoritarian leader would differ from the same promise from an egalitarian group. All of the concerns regarding standing and delegation will also apply as we scrutinize who holds the authority to commit the collective to the values endorsed. We should also seek to make the standards for membership in the collective explicit so that we know precisely who promises to uphold the value. If a president offers a value-declaring apology, does she speak for herself, members of her party, her nation, or "the entire international community"? In addition, does the collective endorse the correct value or does it sermonize in general terms or expound on the "wrong wrong"? Most significantly, does the collective honor the principle selectively or does it uphold its promise without exceptions or excuses?

Some forms of meaning central to categorical apologies may or may not accompany value-declaring collective apologies. They may endorse the value in the context of establishing a historical record in some detail, or they may prefer to look forward to avoid discussing the past. They may choose which victims they wish to recognize as interlocutors, which offenses they acknowledge, and which values they wish to endorse. Because they need not accept blame for past injustice, they may have nothing to regret. They could even claim that although a course of action was justified in the past, it would not be in the future.

A declaration that promises not to breach the value in question need not necessarily provide redress for past injuries. They may support relief efforts in a variety of ways, but members of the collective will probably describe their efforts as charitable contributions rather than payments of moral debt if they do not accept blame for the harm. Even so, we should pay attention to whether a declaration pledges resources to the cause, who it expects to fund these efforts, and whether it has standing to commit the supporters and financiers. I resisted Lazare and Tavuchis' claims that emotions and intentions are largely irrelevant to collective apologies generally, but I agree that such mental states might play a reduced role in value-declaring collective apologies. Institutional members who provide value declarations can also avoid suffering any of the punitive consequences of apologizing.

As I describe them, collective value-declaring apologies significantly differ from collective categorical apologies. Indeed, some will claim that they drift so far from customary practices of repentance that they do not deserve to be described as apologies of any kind. We can appreciate, however, that collective value-declaring apologies serve many important functions. Beyond those previously discussed, value-declaring apologies can provide genuinely profound meaning when the collective cannot provide categorical apologies for whatever reasons. Most basically, institutions sometimes must respond to injuries for which they may not be situated to categorically apologize. The current leaders of the United States, for example, must say *something* about African slavery. Modern Germany cannot remain silent about its past even if the causal links to genocide have been forcefully broken. Such breaks are rarely clean, and asserting that one lacks standing to apologize for the deeds of others does not eliminate the duty to care for injured victims and communities. Value-declaring apologies may palliate such pain. Even if they only metaphorically speak for the guilty dead, referring to this perpetual remainder of responsibility may nourish public normative discourse by articulating our values and recognizing their violation. Merely beginning such conversations about shared values takes a step – even if an unsteady step – toward reconciliation. Collectives can stabilize such progress by building solidarity around the declared value and investing resources in a shared vision of the future. At times the limitations of value-declaring collective apologies may even provide an asset, as a community may find that it cannot survive a fine-grained causal analysis that judges so many guilty. As many modern truth and reconciliation tribunals have decided, stability can be more essential to human flourishing than precise moral accounting. The best path for moving together toward peace may be the one that avoids trekking through the past.

Although some ambiguity may grease the wheels of reconciliation, too much can cause the process to slide off the rails. Having taken some care not to discount the significance of collective value-declaring apologies, I want to stress the importance of asking whether we should receive categorical apologies from individuals of the collective as well. Should this group and its members offer more than a declaration? Is the collective value-declaring apology less benign than it seems? Does it deflect blame onto those who cannot defend themselves when the group and its members should accept accountability? Does it shield leaders and followers from facing the consequences of their contemptible actions? Does it avoid naming those who should be blamed? Does it obfuscate when it should clarify? Does it exploit our confusion and prey on our desperation for the meaning provided by categorical apologies? Does it seek to parlay undeserved moral credit into some self-serving benefit? Does it avoid these questions with evasive rhetoric? Given the examples throughout this text, the suspicions driving these questions seem entirely warranted. We should be equally wary of all other variations of noncategorical collective apologies, including expressions of sympathy, compensatory apologies, purely instrumental apologies, and proxy apologies. In a collective compensatory apology, for instance, we may not be concerned with anything other than receiving payment from the institution. In some cases the check may provide all of the meaning we seek, but if this is provided as a settlement for the wrongful death of a child we would want to understand if it comes without an admission of blame or a promise to reform the deadly behavior.

In the vast majority of cases, victims should seek apologies from those individuals personally responsible for harming them. Collective apologies can supplement this meaning. Instead, we often look to collective apologies first and wrongdoers happily serve us a steady diet of apologetic gravy without meat.

Given their many layers of meaning, collective apologies often resist classification into the varieties I describe. Instead, these landmarks and the questions they raise can guide us toward the meanings we seek from gestures of contrition. Collective apologies can take many forms, and this study introduces us to a few possibilities while equipping us to identify when an apology does not serve the purpose and provide the meaning that we believe it should. Expectations will differ among individuals, cultures, and contexts. Attributions of collective blame should trouble members of individualist cultures, but members of collectivist cultures may be more satisfied with apologies that assert group culpability. Cultures emphasizing shame may expect different emotional content from apologizers than those in guilt-based cultures. We should be watchful, however, for those who abuse the language of diverse moral traditions in order to disorient and manipulate victims. In the aftermath of the Bay of Pigs invasion, John F. Kennedy paraphrased the Italian Fascist Galeazzo Ciano: "Victory has a thousand fathers but defeat is an orphan."[3] I imagine that authoritarian and democratic leaders would also agree regarding the difficulty of finding suitable parents for categorical apologies.

I conclude these considerations of collective apologies by citing in full Clinton's 1997 statement for the infamous Tuskegee studies in which clinicians working for the U.S. Public Health Service withheld treatment for syphilis from a group of poor black men in experiments conducted from 1932 to 1972. I will not analyze this case as I have done with so many in this book. Instead, I leave readers to think through the example. From the introductions of attendees to the closing blessing, readers can determine for themselves which sorts of meanings this apology does and does not provide. They can also judge its adequacy. As you ask of this apology the critical questions that I have repeatedly emphasized, I hope that you see the gesture through new eyes.

Ladies and gentlemen, on Sunday, Mr. Shaw will celebrate his 95th birthday. I would like to recognize the other survivors who are here today and their families: Mr. Charlie Pollard is here. Mr. Carter Howard. Mr. Fred Simmons. Mr. Simmons just took his first airplane ride, and he reckons he's about 110 years old, so I think it's time for him to take a chance or two. I'm glad he did. And Mr. Frederick Moss, thank you, sir.

I would also like to ask three family representatives who are here – Sam Doner is represented by his daughter, Gwendolyn Cox. Thank you, Gwendolyn. Ernest Hendon, who is watching in Tuskegee, is represented by his brother, North Hendon. Thank you, sir, for being here. And George Key is represented by his grandson, Christopher Monroe. Thank you, Chris.

I also acknowledge the families, community leaders, teachers, and students watching today by satellite from Tuskegee. The White House is the people's house; we are glad to have all of you here today. I thank Dr. David Satcher for his role in this. I thank Congresswoman Waters and Congressman Hilliard, Congressman Stokes, the entire Congressional Black Caucus. Dr. Satcher, members of the Cabinet who are here, Secretary Herman, Secretary Slater, members of the Cabinet who are here, Secretary Herman, Secretary Slater. A great friend of freedom, Fred Gray, thank you for fighting this long battle all these long years.

The eight men who are survivors of the syphilis study at Tuskegee are a living link to a time not so very long ago that many Americans would prefer not to remember, but we dare not forget. It was a time when our nation failed to live up to its ideals, when our nation broke the trust with our people that is the very foundation of our democracy. It is not only in remembering that shameful past that we can make amends and repair our nation, but it is in remembering that past that we can build a better present and a better future. And without remembering it, we cannot make amends and we cannot go forward.

So today America does remember the hundreds of men used in research without their knowledge and consent. We remember them and their family members. Men who were poor and African American, without resources and with few alternatives, they believed they had found hope when they were offered free medical care by the United States Public Health Service. They were betrayed.

Medical people are supposed to help when we need care, but even once a cure was discovered, they were denied help, and they were lied to by their government. Our government is supposed to protect the rights of its citizens; their rights were trampled upon. Forty years, hundreds of men betrayed, along with their wives and children, along with the community in Macon County, Alabama, the City of Tuskegee, the fine university there, and the larger African-American community. The United States government did something that was wrong – deeply, profoundly, morally wrong. It was an outrage to our commitment to integrity and equality for all our citizens.

To the survivors, to the wives and family members, the children and the grand-children, I say what you know: No power on Earth can give you back the lives lost, the pain suffered, the years of internal torment and anguish. What was done cannot be undone. But we can end the silence. We can stop turning our heads away. We can look at you in the eye and finally say on behalf of the American people, what the United States government did was shameful, and I am sorry. The American people are sorry – for the loss, for the years of hurt. You did nothing wrong, but you were grievously wronged. I apologize and I am sorry that this apology has been so long in coming.

To Macon County, to Tuskegee, to the doctors who have been wrongly associated with the events there, you have our apology, as well. To our African-American citizens, I am sorry that your federal government orchestrated a study so clearly racist. That can never be allowed to happen again. It is against everything our country stands for and what we must stand against is what it was.

So let us resolve to hold forever in our hearts and minds the memory of a time not long ago in Macon County, Alabama, so that we can always see how adrift we can become when the rights of any citizens are neglected, ignored, and betrayed. And let us resolve here and now to move forward together.

The legacy of the study at Tuskegee has reached far and deep, in ways that hurt our progress and divide our nation. We cannot be one America when a whole segment of our nation has no trust in America. An apology is the first step, and we take it with a commitment to rebuild that broken trust. We can begin by making sure there is never again another episode like this one. We need to do more to ensure that medical research practices are sound and ethical, and that researchers work more closely with communities.

Today I would like to announce several steps to help us achieve these goals. First, we will help to build that lasting memorial at Tuskegee. The school founded by Booker T. Washington, distinguished by the renowned scientist George Washington Carver and so many others who advanced the health and well-being of African Americans and all Americans, is a fitting site. The Department of Health and Human Services will award a planning grant so the school can pursue establishing a center for bioethics in research and health care. The center will serve as a museum of the study and support efforts to address its legacy and strengthen bioethics training.

Second, we commit to increase our community involvement so that we may begin restoring lost trust. The study at Tuskegee served to sow distrust of our medical institutions, especially where research is involved. Since the study was halted, abuses have been checked by making informed consent and local review mandatory in federally funded and mandated research.

Still, 25 years later, many medical studies have little African-American participation and African-American organ donors are few. This impedes efforts to conduct promising research and to provide the best health care to all our people, including African Americans. So today, I'm directing the Secretary of Health and Human Services, Donna Shalala, to issue a report in 180 days about how we can best involve communities, especially minority communities, in research and health care. You must – every American group must be involved in medical research in ways that are positive. We have put the curse behind us; now we must bring the benefits to all Americans.

Third, we commit to strengthen researchers' training in bioethics. We are constantly working on making breakthroughs in protecting the health of our people and in vanquishing diseases. But all our people must be assured that their rights and dignity will be respected as new drugs, treatments and therapies are tested and used. So I am directing Secretary Shalala to work in partnership with higher education to prepare training materials for medical researchers. They will be available in a year. They will help researchers build on core ethical principles of respect for individuals, justice, and informed consent, and advise them on how to use these principles effectively in diverse populations.

Fourth, to increase and broaden our understanding of ethical issues and clinical research, we commit to providing postgraduate fellowships to train bioethicists especially among African Americans and other minority groups. HHS will offer these fellowships beginning in September of 1998 to promising students enrolled in bioethics graduate programs.

And, finally, by executive order I am also today extending the charter of the National Bioethics Advisory Commission to October of 1999. The need for this commission is clear. We must be able to call on the thoughtful, collective wisdom of experts and community representatives to find ways to further strengthen our protections for subjects in human research.

We face a challenge in our time. Science and technology are rapidly changing our lives with the promise of making us much healthier, much more productive and more prosperous. But with these changes we must work harder to see that as we advance we don't leave behind our conscience. No ground is gained and, indeed, much is lost if we lose our moral bearings in the name of progress.

The people who ran the study at Tuskegee diminished the stature of man by abandoning the most basic ethical precepts. They forgot their pledge to heal and repair. They had the power to heal the survivors and all the others and they did not. Today, all we can do is apologize. But you have the power, for only you – Mr. Shaw, the others who are here, the family members who are with us in Tuskegee – only you have the power to forgive. Your presence here shows us that you have chosen a better path than your government did so long ago. You have not withheld the power to forgive. I hope today and tomorrow every American will remember your lesson and live by it. Thank you, and God bless you.[4]

Previewing the Meanings of Apologies in Law

> "Do not argue, admit liability, or disclose the limits of your insurance coverage."
> *Amica Mutual Insurance Company, from the registration envelope kept in the glove compartment of my car*

I refer those seeking a summary of the preceding arguments to the final sections of Parts One and Two. Rather than recapitulating previous chapters, I would like to use this conclusion to explain why it seems worth following this work with a book on apologies in law. I provide this preview not only to promote the sequel, but also to provide those who stop reading here with a hint of just how thoroughly our legal environments structure our thinking about apologies. If religion and its practices of repentance once provided the backdrop that framed our understandings of apologies, law increasingly plays that role in modern life. A specific kind of law driven by adversarial procedures and oriented toward economic outcomes increasingly structures our apologies. Whereas apologies tend to bring people together, adversarial law pushes legal combatants apart in a high-stakes competition.

If one doubts the law's influence over our culture of apologies, place any example from this book within the context of the victim having already brought a legal claim of some sort against the offender. Consider even how my philosophy department's response to fictional allegations of sexism would change if we faced formal charges of harassment or discrimination. The specter of litigation would haunt our discussions even if no one had threatened to bring a claim against us. Similarly, notice how the fear that an apology may void our insurance coverage influences our interactions at the scene of an automobile accident. We often act as if we expect the lawyers circling overhead to descend at the first sign of contrition, and this has a kind of chilling effect on apologetic discourse.

Apologies in both civil and criminal law pull in opposite directions. On the one hand, certain kinds of apologies admit guilt. Whether in criminal hearings, corporate settlement negotiations, or malpractice litigation, admitting guilt is often equivalent to admitting complete defeat. Hence, some view apologizing as legal suicide. For these reasons, many medical malpractice insurers will void their policies if doctors provide too many details to injured patients.[1] As the American Medical Association warned physicians: "Anything you say can and will be held against you."[2]

On the other hand, some apologies provide an astoundingly successful means of mollifying disputants. A strategically timed and worded apology can prevent litigation altogether, reduce damage payments and jury awards by considerable amounts, or shave years from prison sentences. U.S. Supreme Court Justice Anthony Kennedy once claimed that expressions of remorse can be the difference between life and death in capital sentencing procedures.[3] For some, apologies have therefore become tactical weapons that "should be part of the arsenal of resources brought to bear in addressing and resolving legal disputes."[4] Attorneys use apologies as an "attitudinal structuring tactic" in order to "lubricate settlement discussions" and "influence an opponent's bargaining behavior."[5]

Attorneys coach clients to navigate these dangers and benefits of apologizing in legal contexts, sometimes advising them to say just enough to maximize the appearance of contrition without undermining their claims of innocence.[6] Surgeons and lawnmower manufacturers – I will not spell out the grisly connection – innovated these techniques and a wave of literature supported by insurance companies and risk-management firms advised on how to play this advantage.[7] Some recommend that the apology be "carefully crafted to avoid admission of wrongdoing."[8] Others propose offering only expressions of sympathy first to test if that alone is "sufficient to quell a purported 'victim.'"[9] If victims expect more than sympathy, one can dole out a little apologetic meaning at a time to determine how much is required to propitiate them. This allows mediators to reserve admissions of guilt as the trump card if negotiations stall.[10] Some further advise that if "a full apology is to be made, a mediation session preceded by a confidentiality agreement may often be the best place for it because apologies made in that forum are protected by federal law."[11] Offenders should also leave more serious apologies to their lawyers "in order to prevent unwitting exposure to liability or inadvertent admitting of guilt."[12]

When faced with a $100 million claim from a woman paralyzed in one of the many rollover crashes of their sport utility vehicles that resulted in at least 200 deaths, three attorneys for Ford Motor Company apologized to her. They also allowed their apology to be videotaped, but only on the condition that the volume was turned off because "they didn't want anyone hearing what they say."[13] Despite this transparent attempt to limit the public value of the apology, it apparently worked. That day the victim settled for an undisclosed amount, saying that the "gist of the whole thing was that they were truly sorry for what . . . happened to me. And I felt like it was very sincere."[14] Examples of this sort should trigger a series of questions in readers, including those concerns related to ambiguous apologies, expressions of sympathy, value-declaring apologies, conciliatory apologies, compensatory apologies, purely instrumental apologies, coerced apologies, proxy apologies, and collective apologies generally. In other words, just about every issue returns to us as we wonder if legal practices embolden even the most mendacious apologies.

Several distinctive characteristics of modern law, especially as practiced in the United States, complicate matters further. We can note here but a few of the many cultural features that I will consider in relation to apologies in law. We already discussed the importance of shared values for categorical apologies and the difficulty of reaching such agreements within and between pluralistic cultures. I also noted the uncontroversial fact that, for better or for worse, money serves as the prevailing common denominator of value between our diverse worldviews. The law struggles to reduce various kinds of injuries to this broadly valuable currency, but of course something is lost in the translation between an injury like the wrongful death of a child and a cash award. Although there are considerable benefits to a transactional model of justice, law becomes increasingly ill-equipped to accommodate the sorts of apologetic meaning associated with nonmonetary compensation when legal exchanges take on the characteristics of competitive economic markets. The truth lies somewhere between the dueling hyperboles demonizing the commodification of human life and evangelizing blind faith in liberal market forces, but surely these trends carve out a rather peculiar life for apologies in law.

Consider contingency fee arrangements, in which attorneys receive a percentage of their clients' winnings rather than a flat fee or an hourly rate. How does this compensation structure apply to apologies? Perhaps I should be more generous in my estimate of the goodwill of lawyers, but I imagine that most plaintiffs' attorneys will not provide their services on the prospect of receiving one-third of an apology. Contingency fee arrangements enfranchise litigants who otherwise could not afford access to the courts, but they also encourage attorneys to steer clients toward economic remedies. If providing an apology tends to lessen the economic damages that an offender must pay, this also decreases the profits of an attorney paid with contingency fees. Such a conflict of interest may seem inconsequential, but the stakes are very high indeed in the context of multi-billion dollar class-action litigation. In a sexual discrimination case like *Dukes v. Wal-Mart* where attorneys seek to represent 1.6 million women, we can appreciate the difference in potential outcomes. If the attorneys negotiate to maximize payment for themselves and their clients, this would have very different social consequences than if they pursued something like a collective categorical apology from the corporation. Because we now bring so many disputes to the courts that previously would have been resolved through informal channels, these sorts of concerns penetrate more deeply into culture and risk undermining the moral meanings of nonlegal apologies as well.

Criminal law presents an additional set of confounding issues. What, for instance, should we make of courts *ordering* offenders to apologize? Although this might appear like a potentially progressive alternative to incarceration, we have good reasons to wonder about the meanings of such acts. Even without gestures of contrition from offenders, the legal process can establish a factual record, assign blame, excuse accidents, identify and affirm the values breached, recognize the victims as members of the moral community, levy penalties, and oversee the completion of sentences and redress. What, then, does a forced apology from a defendant add? Might it advance primarily retributive, rather than restorative or rehabilitative, justifications for punishment? Should forced apologies provide an inexpensive way to "magnify the humiliation inherent in conviction," as some argue?[15] Rather than reintegrating offenders into the moral community, do such "demeaning rituals" alienate convicts by dehumanizing them instead of recognizing their dignity?[16]

For some injuries, Kant explicitly claims that law should require wealthy offenders to apologize to their "socially inferior" victims so that this "humiliation will compensate for the offense as like for like."[17] This recalls Achilles' desire for an apology from Agamemnon, but what sort of apology does Kant have in mind? Could Kant possibly mean that the state can punish an unrepentant offender by requiring her to lie about her beliefs, values, or feelings? If an offender disagrees with the statute under which a court convicts her, for instance if the state finds an advocate for marijuana legalization guilty of possession, should a judge increase her punishment unless she apologizes? Once again, these questions seem especially important in the absence of a robust set of moral values shared by a community.

Voluntary apologies in criminal contexts introduce additional problems. If a jurisdiction reduces punishment for convicts who express contrition, it invites a parade of purely instrumental apologies into its sentencing procedures. One U.S. federal appellate court warned that reducing sentences for the contrite will result in "lenience toward those who cry more easily, or who have sufficient criminal experience to display sentiment at sentencing."[18] We can also worry that this could undercut the deterrent value of some penalties if offenders believe that they will not suffer the full consequences if they can stage an adequate apology.[19] To take this a step further, should individual defendants benefit from apologies provided by the collective to which they belong, for instance if an executive cites statements of contrition offered by her corporation as evidence of her own remorse?

From a view sympathetic to the religious origins of repentance, categorical apologies might seem like the ultimate objective of the penological theories that are now unfashionable but that once imagined the penitentiary as refuge where the offender could be shepherded back to her true conscience. If we take apologies to signify genuine reform, what sorts of apologetic meanings must the offender demonstrate before deserving leniency? If sentencing guidelines allow judges to consider offenders' contrition, what sorts of meaning should they identify? How do various aspects of apologetic meaning predict recidivism rates? Is, for example, recognizing the victim as a moral interlocutor a better indicator of the offender's future behavior than the emotional content of her apology?

The U.S. Federal Sentencing Guidelines allow judges to reduce punishments by considerable amounts for defendants who accept responsibility for their crimes and express remorse.[20] What do these terms signify, how does case law interpret this language, and do the provisions capture the sorts of meaning that they should?[21] How will officials judge the offender's interior life and determine the nature of her beliefs, values, emotions, or intentions, thereby differentiating genuine contrition from staged attempts to manipulate the system? In both civil and criminal matters, might an attorney's aggressive style of advocacy – by most accounts the sort of representation one should hope for in this system – cause her client to appear remorseless?[22] Must certain elements, like an admission of guilt, come early in the proceedings? Otherwise offenders would be inclined to apologize after convictions but before sentencing in order to maximize the benefit but reduce the risks of accepting blame. Perhaps we should judge a convicts' apology several years into her sentence so that we can better evaluate the sincerity of her commitment to reform? If we seek assurance that the convict does not treat the apology as mere means to earthly ends, maybe the most appropriate moment for repentance is immediately before her execution, as Foucault found in eighteenth-century practice.[23] Once we determine what we seek from an apology, who should judge whether an offender measures up: judges, juries, or some sort of specialists in contrition?

We can also wonder if criminal law has either the time or the place for apologetic interactions. If Markus Dubber is correct in his assessment that within modern penal institutions "offenders and victims alike are irrelevant nuisances, grains of sand in the great machine of state risk management," can the assembly line of justice build in the intricacies of apologetic meaning?[24] Stephanos Bibas and Richard Bierschbach demonstrate this problem quite convincingly, describing how even the most "genuinely remorseful offender who wishes to apologize to his victim and make amends usually has no readily available way to do so."[25] Offenders "almost never" encounter victims until sentencing, instead interacting primarily with their attorneys who are likely to obviate attempts to apologize. Even during sentencing, an offender typically directs her statements to the court and must literally turn her back on the judge if she wishes to face her victim while apologizing.[26]

If an offender does provide a promissory categorical apology, should she accept full punishment rather than seek to reduce her sentence? Interesting examples arise when those working through twelve-step addiction programs confess to and apologize for crimes committed as many as twenty years earlier.[27] If an apology results in clemency, should we understand this as a kind of state-sanctioned collective forgiveness? Does the state possess standing to grant such forgiveness, especially if the primary victim is deceased? These are difficult questions that threaten to strike at the heart of restorative justice. Thankfully, I can consider them in dialogue with the works of sophisticated legal philosophers like John Braithwaite, R. A. Duff, Jean Hampton, Jeffrie Murphy, Philip Petit, Austin Sarat, and others.

If it ultimately accomplishes little else, I hope this book raises new questions about apologies and our shared values. Every question I asked regarding apologetic meaning begat several more questions, each more unruly and interesting than the last. Perhaps others working in these areas can better tame the issues and eliminate many of my questions as irrelevant. I expect, however, that these questions run deep into the core of modern moral consciousness. I do not yet see any bedrock at the bottom of that hole, and I anticipate that my subsequent work on apologies in law will only mine deeper into their dialectical meanings. Every age may worry that its moral roots rot under its feet, but I wonder if there has ever been such strangely sour fruit on so many vines. I am aware that critical reflection often destroys meaning as it demythologizes the values attributed to our social rituals, yet I remain optimistic that asking such questions of apologies can nourish our shared moral lives.

Notes

Epigraph

1. Yusef Komunyakaa, "When in Rome-Apologia," in *Neon Vernacular* (Hanover: Wesleyan University Press, 1993), 97.

Introduction

1. As noted later, Maimonides primarily addressed acts of repentance rather than apologies. His contributions, however, speak to many of the central issues of apologetic meaning. Moses Maimonides, *Hilchot Teshuvah: The Laws of Repentance* (New York: Moznaim, 1987). For extended conversations about apologies in modern philosophical literature, see Glen Pettigrove, "Unapologetic Forgiveness," *American Philosophical Quarterly* 41, no. 1 (2004): 187–204; Pettigrove, "Apology, Reparations, and the Question of Inherited Guilt," *Public Affairs Quarterly* 17, no. 4 (2003): 319–48; Trudy Govier and Wilhelm Verwoerd, "The Promise and Pitfalls of Apology," *Journal of Social Philosophy* 33, no. 1 (2002): 67–82; Paul Davis, "On Apologies," *Journal of Applied Philosophy* 19, no. 2 (2002): 169–73; Nicolaus Mills, "The New Culture of Apology," *Dissent* (Fall 2001): 113–16; Kathleen Gill, "The Moral Functions of an Apology," *Philosophical Forum* 31, no. 1 (2000): 11–27; Jana Thompson, "The Apology Paradox," *Philosophical Quarterly* 55, no. 201 (2000): 470–75; Richard Joyce, "Apologizing," *Public Affairs Quarterly* 13, no. 2 (1999): 159–73; Jean Harvey, "The Emerging Practice of Institutional Apologies," *The International Journal of Applied Philosophy* 9, no. 2 (1995): 57–65; John Wilson, "Why Forgiveness Requires Repentance," *Philosophy* 63, no. 246 (1988): 534–5; and Louis Kort, "What is an Apology?" *Philosophical Research Archives* 1 (1975): 78–87.

2. Richard Conniff, "The Power of 'Sorry,'" *The New York Times*, December 26, 2006. See Conniff's *The Ape in the Corner Office* (New York: Random House, 2005). See also Filippo Aureli and Frans B. M. de Waal, eds., *Natural Conflict Resolution* (Berkeley: University of California Press, 2000).

3. Aaron Lazare also believes that globalization contributes to the rise of apologies. See Aaron Lazare, *On Apology* (Oxford: Oxford University Press, 2004), 12.

4. Homer, *The Iliad*, trans. E. V. Rieu (New York: Penguin, 1950), 171. Notice how Achilles minimizes the importance of the gifts even after he agrees to fight after Patroclus' death: "The gifts can wait. Produce them, if you like, at your

convenience; or keep them with you." Ibid., 358. All references to *The Iliad* are in Rieu's translation unless otherwise noted. Mark Edwards describes Achilles' eventual response to receiving the gifts from Agamemnon as displaying "offhand-edness, or even disdain." Mark Edwards, *The Iliad: A Commentary* V (New York: Cambridge University Press, 1991), 253.

5. Cited in Susan Alter, "Apologizing for Serious Wrongdoing: Social, Psychologi-cal, and Legal Considerations," *Final Report for the Law Commission of Canada* (1999).

6. See, for example, J. Stratton Shartel, "Toro's Mediation Program Challenges Wisdom of Traditional Litigation Model," *Inside Litigation* 9 (1995): 10. See also Jonathan Cohen, "Apology and Organizations: Exploring an Example for Medical Practice," *Fordham Urban Law Journal* 27 (2000): 1447.

7. See 18 U.S.C.S. app. § 3E1.1 (Law. Co-op, 2000).

8. Ken Blanchard and Margaret McBride, *The One Minute Apology* (New York: Harper Collins, 2003); Beverly Engel, *The Power of Apology: Healing Steps to Transform all of Your Relationships* (New York: John Wiley and Sons, 2001).

9. Reuters, "Pope Apologizes to Muslims," September 16, 2006 (emphasis in orig-inal).

10. "Pope Seeks to Calm Storm over 'Evil Islam' Comment," *Observer* (London), September 17, 2006.

11. "Text of Pope's Statement," *BBC News*, September 17, 2006.

12. Ian Fisher, "The Pope Apologizes for Uproar over his Remarks," *New York Times*, September 17, 2006; Reuters, "Pope Apologizes to Muslims."

13. "Pope's Apology Rejected by Some, Accepted by Others," *Der Spiegel*, September 18, 2006.

14. "Pope Sorry for Offending Muslims," *BBC News*, September 17, 2006.

15. "Grand Sheikh Condemns Suicide Bombings," *BBC News*, December 4, 2001.

16. Daniela Petroff, "Pope Expresses 'Deep Respect' for Islam," *ABC News*, Septem-ber 20, 2006.

17. Stephen Brown and Philip Pullella, "Muslims Seek Fuller Apology," *The Boston Globe*, September 20, 2006.

18. Ibid.

19. "Brotherhood Seeks Papal Apology," *Al Jazeera*, September 18, 2006.

20. "Pope Seeks to Calm Storm," *The Observer*.

21. Brown and Pullella, "Muslims Seek Fuller Apology," *The Boston Globe*.

22. "Pope Seeks to Calm Storm," *The Observer*.

23. "Report: Rome Tightens Pope's Security after Fury over Islam Remarks," *Haaretz*, September 17, 2006.

24. "Christian Killed in Iraq in Response to Pope's Speech: Islamic Website," *Assyr-ian International News Agency*, September 16, 2006.

25. "Al-Qaeda Threatens Jihad over Pope's Remark," *Times (London)*, September 18, 2006.

26. Richard Owen, "Nun Shot Dead as Pope Fails to Calm Militant Muslims," *Times (London)*, September 18, 2006.

27. "Iraq Priest 'Killed over Pope's Speech,'" *Al Jazeera*, October 15, 2006.

28. Michel de Montaigne, "Of Repentance," in *Montaigne: Essays*, ed. and trans. John M. Cohen (New York: Penguin, 1993), 235–49.

29. Michel de Montaigne, *Apology for Raymond Sebond*, trans. M. A. Screech (New York: Penguin, 1988).

30. For an overview of the history of the terms "apology" and "apologize" in English, see Marion Owen, *Apologies and Remedial Interchanges: A Study of Language Use in Social Interactions* (Berlin: Mouton de Gruyter, 1985), 109–13.

31. Samuel Johnson, *A Dictionary of the English Language on CD-ROM*, ed. Anne McDermott (New York: Cambridge University Press, 1996).

32. *The Oxford English Dictionary* (London: Oxford, 2005).

33. The 2005 edition provides the following definitions of apology: "1. The pleading off from a charge or imputation, whether expressed, implied, or only conceived as possible; defence of a person, or vindication of an institution, etc., from accusation or aspersion; 2. Less formally: Justification, explanation, or excuse, of an incident or course of action; 3. An explanation offered to a person affected by one's action that no offence was intended, coupled with the expression of regret for any that may have been given; or, a frank acknowledgement of the offence with expression of regret for it, by way of reparation; 4. Something which, as it were, merely appears to apologize for the absence of what ought to have been there; a poor substitute."

34. Nicholas Tavuchis, *Mea Culpa: A Sociology of Apology and Reconciliation* (Stanford: Stanford University Press, 1991); Lazare, *On Apology*.

35. Trudy Govier and Wilhelm Verwoerd, "Taking Wrongs Seriously: A Qualified Defense of Public Apologies," *Saskatchewan Law Review* 65 (2002): 157.

36. Ludwig Wittgenstein, *Philosophical Investigations*, trans. G. E. M. Anscombe (Oxford: Blackwell, 1953).

Part One. Apologies from Individuals

1. Barbara Charlesworth Gelpi and Albert Gelpi, eds., "Women and Honor: Some Notes on Lying," in *Adrienne Rich's Prose and Poetry* (New York: Norton and Company, 1993), 197. I want to thank Timm Triplett for bringing this passage to my attention.

Chapter 1. The Meanings of Apologies

1. Kort, "What Is an Apology?," 83.

2. Lazare, *On Apology*, 13.

3. John Searle, *Speech Acts: An Essay in the Philosophy of Language* (Cambridge: Cambridge University Press, 1969); J. L. Austin, *How to Do Things with Words* (Oxford: Oxford University Press, 1962); and John Searle, "A Classification of Illocutionary Acts," *Language in Society* 5 (1976): 1–24. For examples of Searle's influence on the study of apologies within linguistics and related fields, see Janet Holmes, *Women, Men, and Politeness* (New York: Longman, 1995); Penelope Brown and Stephen Levinson, *Politeness: Some Universals in Language Usage* (New York: Cambridge, 1987); Marion Owen, *Apologies and Remedial Interchanges*; Bruce Fraser, "On Apologizing," in Florian Coulmas, ed., *Conversational Routine: Explorations in Standardized Communication Situations and Prepatterned Speech* (Berlin: Mouton de Gruyter, 1981), 259–71; Florian Coulmas, "'Poison to Your Soul': Thanks and Apologies Contrastively Viewed," in *Conversational Routine*: 69–91; N. R. Norrick, "Expressive Illocutionary Acts," *Journal of Pragmatics* 2 (1978): 277–91; E. Olshtain and A. D. Cohen, "Apology: A Speech Act Set," in *Sociolinguistics and Language Acquisition*, eds. Nessa Wolfson and Elliot Judd (Rowley, Ma.: Newbury House, 1983): 18–35;

K. Barrett, "Apologies as Illocutionary Acts," *Southern California Occasional Papers in Linguistics* (1974): 121–31; and C. J. Fillmore, "Verbs of Judging: An Exercise in Semantic Description," in *Studies in Linguistic Semantics*, eds. C. Fillmore and T. Langendoen (New York: Holt Rinehart, 1971). For examples of treatments of apologies in other social scientific fields, see M. McCullough, E. Worthington, and K. Rachel, "Interpersonal Forgiving in Close Relationships," *Journal of Personality and Social Psychology* 73, no. 2 (1997): 321–36; S. Scher and J. Darley, "How Effective Are the Things People Say to Apologize? Effects of the Realization of the Apology Speech Act," *Journal of Psycholinguistic Research* 26 (1997): 127–40; K. Ohbuchi, M. Kameda, and N. Agarie, "Apology as Aggression Control: Its Role in Mediating Appraisal of and Response to Harm," *Journal of Personality and Social Psychology* 56, no. 2 (1989): 219–27; B. Darby and B. Schlenker, "Children's Reactions to Transgressions: Effects of the Actor's Apology, Reputation and Remorse," *British Journal of Social Psychology* 28 (1989): 353–64; B. Darby and B. Schlenker, "Children's Reactions to Apologies," *Journal of Personality and Social Psychology* 43 (1982): 742–53; B. Schlenker and B. Darby, "The Use of Apologies in Social Predicaments," *Social Psychology Quarterly* 44 (1981): 271–78; and Mary B. Harris, "Mediators Between Frustration and Aggression in a Field Experiment," *Journal of Experimental Social Psychology* 10 (1974): 561–71.

4. Searle, "A Classification of Illocutionary Acts," 12.
5. Ibid., 4. See also Pettigrove, "Unapologetic Forgiveness," 187. Pettigrove also understands an apology primarily as a speech act.
6. See Owen, *Apologies and Remedial Interchanges*; Holmes, *Women, Men, and Politeness*, 154 (describing apologies as "negative politeness devices"); and Brown and Levinson, *Politeness*, 68 (describing apologies as "directly damaging [one's] positive face").
7. Erving Goffman, *Relations in Public* (New York: Basic Books, 1971), 113.
8. Coulmas, "'Poison to Your Soul,'" 70. Florian Coulmas describes his ambition with more sensitivity to cultural contexts: "To treat speech acts such as thanks and apologies as invariable abstract categories is surely a premature stance. What we can do without too much or too little naivety is hence to start out with kinds of speech acts as defined in a given socio-cultural and linguistic system, and then proceed to look for similar or equivalent linguistic acts in another culture. A number of careful analyses of this kind can eventually contribute to a better understanding of a kind of speech act as a generic type."
9. Holmes, *Women, Men, and Politeness*, 155.
10. Gill, "The Moral Functions of an Apology," 14.
11. See S. Blum-Kulka, J. House, and G. Kasper, eds., *Cross-cultural Pragmatics: Requests and Apologies* (Norwood, NJ: Ablex, 1989).
12. See D. C. Barnlund and M. Yoshioka, "Apologies: Japanese and American styles," *International Journal of Intercultural Relations* 14 (1990): 193–206; S. Blum-Kulka and E. Olshtain, "Requests and Apologies: A Cross-cultural Study of Speech Act Realization Patterns (CCSARP)," *Applied Linguistics* 5 (1984): 196–213; Scher and Darley, "How Effective Are the Things People Say to Apologize?"; Darby and Schlenker, "Children's Reactions to Apologies"; Darby and Schlenker, "Children's Reactions to Transgressions"; and Schlenker and Darby, "The Use of Apologies in Social Predicaments."
13. Scher and Darley, "How Effective Are the Things People Say to Apologize?" 132.

14. Pettigrove, "Apology, Reparations and the Question of Inherited Guilt," 327.
15. Searle, *Speech Acts*, 21.
16. Owen, *Apologies and Remedial Interchanges*, 21.
17. Ibid., 63. By page 181 Owen begins to recognize the limitations of such an approach: "Examination of our set of strategies now suggests that we should have cast the net wider still to include such expressions as 'excuse me' and 'forgive me', since these clearly . . . have remedial effect, whether or not they are describable as apologies."
18. Fraser, "On Apologizing," 261.
19. See Kort, "What Is an Apology?" and Joyce, "Apologizing," 165. See also Fraser, "On Apologizing," 261: "A speaker can violate one or more of these positions and still apologize successfully, albeit insincerely. I might, for example, apologize for breaking your valuable vase which, in fact, is still whole. A strange apology, but an apology nonetheless."
20. Olshtain and Cohen, "Apology: A Speech Act Set," 22. In "The Use of Apologies in Social Predicaments." Darby and Schlenker use the term "more full blown apology," which Gill approvingly cites in note 7 of her "The Moral Functions of Apology."
21. See Albert Mehrabian, "Substitute for Apology: Manipulation of Cognitions to Reduce Negative Attitude Toward Self," *Psychological Reports* 20 (1976): 687–92.
22. See G. Kasper and S. Blum-Kulka, eds., *Interlanguage Pragmatics* (New York: Oxford University Press, 1993); Malgorzata Susczynska, "Apologizing in English, Polish and Hungarian: Different Languages, Different Strategies," *Journal of Pragmatics* 31 (1999): 1053–65; R. R. Mehrotra, "How to be Polite in Indian English," *International Journal of the Sociology of Language* 116 (1995): 99–110; M. Lipson, "Apologizing in Italian and English," *International Review of Applied Linguistics in Language Teaching* 32, no. 1 (1994):19–39; Janet Holmes, "Apologies in New Zealand English," *Language in Society* 19 (1990): 155–99; Anna Trosborg, "Apology Strategies in Natives/Non-natives," *Journal of Pragmatics* 11 (1987): 147–67; A. Cohen and E. Olshtain, "Comparing Apologies Across Languages," in *Scientific and Humanistic Dimensions of Language*, ed. Kurt Jankowsky (Amsterdam: John Benjamins, 1985): 175–83; Owen, *Apologies and Remedial Interchanges*; Olshtain and Cohen, "Apology: A Speech Act Set"; Coulmas, "'Poison to the Soul'"; A. Cohen and E. Olshtain, "Developing a Measure of Socio-Cultural Competence: The Case of Apology," *Language Learning* 31(1981):113–34; and A. Borkin and S. Reinhart, "'Excuse me' and 'I'm sorry,'" *TESOL Quarterly* 12 (1978): 57–70.
23. See, for example, the discussion of Tzeltal in Brown and Levinson, *Politeness*, 187–90. See also the discussions in Chapter 4 regarding the relationship between gratitude and thanks in Japanese culture.
24. David Cooper, *Meaning* (Montreal: McGill University Press, 2003), 1–15.
25. Ibid., 12, 84, citing Maurice Merleau-Ponty, *Phenomenology of Perception*, trans. C. Smith (London: Routledge, 1962), xix, 188.
26. Ibid., 22.
27. Ibid., 2.
28. Ibid., 21 (emphasis in original).
29. Ibid.
30. Theodor Adorno, "Trying to Understand Endgame," in *Notes to Literature* 1, ed. Ralph Tiedemann and trans. Shierry Weber Nicholsen (New York: Columbia

University Press, 1991), 243. See Adorno's reading of these moments in *Endgame*: "Hence interpretation of Endgame cannot pursue the chimerical aim of expressing the play's meaning in a form mediated by philosophy. Understanding it can mean only understanding its unintelligibility. Split off, thought no longer presumes, as the Idea once did, to be the meaning of the work.... "

31. Bob Scharff helped me formulate the ideas in this paragraph.

32. Michael Walzer, *Spheres of Justice: A Defense of Pluralism and Equality* (New York: Basic Books, 1983).

33. Lazare shares this worry: "I believe pseudo-apologies are parasitical on that power. With a pseudo-apology, the offender is trying to reap the benefits of apologizing without having actually earned them." *On Apology*, 13.

34. Friedrich Nietzsche, *Human, All Too Human: A Book for Free Spirits*, trans. R. J. Hollingdale (New York: Cambridge University Press, 1993), 316.

35. Martha Minow, *Between Vengeance and Forgiveness: Facing History after Genocide and Mass Violence* (Boston: Beacon, 1998), x.

Chapter 2. Elements of the Categorical Apology

1. Paul Slansky and Arleen Sorkin, *My Bad: 25 Years of Public Apologies and the Appalling Behavior that Inspired Them* (New York: Bloomsbury, 2006), 40.

2. Lazare, *On Apology*, 13.

3. Ibid.

4. Slansky and Sorkin, *My Bad*, 178.

5. Ibid.

6. Ibid., 207.

7. Ibid., 208.

8. Ibid.

9. Minow, *Between Vengeance and Forgiveness*, 103, citing Howard Zehr, *Changing Lenses: A New Focus for Crime and Justice* (Scottsdale, PA: Herald Press, 1990), 26.

10. See Minow, *Between Vengeance and Forgiveness*, 94–102.

11. International Military Tribunal, Trial of the Major War Criminals before the International Military Tribunal, Nuremburg, 14 Nov. 1945–1 Oct. 1946, vol. 3 (Nuremberg: International Military Tribunal, 1947), 92.

12. *Seinfeld*, "The Apology," Episode 909. Executive Producers Larry David, George Shapiro, and Howard West.

13. Jonathan Atler, "High Stakes in New Orleans," *Newsweek*, August 22, 1988, 15.

14. Deborah Tannen notes this distinction in *You Just Don't Understand: Women and Men in Conversation* (New York: Ballantine Books, 1990), 233.

15. Slansky and Sorkin, *My Bad*, 168.

16. See, for example, William K. Bartels, "The Stormy Sea of Apologies: California Evidence Code Section 1160 Provides a Safe Harbor for Apologies Made after Accidents," *Western State University Law Review* 28 (2000/2001): 141–57; Jonathan R. Cohen, "Advising Clients to Apologize," *Southern California Law Review* 72 (1999): 1009–69, 1061–4; Jonathan R. Cohen, "Nagging Problem: Advising the Client Who Wants to Apologize," *Dispute Resolution Magazine* (Spring 1999): 19; Jonathan R. Cohen, "Legislating Apologies: The Pros and Cons," *University of Cincinnati Law Review* 70 (2002): 1–29; Steven Keeva, "Does Law Mean Never Having to Say You're Sorry?" *American Bar*

Association Journal 85 (1999): 64; Elizabeth Latif, "Apologetic Justice: Evaluating Apologies Tailored Toward Legal Solutions," *Boston University Law Review* 81 (2001): 289–318; Aviva Orenstein, "Apology Excepted: Incorporating a Feminist Analysis into Evidence Policy Where You Would Least Expect It," *Southwestern University Law Review* 28 (1999): 221–75; and Peter Rehm and Denise Beatty, "Legal Consequences of Apologizing," *Journal of Dispute Resolution* (1995): 115–30. See also Lee Taft, "Apology Subverted: The Commodification of Apology," *Yale Law Journal* 109 (2000): 1135–60 (critically evaluating such legislation).

17. See, for example, Mass. Gen. Laws. ch. 233, 23D (1999) (rendering "statements, writings or benevolent gestures expressing sympathy or a general sense of benevolence" inadmissible "as evidence of an admission of liability in a civil action"); Tex. Civ. Prac. & Rem. Code Ann. 18.061(a) (1) (West 1999) (rendering inadmissible expressions of "sympathy or a general sense of benevolence relating to the pain, suffering, or death of an individual involved in an accident"); Assembly 2804, 1999 Reg. Sess. (Cal. 2000).

18. "Apology Australia, http://apology.west.net.au/. Archived at the National Library of Australia's web archive at http://pandora.nla.gov.au/pan/10736/20050711/apology.west.net.au/index.html.

19. "Bush Reaches Out to Quell Arab Rage at Inmate Abuse," *The Boston Globe*, May 6, 2004.

20. David Stout and Terence Neilan, "Bush Tells Arab World that Prisoner Abuse was Abhorrent," *New York Times*, May 5, 2004.

21. "Bush Calls Iraq Abuse Abhorrent," *BBC News*, May 5, 2004. Rice also stated: "We are deeply sorry for what has happened to these people and what the families must be feeling. It's just not right. And we will get to the bottom of what happened. It is simply unacceptable that anyone would engage in the abuse of Iraqi prisoners." Slansky and Sorkin, *My Bad*, 150–51.

22. Elisabeth Bumiller and Eric Schmitt, "President Sorry for Iraq Abuse; Backs Rumsfeld," *New York Times*, May, 7, 2004. The White House, "Interview of the President by Al-Ahram International," http://www.whitehouse.gov/news/releases/2004/05/20040507-7.html. Bush made similar statements during an interview on Al-Ahram International on May 6, 2004: "I am sorry for the humiliation suffered by those individuals. It makes me sick to my stomach to see that happen. I'll tell you what else I'm sorry about. I'm sorry that the truth about our soldiers in Iraq becomes obscured. In other words, we've got fantastic citizens in Iraq; good kids; good soldiers, men and women who are working every day to make Iraqi citizens' lives better. And there are a thousand acts of kindness that take place every day of these great Americans who really do care about the citizens in Iraq. It's an awful, awful period for the American people, just like it's awful for the Iraqi citizens to see that on their TV screens." The interviewer then asked: "Again, sir, do you feel like you need to apologize to the Iraqis and the Arab world after you said that, 'I'm sorry'?" Bush replied: "Well, I'm sorry for the prisoners, I really am. I think it's humiliating. And it is, again – what the Arab world must understand is a couple of things. One, under a dictatorship, these – this wouldn't be transparent. In other words, if there was torture under a dictator, we would never know the truth. In a democracy, you'll know the truth. And justice will be done. And that's what people need to know."

23. "Rumsfeld Testifies Before Senate Armed Services Committee," *The Washington Post*, May 7, 2004.

24. Jackie Spinner, "Soldier: Unit's Role Was to Break Down Prisoners," *The Washington Post*, May 8, 2004.

25. Slansky and Sorkin, *My Bad*, 151.

26. Ibid., 39.

27. Ibid.

28. Elisabeth Bumiller and Richard Stevenson, "President Says He's Responsible in Storm Lapses," *The New York Times*, September 14, 2005.

29. Darren Fonda and Rita Healy, "How Reliable is Brown's Resume?" *Time Magazine*, September 8, 2005.

30. Slansky and Sorkin, *My Bad*, 38.

31. For a sampling of theories of physical causation, see Phil Dowe, *Physical Causation* (Cambridge: Cambridge University Press, 2000); Judea Pearl, *Causality* (Cambridge: Cambridge University Press, 2000); Wesley Salmon, *Causality and Explanation* (Oxford: Oxford University Press, 1998); D. H. Mellor, *The Facts of Causation* (London: Routledge, 1995); Michael Tooley, *Causation: A Realist Approach* (Oxford: Clarendon Press, 1987); Wesley Salmon, *Scientific Explanation and the Causal Structure of the World* (Princeton: Princeton University Press, 1984); and J. L. Mackie, *The Cement of the Universe* (Oxford: Oxford University Press, 1974). For discussions of direct causation in law, see M. Moore, "The Metaphysics of Causal Intervention," *California Law Review* 88 (2000): 827–78; J. Stapleton, "Law, Causation and Common Sense," *Oxford Journal of Legal Studies* 8 (1988): 111–31; Jane Stapleton, "Legal Cause: Cause-in-Fact and the Scope of Liability for Consequences," *Vanderbilt Law Review* 54 (2001): 941–1000; and W. S. Malone, "Ruminations on Cause-in-fact," *Stanford Law Review* 9 (1956–7): 60–99.

32. For discussions of moral responsibility and proximate causation in law, see J. M. Fischer and Mark Ravizza, eds., *Perspectives on Moral Responsibility* (Ithaca: Cornell University Press, 1993); H. L. A. Hart and Tony Honoré, *Causation in the Law*, 2nd ed. (Oxford: Clarendon Press, 1985); Joel Feinberg, *Doing and Deserving: Essays in the Theory of Responsibility* (Princeton: Princeton University Press, 1970); L. Green, *Rationale of Proximate Cause* (Kansas City: Vernon Law Book Company, 1927); and J. M. Fischer, "Recent Work on Moral Responsibility," *Ethics* 110 (1999): 93–139.

33. Hart and Honoré, *Causation in the Law*, 341.

34. *Palsgraf v. Long Island R.R.*, 162 N.E. 99, 103 (N.Y. 1928).

35. *Prosser and Keaton on the Law of Torts*, 5th ed., (American Law Institute, 1984), § 41.

36. Ibid., § 440.

37. See my "When Selling Your Soul Isn't Enough," *Social Theory and Practice*, 30–4 (2004): 599–612.

38. On these issues, see R. J. Wallace, *Responsibility and the Moral Sentiments* (Cambridge, MA: Harvard University Press, 1994); Daniel Dennett, *Freedom Evolves* (New York: Viking Press, 2003); and Dennett, *Elbow Room: The Varieties of Free Will Worth Wanting* (Cambridge, MA: MIT Press, 1984).

39. P. F. Strawson, "Freedom and Resentment," *Proceedings of the British Academy* 48 (1962): 1–25.

40. Marion Smiley, *Moral Responsibility and the Boundaries of Community* (Chicago: University of Chicago Press, 1992).

41. Leo Katz, *Bad Acts and Guilty Minds: Conundrums of the Criminal Law* (Chicago: University of Chicago Press, 1987), 210.

42. G. Calabresi, "Concerning Cause and the Law of Torts," *University of Chicago Law Review*, 43 (1975): 69–108.

43. See Deborah Tannen, *The Argument Culture* (New York: Random House, 1998), 47 (making a similar point).

44. Janet Holmes, *Women, Men, and Politeness* (New York: Longman, 1995) 182.

45. Tannen, *Talking from 9 to 5: Women and Men at Work* (New York: Harper Collins, 1994), 46.

46. Sara Mills, *Gender and Politeness* (Cambridge: Cambridge University Press, 2003), 231.

47. Minow, *Between Vengeance and Forgiveness*, 115.

48. See Owen, *Apologies and Remedial Interchanges*, 149 (generally agreeing).

49. Lazare appears committed to the position that we should apologize for accidents such as oversleeping, misspeaking, or bumping into someone. See *On Apology*, 36, 121, 123.

50. Walt Whitman, *Leaves of Grass*, ed. Emory Holloway (Garden City: Doubleday, 1926), 41.

51. Rieu translates Nestor as requesting a "humble apology" from Agamemnon, Homer, *The Iliad*, 164, but Fagles has him calling for "warm, winning words." See Homer, *The Iliad*, trans. Robert Fagles (New York: Penguin, 1990), 255.

52. Homer, *The Iliad*, 164.

53. Ibid., 356.

54. See Edwards, *The Iliad: A Commentary* V, 246–9.

55. For an illuminating discussion of these passages and the subtleties of attributing blame for human action on the gods, see Edwards, *The Iliad: A Commentary* V, 245–7.

56. Edwards, *The Iliad: A Commentary* V, 244, 246–47.

57. Homer, *The Iliad*, 357 (emphasis in original). Fagles translates Agamemnon's description of the gifts offered by the embassy as a "priceless ransom paid for friendship." *The Iliad*, trans. Fagles, 255.

58. Montaigne, "Of Repentance," 245–6.

59. Paul Robinson, *Criminal Law Defenses* (St. Paul: West Publishing, 1984), 91.

60. Slansky and Sorkin, *My Bad*, 210–11.

61. We can find various methods of denying intent in Slansky and Sorkin's *My Bad*, for instance, on the following pages: 9, 16, 27, 28, 29, 30, 32–33, 35, 36, 36–37, 50, 65, 67, 71, 75, 77, 78, 80, 87, 97, 97, 97–98, 98, 100, 100, 105–6, 109, 119, 126, 132–33, 136, 138, 144–45, 155, 186, 186, 190, 197, 198, 201, 206, and 215.

62. Ibid., 99.

63. Ibid., 95.

64. Ibid., 192.

65. Ibid.

66. Ibid., 232.

67. Ibid., 233.

68. Ibid.

69. Ibid., 229.

70. Ibid., 221.

71. Ibid., 181.

72. Ibid., 195–96.

73. Ibid., 233. Cincinnati Reds owner Marge Schott made a similar distinction, claiming that it was "my mouth but not my heart speaking" her recurrent racist comments. Ibid., 128–29.

74. Ibid., 32.

75. Ibid., 120–21.

76. Ibid., 135–36.

77. Ibid., 145–46.

78. Ibid., 101.

79. Ibid., 166–67.

80. See Tavuchis, *Mea Culpa*, 49. ("An authentic apology cannot be delegated, consigned, exacted, or assumed by the principals, no less outsiders, without totally altering its meaning and vitiating its moral force.")

81. Michele Parente, "Boy's Uncle Apologizes to Blacks: Aims to Ease Tensions over Mom's Abduction Claim," *Buffalo News*, November 9, 1994.

82. For a further discussion of this point, see Pettigrove, "Apology, Reparations and the Question of Inherited Guilt," 321–22.

83. Lazare, *On Apology*, 41. See also Pettigrove, "Apology, Reparations and the Question of Inherited Guilt," 333 (taking a similar position with respect to innocence and guilt).

84. See David Lewis, "Collective Responsibility," in Larry May and Stacy Hoffman, ed., *Collective Responsibility* (Lanham, MD: Rowman & Littlefield, 1991), 22.

85. See M. McLean, "Circle Sentencing" *Jurisfemme* 18, no. (1998): 4.

86. Slansky and Sorkin, *My Bad*, 184.

87. Ibid., 193.

88. James Bennet, "Clinton Admits Lewinsky Liaison to Jury; Tells Nations 'It was Wrong,' but Private," *The New York Times*, August 19, 1998.

89. "Excerpts from Apologies by Clinton," *The New York Times*, September 11, 1998.

90. Ian Fisher, "Berlusconi Flirts. His Wife's Fed Up. Read All About It." *The New York Times*, February 1, 2007. See also "Wife Wins Apology from Berlusconi," Reuters, January 31, 2007.

91. "Wife Wins Apology from Berlusconi," Reuters. Berlusconi subsequently stated, "Your dignity has nothing to do with it, I treasure it as a precious good in my heart, even when I make carefree jokes, a gallant remark."

92. Slansky and Sorkin, *My Bad*, 151.

93. "Further Statement of Joseph Ellis," at http://www.mtholyoke.edu/offices/comm/news/ellisstatement.html.

94. For differing opinions, see Govier and Verwoerd, "The Promise and Pitfalls of Apology," 70; and Gill, "The Moral Functions of an Apology," 13.

95. See Slansky and Sorkin, *My Bad*, 174 and 236–38.

96. See Lazare, *On Apology*, 92–93.

97. Slansky and Sorkin, *My Bad*, 70.

98. Ibid., 203.

99. David Kocieniewski, "McGreevey Apologetic but Proud at Farewell," *New York Times*, November 9, 2004.

100. Erving Goffman, *Relations in Public: Micro-Studies of the Public Order* (New York: Basic Books, 1971), 113–14.

101. James Sterngold, "Sailor Gets Life for Killing Gay Shipmate," *New York Times*, May 27, 1993.

102. See Govier and Verwoerd, "The Promise and Pitfalls of Apology," 69 (emphasizing how apologies recognize the moral status of the victim).

103. Bill de Vries helped me formulate this important thought. I hope to consider the distinctions between Kant and Hegel on this point in later work.

104. Tavuchis, *Mea Culpa*, 36. See also Gill, "The Moral Functions of an Apology," 14.

105. Angela Doland, "Zidane Explains – Partly – What Caused his World Cup Outburst," *The Washington Post*, July 13, 2006.

106. Lazare, *On Apology*, 36–37.

107. Kort, "What is an Apology?," 84.

108. Joyce, "Apologizing," 167.

109. Alison Bass, "When Apologizing, 'Sorry' Just the Start," *The Boston Globe*, April 3, 1994.

110. Thompson, "The Apology Paradox."

111. Stanley Fish, "Politics Means Always Having to Say You're Sorry," *The New York Times*, February 25, 2007.

112. Matthew Mosk, "Edwards Again Says He Was Wrong to Vote for War," *The Washington Post*, February 5, 2007.

113. Fish, "Politics Means Always Having to Say You're Sorry."

114. Ibid.

115. See Charles Paul Hoffman, commentary appended to Fish, "Politics Means Always Having to Say You're Sorry." In general, the comments posted by readers in response to Fish's analysis were quite insightful.

116. Adrienne Rich, "Women and Honor: Some Notes on Lying," 197.

117. Patrick Healey, "Politics Means Sometimes Having to Say You're Sorry," *The New York Times*, March 4, 2007.

118. Ibid., citing Graham Dodds: "It's a hallmark of Bush that he sticks to his guns no matter what." "If she were to apologize now, she would open herself up to the charge of flip-flopping"

119. "Holy Land Farewell to the Pope," *BBC News*, March 26, 2000.

120. Lazare, *On Apology*, 38.

121. Slansky and Sorkin, *My Bad*, 14–5. For more on Jason Schechterle, see www.officerjason.org.

122. Immanuel Kant, *The Metaphysical Elements of Justice*, trans. John Ladd (Indianapolis: Hackett, 1999), 101.

123. See *Letitia Baldrige's New Manners for a New Times: A Complete Guide to Etiquette* (New York: Scriber, 2003), 630. Baldrige advises delivering a written apology within twenty-four hours of the incident. See also Stephen Goldberg, Eric Green, and Frank Sander, "Saying You're Sorry," *Negotiation Journal* (July 1997), 223 (suggest a similar tactic in negation contexts).

124. Tavuchis, *Mea Culpa*, 22, and Orenstein, "Gender and Race in the Evidence Policy," 104n.

125. Govier and Verwoerd offer a rather successful example of this sort of process. "Taking Wrongs Seriously," 156–57.

126. Tavuchis claims that promises of reform are "inessential" because they are "implicit in the state of 'being sorry.'" Tavuchis, *Mea Culpa*, 36.

127. Slansky and Sorkin, *My Bad*, 86.

128. Amitai Etzioni, "Preface," in ed. Etzioni, *Civic Repentance* (Lanham, MD: Rowman & Littlefield, 1999), vii.

129. Robert Pearce, ed., *The Sayings of Leo Tolstoy* (London: Duckworth Publishing, 1995), 52.

130. For examples of this suggestion that apologies are commensurate with harms see Tavuchis, *Mea Culpa*, 19; Max Bolstad, "Learning from Japan: The Case for Increased Use of Apology in Mediation," *Cleveland State Law Review* 48 (2000): 578; Aviva Orenstein, "Apology Excepted," 243; and Deborah Levi,

"The Role of Apology in Mediation," *New York University Law Review* 72 (1997): 1165–1220, 1178.

131. Montaigne, "Of Repentance," 245.

132. See Minow, *Between Vengeance and Forgiveness*, 117: "Yet nothing in this discussion should imply that money payment, returned property, religious sites, or apologies seal the wounds, make victims whole, or clean the slate."

133. Benjamin Disraeli, "Prosecution of War, May 24, 1855," in *Selected Speeches of the Late Right Honourable the Earl of Beaconsfield*, ed. T. E. Kebbel, vol. II (London: Longman's Green, 1882), 55.

134. Tavuchis, *Mea Culpa*, 34. At one point, Tavuchis describes an apology as "a speech act that is predicated on the impossibility of restitution."

135. See Minow, *Between Vengeance and Forgiveness*, 93.

136. Ibid., 5: "Closure is not possible. . . . So this book inevitably becomes a fractured meditation on the incompleteness and inescapable inadequacy of each possible response to collective atrocities."

137. Ibid., x.

138. Pettigrove, "Apology, Reparations and the Question of Inherited Guilt," 327.

139. For a collection of such codes, see Gordon Bazemore, "Communities, Victims, and Offender Reintegration: Restorative Justice and Earned Redemption," in ed. Etzioni, *Civic Repentance*, 49–50.

140. Immanuel Kant, *Foundations of the Metaphysics of Morals*, trans. Lewis White Beck (Indianapolis: Bobbs-Merrill, 1959), 53.

141. *Kelly v. Robinson*, 479 U.S. 36, 49, n.10 (1986).

142. H. Wagatsuma and A. Rosett, "The Implications of Apology: Law and Culture in Japan and the United States," *Law and Society Review* 20 (1986): 461–98, 464.

143. Ibid., 478.

144. Minow, *Between Vengeance and Forgiveness*, 104 (describing this as "crossing over different lexicons of value").

145. Taft, "Apology Subverted," 1156.

146. Oscar Wilde, *The Picture of Dorian Gray* (New York: Penguin, 1983), 110.

147. Slansky and Sorkin, *My Bad*, 24.

148. "O'Reilly Apologizes, Says He's Now Skeptical of Bush," Reuters News Agency, February 10, 2004.

149. Slansky and Sorkin, *My Bad*, 112.

150. *The Oxford English Dictionary* provides the following definitions of sincere: "1. Not falsified or perverted in any way: a. Of doctrine, etc.: Genuine, pure; b. True, veracious; correct, exact; c. Morally uncorrupted, uncontaminated. 2. Pure, unmixed; free from any foreign element or ingredient: a. Of immaterial things; b. Of colours or substances; c. *spec.* Unadulterated; genuine; d. Free from hurt; uninjured. Devoid *of* something. *rare.* 3. Containing no element of dissimulation or deception; not feigned or pretended; real, true. 4. Characterized by the absence of all dissimulation or pretence; honest, straightforward: a. Of life, actions, etc; b. Of persons, their character, etc."

151. Lazare, *On Apology*, 157.

152. Ibid.

153. Ibid.

154. Ibid., 158.

155. Joyce, "Apologizing," 171.

156. See Lazare, *On Apology*, 134–58.

157. Slansky and Sorkin, *My Bad*, 41.

158. *The Big Book*, 4th ed. (Center City, MN: Hazelden, 2001), 59.

159. Ibid.

160. Jeffrie Murphy, "Repentance, Punishment, and Mercy," in eds. Amitai Etzioni and David Carney, *Repentance: A Comparative Perspective* (Lanham, MD: Rowman & Littlefield, 1997), 158.

161. Jay Rayner, *Eating Crow* (New York: Simon & Schuster, 2004), 58.

162. Ibid., 55, 58.

163. Ibid., 47, 46, 56, 70.

164. Montaigne, "Of Repentance," 245.

165. See Murphy, "Repentance, Punishment, and Mercy," 43n.

166. David Hume, *A Treatise of Human Nature*, 2nd ed., eds. L. A. Selby-Bigge and P. H. Niditch (Oxford: Clarendon Press), 415.

167. Friedrich Nietzsche, *The Genealogy of Morals*, in trans. Walter Kaufmann, *The Portable Nietzsche* (New York: Penguin, 1977).

168. Jean-Jacques Rousseau, *Emile: Or a Treatise on Education*, trans. William Payne (Amherst, NY: Prometheus Books, 2003); Arthur Schopenhauer, *On the Basis of Morality*, trans. E. F. J. Payne (Indianapolis: Hackett, 1998); and Adam Smith, *The Theory of Moral Sentiments* (New York: Cambridge University Press, 2002).

169. Gilbert Ryle, *The Concept of Mind* (Chicago: University of Chicago Press, 2000); Franz Brentano, "On the Origin of our Knowledge of Right and Wrong," in *What Is an Emotion?* eds. Cheshire Calhoun and Robert Solomon (New York: Oxford University Press, 2003); Max Scheler, *The Nature of Sympathy*, trans. Peter Heath (Hamden, CT: Archon, 1954); Martin Heidegger, *Being and Time*, trans. John Macquarrie and Edward Robinson (New York: Harper and Row, 1962); and Paul Ricoeur, *The Rule of Metaphor*, trans. R. Czerny (New York: Routledge, 2003).

170. Martha Nussbaum, *Upheavals of Thought: The Intelligence of Emotions* (New York: Cambridge University Press, 2001), 24.

171. Ibid., 23–24, 100–103.

172. For two excellent collections of essays, see Robert Solomon, ed., *Thinking About Feelings: Philosophers on Emotions* (New York: Oxford University Press, 2003); and Amélie Rorty, ed., *Explaining Emotions* (Los Angeles: University of California Press, 1980).

173. See Gabriele Taylor, "Justifying the Emotions," *Mind* 84 (1975): 390–402; and Nussbaum, *Upheavals of Thought*.

174. Bernard Williams, "Morality and the Emotions," in *Problems of the Self: Philosophical Papers 1956–1972* (Cambridge: Cambridge University Press, 1973), 207–29.

175. Martha Nussbaum, "Morality and Emotions," in ed. Edward Craig, *Routledge Encyclopedia of Philosophy* 6 (New York: Routledge, 1998), 559.

176. Philosophers disagree about whether certain emotions are "required." Gill claims that regret and remorse are necessary conditions of apologizing in "The Moral Functions of Apology" (14). Harvey describes certain emotions as "basic conditions of moral soundness" in "The Emerging Practice of Institutional Apologies" (63). Pettigrove asserts that while apologies lacking certain emotional states "may be morally deficient, we are not generally inclined to say they fail to be apologies" in "Apologies, Reparations, and the Question of Inherited Guilt" (323).

177. For treatments of empathy from diverse theoretical orientations, see Karsten Stueber, *Rediscovering Empathy Agency, Folk Psychology, and the Human Sciences* (Cambridge: MIT Press, 2006); N. Eisenberg, "Empathy-related Emotional Responses, Altruism, and their Socialization," in eds. R. J. Davidson and A. Harrington, *Visions of Compassion: Western Scientists and Tibetan Buddhists Examine Human Nature* (London: Oxford University Press, 2002), 131–64; J. Hkansson and H. Montgomery, "Empathy as an Interpersonal Phenomenon," *Journal of Social and Personal Relationships*, 20, no. 3 (2003), 267–84; Stephanie Preston and Frans B. M. de Waal, "Empathy: Its Ultimate and Proximate Bases," *Behavioral and Brain Sciences* 25 (2002): 1–72; M. L. Hoffman, *Empathy and Moral Development* (Cambridge: Cambridge University Press, 2000); and N. Eisenberg and J. Strayer eds., *Empathy and its Development* (Cambridge: Cambridge University Press, 1987).

178. Stephen Darwell, *Welfare and Rational Care* (Princeton: Princeton University Press, 2004), 3.

179. See Michael Stocker and Elizabeth Hegeman, *Valuing Emotions* (Cambridge: Cambridge University Press, 1996), 214–17, and Nussbaum, "Equity and Mercy," *Philosophy and Public Affairs* 22 (1993): 83–125.

180. Ana Areces, "I'm Sorry, I Won't Apologize," *The New York Times*, August 25, 1996.

181. John Rawls, *A Theory of Justice* (Cambridge, MA: Harvard University Press, 1971). See also R. J. Wallace, *Responsibility and the Moral Sentiments* (Cambridge, MA: Harvard University Press, 1998); J. P. Tangney and K. Fischer eds., *Self-Conscious Emotions: The Psychology of Shame, Guilt, Embarrassment, and Pride* (New York: Guilford Press, 1995); Bernard Williams, *Shame and Necessity* (Berkeley: University of California Press, 1994); G. Taylor, *Pride, Shame, and Guilt: Emotions of Self-Assessment* (Oxford: Oxford University Press, 1985); Herbert Morris ed., *Guilt and Shame* (Belmont: Wadsworth Press, 1971); Calhoun, Cheshire, "An Apology for Moral Shame," *The Journal of Political Philosophy* 12, no. 2 (2004): 127–46; J. Deigh, "Shame and Self-Esteem: A Critique," *Ethics* 93 (1983): 225–45.

182. Rawls, *A Theory of Justice*, 443.

183. Ibid., 445.

184. Ibid.

185. Ibid.

186. Ibid., 445; and Williams, *Shame and Necessity*, 90.

187. Williams, *Shame and Necessity*, 89.

188. Nussbaum, *Upheavals of Thought*, 216.

189. Ibid.

190. See E. R. Dodds, *The Greeks and the Irrational* (Berkeley: University of California Press, 2004); Gerhart Piers and Milton Singer, *Shame and Guilt: A Psychoanalytic and a Cultural Study* (New York: W. W. Norton Press, 1971); and A. C. Baier, "Moralism and Cruelty: Reflections on Hume and Kant," *Ethics* 103 (1993): 436–57.

191. Although little hangs on the distinction for my account, various philosophers dispute whether regret qualifies as an emotion. Contrast A. O. Rorty, "Agent Regret," *Explaining Emotions*, ed. Rorty (Berkeley: University of California Press, 1980), 501; Stuart Hampshire, *Thought and Action* (New York: Viking Press, 1960), 241; and Errol Bedford, "Emotions," *Proceedings of the Aristotelian Society* (1956): 281–304.

192. Kant, *The Metaphysical Elements of Justice*, 139.
193. See Ohbuchi, Kameda, and Agarie, "Apology as Aggression Control"; and Darby and Schlenker, "Children's Reactions to Apologies."Searle, "A Classification of Illocutionary Acts," 12.
194. Ohbuchi, Kameda, and Agarie, "Apology as Aggression Control," 219.
195. Ibid.
196. See ibid. See also Scher and Darley, "How Effective Are the Things People Say to Apologize"; Darby and Schlenker, "Children's Reactions to Apologies"; G. S. Schwartz, T. R. Kane, J. M. Joseph, and J. T. Tedeschi, "The Effects of Post-Transgression Remorse on Perceived Aggression, Attribution of Intent, and Level of Punishment," *Journal of Social and Clinical Psychology*, 17 (1987): 293–97; and J. T. Tedeschi and C. A. Riordan, "Impression Management and Prosocial Behavior Following Transgression," in ed. J. T. Tedeschi, *Impression Management Theory and Social Psychological Research* (New York: Academic Press, 1981), 223–44.
197. Nietzsche, *The Genealogy of Morals*.
198. See Jean-Paul Sartre, *The Emotions: Outline of a Theory* (New York: Philosophical Library, 1948). See also Robert Solomon, "Emotions and Choice," in *Explaining Emotions*.
199. See Ronald de Sousa, *The Rationality of Emotion* (Cambridge, MA: MIT Press, 1987).
200. See Nussbaum, "Morality and Emotions." For studies of the relationship between culture and emotion, see Jean Briggs, *Never in Anger: Portrait of an Eskimo Family* (Cambridge, MA: Harvard University Press, 2006); Richard Lazarus, *Emotion and Adaptation* (Oxford: Oxford University Press, 1994); and Catherine Lutz, *Unnatural Emotions: Everyday Sentiments on a Micronesian Atoll and Their Challenge to Western Theory* (Chicago: University of Chicago Press, 1988).
201. Catherine MacKinnon, *Feminism Unmodified: Discourse on Life and Law* (Cambridge, MA: Harvard University Press, 1988); and J. S. Mill, *The Basic Writings of John Stuart Mill: On Liberty, the Subjection of Women, and Utilitarianism* (New York: Random House, 2002).
202. Antonio Damasio, *The Feeling of What Happens: Body and Emotion in the Making of Consciousness* (New York: Harcourt Brace, 1999).
203. See Uta Frith, *Autism: Explaining the Enigma* (Oxford: Blackwell, 2002); Simon Baron-Cohen, *Mindblindness: An Essay on Autism and Theory of Mind* (Cambridge, MA: MIT Press, 1995); and J. Kennett, "Autism, Empathy and Moral Agency," *Philosophical Quarterly* 52, no. 208 (2002): 340–57. For discussions of psychopathy and emotions, see Robert D. Hare, *Without Conscience: The Disturbing World of the Psychopaths Among Us* (New York: Guilford Press, 1999), 40–46. The American Psychiatric Association lists "lack of remorse" as a diagnostic criterion for antisocial personality disorder. *Diagnostic and Statistical Manual of Mental Disorders* (Washington, D.C.: American Psychiatric Association, 1994), 292.
204. Lazare, *On Apology*, 157.

Chapter 3. Apologies and Gender

1. *She Wore a Yellow Ribbon*, directed by John Ford, 1949.
2. Jim Belushi, *Real Men Don't Apologize* (New York: Hyperion, 2006).

3. Carrie Petrucci, "Apology in the Criminal Justice Setting," *Behavioral Sciences and the Law* 20 (2002): 345, citing M. Timmers, A. H. Fischer, and A. S. R. Manstead, "Gender Differences in Motives for Regulating Emotions," *Personality and Social Psychology Bulletin* 24 (1998): 974–85; and J. M. Stoppard and C. D. Gruchy, "Gender, Context, and Expression of Positive Emotion," *Personality and Social Psychology Bulletin* 19 (1993): 143–50). See also Janet Holmes, "Sex Differences and Apologies: One Aspect of Communication Competence," *Applied Linguistics* 10, no. 2 (1989): 194; and M. H. Gonzales, J. A. Haugen, and D. J. Manning, "Victims as 'Narrative Critics:' Factors Influencing Rejoinders and Evaluative Responses to Offenders' Accounts," *Personality and Social Psychology Bulletin* 20 (1994): 691–704.

4. Lazare, *On Apology*, 16.

5. For examples of arguments citing Tannen for the claim that women apologize more than men, see Bolstad, "Learning from Japan," 562–63; Levi, "The Role of Apology in Mediation," 1185; Carol Lynn Mithers, "Don't Be Sorry," *Ladies Home Journal* (September 1994): 62; Orenstein, "Gender and Race in the Evidence Policy," 250; Pavlick, "Apology and Mediation: The Horse and Carriage of the Twenty-First Century," *Ohio State Journal on Dispute Resolution* 18 (2003), 851; and Rehm and Beatty, "Legal Consequences of Apologizing," 118.

6. Tannen, *The Argument Culture*, 45–46. Tannen claims elsewhere: "Rituals of apologizing, softening criticism, and thanking can be used by women or men. But they are more often found in the speech of women." See Tannen, *Talking from 9 to 5*, 56–57.

7. Tannen, "I'm Sorry, I Won't Apologize," *New York Times Magazine*, July 21, 1996, 35.

8. Tannen, *You Just Don't Understand*, 232. Tannen also states: "Many women are frequently told, 'Don't apologize' or 'You're always apologizing.' The reason 'apologizing' is seen as something they shouldn't do is that it seems synonymous with putting oneself down." Tannen, *Talking from 9 to 5*, 45.

9. Tannen, *You Just Don't Understand*, 232.

10. Tannen, *Talking from 9 to 5*, 45.

11. Ibid., 47.

12. Ibid. Here Tannen also cites Nessa Wolfson, "Pretty Is as Pretty Does: A Speech Act View of Sex Roles," *Applied Linguistics* 5, no. 3 (1984): 236–44.

13. Holmes, *Women, Men, and Politeness*, 155.

14. Ibid., 157.

15. Ibid., 187.

16. Ibid., 175.

17. Ibid., 185. Holmes also states on page 178: "There are twice as many examples of men apologizing to those who are strangers or acquaintances as to friends. Women however, apologize as often to their friends as to strangers. Again this supports the view that men regard apologies to friends as less crucial and as more dispensable than those to strangers. Men may reflect or signal friendship by *not* apologizing for what they regard as 'trivial' offenses."

18. Ibid.

19. Ibid.

20. Ibid. See also page 169.

21. Ibid., 162.

22. Ibid., 185.
23. Ibid., 182.
24. Ibid., 156.
25. Mills, *Gender and Politeness*, 221.
26. Holmes, *Women, Men, and Politeness*, 159.
27. Mills, *Gender and Politeness*, 222–23.
28. Fraser, "On Apologizing," 269.
29. Compare Judith Mattson Bean and Barbara Johnstone, "Workplace Reasons for Saying You're Sorry: Discourse Task Management and Apology in Telephone Interviews," *Discourse Processes* 17 (1994); and Miriam Meyerhoff, "Sorry in the Pacific: Defining Communities, Defining Practices," *Language in Society* 28 (1999): 225–38.
30. Holmes, *Women, Men, and Politeness*, 160.
31. Ibid., 162–63.
32. Mills, *Gender and Politeness*, 229, 231.
33. Mills accuses Holmes of such sexist speculation: "Holmes' analysis, whilst based on the analysis of speaker intentions, finds that analysis of differential judgment of the impact of apologies on hearers is necessary. However, she does not have the means to call on the judgments of the interactants apart from her own intuitions and stereotypes which she assumes the readers are drawing on." Ibid., 223. Holmes also makes the following claim: "Men seem to avoid apologies where possible, using them only in cases where they judge they are likely to cause greater offense by the omission of an apology." Holmes, *Women, Men, and Politeness*, 185–86.
34. Holmes, *Women, Men, and Politeness*, 175.
35. Lazare, *On Apology*, 29.
36. Taft explains: "In the call to apologize ... the offender sets out on a course that is difficult, pain-filled, and potentially humiliating, yet also one of great courage and strength." Taft, "Apology Subverted," 1142.
37. Tannen, *Talking from 9 to 5*, 46.
38. Tannen, *You Just Don't Understand*, 234.
39. Tannen, *Talking from 9 to 5*, 46.
40. For Mills' emphasis on the difficulty of quantifying individual incidence rates of such collaborative acts, see *Gender and Politeness*, 231, 234, and 235.
41. See Orenstein, "Gender and Race in the Evidence Policy," 251; and Rehm and Beatty, "The Legal Consequences of Apologizing," 118.
42. Michael Woods, *Healing Words: The Power of Apology in Medicine* (Santa Fe: Doctors in Touch, 2007), 38.
43. See Gonzales, Haugen, and Manning, "Victims as 'Narrative Critics.'"
44. See Bean and Johnstone, "Workplace Reasons for Saying You're Sorry," 79; Fraser, "On Apologizing," 261; Levi, "The Role of Apology in Mediation," 1186; Mills, *Gender and Politeness*, 234–35; Orenstein, "Gender and Race in the Evidence Policy," 161n.; Erin O'Hara and Douglas Yarn, "On Apology and Consilience," *Washington Law Review* 77 (2002): 1145; and Jeffrey Z. Rubin and Bert R. Brown, *The Social Psychology of Bargaining and Negotiation* (New York: Academic Press, 1975), 173–74.
45. Sandra Bartky, "The Pedagogy of Shame," in *Feminisms and Pedagogies of Everyday Life*, ed. Carmen Luke (New York: Routledge, 1996), 85.
46. Ibid.

47. Ibid., 84.
48. Ibid., 86.
49. Bartky, *Sympathy and Solidarity* (Lanham, MD: Rowman & Littlefield, 2002), 146.

Chapter 4. Apologies in Diverse Religious and Cultural Traditions

1. Murphy, "Repentance, Punishment, and Mercy," 147.
2. Montaigne, "Of Repentance."
3. Etzioni, "Preface," in *Civic Repentance*, ed. Etzioni, vii.
4. See Joseph Epes Brown, *Teaching Spirits: Understanding Native American Religious Traditions* (New York: Oxford University Press, 2001), 83–105.
5. See Jacob Neusner, "Repentance in Judaism," *Repentance*, eds. Etzioni and Carney eds., 61. For more on *teshuvah*, see Chaim Nussbaum, *The Essence of Teshuvah: A Path to Repentance* (Northvale, NJ: Jason Aronson, 1993); W. Eichrodt, *Theology of the Old Testament*, 2 (Stuttgart: Westminster John Knox Press, 1967), 380–495; and A. Buechler, *Studies in Sin and Atonement* (Oxford: Oxford University Press, 1928).
6. See Estelle Frankel, "Repentance, Psychotherapy, and Healing: Through a Jewish Lens," in *Civic Repentance*, ed. Etzioni, 139. The book of Numbers outlines the relevance of the intentions of the repentant wrongdoer: "You shall have one law for him who does anything unwittingly, for him who is naïve among the people of Israel, and for the stranger who sojourns among them. But the person who does anything with a high hand, whether he is native or a sojourner, reviles the Lord, and that person shall be cut off from among his people. Because he has despised the word of the Lord, and has broken his commandment, that person shall be utterly cut off; his [the Lord's] iniquity shall be upon him." Numbers 15:29–31.
7. Frankel, "Repentance, Psychotherapy, and Healing," 125.
8. See Neusner, "Repentance in Judaism," 63. For a discussion of how to conceptualize a sin as against god or a human, see Emmanuel Levinas, "Toward the Other," in *Nine Talmudic Readings*, trans. Annette Aronowicz (Bloomington: Indiana University Press, 1990), 16.
9. Jacob Milgrom, Louis Jacobs, Samuel Rosenblatt, and Alan Unterman, "Repentance," *Encyclopaedia Judaica* 17, eds. Michael Berenbaum and Fred Skolnik (Detroit: Macmillan Reference USA, 2007), 222.
10. Maimonides, *Hilchot Teshuvah*, 6–9.
11. Ibid., 26.
12. Milgrom, Jacobs, Rosenblatt, and Unterman, "Repentance," 222.
13. Maimonides continues with an example: "For example, a person engaged in explicit sexual relations with a woman. Afterwards, they meet in privacy, in the same country, while his love for her and physical power still persisted, and nevertheless, he abstained and did not transgress." *Hilchot Teshuvah*, 26.
14. But note: "If he does not repent until old age, at a time when he is incapable of doing what he did before, even though this is not a high level of repentance, he is Baal-Teshuvah." Ibid., 22.
15. See Murphy, "Repentance, Punishment, and Mercy," 167.
16. See Neusner, "Repentance in Judaism," 62–63, citing the Mishnah-tractate Yoma 8:9.

17. Maimonides, *Hilchot Teshuvah*, 218–19.
18. Maimonides explains: "When one teaches children, women, and most of the common people, one should teach them to serve out of fear and in order to receive a reward. As their knowledge grows and their wisdom increases, this secret should be revealed to them [slowly,] bit by bit." Ibid.
19. Maimonides states: "Whenever they are embarrassed for the deeds they committed and shamed because of them, their merit increases and their level is raised." Ibid., 172. See also Frankel, "Repentance, Psychotherapy, and Healing," 142.
20. Maimonides, *Hilchot Teshuvah*, 156.
21. Ibid., 12, 22; and Milgrom, Jacobs, Rosenblatt, and Unterman, "Repentance," 222.
22. Maimonides, *Hilchot Teshuvah*, 114.
23. Ibid., 126.
24. Ibid., 160.
25. Frankel, "Repentance, Psychotherapy, and Healing," 136.
26. Ibid., 172.
27. Ibid., 46.
28. Ibid.
29. Neusner, "Repentance in Judaism," 72.
30. Ibid., 69.
31. Ibid., 72.
32. Abraham Kook, *Rabbi Kook's Philosophy of Repentance* (New York: Yeshiva University Press, 1978).
33. The term comes from historian Marshall Hodgson who defined Islamicate as something that "would refer not directly to the religion, Islam, itself, but to the social and cultural complex historically associated with Islam and the Muslims, both among Muslims themselves and even when found among non-Muslims." *Venture of Islam* vol. 1 (Chicago: University of Chicago Press, 1977), 59. See M. S. Stern, "Al-Ghazzali, Maimonides, and Ibn Paquda on Repentance: A Comparative Perspective," *Journal of the American Academy of Religion* 47, no. 4 (1979): 589–607.
34. Mahmoud Ayoub, "Repentance in the Islamic Tradition," in *Repentance*, eds. Etzioni and Carney, 108.
35. See Frederick M. Denny, The Qur'anic Vocabulary of Repentance: Orientations and Attitudes," *Journal of the American Academy of Religion Thematic Issue* S X-4 (1980): 649–64; and Ayoub, "Repentance in the Islamic Tradition," 96. Arthur Jeffery traces the term to Aramaic or possibly Akkadian roots. *The Foreign Vocabulary of the Qur'an* (Lahore: al-Biruni, 1977), 87, 95.
36. See, for example, Denny, "The Qur'anic Vocabulary of Repentance," 650, 653, 657; Frederick Denny, "Tawba," in *The Encyclopedia of Islam* 10, ed. B. Lewis (Boston: Brill, 1997), 385; and Ayoub, "Repentance in the Islamic Tradition," 98. On blood money, see Uri Rubin, "Repentance and Penance," in *Encyclopaedia of the Quran*, ed. Jane Dammen McAuliffe (Boston: Brill, 2005).
37. Abdul Hamid Siddiqi, trans., *Sahih Muslim* (Delhi: Adam Publishers, 1996), 238. But note that according to Ayoub, Islamic jurists disagree regarding cases where the usurper dies before repaying her debt. Ayoub, "Repentance in the Islamic Tradition," 106. See also *Sahih Muslim*, 264.
38. *Sahih Muslim*, 257.
39. Ibid., 259.

40. Denny, "The Qur'anic Vocabulary of Repentance," 658.
41. For a discussion of distinctions between sins against god and those against humans, see Ayoub, "Repentance in the Islamic Tradition," 102.
42. See *Sahih Muslim* , 264–65; Denny, "The Qur'anic Vocabulary of Repentance," 655, 657, and Ayoub, "Repentance in the Islamic Tradition," 99.
43. Denny, "The Qur'anic Vocabulary of Repentance," 657. See also Ayoub, "Repentance in the Islamic Tradition," 102: "Sincere intention therefore to turn toward God with true repentance and the resolve not to repeat the same offense are necessary conditions for true repentance. But since inner thoughts and repentance are known to God alone, sincere repentance must be demonstrated through outward behavior."
44. See Nasr Hamid Abu Zayd, "Intention," in *Encyclopedia of the Quran.*
45. Ayoub, "Repentance in the Islamic Tradition," 100 (emphasis added).
46. Ibid., 111.
47. See Ayoub, "Repentance in the Islamic Tradition," 102.
48. See ibid., 99; Denny, "The Qur'anic Vocabulary of Repentance," 652, 657; and Rubin, "Repentance and Penance."
49. Ibid., 107; and Denny, "Tawba," 385.
50. Gerhard Kittel ed., *Theological Dictionary of the New Testament* VI (Grand Rapids: Eerdmans, 1981), 975–1008.
51. I thank Charlotte Witt for this explanation. We also have reason to believe that the transformation of *metanoia* may parallel the development of *pnuema*, which was for the Greeks a material substance associated with life but came to be translated as "holy spirit" in the Gospels. In both cases we see a tension between material and immaterial views, as would be expected given the historical debates in early Christian thought recorded by Augustine and others. This also underscores how such meanings develop within traditions of commentary rather than simply inhering within the definition of a word.
52. Kittel, *Theological Dictionary of the New Testament*, 976.
53. Mark 1:15. See also Mark 6:12; Luke 13:3, 15:11, 24:47; Matthew 21–29, 3:8–10; Acts 2:38, 20:21, 17:30.
54. Matthew 3:2.
55. Revelation 9:20–21; 16:9–11.
56. Kittel, *Theological Dictionary of the New Testament*, 1000.
57. Ibid., 1003.
58. Ibid., 1002.
59. David Noel Freedman, *Eerdmans Dictionary of the Bible* (Cambridge: Eerdmans, 2000), 118–19.
60. Kittel, *Theological Dictionary of the New Testament*, 979.
61. Ibid., 980.
62. Harvey Cox, "Repentance and Forgiveness: A Christian Perspective," in *Repentance*, eds. Etzioni and Carney, 24.
63. See Anselm of Canterbury, *Saint Anselm: Basic Writings*, trans. S. N. Deane (LaSalle, IL: Open Court, 1962), 224–25, 245–46, 284. See also John Lyden, "From Sacrifice to Sacrament: Repentance in a Christian Context," in *Repentance*, eds. Etzioni and Carney, 45.
64. See Lyden, "From Sacrifice to Sacrament," 47.
65. Etzioni, "Introduction," in *Repentance*, eds. Etzioni and Carney, 15.
66. David Carney, "Repentance in Political Life: Case Studies of American Political Figures," in ed. Etzioni, *Civic Repentance*, 167.

67. Guy Beck, "Fire in the Atman: Repentance in Hinduism," *Repentance*, eds. Etzioni and Carney, 77.
68. Luke 23:43.
69. Cited in Edward J Hanna, "Penance," in *The Catholic Encyclopedia* (New York: Robert Appleton Company, 1913), 631. See also Harold Brown, "Godly Sorrow, Sorrow of the World: Some Christian Thoughts on Repentance," in *Repentance*, eds. Etzioni and Carney, 36–37. Leibniz stated: "This whole work of sacramental penance is indeed worthy of the Divine wisdom and if aught else in the Christian dispensation is meritorious of praise, surely this wondrous institution. For the necessity of confessing one's sins deters a man from committing them, and hope is given to him who may have fallen again after expiation. The pious and prudent confessor is in very deed a great instrument in the hands of God for man's regeneration. For the kindly advice of God's priest helps man to control his passions, to know the lurking places of sin, to avoid the occasions of evil doing, to restore ill-gotten goods, to have hope after depression and doubt, to have peace after affliction, in a word, to remove or at least lessen all evil, and if there is no pleasure on earth like unto a faithful friend, what must be the esteem a man must have for him, who is in very deed a friend in the hour of his direst need?" Leibniz, *Systema Theologicum* (Paris, 1819), 270, cited in Hanna, "Penance," 634.
70. Henry Charles Lea devoted three volumes to the subject in *A History of Auricular Confession and Indulgences in the Latin Church* (Philadelphia: Lea Brothers, 1896).
71. John P. Beal, James A. Coriden, and Thomas Green, eds., *New Commentary on the Code of Cannon Law* (Mahwah, NJ: Paulist Press, 2002), 199.
72. See Matthew 5:23 and James 5:16.
73. Augustine explained: "If his sin is not only grievous in itself, but involves scandal given to others, and if the bishop [*antistes*] judges that it will be useful to the Church [to have the sin published], let not the sinner refuse to do penance in the sight of many or even of the people at large, let him not resist, nor through shame add to his mortal wound a greater evil." Augustine, *Sermon CLI* (cited in Hanna, "Penance," 630). For an alternative translation, see Augustine, *Sermons 148–183*, trans. Edmund Hill (New York: New City Press, 1990).
74. Hanna, "Penance," 619.
75. Lyden, "From Sacrifices to Sacrament," 43.
76. Beck, "Fire in the Atman," 77.
77. Ibid., 78. See also Jeanine Miller, *The Vision of Cosmic Order in the Vedas* (London: Routledge, 1985), 42.
78. Beck, "Fire in the Atman," 83.
79. Ibid., 81.
80. Ibid., 82.
81. Ibid., 84.
82. Ibid., 85.
83. Ibid., 91–92.
84. Malcolm David Eckel, "A Buddhist Approach to Repentance," in eds. Etzioni and Carney, *Repentance*, 122. See also Margaret Childs, *Rethinking Sorrow: Revelatory Tales of Late Medieval Japan* (Ann Arbor: University of Michigan Press, 1991).
85. Eckel, "A Buddhist Approach to Repentance," 133.
86. Ibid., 132.

87. Ibid., 137.
88. See Pavlick, "Apology and Mediation," 848–49.
89. See for example Naomi Sugimoto, *Japanese Apology Across Disciplines* (Commack, NY: Nova Science, 1999); N. Tanaka, H. Spencer-Oatey, and E. Cray, "'Its Not my Fault': Japanese and English Responses to Unfounded Accusations," in *Culturally Speaking: Managing Rapport through Talk Across Cultures*, ed. Helen Spencer-Oatery (London: Continuum, 2000); J. O. Haley, "Apology and Pardon: Learning from Japan," in *Repentance*, eds. Etzioni and Carney; *American Behavioral Scientist* 41 (1998): 842–67; Wagatsuma and Rosett, "The Implications of Apology"; and Wu Pei-yi, "Self-Examination and Confession of Sins in Traditional China," *Harvard Journal of Asiatic Studies* 39, no. 1 (1978): 5–38.
90. PBS NewsHour, "The Ambassador's Report," April 11, 2001, http://www.pbs.org/newshour/bb/asia/china/plane/letter_4-11.html.
91. See Haley, "Apology and Pardon," 98, 105, 110.
92. Ibid., 105. See also Goldberg, Green, and Sander, "Saying You're Sorry," 222 and Haley, "Apology and Pardon," 99.
93. V. L. Hamilton and J. Sanders, *Everyday Justice* (New Haven: Yale University Press, 1992), 40, cited by Haley, "Apology and Pardon," 117.
94. Florian Coulmas, "'Poison to Your Soul': Thanks and Apologies Contrastively Viewed," in *Conversational Routine*, ed. Coulmas, 79.
95. Ibid., 89.
96. Ibid., 89.
97. Ibid., 88.
98. Ibid., 83.
99. Ibid., 84.

Chapter 5. Unusual Cases: Apologizing to Animals, Infants, Machines, the Deceased, and Yourself

1. See Brown, *Teaching Spirits*, 83–105.
2. For discussions of the emotional abilities of machines, see John Haugeland, *Having Thought: Essays in the Metaphysics of Mind* (Cambridge: Harvard University Press, 2000); Rosalind Picard, *Affective Computing* (Cambridge: M.I.T. Press, 2000) and Marvin Minsky, *The Emotion Machine* (New York: Simon & Schuster, 2007).

Chapter 6. The Relationship Between Apologies and Forgiveness

1. See Seneca, "De Ira," in *Seneca: Moral and Political Essays*, eds. John M. Cooper and J. F. Procopé (New York: Cambridge, 1995); Joseph Butler, *Fifteen Sermons Preached at the Rolls Chapel*, ed. Robert Carmichael (London: Longman, 1856); G. W. F. Hegel, *Phenomenology of Spirit*, trans. A. V. Miller (Oxford: Oxford University Press, 1977), §670; Nietzsche, *Beyond Good and Evil* (see discussions of ressentiment); Hannah Arendt, *The Human Condition* (Chicago: University of Chicago Press, 1968); Jacques Derrida, *Cosmopolitanism and Forgiveness*, trans. M. Dooley and R. Kearney (London: Routledge, 2001); and Derrida, "On Forgiving" in *Questioning God*, eds. John Caputo, Mark Dooley, and Michael J. Scanlon (Bloomington: Indiana University Press, 2001).
2. For a few examples, see Charles Griswold, *Forgiveness: A Philosophical Exploration* (New York: Cambridge University Press, 2007); Margaret Urban Walker,

Moral Repair: Reconstructing Moral Relations After Wrongdoing (New York: Cambridge University Press, 2006); Trudy Govier, *Forgiveness and Revenge* (New York: Routledge, 2002); Jeffrie Murphy and Jean Hampton, *Forgiveness and Mercy* (Cambridge: Cambridge University Press, 1988); Peter Digeser, *Political Forgiveness* (Ithaca: Cornell University Press, 2001); Minow, *Between Vengeance and Forgiveness*; Joram Haber, *Forgiveness: A Philosophical Study* (Lanham, MD: Rowman & Littlefield, 1991); Sharon Lamb and Jeffrie Murphy eds., *Before Forgiving: Cautionary Tales of Forgiveness in Psychotherapy* (Oxford: Oxford University Press, 2004); Kelly Oliver, "Forgiveness and Community," *Southern Journal of Philosophy* 42 (2004): Mary Beth Mader, "Fore-given Forgiveness," *Southern Journal of Philosophy* 42 (2004): 16–24; Pettigrove, "The Forgiveness We Speak"; Patrick Boleyn-Fitzgerald, "What Should 'Forgiveness' Mean?" *Journal of Value Inquiry* 36 (2002): 486–98; Eve Garrard and David McNaughton, "In Defense of Unconditional Forgiveness," *Proceedings of the Aristotelian Society* (2002): 39–60; Robin Dillon, "Self-Forgiveness and Self-Respect," *Ethics* 112 (2001): 53–83; David Novitz, "Forgiveness and Self-Respect," *Philosophy and Phenomenological Research* 58, no. 2 (1998): 299–315; Uma Narayan, "Forgiveness, Moral Reassessment and Reconciliation," in *Explorations of Value*, ed. Thomas Magnell (Amsterdam: Rodopi, 1997); Robert C. Roberts, "Forgivingness," *American Philosophical Quarterly* 32, no. 4 (1995): 293–306; J. M. Bernstein, "Conscience and Transgression: The Persistence of Misrecognition," *The Bulletin of the Hegel Society of Great Britain* 29 (1994); Jean Harvey, "Forgiveness as an Obligation of the Moral Life," *International Journal of Moral and Social Science* 8, no. 3 (1993): 211–21; Margaret Holmgren, "Forgiveness and the Intrinsic Value of Persons," *American Philosophical Quarterly* 30, no. 4 (1993): 341–451; Martha Nussbaum, "Equity and Mercy," *Philosophy and Public Affairs* 22, no. 2 (1993): 83–125; Cheshire Calhoun, "Changing One's Heart," *Ethics* 103 (1992): 76–96; Norvin Richards, "Forgiveness," *Ethics* 99 (1988): 77–97; Wilson, "Why Forgiveness Requires Repentance"; Joanna North, "Wrongdoing and Forgiveness," *Philosophy* 62, no. 242 (1987): 499–508; Martin Golding, "Forgiveness and Regret," *Philosophical Forum* 16 (1984–5): 121–37; Martin Hughes, "Forgiveness," *Analysis* 35, no. 4 (March 1975): 113–17; Aurel Kolnai, "Forgiveness," *Proceedings of the Aristotelian Society* 74 (1973–74): 91–106; and Claudia Card, "Mercy," *Philosophical Review* 81 (1972): 182–207.

3. Richards, "Forgiveness," 79.
4. Wilson, "Why Forgiveness Requires Repentance," 534–35.
5. See, for example, Derrida, *Cosmopolitanism and Forgiveness*, 42, 49, 50, 51, and 65.
6. See Oliver, "Forgiveness and Community"; and Mader, "Fore-given Forgiveness."
7. Pettigrove, "The Forgiveness We Speak," 373.
8. Ibid., 387. Pettigrove takes this position despite suggestions that it "might be the case that we have more than one type of activity in which we engage on different occasions when uttering 'I forgive you' and that these reflect or create competing ideals of forgiveness. Occam's razor need not carve out for us a unitary illocutionary act performed in all utterances of 'I forgive you.'" Ibid., 386.
9. See Bernstein, "Conscience and Transgression."
10. Arendt, *The Human Condition*, 237.
11. Ibid.

12. See Murphy and Hampton, *Forgiveness and Mercy*; Calhoun, "Changing One's Heart"; Harvey, "Forgiveness as an Obligation of the Moral Life"; and Narayan, "Forgiveness, Moral Reassessment and Reconciliation."

13. See Fred Luskin, *Forgive for Good: A Proven Prescription for Health and Happiness* (New York: Harper Collins, 2001); and Redford Williams, *Anger Kills: Seventeen Strategies for Controlling the Hostility that Can Harm Your Health* (New York: Harper Collins, 1998).

14. See Murphy, *Forgiveness and Mercy*.

15. Homer, *The Iliad*, 355. Fagles' translation draws further attention to Achilles' conflict: "Despite my anguish I will beat it down, the fury mounting inside me, down by force. Now, by god, I call a halt to my anger." *The Iliad*, trans. Fagles, 490.

16. The Dalai Lama, *Healing Anger: The Power of Patience from a Buddhist Perspective* (Ithaca: Snow Lion, 1997).

17. See *Quran* 42:37 ("Those who avoid the greater sins and indecencies and, when they are angry, even then forgive"), 42:40 ("if a person forgives and makes reconciliation, his reward is due from Allah"), and 42:43 ("But indeed if any show patience and forgive, that would truly be an affair of great Resolution").

18. See Pope John Paul II, *Forgiveness: Thoughts for a New Millennium* (Kansas City: Andrews McMeel, 1999); M. M. Adams, "Forgiveness: A Christian Model," *Faith and Philosophy* 8, no. 3 (1991): 277–304. For Biblical discussions of forgiveness, see Ephesians 4:32; Matthew 18:34–35; Mark 11:25; and Luke 23:34.

19. Arendt, *The Human Condition*, 238.

20. Matthew 18:21–22.

21. See L. E. Newman, "The Quality of Mercy: On the Duty to Forgive in the Judaic Tradition," *Journal of Religious Ethics* 15 (1987): 155–72; and Neusner, "Repentance in Judaism."

22. See Kant, *The Metaphysics of Morals* (New York: Cambridge University Press, 1996), 140–45, 168–69; K. D. Moore, *Pardons: Justice, Mercy, and the Public Interest* (Oxford: Oxford University Press, 1989); and P. Twambley, "Mercy and Forgiveness," *Analysis* 36 (1976): 84–90.

23. See Minow, *Between Vengeance and Forgiveness*, 16.

24. Pettigrove, "The Forgiveness We Speak," 383. Desmond Tutu, *No Future without Forgiveness* (New York: Random House, 1999), 272.

25. Pettigrove's distinctions between commissive and behabitive accounts of forgiveness is helpful here. Commissive forgiveness allows the victim to continue to feel no reduction in anger toward the offender as she refrains from acting on that anger, while behabitive forgiveness attests to a reduction in hostile attitudes toward the offender. "The Forgiveness We Speak," 383.

26. Consider Arendt's strong opinion here: "It is . . . a structural element in the realm of human affairs, that men are unable to forgive what they cannot punish and that they are unable to punish what has turned out to be unforgivable. This is the true hallmark of those offenses which, since Kant, we call 'radical evil' and about whose nature so little is known, even to us who have been exposed to one of their rare outbursts on the public scene. All we know is that we can neither punish nor forgive such offenses and that they therefore transcend the realm of human affairs and the potentialities of human power, both of which they radically destroy whenever they make their appearance. Here, where the deed itself dispossesses us of all power, we can indeed only repeat with Jesus: 'It

were better for him that a millstone were hanged about his neck, and he cast into the sea.'" *The Human Condition*, 241.

27. See Peter Haas, "Forgiveness, Reconciliation and Jewish Memory after Auschwitz," in *After-Words: Post-Holocaust Struggles with Forgiveness, Reconciliation, Justice* (Seattle: University of Washington Press, 2004).

28. Minow, *Between Vengeance and Forgiveness*, 116.

29. Levinas, "Toward the Other," 19.

30. Kolnai, "Forgiveness"; Murphy and Hampton, *Forgiveness and Mercy*, 17–18; and Novitz, "Forgiveness and Self-Respect," 299. See also Murphy, *Forgiveness and Mercy*. Pettigrove argues that it is possible and permissible to forgive the unapologetic. See "Unapologetic Forgiveness."

31. Contrast H. Rashdall, *A Theory of Good and Evil* (London: Oxford University Press, 1924) and Murphy and Hampton, *Forgiveness and Mercy*; and D. Heyd, "Beyond the Call of Duty in Kant's Ethics," *Kant-Studien* 71(1980): 308–24.

32. See Butler, *Fifteen Sermons*, and Martin Luther King, Jr., "Loving Your Enemies," in *Strength to Love* (Philadelphia: Fortress Press, 1981), 49–50.

33. Arendt, *Human Condition*, 241.

34. See Luskin, *Forgive for Good*; Williams, *Anger Kills*; Robert Enright, *Forgiveness Is a Choice: A Step-by-Step Process for Resolving Anger and Restoring Hope* (Washington, DC: American Psychological Association, 2001); Sharon Lamb, "Reasons to Be Cautious about the Use of Forgiveness in Psychotherapy," in *Before Forgiving*; and Roy F. Baumeister, Julie Juola Exline, and Kristin L. Sommer, "The Victim Role, Grudge Theory, and Two Dimensions of Forgiveness," in *Dimensions of Forgiveness: Psychological Research and Theological Perspectives*, ed. Everett L. Worthington, Jr. (Philadelphia: Templeton Foundation Press, 1998), 79–104.

35. Jeffrie Murphy thinks not. "Forgiveness and Mercy," *Routledge Encyclopedia of Philosophy* vol. 3, 698.

36. Arendt, *The Human Condition*, 237, 243. Julia Kristeva, *Black Sun: Depression and Melancholy*, trans. Leon Roudiez (New York: Columbia University Press, 1987), 216.

37. Emmanuel Levinas, *Difficult Freedom: Essays on Judaism*, trans. Sean Hand (Baltimore: Johns Hopkins University Press, 1997), 20.

Chapter 7. Varieties of Apologies

1. Iris Murdoch, "The Sublime and the Good," in *Existentialists and Mystics: Writings on Philosophy and Literature*, ed. Peter Conradi (New York: Penguin, 1997, 206). Pettigrove applies the terms to examples of forgiveness. "The Forgiveness We Speak," 373.

2. See "Apology Australia," http://apology.west.net.au/.

3. Homer, *The Iliad*, trans. Fagles, 255.

4. For an excellent bibliography and overview of philosophical conceptions of coercion, see Scott Anderson's entry for the online *Stanford Encyclopedia of Philosophy* at http://plato.stanford.edu/entries/coercion/.

5. On coercive offers, see Anderson's discussion and bibliography. Ibid.

6. Elisabeth Rosenthal, "For a Fee, This Chinese Firm will Beg Pardon for Anyone," *The New York Times*, January 3, 2001. See also Damien McElroy, "Chinese Entrepreneur Opens Business to Say Sorry," *Telegraph UK*, June 19, 2001.

Chapter 8. The Collective Categorical Apology

1. For a collection of political apologies, see the materials gathered by Rhoda E. Howard-Hassmann at http://political-apologies.wlu.ca/about.php.

Chapter 9. The Problem of Consensus

1. "Clinton's Painful Words of Sorrow and Chagrin," *The New York Times*, March 26, 1998.

Chapter 10. Issues Specific to Collective Apologies

1. Tavuchis, *Mea Culpa*, 117.
2. Ibid.
3. R. W. Apple, Jr., "Clinton's Contrition," *The New York Times*, April 1, 1998.
4. See, for example, William Glaberson, "Swiss Banks Publish Names from Holocaust," *The New York Times*, January 13, 2005.
5. See Suzy Hansen, "The Price of Pain," *Salon.com*, July 15, 2005, at http://archive.salon.com/ books/int/2002/07/15/wolffe/.
6. See John Authers and Richard Wolffe, *The Victim's Fortune: Inside the Epic Battle over the Debts of the Holocaust* (New York: Harper Collins, 2002), 33–36.
7. Ibid., 32–36, 99–102.
8. For an insightful discussion of de Klerk's statements, see Govier and Verwoerd, "The Promise and Pitfalls of Apology," 77–79.
9. The Chief Cabinet Secretary provided the following statement in 1993: "As a result of the study which indicates that comfort stations were operated in extensive areas for long periods, it is apparent that there existed a great number of comfort women. Comfort stations were operated in response to the request of the military authorities of the day. The then Japanese military was, directly or indirectly, involved in the establishment and management of the comfort stations and the transfer of comfort women. The recruitment of the comfort women was conducted mainly by private recruiters who acted in response to the request of the military. The Government study has revealed that in many cases they were recruited against their own will, through coaxing coercion, etc., and that, at times, administrative/military personnel directly took part in the recruitments. They lived in misery at comfort stations under a coercive atmosphere. As to the origin of those comfort women who were transferred to the war areas, excluding those from Japan, those from the Korean Peninsula accounted for a large part. The Korean Peninsula was under Japanese rule in those days, and their recruitment, transfer, control, etc., were conducted generally against their will, through coaxing, coercion, etc. Undeniably, this was an act, with the involvement of the military authorities of the day, that severely injured the honor and dignity of many women. The Government of Japan would like to take this opportunity once again to extend its sincere apologies and remorse to all those, irrespective of place of origin, who suffered immeasurable pain and incurable physical and psychological wounds as comfort women. It is incumbent upon us, the Government of Japan, to continue to consider seriously, while listening to the views of learned circles, how best we can express this sentiment. We shall face squarely the historical facts as described above instead of evading them, and take them to heart as lessons of history. We hereby reiterated our firm determination never

to repeat the same mistake by forever engraving such issues in our memories through the study and teaching of history. As actions have been brought to court in Japan and interests have been shown in this issue outside Japan, the Government of Japan shall continue to pay full attention to this matter, including private research related thereto." "Japan's Official Responses to Reparations," in *When Sorry Isn't Enough: The Controversy over Apologies and Reparations for Human Injustice*, ed. Roy Brooks (New York: New York University Press, 1999), 127–28. On Abe's subsequent denials, see "Sex Slave Denial Angers S. Korea," *BBC News*, March 3, 2007.

10. Atler, "High Stakes in New Orleans," 15.
11. California Senate Bill 670, introduced by Senator Joe Dunn and filed with the Secretary of State on October 7, 2005. See also Senator Joe Dunn, interview by Melissa Block, *National Public Radio*. "Remembering California's 'Repatriation Program,'" *All Things Considered*, January 2, 2006.
12. For a comparison of coverage of the Mexican Repatriation and Japanese-American Internment in textbooks, see Kasie Hunt, "Some Stories Hard to Get into History Books," *USA Today*, April 5, 2006.
13. See "U.S. Urged to Apologize for 1930s Deportations," *USA Today*, April 5, 2006.
14. See "Remembering California's 'Repatriation Program.'"
15. See "U.S. Urged to Apologize for 1930s Deportations."
16. See "Remembering California's 'Repatriation Program.'"
17. Ibid.
18. See ibid., where Melissa Block describes the legislation as an "official apology."
19. Bumiller and Schmitt, "President Sorry for Iraq Abuse; Backs Rumsfeld." Also see similar statements cited in 96n.
20. See George Hicks, "The Comfort Women Redress Movement," in *When Sorry Isn't Enough*, ed. Roy Brooks, 113–26.
21. Joyce, "Apologizing," 160.
22. Govier and Verwoerd, "The Promise and Pitfalls of Apology," 76.
23. Harvey, "The Emerging Practice of Institutional Apologies," 58.
24. For an overview of collective responsibility and a thorough bibliography, see Marion Smiley's entry for the *Stanford Encyclopedia of Philosophy* at http://plato.stanford.edu/ entries/collective-responsibility/. I draw upon it extensively. For an influential collection of essays, see Larry May and Stacy Hoffman, eds., *Collective Responsibility: Five Decades of Debates in Theoretical and Applied Ethics* (Lanham, MD: Rowman & Littlefield, 1991).
25. Manuel Velasquez, "Why Corporations are Not Responsible for Anything They Do," in *Collective Responsibility*, eds. May and Hoffman, 111–32.
26. David Cooper, "Collective Responsibility," *Philosophy*, 43 (1968): 258.
27. Joel Feinberg, "Collective Responsibility," in *Collective Responsibility*, eds. May and Hoffman, 54.
28. Ibid.
29. Ibid., 56.
30. Ibid.
31. Ibid., 57.
32. Ibid., 60–61 (italics in original).
33. Ibid., 67.
34. For discussions of moral luck, see D. Statman, ed., *Moral Luck* (Albany: State University of New York Press, 1993) and Bernard Williams, *Moral Luck* (Cambridge: Cambridge University Press, 1991).

35. Ibid.

36. Ibid., 72 (italics in original).

37. See Peter French, *Collective and Corporate Responsibility* (New York: Columbia University Press, 1984).

38. Ibid., 5.

39. Ibid., 13.

40. French, "The Corporation as a Moral Person," in *Collective Responsibility*, eds. May and Hoffman, 133.

41. Ibid., 141.

42. Ibid., 143.

43. Ibid.

44. Ibid., 147.

45. See Peter French, ed., *Individual and Collective Responsibility* (Rochester, VT: Schenkman, 1998), 25.

46. "Profile: Timothy McVeigh," *BBC News*, May 11, 2001.

47. Harvey, "The Emerging Practice of Institutional Apologies," 59. Govier and Verwoerd follow Harvey in their "The Promise and Pitfalls of Apology," 74.

48. Harvey, "The Emerging Practice of Institutional Apologies," 59.

49. Ibid.

50. Dana Priest and Anne Hull, "Soldiers Face Neglect, Frustration at Army's Top Medical Facility," *The Washington Post*, February 18, 2007.

51. The essays in May and Hoffman's *Collective Responsibility* consider the salient distinctions between such groups.

52. John Poynder, ed., *Literary Extracts from English and Other Works* 1 (1814), 268.

53. The notion of collective sacrifice to the gods, however, seems well established.

54. Karl Jaspers, *The Question of German Guilt*, trans. E. B. Ashton (New York: Capricorn, 1961), 36.

55. Larry May, *The Morality of Groups* (Notre Dame: University of Notre Dame Press, 1987), 64.

56. Ibid., 65.

57. See Smiley's entry on collective responsibility for *The Stanford Encyclopedia of Philosophy*.

58. Juha Raikka, "On Dissociating Oneself from Collective Responsibility," *Social Theory and Practice* 23 (1997): 1–9.

59. Hannah Arendt, "Organized Guilt and Universal Responsibility," in *Collective Responsibility*, eds. May and Hoffman, 280.

60. Hannah Arendt, "Collective Responsibility," in *Responsibility and Judgment*, ed. Jerome Kohn (New York: Schocken Books, 2003), 147.

61. Arendt, "Organized Guilt and Universal Responsibility," 278 (italics in original).

62. Ibid., 281.

63. Ibid.

64. Ibid., 278.

65. Ibid., 282.

66. Ibid., 281–82.

67. See Jan Narveson, "Collective Responsibility," *Journal of Ethics*, 6 (2002): 179–98; and Max Weber, *Economy and Society* I (Berkeley: University of California Press, 1978).

68. H. D. Lewis, "Collective Responsibility," in *Collective Responsibility*, eds. May and Hoffman, 21–22.

69. Ibid., 28.
70. Govier and Verwoerd, "Taking Wrongs Seriously," 149.
71. Lewis, "Collective Responsibility," 28.
72. Ibid., 30.
73. Ibid., 24.
74. Arendt, "Collective Responsibility," 147.
75. Michael Cunningham claims that conservatives from Britain, Australia, and the United States tend to respond similarly to national gestures of contrition. Michael Cunningham, "Saying Sorry: The Politics of Apology," *Political Quarterly* 70, n. 3 (1999): 288.
76. Cited in Jacob Weisberg, "Sorry Excuse: Rules for National Apologies," *Slate*, April 4, 1998.
77. J. Ryle, "City of Words: A Sorry Apology from Clinton," *Guardian*, April 13, 1998.
78. Recall his statement: "I will never apologize for the United States of America, I don't care what the facts are." Atler, "High Stakes in New Orleans," 15.
79. "Excerpts From Frist's Speech on Ex-Official," *The New York Times*, March 27, 2005.
80. William Kristol, "The Sorry Mr. Clarke," *The Weekly Standard*, April 5, 2004.
81. Michael Putzel, "Move Was My Call, Says Reno," *The Boston Globe*, April 20, 1993.
82. Michael Oreskes, "Where Does the Buck Stop? Not Here," *The New York Times*, March 28, 2004.
83. R. S. Downie, Collective Responsibility," in *Collective Responsibility*, eds. May and Hoffman, 47–51.
84. Ibid., 50–51.
85. Ibid.
86. Ibid. See also Narveson, "Collective Responsibility"; and Linda Radzik, "Collective Responsibility and Duties to Respond," *Social Theory and Practice*, 27 (2001): 455–71.
87. See J. Angelo Corlett, "Collective Moral Responsibility," *Journal of Social Philosophy*, 32 (2001): 575.
88. John Ladd, "Morality and the Ideal of Rationality in Formal Organizations," *Monist*, 54, 1 (1970): 488–516.
89. Ibid. See also Lewis, "Collective Responsibility," 24.
90. Lewis, "Collective Responsibility," 32.
91. Ibid.
92. Ibid.
93. See Vinit Haksar, "Moral Agents," *Routledge Encyclopedia of Philosophy*, vol. 6 (1998): 499–504.
94. Alasdair MacIntyre, *After Virtue: A Study in Moral Theory* (London: Duckworth, 1985), 220–21.
95. Ibid.
96. Conversations with Guyora Binder helped me to articulate this point.
97. See John Searle, *The Social Construction of Reality* (New York: Free Press, 1995); and Michael Bratman, *Faces of Intention* (New York: Cambridge University Press, 1999): 109–29.
98. Margaret Gilbert, *On Social Facts* (Princeton: Princeton University Press, 1992).
99. See Margaret Gilbert, *Living Together* (Lanham, MD: Rowman & Littlefield, 1996).

100. See Raimo Tuomela, *The Philosophy of Social Practices* (New York: Cambridge University Press, 2002); *Cooperation: A Philosophical Study* (Dordrecht: Kluwer Academic Publishers, 2000); and *The Importance of Us* (Stanford: Stanford University Press, 1995).

101. Pettigrove, "Apology, Reparations and the Question of Inherited Guilt," 328.

102. Pettigrove takes a similar position. See ibid., 342.

103. Gill, "The Moral Functions of an Apology," 26.

104. Tavuchis does appreciate this issue: "An authentic apology cannot be delegated, consigned, exacted, or assumed by the principals, no less outsiders, without totally altering its meaning and vitiating its moral force." *Mea Culpa*, 49.

105. Orenstein, "Apology Excepted," 238.

106. Gill, "The Moral Functions of an Apology," 19.

107. Cunningham, "Saying Sorry: The Politics of Apology," 291.

108. Govier and Verwoerd, "The Promise and Pitfalls of Apology," 76.

109. Harvey, "The Emerging Practice of Institutional Apologies," 59.

110. *Canadian Press Wire Service*, April 21, 1996, cited in Susan Alter, "Apologising for Serious Wrongdoing," *Final Report of the Law Commission of Canada* (1999).

111. C. S. Lewis, "The Dangers of National Repentance," *Guardian*, March 15, 1940. Pettigrove brought this passage to my attention in "Apology, Reparations and the Question of Inherited Guilt," 327.

112. See Alexander Chancellor, "Guide to Age," *Guardian*, October 16, 2004: "Such breast-beating over complex historical episodes for which subsequent generations can bear no responsibility has been widely ridiculed, but it is precisely because they are clearly blameless that governments find it so easy to say sorry for ancient injustices. And they hope thereby to curry favour with the descendants of the victims at no cost to themselves."

113. Clyde Farnsworth, "Australians Resist Facing up to Legacy of Parting Aborigines from Families," *The New York Times*, June 8, 1997.

114. Camille Paglia, "Who is Really to Blame for the Historical Scar of Black Slavery?," in *When Sorry Isn't Enough*, ed. Roy Brooks, 352–54.

115. Rayner, *Eating Crow*, 98.

116. Ibid., 207.

117. Ibid., 95.

118. Ibid., 230.

119. Ibid., 238–39.

120. Ibid., 239.

121. Ibid., 254.

122. Slansky and Sorkin, *My Bad*, 82–83.

123. Apple, "Clinton's Contrition."

124. Govier and Verwoerd, "Taking Wrongs Seriously," 148.

125. Joyce, "Apologizing," 162.

126. Slansky and Sorkin, *My Bad*, 214.

127. See Kate Connolly, "Pope Says Sorry for Crusader's Rampage in 1204," *Telegraph UK*, June 30, 2004, and "Pope Sorrow over Constantinople," *BBC News*, June 29, 2004.

128. For the full text of the Pope's speech, see the Vatican's electronic archives: http://www.vatican.va/holy_father/john_paul_ii/speeches/2001/documents/hf_jp-ii_spe_20010504_archbishop-athens_en.html.

129. Joyce, "Apologizing," 164.
130. Ibid.
131. "Clinton's Painful Words of Sorrow and Chagrin," *The New York Times*.
132. The Convention on the Prevention and Punishment of the Crime of Genocide, adopted by the United Nations General Assembly in 1948 and ratified by the United States in 1988, requires signatories to prevent and punish acts of genocide. The U.S. Senate delayed forty years in passing the act due to fears that African-American or Native-American groups would charge the United States with violating the convention. The Congress attached so many reservations to the law – including a requirement that the United States could not be brought before the International Court of Justice – that some claim that its passage is largely meaningless. See Samantha Power, *"A Problem from Hell": America and the Age of Genocide* (New York: Basic Books, 2002).
133. "Truth and Reconciliation Hearing Testimony of Former President F. W. de Klerk," in *When Sorry Isn't Enough*, ed. Roy Brooks, 505.
134. See Power, *"A Problem from Hell."*
135. See Harvey, "The Emerging Practice of Institutional Apologies," 61, and Gill, "The Moral Functions of an Apology," 20.
136. See Mark Gibney and Erik Roxstrum, "The Status of State Apologies," *Human Rights Quarterly* 23, no. 4 (2001): 911–39.
137. Bernard Siegan, "The United States Has Already Apologized for Racial Discrimination," in *When Sorry Isn't Enough*, ed. Roy Brooks, 413–16.
138. Office of the Surgeon Multinational Force – Iraq and Office of the Surgeon General United States Army Medical Command, "Final Report: Mental Health Advisory Team Operation Iraqi Freedom," (2006): 35.
139. James Bennett, "In Uganda, Clinton Expresses Regret on Slavery in U.S.," *The New York Times*, March 25, 1998.
140. Ibid.
141. Marc Lacey, "Clinton Tries to Subdue Greeks' Anger at America," *The New York Times*, November 21, 1999.
142. Weisberg, "Sorry Excuse."
143. Thompson, "The Apology Paradox," 476.
144. Lazare, *On Apology*, 109.
145. See Weisberg, "Sorry Excuse: Rules for National Apologies."
146. R. W. Apple, Jr., "From Mandela, A Gentle Admonishment," *The New York Times*, March 28, 1998.
147. "Report Sets Holocaust Damage," *Associated Press*, Wednesday, April 20, 2000. See also "$5bn Nazi Slave Fund Agreed," *BBC News*, November 14, 1997.
148. See Alan Ray, "Native American Identity and the Challenge of Kennewick Man," 79 *Temple Law Review* (2006): 89–154.
149. Minow, *Between Vengeance and Forgiveness*, 4–5.
150. See "Clinton's Painful Words of Sorrow and Chagrin." In addition to the $2 million Clinton provided to the Genocide Survivors Funds, he promised improved genocide warning procedures and general support in rebuilding and reestablishing rule of law.
151. Thurlow, cited in *Literary Extracts from English*, 268.
152. See Christopher Stone, *Where the Law Ends: The Social Control of Corporate Behavior* (New York: Harper and Row, 1975); David Risser, "Punishing Corporations: A Proposal," *Business and Professional Ethics Journal* 8, no. 3

(1989); and Peter French, "The Hester Prynne Sanction," *Business and Professional Ethics Journal* 4, no. 2 (1985).
153. Lazare, *On Apology*, 118.
154. Rayner, *Eating Crow*, 171.
155. One commentator wondered if Clinton did not offer a formal apology for slavery because doing so would increase demands for reparations. See "Clinton Opposes Slavery Apology," in *When Sorry Isn't Enough*, ed. Roy Brooks, 352.
156. Joel Bakan, *The Corporation: The Pathological Pursuit of Profit and Power* (New York: Free Press, 2004).
157. See Pettigrove's discussion of these possibilities in the context of collective forgiveness in "Hannah Arendt and Collective Forgiving," *Journal of Social Philosophy* 37, no. 4 (2006): 483–500.
158. See ibid., 492–93.
159. See ibid., 491.
160. Tavuchis, *Mea Culpa*, 117.
161. Govier and Verwoerd, "The Promise and Pitfalls of Apology," 74.

Chapter 11. Varieties of Collective Apologies

1. Ingvar Carlsson, Han Sung-Joo, and Rufus Kupolati, *Report of the Independent Inquiry Into the Actions of the United Nations During the 1994 Genocide in Rwanda*, December 15, 1999.
2. "The Apology Paradox," 473–74. Jana Thompson describes political apologies as "forward- rather than backward-looking." Peter Digeser argues for a forward-looking account of political forgiveness. *Political Forgiveness* (Ithaca: Cornell University Press, 2001).
3. Gregory Titleman, *Random House Dictionary of Popular Proverbs and Sayings* (New York: Random House, 1996), 352.
4. For a collection of stories on Clinton's apology, see Tuskegee University's web page: http://www.tuskegee.edu/Global/story.asp/S/1211608.

Conclusion

1. Michael Woods, *Healing Words: The Power of Apology in Medicine* (Santa Fe: Center for Physician Leadership, 2007), 52–53.
2. American Medical Association, Office of the General Counsel, Division of Health Law, "Medical Professional Liability Insurance" (1998), 133. I learned of this resource from Cohen, "Advising Clients to Apologize," 60n.
3. *Riggins v. Nevada*, 504 U.S. 127, 144 (1992)(concurring opinion).
4. Marshall Tanick and Teresa Ayling, "Alternative Dispute Resolution by Apology: Settlement by Saying 'I'm Sorry,'" *The Hennepin Lawyer* (1996): 22.
5. Ibid.; Deborah Levi, "The Role of Apology in Mediation," *New York University Law Review* 72 (1997): 1175.
6. See Robin Topping, "Attorneys Balance 'Safe' with 'Sorry,'" *New York Newsday*, February 4, 2004.
7. For an argument that doctors should apologize after they commit medical errors, see Lucian Leape, "Understanding the Power of Apology: How Saying 'I'm Sorry' Helps Heal Patients and Caregivers," *National Patient Safety Foundation Newsletter*, 8, no. 4 (2005).

8. Tanick and Ayling, "Alternative Dispute Resolution by Apology," 22.
9. Ameeta Patel and Lamar Reinsch, "Corporations Can Apologize: Corporate Apologies and Legal Liability," *Business Communication Quarterly*, 66, no. 1 (2003): 22.
10. Ibid., 23.
11. Ibid.
12. Ibid.
13. "Tire Victim: Apology Seemed Sincere," *CBS News*, January 9, 2001.
14. Ibid.
15. Dan Kahan, "What Do Alternative Sanctions Mean?" *University of Chicago Law Review* 6 (1996). Kahan has since recanted views in this paper. See "What's Really Wrong with Shaming Sanctions," *Texas Law Review* 84 (2006): 2075.
16. See Andrew von Hirsch, *Censure and Sanctions* (New York: Oxford University Press, 1996): 82–83; Stephen Garvey, "Can Shaming Punishments Educate?" *University of Chicago Law Review* 65 (1998); and James Q. Whitman, "What Is Wrong with Inflicting Shame Sanctions?," *Yale Law Journal* 107 (1998).
17. Kant states: "Now, it might seem that the existence of class distinctions would not allow for the [application of the] retributive principle of returning like for like. Nevertheless, even though these class distinctions may not make it possible to apply this principle to the letter, it can still always remain applicable in its effects if regard is had to the special sensibilities of the higher classes. Thus, for example, the imposition of a fine for a verbal injury has no proportionality to the original injury, for someone who has a good deal of money can easily afford to make insults whenever he wishes. On the other hand, the humiliation of the pride of such an offender comes much closer to equaling an injury done to the honor of the person offended; thus the judgment and Law might require the offender, not only to make a public apology to the offended person, but also at the same time to kiss his hand, even though he be socially inferior. Similarly, if a man of a higher class has violently attacked an innocent citizen who is socially inferior to him, he may be condemned, not only to apologize, but to undergo solitary and painful confinement, because by this means, in addition to the discomfort suffered, the pride of the offender will be painfully affected, and thus his humiliation will compensate for the offense as like for like." *Metaphysical Elements of Justice*, 139.
18. *United States v. Vance*, 62 F.3d 1152, 1158 (9th Cir. 1995).
19. For an excellent overview of these and related concerns, see Stephanos Bibas and Richard A. Bierschbach, "Integrating Remorse and Apology into Criminal Procedure," *Yale Law Journal* 114 (2004).
20. See 18 U.S.C.S. app. § 3E1.1 (Law. Co-op, 2000).
21. For a sample of cases interpreting these guidelines, see *United States v. Fagan*, 162 F.3d 1280, 1284 (10th Cir. 1998); *United States v. Camargo*, 908 F.2d 179 (7th Cir. 1990); and *United States v. Hammick*, 36 F.3d 594, 600 (7th Cir. 1994).
22. See Margareth Etienne, "Remorse, Responsibility, and Regulating Advocacy: Making Defendants Pay for the Sins of Their Lawyers," *New York University Law Review* 78 (2003); and Michael O'Hear, "Remorse, Cooperation, and 'Acceptance of Responsibility': The Structure, Implementation, and Reform of Section 3E1.1 of the Federal Sentencing Guidelines," *Northwestern University Law Review* 91 (1997).

23. Michel Foucault, *Discipline and Punish: The Birth of the Prison*, trans. Alan Sheridan (New York: Vintage Books, 1995). See also Stuart Banner, *The Death Penalty* (Cambridge: Harvard University Press, 2003), 16–23; and Lawrence Friedman, *Crime and Punishment in American History* (New York: Basic Books, 1993), 26.

24. Markus Dubber, "Policing Possession: The War on Crime and the End of Criminal Law," *Journal of Criminal Law and Criminology* 91 (2001): 849.

25. Bibas and Bierschbach, "Integrating Remorse and Apology into Criminal Procedure," 97.

26. Ibid., 136.

27. Kristen Gelineau, "Man Gets 18 Months for '84 Attack," *Associated Press*, March 16, 2007.

Index